Guy Julier,
a graduate of Manchester University
(History of Art) and the Royal College of Art, London
(History of Design), is a contributor to *Modernism in Design*
and author of *New Spanish Design*. He has written for several
design magazines including *Blueprint*, *Design*, *Designer's
Journal*, *Industrieel Ontwerpen* and *World Architecture*. He is
presently a Senior Lecturer in the History and Theory of
Design in the School of the Environment,
Leeds Metropolitan University.

WORLD OF ART

This famous series
provides the widest available
range of illustrated books on art in all its aspects.
If you would like to receive a complete list
of titles in print please write to:
THAMES AND HUDSON
30 Bloomsbury Street, London WC1B 3QP
In the United States please write to:
THAMES AND HUDSON INC.
500 Fifth Avenue, New York, New York 10110

Printed in Singapore

THE THAMES AND HUDSON

ENCYCLOPAEDIA
OF 20ᵀᴴ CENTURY DESIGN
AND DESIGNERS

GUY JULIER

211 illustrations

THAMES AND HUDSON

For Robert, Mary and Rebecca Julier

ACKNOWLEDGMENTS

I should like to thank the librarians of the Study Centre at
the Design Museum in London for their consistent and
good-natured help during the preparation of this book.
Thanks are also due to several scholars for their useful
comments and contributions. These are: Julia Bigham,
Mary Godwin, Fiona Hackney, Michael Horsham, Jane
Pavitt, Melanie Tomlinson and, in particular, David
Crowley.

First published in the United States of America in 1993 by
Thames and Hudson Inc., 500 Fifth Avenue,
New York, New York 10110

Library of Congress Catalog Card Number 93-60123

ISBN 0-500-20269-9

Printed and bound in Singapore

Contents

How to use this book

The dominant, 'modern' definition of design, which this book takes as its starting point, focuses on the creation of artefacts within multiple reproduction. But the scope has been extended beyond this **industrial** and **graphic design** to embrace the intellectual and institutional systems which shape their conception and reception. This includes, for instance, the means by which design, and the ideas underlying it, are disseminated by important **magazines**, **journals** and **exhibitions**, as well as **schools**, **colleges** and **universities**. Similarly, **interior design** and **architecture** are admitted in instances where they provide platforms for the development, presentation and perception of design and design theory. Political and ideological concepts, such as **feminism** or **green design**, different **modes of production**, such as CAD-CAM, and influential **materials** and **techniques** are also considered. **Terms**, **concepts** and **movements** that have been influential in art history appear where they have also been used in design, their application being discussed. Finally, at the risk of falling into 'designer-hero' worship, much of this encyclopaedia is devoted to biographies of its important practitioners. Given the breadth of such an approach, the choice is inevitably selective, but the book aims to provide an accessible introduction, a useful quick guide for both students and everyone with an interest in 20th-c. design and a permanent source of reference.

The huge range of entries is outlined in the **subject index** (opposite), which is intended to help the reader draw parallels between entries that may appear some distance apart in the alphabetical order of the encyclopaedia. Such interrelationships are further indicated by the **cross references** in the text which appear in SMALL CAPITALS.

To enable the reader to investigate further the necessarily concise information contained within the text, many of the individual entries are provided with a selected bibliography. Works which recur frequently are indicated by the author's name followed by the date of publication, e.g., Banham (1960). Full details will be found in the general **bibliography** at the end of the book, where titles are grouped thematically and alphabetically. 'Exh. cat.' after a title denotes an exhibition catalogue.

Black-and-white **illustrations** have been selected to provide as complete a visual record as possible of the subjects discussed. Entries to which illustrations relate are identified in the captions by the headword in **bold**.

The **chronological chart** on pp. 206–11 is subdivided by country and is provided to give the reader a general view of developments through the 20th c. The **sources** of the illustrations appear on pp. 215–16.

Subject index

Subject index

Subject index

Introduction

The study of design history is an extremely recent phenomenon. It has seen rapid development as a discipline in the UK, but has also emerged in other countries, particularly the USA, Scandinavia and Australasia. Since the late 1960s it has developed internationally as a taught subject, mostly within art, architecture and design colleges and departments where – to date – it has largely remained. It has thus been taught in an environment in which it has been seen very much as a 'complement' to a student's practical studies. While such a context is as valid as any, it has shaped a particular, dominant form of the subject. This has been mostly conditioned by the continued struggle to make the subject 'relevant' to the student's studies as a practising designer. Thus the tendency has been to read design within a 'modern' definition, that of being about the Industrial Revolution, mass-production manufacture, the Modern Movement and the consumer society. In other words, the study of design history has largely been concerned with the creation of objects that are re-produced and has mostly been taken to mean 'industrial design', existing within the complexities of advanced, Western capitalist society. As such, it has been defined in opposition to concepts that precede the birth of the 'designer', such as decorative art, commercial art and the crafts.

Design is therefore seen as a 20th-c. development, and the dominance of the Modern Movement during the same period has shaped perceptions of its practice. A seminal text which helped to form this view is Nikolaus Pevsner's *Pioneers of the Modern Movement* (1936). It traced a linear, progressive perception of art history; a steady development of architectural style, based on the work and aspirations of individual architects and designers, from the historicism of William Morris and the Arts and Crafts movement to the 'machine aesthetic' of Walter Gropius and the Modern Movement. In this book Pevsner established the canon of 'form follows function' as the governing design ideology of the 20th c. His view no doubt reflects the dominance of German art and architectural history wherein, as Gropius himself professed, architecture is the leading edge in the development of design.

A second important work is Sigfried Giedion's *Mechanization Takes Command: A Contribution to Anonymous History* (1948). Giedion was closely involved with Pevsner's heroes of modern design; he was a friend of the architects Gropius and Le Corbusier and a secretary of the Congrès Internationaux d'Architecture Moderne (CIAM). None the less, in his text he consciously distances his approach from Pevsner's 'great designers' view and from a charting of design's development in terms of nodes of events or classic works. Instead, the main theme is the effect of mechanization on factory production, agriculture and the home. Thus, in addition to the history of the design process, the account becomes that of the history of industry, technology and social customs. The net of analysis is spread wider so that design is seen as a function of technology and consumption. Later writings on design have included anthropological studies such as Daniel Miller's analyses of kitchens on a north London council estate or Dick Hebdige's sociology of popular culture, both cases in which 'taste' and 'style' – and the processes that form them – play a role in shaping design.

If the net of design analyses has broadened horizontally – encompassing considerations beyond the individual designer – then it has extended vertically as well, taking design history further back than the modern period of the 20th c. Such a view can be justified in that the definition of design stems from the Italian word, *disegnare*, which essentially means *drawing*, but taken outside its Renaissance context signifies, by extension, preliminary study and planning. Thus it separates creative invention from the finished product. The result is to see design as anything 'that doesn't happen by accident'. This definition of design eliminates from consideration any limiting factor, such as modes of production and distribution, reception and perception, or commercial context. Using such a broad definition, studies traditionally rooted in the decorative arts, particularly those stemming from decorative arts museums, have claimed that they too are concerned with 'design'. The effect has been to confuse creation of the unique object – design in the decorative arts – with the more modern definition of design as being for mass production.

Other historians agree with the premise that design existed before 1900, but their argument is very different. Firstly, some have suggested that the so-called Industrial Revolution was not in fact a violent rupture, as is generally thought, but instead overlapped with a preceding proto-industrial revolution during which goods were produced on a semi-artisanal basis for a mass market. This view, supported by studies of, among other things, the cloth trade around Halifax in the late 17th c. or the 18th-c. silk industry of Lyons, confounds the accepted thesis that the Industrial Revolution involved the *wholesale* division of labour (including that between designer and producer), alienation, machine production, de-skilling and product standardization. Secondly, further studies within spheres of production traditionally associated with the classical Industrial Revolution, such as iron-casting industries in Britain's Midlands or the manufacture of furniture in the USA in the late 19th c., have shown that there was a continuing need for 'traditional' skilled workers despite mechanization, and that the degree of flexibility (as opposed to standardization) of products did in fact intensify. It may thus be plausible to talk of 'design' in its modern sense before the term came into common usage, by showing how it developed in pre-20th-c. manufacture. However, at the same time, that sense of mechanized mass production with which it is fundamentally associated is undermined by such an approach. It is for this reason that my primary definition of design is that it is the creative invention of objects destined for serial reproduction (i.e., manufactured in numbers greater than one). This prevents the blurring with decorative arts that it has suffered.

The kind of analysis described above is symptomatic of many re-evaluations that have taken place in the late 20th c. It corresponds to what is called the 'Post', the blanket term for political and economic philosophies that under-

went radical criticism, which is made up of Postindustrialism, Postmodernism, Post-Fordism, Post-Marxism, Post-feminism . . . In the case of the analyses of modes of production just cited, the approach may stem from a Post-Marxist philosophy. Marxism has undergone a crisis since the 1960s, brought about by the growth of consumer-led society (rather than producer-led society), the re-evaluation of the nature of the productive systems on which Marxist analysis was based and finally by contemporary shifts in the world political balance with the move of many Eastern bloc countries away from centrally planned economies. Design historians such as Gillian Naylor have subsequently questioned our acceptance of positions adopted by William Morris, John Ruskin and Henry Cole in the face of aesthetics and industrialism, suggesting that theirs was an ideological response, as opposed to a direct response to real physical conditions. In turn, this questions the traditionally accepted bases of the Modern Movement in particular, and much study of design history in general.

The re-evaluation of the past has been matched by important shifts in the economic and cultural framework in which design is held. Economic historians talk of the move that Western capitalism has made into a Post-Fordist, or Postindustrial phase. Various events, in particular the international economic crisis of the 1970s, have undermined the Western industries on which the Fordist ideology was founded (motorcars, textiles and domestic machinery, for instance). Far Eastern countries, on the other hand, have taken an increasingly prominent role in the global economy; they have competed with the West, and often replaced its lead in certain industries such as textiles and have provided new models for industrial production and commercialization. These 'new models' have come primarily from Japan where, with computer-controlled tooling in production processes and the establishment of distinctive management systems, the traditional Western conception of Fordism has been challenged. Fordism was based on the idea of continuous-line assembly and specialized tooling for manufacture: the more that was produced and sold, the greater the initial high investment in plant was offset, effectively pushing up profit margins. The Post-Fordist models do not make the basic assumption that the market is going to be stable. Instead, production, management and distribution systems are structured to respond quickly to market fluctuations. This may be achieved through the use of computer-aided manufacture (CAM). It may also be achieved by the revitalization and adjustment of a traditional artisanal base to manufacture modern products. In parts of Italy, for example, goods ranging from shoes to tractor machinery, which one might expect to be produced under centralized, factory conditions, are produced by networks of garage-sized workshops.

A global account of design in the 20th c., presented by way of an encyclopaedia, must take account of such developments in the world economy. Any account of design must now also spread outside the boundaries of Western capitalism. In the closing two decades of the 20th c., more countries have been drawn into the sphere of influence of Western capitalism. Countries such as Spain, Argentina and the Philippines have each shrugged off a history of right-wing dictatorship, while Eastern bloc countries have undergone democratization. They too have allowed new expressions in design. Furthermore, their national pasts have been opened up for re-examination. The events that form part and parcel of the 'Post' have shown that analysis of many aspects outside or even in opposition to the notion of design being wholly concerned with mass production, mass consumption and mass communication is required to give a full picture. The rise of design in Italy since World War II has had much to do with the interactions of art, craft, architecture and design, as well as industrial and artisanal production; so did the rise of furniture production in Scandinavia in the 1940s and 1950s. British designers such as Tom Dixon or Ron Arad, although they worked largely on one-off, unique pieces, were none the less influential in the development of a Postindustrial aesthetic in design in the 1980s. The 1980s also saw the growth of 'soft-tech' design; products such as amplifiers or computers which had traditionally been subject to a rigorous, if not stylized treatment of 'form follows function', were thus now being approached with greater expression and sensuousness. All aspects of design have been subject to all sorts of incursions from outside its narrow confines.

These incursions are not a recent phenomenon. They have always existed. In studying the early 20th c., it is necessary to trace the activities and debates of individuals and institutions from artistic, architectural, decorative arts or philosophical backgrounds as they came to terms with the growth of mechanized production. These initiatives were important in the formation of the modern definition and practice of design.

Design, then, is not only a process but it is also a vehicle of ideology and a means of expressing national, institutional or corporate aspirations, a point underlined in the 1980s by the importance given to it in many countries. Increased global competition, mostly brought about by those new dynamics in the world economy, was met by increasing government interest in and promotion of design in many countries. The 1980s also saw the growth of many giants in the design business. A design consultancy numbering over 400, as a public limited company (which incorporated not just interior, graphic or product designers, but also marketing specialists, product managers and public relations experts) was established. Such a development has emphasized the inter-disciplinary nature of design. Events in the early 1990s, however, began to show that it was not necessarily to be permanent. Many of these giants began to break up under economic pressure, illustrating once again that no single conception of design is permanent.

Design historians have been accused of being unimaginative and unadventurous in sticking to dominant types of design such as products, furniture or graphics. Why, it is asked, do they not also investigate military weaponry, the design of computer hardware systems or food, or the relationship of politics to design? While agreeing with the point, the author does not pretend fully to rectify this imbalance. Design history, it should be repeated, is still a young subject; there is still a lot of research to be done. None the less, consistent with the policy of starting with the dominant 20th-c. definition of design but then allowing in issues and analyses from outside, entries on such issues as feminism and crafts (and their subsequent effect on mainstream design) are admitted.

In such a way, it is hoped that this encyclopaedia will represent a summation of the history and historiography of design and designers in the 20th c. In doing so it provides an easy and accessible system of reference to many facts and arguments in design as it has developed and undergone transformations. It therefore aims to be of use to those with both specialist and general interests in the subject and its history.

A

A & E Design (f.1968) is a Swedish industrial design office founded by Tom Ahlström and Hans Ehrich. It specialized from an early stage in the use of PLASTICS and has developed much DESIGN FOR DISABILITY.

Aalto, Alvar (1898–1976) was a Finnish architect and furniture designer who studied architecture at the Helsinki Polytechnic (1916–21), after which he travelled extensively in Europe. In 1923 he opened his first office in Jyväskylä and married the architect Aino Marsio in 1925. She was to be his most important collaborator until her death in 1949, particularly in directing the ARTEK company, which manufactured his furniture designs from 1935. In 1927 he moved his office to Turku; the house he designed for himself there is noted as one of the first expressions of Scandinavian Modernism (*see* MODERN MOVEMENT). From 1929 he became connected with internationally renowned artists, such as László MOHOLY-NAGY, Fernand Léger and Georges Braque, as well as the CONGRÈS INTERNATIONAUX D'ARCHITECTURE MODERNE. He also began to design furniture, exploiting PLYWOOD as a malleable and cheap material for seating. Prior to the establishment of Artek, the Otto Korhonen company manufactured his furniture designs.

In 1933 he moved to Helsinki and patented a method of bending wood for stools, seen in his famous Stacking Stool. In 1937 he designed curvilinear vases for the Savoy Restaurant in Turku; these were manufactured by the Iittala glass works and were shown at the NEW YORK WORLD'S FAIR, 1939, where he designed the Finnish Pavilion. The pavilion itself was of a free, expressive nature and established his reputation in the USA. He was a visiting professor of architecture at the Massachusetts Institute of Technology (1946–47). His architectural work was characterized by its sensitivity to the local environment; buildings such as the town hall at Säynâtsalo (1949–52) sit comfortably and unostentatiously in the landscape without any loss of expressive power. His moulded plywood furniture achieves the same effect in the interior.

□G. Labò, *Alvar Aalto* (1948); F. Gutheim, *Alvar Aalto* (1960); L. Mosso, *L'Opera di Alvar Aalto* (1965); P.D. Pearson, *Alvar Aalto* (1978); M. Quantill, *Alvar Aalto: A Critical Study* (1983); *Aalto Furniture and Glass* (exh. cat., Museum of Modern Art, New York, 1984); J. Pallasmaa (ed.), *Aalto Furniture* (1985); G. Schildt, *Aalto Interiors* (1986)

Aarnio, Eero (b.1932) studied industrial design in Helsinki (1954–57) and has worked freelance ever since. His early furniture design was within the traditional mode of Finnish craft. In the 1960s he veered towards POP design with the bulbous, space-age forms of his Tomato chair (1964) and Bubble chair (1967),

Armchair 406 in bent and laminated birch designed by **Aalto** *for Artek (1946).*

Aarnio's *Pastille chair (1968) made in fibreglass resin.*

both produced by the Finnish furniture manufacturer Asko. In the 1980s he designed modular furniture using COMPUTER-AIDED DESIGN and COMPUTER-AIDED MANUFACTURE.

adhocism is a design method which is particularly associated with POSTMODERNISM. The term was first used by Charles Jencks and was employed in architectural criticism in 1968 to describe a process by which parts of a whole design are produced independently or 'found' and later combined. Thus it is no longer necessary to invent new forms, instead pre-existing styles may be plundered and put together in new configurations. This implies that objects may take on new usages and meanings (e.g., a safety-pin can be worn as an earring), and that the emphasis in the design process may be in the choosing rather than in the origination of elements.
☐C. Jencks and N. Silver, *Adhocism* (1972)

advertising agencies first appeared in the second half of the 19th c. when their mandate was to provide everything from posters to the frames in which to hang them. The modern advertising agency has, however, only come into existence with the medium of television (i.e., since the 1960s) and is now expected to co-ordinate all aspects of a campaign across the range of modern advertising media. It is responsible for such aspects as above the line (any advertising where media time or space is purchased) and below the line (point of sale, pack advertising and mailshots) advertising, the generation of the idea and the management of the advertising budget of the client company.
☐B. Elliot, *A History of English Advertising* (1962); J. Pearson and G. Turner, *The Persuasion Industry* (1966); W. Fletcher, *The Ad Makers* (1973); T. Nevett, *Advertising in Britain: A History* (1982); E. Clark, *The Want Makers: Lifting the Lid off the World Advertising Industry: How They Make You Buy* (1989)

AEG (f.1883) (Allgemeine Elektrizitäts Gesellschaft) was successor to DEG (Deutsche Edison Gesellschaft, the German Edison Company for Applied Electricity), formed by Emil Rathenau, who had been impressed by Edison's light bulb, seen at the Paris Exposition Internationale d'Electricité in 1881. His son, Walther, described Emil's vision as follows: when he 'saw this little bulb alight for the first time, he had a

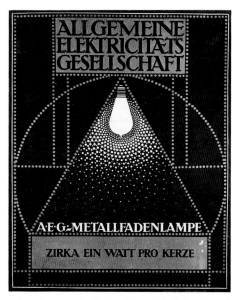

*Behrens's poster for **AEG** electric light bulbs (c.1910) demonstrates his concern for classical proportion.*

vision of the whole world covered with a network of copper wires. . . . In his mind's eye he saw changes in the structure of populations as communications took on a new form.' The company is best known for the work of Peter BEHRENS between 1905 and 1906 in establishing the first ever CORPORATE IDENTITY. AEG's production-engineer, Michael von Dolivo-Dobrowolsky, had realized in the earlier years of the century that mass production was most effective when concentrated on the mechanized manufacture of high-quality standardized components that were interchangeable between products, rather than concentrating on specific artefacts. With the final product as an assemblage of components, less attention was paid to the external form. AEG's technical director, Paul Jordans, was probably responsible for appointing Behrens as artistic advisor in order to concentrate on the latter aspect.

Unlike the occasionally appointed architect or artist (which had included Otto Eckmann and Alfred Messel), Behrens had a permanent position within the company, which allowed him complete control over all visual aspects of AEG's installation, products and publications.

Thus a new awareness of the importance of a corporate image as a competitive tool was fostered in the company. Behrens's projects included the redesigning of the company's logotype which, by 1912, displayed the same clear FUNCTIONALISM as that found in AEG's products. This logotype has been used throughout the 20th c.

In 1909, in keeping with Dolivo-Dobrowolsky's concept of component-standardization, Behrens designed three standard kettles with interchangeable features, such as different surface finishes, allowing, ultimately, 81 possible variations. In spite of the innovative nature of his appointment, his designs for the domestic market followed traditional prototypes, while his industrial design, for the most part, was confined to the modification of existing products. None the less,.while Behrens's interventions initially predated the foundation of the DEUTSCHE WERKBUND, the debate over the standardization of form and the bringing together of art and technology that they generated no doubt coincided with currents of thought in Germany at that time.
□ T. Buddensieg and H. Rogge, *Industriekultur: Peter Behrens und die AEG 1907–1914* (exh. cat., Internationales Design Zentrum, Berlin, 1978); T. Buddensieg, *Industriekultur: Peter Behrens and the AEG* (1984)

Agha, Mehemed Fehmy (1896–1978) was born in the Ukraine of Turkish parents. In 1928, while working as a graphic artist on German *Vogue* in Berlin, he met Condé Nast, who invited him to become art director of *Vogue* in the USA. He worked for Nast from 1929 to 1943, during which time he changed the face of *Vogue*, making bold use of WHITE SPACE, altering the shape of headlines and introducing European SANS-SERIF typefaces. He was also an innovator with the use of photography, hiring photographers such as Edward Steichen and Cecil Beaton, and placing images asymmetrically on a page. He is also credited with introducing colour photographs and full-bleed pages to the modern magazine.

Aicher, Otl (1922–91) was a German graphic designer who studied at the Academy of Fine Arts in Munich (1946–47). In 1948 he established a studio in Ulm, where he co-founded the ULM HOCHSCHULE FÜR GESTALTUNG in 1955 (he was its Vice-Chancellor from 1962 to 1964). He was greatly influenced by Max BILL,

Aicher's *sober pictograms designed for the 1972 Munich Olympics.*

his design being geometric and simple, though this could at times give way to a more sensuous effect. He is most noted for developing the complete graphics programme for the Munich Olympics (1972) and, although much of his work was in CORPORATE IDENTITY, he was also noteworthy for the development of radically Utopian theories in his teaching and writing.

Albers, Josef (1888–1976) was born in Bottrop, Westphalia, and was the first BAUHAUS student to become a 'master'. After Johannes ITTEN resigned in 1923 as head of the Preliminary Course, Albers assisted Itten's successor, László MOHOLY-NAGY. Albers developed the craft element as a complement to Moholy's visual education course. His teaching stressed the constructive rather than the expressive nature of materials, bringing in the constructional use of paper as well as wire mesh, Cellophane and even razor blades. In 1928 he succeeded Marcel BREUER as head of the furniture workshop and stayed at the Bauhaus until its demise in 1933. Moving to the USA, he taught at BLACK MOUNTAIN COLLEGE until 1949, also lecturing at Harvard and Yale and acting as visiting professor at the ULM HOCHSCHULE FÜR GESTALTUNG (1953–54). His work at the Bauhaus in both Weimar and Dessau demonstrates an eclecticism as well as a

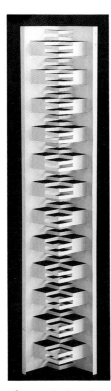

Reconstruction of an exercise in cutting paper (1927–28), part of **Albers**'s *course at the Bauhaus.*

apartment in 1940 he restyled traditional shelving, giving it a proto-HIGH-TECH form and a new function as a space divider, a use destined to become a cliché of interior decoration in the 1940s and 50s. Elements from sources traditionally outside accepted visual languages (e.g., naval architecture) persisted in his interior designs, particularly in his repeated spiral staircases. The formal solutions in his furniture of the 1950s and 60s were constantly innovative, each design responding to the demands of the material. In 1964, along with Franca Helg and Bob NOORDA, Albini redesigned furniture and fittings for Milan's Metro system.

☐ M. Fagiolo, F. Helg and C. De Seta, *Franco Albini 1930–1970* (1979)

Alchymia *see* STUDIO ALCHYMIA

Alessi (f. 1921) was founded by Giovanni Alessi in Omegna, Italy, as an auxiliary industry in metal-plate turning, with a foundry in nickel silver and brass. In 1927 the firm began to concentrate exclusively on manufacturing household items, mostly working in nickel-plated brass, silver-plated brass, German silver and silver-plated German silver. Its products included all types of dinner-table ware, based on the designs of the Austrian company, Berndorf Krupp. Alessi used traditional turning processes (except in the manufacture of trays, which were pressed) that allowed production

growing concentration on simplicity of form and the minimum use of materials. In 1926 he also designed a stencil lettering set for advertising purposes made up of geometric shapes – the square, triangle and quarter section of the circle – which could easily be read from a distance.

☐ *Josef Albers: A Retrospective* (exh. cat., Guggenheim Museum, New York, 1988)

Albini, Franco (1905–77) was born in Robbiate, Como, and studied architecture at Milan Polytechnic, graduating in 1929, following which he set up in private practice. Unlike many of his contemporaries and successors, Albini tended not to expound his opinions, although his furniture designs from the 1930s demonstrated a keen awareness of the theoretical positions that informed Italian RATIONALISM. These designs showed a commitment to new materials and forms: in a set of tensile-structure bookshelves designed for his own

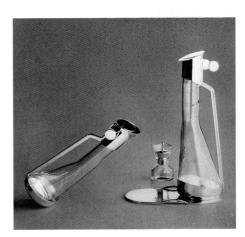

Achille Castiglioni's oil and vinegar set was manufactured by **Alessi** *from 1984.*

lines to be changed quickly. From 1932, under Giovanni's son, Carlo, the firm began to develop its own design identity, mostly through its coffee sets and, in particular, the Bombé set (designed in 1945). With the post-war shortage of nickel silver and brass, Alessi moved into stainless steel pressing (already used by the Lagostina company in 1934), specializing in it entirely from 1964. From the 1950s Italian companies such as Lagostina, Dervas and Alessi began to employ major designers in an effort to compete with more traditional companies such as the Danish GEORG JENSEN silversmiths and De Forenede Jernstoberier or the German Württembergische Metallwarenfabrik. Subsequently, Alessi made significant inroads into the American market. Its production now varies from basic cutlery and pressed trays to exclusive designs which appear under its Alessi Officina trade mark. The latter was launched with its Programma 6 in 1983: eleven of the world's leading architects, including Alessandro MENDINI and Michael Graves, were invited to submit designs for a tea and coffee set. Its subsequent aim has been to foster research and experimentation, free from the limits usually imposed by industrial mass production.
□P. Scarzella, *Steel & Style: The Story of Alessi Household Ware* (1987)

Alfa Romeo (f.1909) was founded in Milan as Anomina Lombarda Fabbrica Automobili – Alfa (the Lombardy Car Manufacturing Company). It took on the engineer Niccolò Romeo in 1914, and his name was added after World War II to make Alfa Romeo. It produced several successful racing cars in the 1930s but it was not until after the War that it went into volume production of cars such as the elegantly styled Giulietta Sprint (1953). Another important Alfa Romeo car is the Alfasud (1971), developed by Rudolf Hruska, which broke new ground by offering a short, front-wheel-drive four-seater. In its time, Alfa Romeo has collaborated with many designers including Nuccio BERTONE, Giorgietto GIUGIARO, Touring and GHIA.
□P. Hull and R. Slater, *Alfa Romeo: A History* (1969); D. Owen, *Alfa Romeo* (1985); P. Altieri, G. Lurani and M. Matteucci, *Alfa Romeo: Catalogue Raisonné 1910–1989* (1988); R. Piatti, *Alfa Romeo S.Z.* (1989); D.G. Styles, *Alfa Romeo: The Legend Revived* (1989); G. Borgeson and J. Fenster, *The Alfa Romeo Tradition (1990);* F. Carmagnola, *Alfa Romeo: Sport Through Design* (exh. cat., Design Museum, London, 1991)

aluminium is a silvery metal which is produced from bauxite ore. In the 1880s the successful use of electrolysis as a method of extracting aluminium from bauxite greatly reduced its price. Initially, the metal had purely industrial applications; by the 1930s, however, it had become a popular material for use in the consumer goods industry, mainly in the USA.

Its key properties are lightness and resistance to corrosion; it is also non-toxic. In its pure form, aluminium is relatively weak, but alloyed with other materials, such as manganese or copper, it can be made as strong as steel. It can also be pressed, machined or spun. Industrial designers made use of these qualities. Kitchenware and food-packaging manufacturers found the metal's lightness and non-toxic qualities ideal for use with food. Its strength and lightness in alloy form increased dramatically the shape, speed and stability of the Douglas DC1 airliner (1933). Hans CORAY's Landi chair (1938) is perhaps the most famous example of the metal's use in furniture design. Today, PLASTICS have displaced many of aluminium's uses.

Ambasz, Emilio (b.1943) was born in Argentina and studied architecture at Princeton University, USA (1960–65). He was curator of design at the MUSEUM OF MODERN ART, New York (1970–75), and organized the important exhibition, Italy: The New Domestic Landscape (1972). This exhibition publicized the RADICAL DESIGN proposals of, among others, UFO, ARCHIZOOM and Gaetano PESCE and articulated the belief that design was not centred around the single object, rather objects themselves functioned as part of a total environment, and thus the study and practice of design necessarily incorporated sociology, politics and anthropology. He established industrial design offices in New York and Bologna in 1976 and in the same year designed his famous Vertebra seating system, which responded automatically to the user's motions. Both his architecture and his design are very much concerned with giving the object poetic form.
□*Emilio Ambasz: Arquitectura, Diseño Gráfico e Industrial* (exh. cat., Centro de Diseño and Galería Yuguanzo, Madrid, 1984); M. Bellini et al., *Emilio Ambasz: The Poetics of the Pragmatic* (1989)

Anonymous Design is the title of an exhibition held in 1974 at the Louisiana Museum near Copenhagen. It consisted of mass-produced articles, each with an anonymous designer. The items were selected on the grounds that they possessed 'genuine character, good form, fine performance and honest use of materials'. In other words, they were considered examples of 'GOOD DESIGN'. In 1991 the Design Museum in London revived the notion of 'non-designed' design with an exhibition entitled Designing Yourself.

anthropometrics is the science of measuring the human form, with particular reference to stature, body weight and the length of limbs. The application of the results of anthropometric studies to the design of everyday objects is now standard practice for many manufacturers and designers.

anti-design was a movement that rejected mainstream design practice. It emerged as a practice in the second half of the 1960s, particularly in Italy. It grew out of a rejection of the spectacular rise in consumerism in the 1950s and early 1960s, which was felt to have turned the original aims of the MODERN MOVEMENT and its residual belief in 'GOOD DESIGN' into a cheap marketing ploy. Design, in other words, was seen as a tool for creating false requirements and thereby increasing sales, rather than as a way of enhancing the domestic environment. At the same time, the formalist aesthetic of Modernism divorced objects from their socio-economic context (something already noted by Gio PONTI and the exponents of REALISM in the 1950s), thus facilitating their appropriation by another ideological framework – that of capitalism and consumerism. As a result, some Italian architect-designers, spearheaded by Ettore SOTTSASS, set out in the late 1960s to redefine Italian design and renew its earlier cultural and political role. This was to be done initially by invalidating the so-called good taste of many Italian products, by means of distortions of scale and form, the shocking use of colour, visual puns or the undermining of an object's functional value. Invariably links would be drawn with fine art practice, particularly that of POP. DE PAS, D'URBINO AND LOMAZZI's Joe sofa for ZANOTTA in 1971 was inspired by Claes Oldenburg's 'soft' sculptures and was a giant baseball glove made of leather-covered polyurethane foam – thus it recontex-

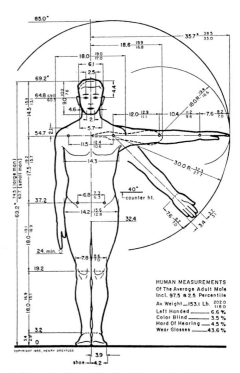

A diagram by Henry Dreyfuss demonstrating the proportions of **anthropometrics**.

tualized a popular object, suggesting that forms might be reused rather than purely 'invented'. Gaetano PESCE's Sit Down chair of 1970 for CASSINA was also inspired by Oldenburg. Its anthropomorphic forms represented comfort rather than pure form; blatantly un-chic, they stood in opposition to the culture of conspicuous consumption prevalent in Italian mainstream design. The Sit Down chair is an example of the desire, expressed by the exponents of anti-design, to negate the idea that an object's aesthetic function is more significant than its more abstract socio-cultural one.

The two examples cited show that, with the support of some manufacturers, artefacts of anti-design were produced and sold. Indeed the fact that the concept was put into production in the long run accounted for a revitalization of Italian modern design, later consolidated by the activities of the MEMPHIS group in the early 1980s. It must be seen against the international backdrop of the growing radicalization of

Apple

The **Apple** *Macintosh Classic computer was launched in 1990.*

designers and architects alongside students and the intelligentsia in the late 1960s, but also in the light of a wider economic, social and cultural crisis that dominated Italian everyday life in the late 1960s.

Sottsass, among others, produced unmanufactured prototypes for furniture, as well as ceramic pieces, which explored the objects of mass culture and questioned the relevance of the concept of 'taste'. In doing so, he produced design about design, or 'meta-design'. Other studios, such as the Florentine architectural groups, SUPERSTUDIO and ARCHIZOOM, produced radical plans for architecture, echoing those of the British group, ARCHIGRAM, which challenged accepted tenets of building, planning and interior design. Thus anti-design found alliances beyond furniture of limited production. Parallels of ideological intent may be found in crafts activity in Britain and the USA after 1970, but by the 1980s anti-design had also created a knock-on effect far into product design, in which traditionally accepted formal values for objects were challenged, as may be seen in Daniel WEIL's famous radio set of 1981.
□ Sparke (1988)

Apple (f. 1977) is the computer company that is invariably credited with one of the most important technical innovations in 20th-c. typesetting. The notion of storing type as mathematical formulae in digital form had been introduced by the German firm Hell in 1965, but the development of the Apple Macintosh personal computer was to revolutionize its application.

In 1975 two Californians, Steve Jobs and Steve Wozniak, designed the Apple I, a single-user computer, and Apple Computer Inc. was founded in 1977 with the launch of the Apple II. This was the first personal computer to be sold complete with all the necessary elements and could thus be used right off the shelf – effectively founding the personal computer (PC) industry. In 1983 Jobs and Wozniak introduced Lisa, a highly user-friendly piece of software that revolutionized the industry with its use of windows, pull-down menus, bit-mapped graphics (see BIT MAPPING) and a mouse. The following year they launched the Macintosh PC, which incorporated the Lisa interface but at an affordable price for many designers. The software for this, which introduced a digitized language of page layout called PostScript, was, in fact, developed by another Californian company, Adobe.

The 'Apple Mac' rapidly gained acceptance in the mid-80s as *the* standard computer equipment for graphic designers. Apple software subsequently developed at an astonishing rate (often way in advance of its hardware), with new programmes such as Pagemaker, which facilitated digital page layout, and Fontographer, which allowed graphic designers to create their own typefaces. For some this meant a more efficient design process than, for instance, the 'traditional' and sometimes messy paste-up approach of sticking images and type down for PHOTOSETTING. Images could be 'scanned' and held in digital format alongside type. In turn they could be sized (blown up or reduced), altered or distorted, although the scope for this was limited by the method of presentation on screen: curves were represented by PIXELS in a stepped, rectilinear fashion. More powerful and expensive computer systems than the Apple, such as the Quantel Paintbox or the Sun workstation, carried out these functions with a much higher finish.

Apple's innovations, however, meant that the designer could now undertake the role of typesetter. This in turn led to 'desk-top publishing' (DTP), whereby corporations and institutions could, with the aid of Apple equipment, carry out virtually the complete production process in-house, from origination and designing to printing, without reliance on outside expertise. Specialist designers were sometimes employed by corporations or institutions to carry this out. Otherwise the job would be undertaken by staff without, necessarily, a design background. The upshot was a blurring of the divisions of labour between editors, designers and printers in this chain.

Within the design profession, this 'democratization' in graphic design – whereby the designer maintains greater control over the type and image at all stages in the production process – is also visible in the typographic work of Neville BRODY, in *ÉMIGRÉ*, in the complex visual structures of April GREIMAN and in the fonts of Matthew CARTER's pioneering computer typefoundry, Bitstream Inc. With its facility for introducing and manipulating type and images, the Apple Mac has also allowed their subversion and recontextualization, which has in turn given rise to the multilayering of visual information and even to DECONSTRUCTION in design. This was promoted, in particular, by staff and students at the CRANBROOK ACADEMY OF ART in the late 1980s.

The Apple revolution also sparked off a debate among the design disciplines on the primacy of traditional drawing skills: ultimately the digital format of Apple Mac equipment could not surpass the expressive power of more conventional materials. A clear understanding of the limitations and potentialities of *both* mediums often led to the most effective results in design.

☐ J. Sculley and J. Byrne, *Odyssey: Pepsi to Apple: A Journey of Adventure, Ideas and the Future* (1987); L. Butcher, *Accidental Millionaire: The Rise and Fall of Steve Jobs at Apple Computer* (1988)

Arabia (f.1873) was founded on the outskirts of Helsinki by the Swedish ceramics factory RÖRSTRAND, to take advantage of the Russian market. Under the art direction of Thure Öberg (late 19th c. to 1931) the firm adopted the ideals earlier expressed by the ARTS AND CRAFTS movement, though its line was more broadly controlled by Rörstrand. By 1916 Arabia was under Finnish ownership and was largely supplying a home market; in 1939, with over 1,000 employees, it had a larger production of porcelain than any other firm in Europe. With the appointment of Kaj FRANCK as art director in 1945, Arabia's ceramics became increasingly utilitarian.

Arad, Ron (b.1951) was born in Tel Aviv and studied at the Jerusalem Academy of Art. He then moved to London and the Architectural

Arad *embedded electronic components in concrete to create his Concrete Stereo (1984).*

Association (1974–79), where he studied under Peter Cook, the founder of ARCHIGRAM. In 1981, after a brief stint in a North London architectural office, Arad, together with furniture entrepreneur Dennis Groves, founded One Off, a furniture workshop and showroom. Initially Arad worked in a broadly HIGHTECH manner, domesticating constructional elements such as scaffolding. He soon moved into a style closer to ADHOCISM, reusing a Rover leather car seat and Puch moped saddle. Conceptually these works had some parallels with those of, for instance, Achille CASTIGLIONI. However, in the context of Britain of the early 1980s, with the laying to waste of much of its manufacturing base, Arad's rough-edged use of crumbling concrete, twisted steel and other elements suggestive of industrial decay constituted, for some critics, an ironic postindustrial statement (*see* POSTINDUSTRIALISM). As the name of his company suggests, Arad's pieces were made individually or in batches; most furnished fashionable retail interiors or offices. With its logotype designed by Neville BRODY, One Off was a well-known point of reference for post-punk British design of the 1980s. By the mid-80s Arad was regularly exhibiting abroad (e.g., at the 1987 Nouvelles Tendences exhibition at the Pompidou Centre in Paris, organized by the CENTRE DE CRÉATION INDUSTRIELLE). By the end of the decade he was also designing interiors, including the foyer of the Tel Aviv opera house and furniture for manufacture by the Swiss company Vitra and the Milanese Poltronova.

□ D. Sudjic, *Ron Arad: Restless Furniture* (1989)

Archigram (1963–75) was an organization of architects, designers and environmental researchers led by Peter Cook and based in London. Its members included Warren Chalk, Peter Cook, Dennis Crompton, Ron Herron, David Greene and Mike Webb. These six came together originally in 1960 while working for Taylor Woodrow Construction Co. on the redevelopment of Euston Station, London, under the direction of Theo Crosby. From 1961 they produced a broadsheet called *Archigram* – a contraction of 'architecture' and 'telegram' or 'aerogram'. This title came from the notion of an urgent imperative on architecture in the face of what Archigram's members saw as the sterile nature of monumental architecture in postwar Britain. They were identified publicly as a group in 1963 after their first exhibition – Living City – at the Institute of Contemporary Arts in London.

The title Archigram was also a statement of their method: architecture by drawing. This approach marked the character of their beliefs – their projects were invariably Utopian and included the Walking City (1964), the Plug-in City (1964–66) and the Instant City (1968). These schemes proposed the use of advanced technology, as found in the American space programme, inflatables and DYMAXION domes. In rejecting formal architectural conventions of traditional building structures, they instead created a consumer-oriented architecture, whereby units, services and appliances could be added on according to need. The implication here is that greater personal choice is exercised as against the imposition of schema by individual architects. This led to a sense of architecture being developed by free association, incorporating popular culture and expendable elements.

Some of their designs were realized, including the Archigram Capsule at the Expo '70 in Osaka and a review of contemporary British design at the Louvre in Paris (1971). However, it is through their writings and exhibitions, as well as the writings of their supporter, Reyner BANHAM, that their theories of design became influential throughout the world. Their concept of expendability was adopted by the Metabolism architectural school in Japan but, together with the increasing prominence of the consumer, the incorporation of POP culture and the rejection of traditional conventions of design, it may also be seen in a broader sense as important in the development of POST-MODERNISM and pop design. The group received particular interest in Italy and influenced such RADICAL DESIGN studios as ARCHIZOOM in the late 1960s.

□ *Archigram* (1961–70); P. Cook, *Architecture: Action and Plan* (1967); *Experimental Architecture* (1970); *Archigram* (1974)

Architectural Review, The (f.1896) is a London-based architectural journal, which was an important promoter of the MODERN MOVEMENT in Britain from the mid-1920s. Critics who were closely associated with it include Nikolaus PEVSNER and Reyner BANHAM.

Archizoom (f.1966) was an architectural studio founded in Florence, inspired partly by the work of the British RADICAL DESIGN group, ARCHIGRAM. In 1967, along with another Florentine group, SUPERSTUDIO, it was represented in an exhibition of so-called 'Super-architecture' in Pistoia. Archizoom's designers included Andrea BRANZI, Gilberto Corretti, Paolo DEGANELLO, Dario and Lucia Bartolini and Massimo Morozzi. Its objects acted as ironic, post-Functionalist (*see* FUNCTIONALISM) commentaries on the MODERN MOVEMENT – its Mies chair of 1969, with its elastic seat, commented on the inadequacies of the Modernist aesthetic. In addition, the group made references to POP, KITSCH and stylistic revivalism. Its 1970 No-stop city, like Super-studio's Continuous Monument, extended the idea of the city into infinity. In 1971 it took part in the exhibition at the MUSEUM OF MODERN ART, New York, entitled the New Domestic Landscape, showing in the 'Counterdesign as Postulation' section.

□ Ambasz (1972)

Art Center College of Design (f.1930) was established in Pasadena, California, by the Los Angeles advertising art director, E.A. Adams. His aim was to bridge the gap between the quality of design services demanded by clients and the lack of formal training then available. In 1986 a European sister campus was opened in Switzerland.

Art Deco was not a movement, but rather a tendency in design. It emanated from France in

George Barbier's Au Revoir *(1924) shows the eclectic range of sources used in* **Art Deco**.

the 1920s but appeared in increasingly hybrid forms in Britain and the USA in the 1930s. It took its name from the PARIS EXPOSITION DES ARTS DÉCORATIFS ET INDUSTRIELS, 1925, where the style was represented at its most lavish. Its sources, however, are diverse. It was influenced by the fine art movements of Cubism and Fauvism, but was equally affected by the Ballets Russes, African and other non-European art forms, in particular Egyptian art, as well as the designs of such proto-Modernists as Josef HOFFMANN, Frank Lloyd WRIGHT and Adolf LOOS. It was often luxurious, incorporating costly materials such as ivory, enamel, shagreen and ebony. Stylistically, its furniture, products and architecture show a heavy, distorted and markedly rectilinear classicism and are egyptianized with little ornament. Important exponents of Art Deco include Jacques-Emile RUHLMANN, René LALIQUE, Jean Dunand and A.M. CASSANDRE, whose graphic design work is also distinguished by its classicism, as well as a strong Futurist or Cubist influence.

Art Deco was not purely a luxury style, however. Applied in the public domain to the many Odeon cinemas opened during the 30s in Britain and the USA, for instance, it was a way of creating lavish effects at reasonably low cost, using CHROMIUM, coloured glass and painted concrete. This has come to be known as the ODEON STYLE; its cheap opulence has been interpreted as an attempt at providing an antidote to the general economic hardship of the decade. Such new materials as BAKELITE could also be used in an Art Deco style, its lack of ornament making moulding easy, and Bakelite's versatility (it could be made either translucent or marbled) being appropriate for such new products as radios.

On the whole, Art Deco was an artisanal style. Its exposure at the Paris 1925 exhibition also brought much criticism for its lavishness, in particular from more Modernist-inspired designers. Interest in Art Deco was revived in the 1960s, partly as it provided an irreverent counterpoint to the MODERN MOVEMENT. (Art Deco had, though, demonstrated some overlap with Modernism, as may be seen in the work of Eileen GRAY, and even in some designs by LE CORBUSIER. It was also to be found in the ocean liners that Le Corbusier so admired.) Subsequently, it was often pastiched in expressions of POSTMODERNISM.

☐ M. Battersby, *The Decorative Thirties* (1988); A. Duncan, *Art Deco* (1988)

Art et Décoration (f.1897) is published by the Parisian Librairie Centrale des Beaux-Arts. It began as a mouthpiece for commentators calling for design reform, but progressively moved towards a more middle-of-the-road position by the end of the 20th c.

art furniture is a term which originated in the 1860s in England to refer to furniture that eschewed the dominant taste for neo-Rococo and instead used a simpler style which prefigured the ARTS AND CRAFTS movement. In the 20th c. it re-emerged as part of the CRAFTS

REVIVAL and was the furniture equivalent of studio pottery (i.e., one-off, hand-made pieces that were invariably exhibited as art objects). This was particularly so in the USA, where examples of art furniture may often be seen in the New York magazine *Metropolis*.

Art Nouveau was a decorative arts style which developed simultaneously across Europe in the 1880s. It peaked in *c.*1900, but petered out again before World War I. It was characterized by the conscious exaggeration of organic forms which 'grew', almost like ivy, over the basic structure; the whiplash curve was its most common feature. The name derives from a Parisian shop (the Maison de l'Art Nouveau), which opened in 1896, but in different countries it was given different titles: STILE LIBERTY in Italy, MODERNISME in Spain, JUGENDSTIL in Germany and Scandinavia and Le Style Moderne in France. Its internationalization was due partly to the publication of magazines such as *Jugend* and *The Studio* and partly to the frequent international expositions at the turn of the century. Its historical sources comprised Japonisme, Celtic influences, Rococo, the Auricular style and many others. Apart from some regional variations, two broad types of Art Nouveau emerged. One was the fastidious, intricate style seen in the work of French and Belgian exponents such as Alphonse Mucha, Hector Guimard and Victor HORTA. The other was a purer, more rectilinear style developed by the Glaswegian, Charles Rennie MACKINTOSH, and seen in the work of members of the SECESSION. It was this style that was carried through by Josef HOFFMANN and Joseph Maria OLBRICH to the WIENER WERKSTÄTTE and thence to the DEUTSCHE WERKBUND, where, in a more simplified form, it was applied to industrial design. It is not surprising that the latter rather than the former version should feed into industrial design – the chief appeal of the more complex form of Art Nouveau was in the virtuosic display of craftsmanship, thus making it inapplicable to machine-based manufacture. □P. Selz and M. Constantine (eds), *Art Nouveau: Art and Design at the Turn of the Century* (1959); T. Benton and S. Millikin, *Art Nouveau 1890–1902* (1978); G.P. Weisberg, *Art Nouveau Binge: Paris Style, 1900* (1986)

Artek (f.1935) is a Finnish firm that was founded to manufacture and distribute the furniture designs of Alvar AALTO.

A detail of Alphonse Mucha's **Art Nouveau** *poster promoting Austria at the Paris World Fair of 1900.*

Arteluce (f.1946) was founded in Milan as a small lighting firm. Initially, it produced the designs of Gino Sarfatti, and these exotic 'light sculptures', combining function with flamboyance, became internationally appreciated as the hallmarks of Italian design in the 1950s. Among its most successful designs is KINGMIRANDA's minimalist Jill light (1977).

Arts and Crafts is a term primarily used to describe the English movement led by John Ruskin, William Morris and C.R. ASHBEE, although similar groups existed in most European countries and the USA. It was in its prime from 1888 to *c.*1910 and was directly or indirectly influential throughout the 20th c.

The term originated with an exhibition held in 1888 by an offshoot of the Art Workers' Guild in London. The aim of its exhibitors, who collectively called themselves the Arts and Crafts Exhibition Society, was to promote the ideals of craftsmanship, in particular in the face of the industrialization of production. This was an aim held by many reforming architects, designers and theorists who deplored the aesthetic and social effects of the Industrial Revolution. The virtues of craftwork, individualism and the designer's right to experiment and explore materials were all highlighted. This did not necessarily mean the creation of an avantgarde, as was later to be the case in the MODERN MOVEMENT, but rather the recovery of the vernacular tradition. A.W.N. Pugin had previously argued that the architecture and design of the Middle Ages was invariably seen as both the cause and symptom of ideal social conditions, and this was now recognized by exponents of the Arts and Crafts movement.

By establishing medieval-style guilds of handiwork and rural craft communities, such as those set up in the Cotswolds by C.R. Ashbee, Ernest Gimson and the Barnsley brothers, members of the Arts and Crafts Exhibition Society have subsequently been accused of turning their backs on machine production and wallowing in an over-romantic and economically impractical solution to the traumas of industrialization. Much has been made of the inherent and ongoing contradiction in the ethic of craft production: it narrowed the gaps between designer, producer, seller and consumer and arguably instilled a greater love for the object in conception and production; at the same time, while mass production implied the net reduction of cost and therefore cheaper goods, craft production made objects – including most of those produced by English exponents of the Arts and Crafts – prohibitively expensive for most people.

None the less, a by-product of the Arts and Crafts in England was that it stimulated a campaign, mostly conducted by Gordon RUSSELL and Ambrose HEAL, for better standards in mass production. Thus craft values were extended to the field of industrial design. Another important Arts and Crafts figure is W.R. LETHABY, who gave his full support to the DESIGN AND INDUSTRIES ASSOCIATION in 1914. In stylistic terms it is difficult to trace any links from the Arts and Crafts to design for mass production. After all, it was not just one style but many, incorporating Gothic, Japonisme, neo-Georgian and ART NOUVEAU. However, ideologically and methodologically it was an important forerunner of the Modern Movement, most generally in the belief that

*Firedogs (1904) designed by Ernest Gimson, a leading member of the **Arts and Crafts** movement.*

good art and design could reform society, but also in expounding the virtues of honesty and simplicity in the object and in eschewing showy ornament and the disguising of materials. Nikolaus PEVSNER in particular traced a route after 1900 from the Arts and Crafts via Hermann MUTHESIUS and the WIENER WERKSTÄTTE to the DEUTSCHE WERKBUND. While theoretical influences are clear, however, to place the English Arts and Crafts movement at the head of all subsequent design movements in the 20th c. would not only be ironic, given its antipathy towards mass production, but would also ignore specific developments in different countries at the same time. In addition it would disregard the theoretical advances of figures such as Frank Lloyd WRIGHT and Walter GROPIUS.

In many countries, in particular in Scandinavia and middle Europe (Austria, Hungary and Germany), the Arts and Crafts movement helped provide the impetus for the recuperation of national styles. This coincided with a vigorous restatement of national identities, and the adoption of Arts and Crafts values may be read as an expression of national Romanticism. Such countries showed a profound awareness of the British Arts and Crafts movement: their design reform leaders read Morris and Ruskin, and most of them came to Britain to see their work. Key names in this process at the turn of the century were Axel Gallen-Kallela (Finland),

Eliel SAARINEN, Herman Gesellius and Armas Lindgren (Sweden), the GÖDÖLLŐ Artists' Colony (Hungary), Josef HOFFMANN (Austria) and Peter BEHRENS (Germany). In the USA, the Arts and Crafts movement also had some influence, in particular in the furniture production of the Charles P. Limbert Company of Grand Rapids and of the Stickley brothers. In the very early 20th c., Arts and Crafts was widely recognized in the USA as a style discernible in catalogues and when shopping in department stores. Moreover it was seen as a style which could pervade all of a building from its architecture to its interior fittings.

The Arts and Crafts, along with many tendencies that preceded the Modern Movement, received a revival of interest in the late 1960s, when HABITAT and LIBERTY & CO. began to market designs by William Morris. Other revivals of interest included its 1920s spin-off, the OMEGA workshops. Omega also had some similarities with the CRAFTS REVIVAL and later the NEW DESIGN, although the Arts and Crafts movement's ruralist and medievalist connotations had been left behind. For many, however, the Arts and Crafts signified a rejection of industrialized production and distribution and the embracing of traditional

Ashbee's silver-mounted decanter (c.1904) was made for the Guild of Handicraft.

materials and construction methods. For others it signalled an ongoing failure to resolve the moral debate of design in society.

□G. Naylor, *The Arts and Crafts Movement* (1971); I. Anscombe and C. Gere, *Arts and Crafts in Britain and America* (1978); L. Lambourne, *Utopian Craftsmen* (1980); W. Kaplan, *The Art That Is Life: The Arts and Crafts Movement in America 1875–1920* (exh. cat., Museum of Fine Arts, Boston, 1987); E. Cumming and W. Kaplan, *The Arts and Crafts Movement* (1991)

Ashbee, Charles Robert (1863–1942) trained as an architect and was an influential member of the ARTS AND CRAFTS movement. From the 1880s he designed ART NOUVEAU style silver and metalwork, and his work was exhibited widely in England as well as in Vienna, Munich, Düsseldorf and Paris. He was a founder of the School and Guild of Handicraft (f.1888), which was based in the East End of London until 1902 and then moved to Chipping Campden in the Cotswolds, where it remained until its liquidation in 1908. It was partly this experience that led to Ashbee's partial rejection of handicrafts and his adoption of machine-oriented production. He had also met Frank Lloyd WRIGHT in 1900 and was important in introducing the latter's theories to Europe. Ashbee's own writings were influential both in Britain, where he broke from Victorian traditions of ornament

*A desk in the **Arts and Crafts** style by Stickley Brothers Co. of Grand Rapids, Michigan (c.1904).*

and HISTORICISM, and in Austria, where they reached Josef HOFFMANN and other members of the WIENER WERKSTÄTTE. In 1915 he moved to Cairo University as a lecturer in English.

☐F. MacCarthy, *The Simple Life: C.R. Ashbee in the Cotswolds* (1981); A. Crawford, *C.R. Ashbee: Architect, Designer and Romantic Socialist* (1985)

Aspen International Design Conference (f.1951) is a week-long event held in Aspen, Colorado, and is famous among designers. It brings together international designers and architects for discussion on a different theme each year. It was inaugurated in 1951 by Walter Paepcke of the CONTAINER CORPORATION OF AMERICA.

Asplund, Gunnar (1885–1940) is regarded as Sweden's leading architect of the early 20th c. He designed furniture for the Stockholm City Hall in 1921 as well as furniture and fittings for the Stockholm City Library (1921–28). These represented a break from the heavy ornamentalism of traditional Swedish architecture and a move towards a refined neo-Classicism that verged on Modernism (*see* MODERN MOVEMENT). As the architect of the Stockholm Exhibition in 1930 he was also responsible for attracting international attention to the emergence of Swedish Modernism. Some of his furniture is manufactured by CASSINA.

Auböck, Carl (b.1925) is a Viennese architect and industrial designer who studied architecture at the Technical University in Vienna (1943–49) and briefly thereafter at the Massachusetts Institute of Technology. His designs often show the influence of his Austrian background, in particular that of the work of his fellow-countrymen, Otto WAGNER, Adolf LOOS and Josef HOFFMANN. Auböck received a strong foundation in craft approaches from his parents, who were both students at the BAUHAUS and were involved in the WIENER WERKSTÄTTE. Some of his designs are produced and distributed by his family firm, Firma Ostovics. He is also interested in ERGONOMICS

Asplund's *Göteborg 1 chair was originally made in 1934–37. Cassina re-edited it in 1983.*

and has designed a great deal of innovatory ski equipment.

Aulenti, Gae (b.1927) studied architecture in Milan, graduating in 1954, since when she has worked as a freelance designer and architect. While she is known as a teacher and theoretician, her greatest impact has been as an interior and exhibition designer, in particular for FIAT and OLIVETTI. Her furniture and product design, however, are typical of the 'second wave' of postwar Italian designers.

austerity binge was the term used by Bevis Hillier to describe European decorative arts of the 1940s and 1950s. He argues that running through the years of rationing and shortages of the 1940s and the more affluent 1950s one may detect a rejection of prewar FUNCTIONALISM in design. This meant that a more playful style, incorporating balloons, mermaids and winged horses, was to be found alongside an interest in such popular arts as canal-boat painting, heraldry and fairground art.

☐B. Hillier, *Austerity/Binge: The Decorative Arts of the Forties and Fifties* (1974)

B

B&B Italia (f.1974) began as C&B Italia, founded in 1966 by the partnership of Cesare Cassina and Pietro Busnelli. The latter had owned a mainstream furniture-making business in Brianza, Italy, called Fratelli Busnelli fu Giuseppe, with his brother, Franco. Following a trip to Interplast in London, they started experimenting with POLYURETHANE foam, a material that revolutionized manufacture by allowing the use of assembly-line production rather than relying on master-upholsterers. Breaking with Franco, Pietro then set up C&B Italia to exploit these new methods. C&B Italia expanded rapidly, pushing into world markets with work by designers such as Joe COLOMBO, the CASTIGLIONIS, ARCHIZOOM and Gaetano PESCE. As a result, it proved serious competition for CASSINA itself – thus, in 1974 Cesare Cassina withdrew, and the company became B&B Italia (the second 'B' being the banks that bought up Cassina's share).
☐ M. Mastropietro (ed.), *An Industry for Design: The Research, Designers and Corporate Image of B&B Italia* (1982)

Baier, Fred (b.1949) is a British DESIGNER-MAKER who studied furniture design at the ROYAL COLLEGE OF ART, London (1973–76). His furniture is marked by its complexity, structural bravura and strong play on visual imagery.
☐ J. Houston, *Fred Baier: Furniture in Studio* (1990)

Baillie Scott, Mackay Hugh (1865–1945) was a British architect of strong ARTS AND CRAFTS persuasion. His design work became known in Germany and Austria, as he decorated and furnished part of the Grand Ducal palace in Darmstadt in 1898, and was much published there, particularly with the support of Hermann MUTHESIUS. His cottagey design became associated in Germany with an English style of that period.
☐ J.D. Kornwolf, *M.H. Baillie Scott and the Arts and Crafts Movement* (1971); K. Medici-Mall, *Das Landhaus Waldbühl von M.H. Baillie Scott* (1979).

Bakelite was the trade name used by the Belgian-born chemist and inventor Leo H. Baekeland for his thermosetting plastic, Phenol-Formaldehyde, patented in 1907. It is a brittle plastic (*see* PLASTICS), usually reinforced with a filler of fibre and wood flour (finely ground sawdust). Its first applications were in the electrical industry, but its cheapness and its resemblance to wood made it ideal for use in mass consumer products. Bakelite provided designers with an appropriate modern symbol during the late 1920s and 30s, when consumer interest in technological products was rising. Raymond LOEWY's restyled Gestetner duplicating machine (1929) and Wells COATES's Ekco radio (1934) helped to popularize Bakelite.

Balla, Giacomo (1871–1958) was an exponent of Italian FUTURISM. He is primarily recognized as a painter, but, like many Futurists, did not restrict himself to that medium. He produced painted furniture for the Lowenstein House, Düsseldorf (1912–15), and attempted to industrialize his modern design. He designed ceramics at Albisola, Italy, in the 1920s.
☐ V.C. Dorazio, *Giacomo Balla* (1970); E.

Gaetano Pesce designed the seating series Up (1969) for C&B Italia, which later became **B&B Italia**.

Crispolti, *La Ceramica Futurista di Balla e Tullio d'Albisola* (1982); *Il Futurismo e la Moda: Balla e gli Altri* (1986); E. Crispolti and M. Scudiero, *Balla/Depero: Recostruzione Futurista dell'Universo* (1989)

Ballmer, Théo (1902–65) was a graphic designer, who was born in Lausanne, Switzerland. After employment with a printing firm in Lausanne, he travelled to Zurich in the early 1920s and became a student at the School of Arts and Crafts under Ernst KELLER. In the late 1920s he spent a period at the Dessau BAUHAUS. In his poster designs of 1928 Ballmer combined DE STIJL principles and an ordered grid to create harmonious visual forms. From 1931 he was an instructor at the Basle School of Arts and Crafts.

Banham, (Peter) Reyner (1922–88) played a key role in the emergence of the serious study of design history and popular culture. Before World War II he worked as an engineering apprentice with the Bristol Aeroplane Co., but also developed an interest in the arts. In 1948 he entered the Courtauld Institute, London, to study art history under Anthony Blunt. He then went to work at the *ARCHITECTURAL REVIEW* under Nikolaus PEVSNER, with whom he also registered for a Ph.D. on the history of Modernism. This important text was subsequently published in 1960 as *Theory and Design in the First Machine Age* and rethought the history of the MODERN MOVEMENT, challenging Pevsner's own account – *Pioneers of the Modern Movement*. It picked up where Pevsner had left off (*c.*1910) and highlighted the way in which Modernists had embraced the expressive aesthetics of modern life, be they of machinery or popular culture. This undermined the claims of some supporters of the Modern Movement who adhered to pure FUNCTIONALISM.

During the late 1950s, Banham was also a leading member of the INDEPENDENT GROUP, which pioneered POP design. In 1964 he joined the staff of the Bartlett School, University of London, as an architectural historian, becoming professor in 1969. While architectural studies there at the time were dominated by a technocratic approach, which he himself supported, at the same time he encouraged a greater attention to urban, economic and political factors. In 1976 he moved to the USA, taking up posts at the State University of New York (1976), the University of California,

OTTO PREMINGER PRESENTS
PAUL NEWMAN · EVA MARIE SAINT
RALPH RICHARDSON · PETER LAWFORD
LEE J. COBB · SAL MINEO · JOHN DEREK
HUGH GRIFFITH IN "EXODUS"

WITH GREGORY RATOFF, FELIX AYLMER, DAVID OPATOSHU AND JILL HAWORTH. SCREENPLAY BY DALTON TRUMBO FROM THE BEST-SELLING NOVEL BY LEON URIS. IN SUPER PANAVISION 70, TECHNICOLOR® AND TODD AO STEREOPHONIC SOUND. A UNITED ARTISTS RELEASE

Bass's poster for the film Exodus *(1960).*

Santa Cruz (1980), and then at the Institute of Fine Arts in New York (1987). Apart from his many energetic and exuberant activities with organizations such as the INTERNATIONAL COUNCIL OF SOCIETIES OF INDUSTRIAL DESIGN, Banham left a subtle reinterpretation of the Modern Movement which made POSTMODERNISM's rejection of it indefensible. However, at the same time, his understanding of design in the context of mass culture was that the development of design history need not necessarily depend on either the historical period or the theoretical underpinning of the Modern Movement. Equally, his contribution to design history and practice was in moving his reading between the analysis of the individual object and a broader world view.

☐ Banham (1960); *Guide to Modern Architecture* (1962); *The New Brutalism* (1966); *The Architecture of the Well-Tempered Environment* (1969); *Los Angeles: The Architecture of Four Ecologies* (1971); *Megastructures* (1977); *Scenes in America Deserta* (1982); *A Concrete Atlantis* (1986); P. Sparke (ed.), *Design by Choice* (1981); obituary in *Journal of Design History* Vol. 1, No. 2 (1988)

Bass, Saul (b. 1920) studied at the Art Students League in New York (1936–39) before starting work as a graphic designer in the art department of Warner Brothers. Movie advertisements at that time were all inclusive (i.e., they attempted to represent everything that was in the film rather than capture its essence). Dissatisfied with this approach, he left Warner Brothers in 1946 and moved to Los Angeles to work for various ADVERTISING AGENCIES. In 1949 his minimalist full-page magazine advertisement for *Champion* – the Kirk Douglas picture – appeared, with a dramatic black page and tiny half-tone logo and the film title in the centre. He went freelance in the mid-1950s. His subsequent work for Otto Preminger of Paramount Pictures enabled him to explore new ground in credit sequences and film advertising: his symbol for *The Man with the Golden Arm* (1956) used both pictograms and strong abstract elements to create an erratic and strident atmosphere. Bass's reductionism was later carried through to CORPORATE IDENTITY work from the 1970s.

batch production or flexible production has been developing since the late 1960s as a means of reacting more efficiently and more rapidly to the changing demands of the market place, in terms of both production volume and production variety. The rise of pluralism in design has meant that manufacturers have been less able to think in terms of high-volume continuous runs of standardized products, but instead must use short runs, or batch-produced sets, of varied products.

Batch or flexible manufacturing systems most often make use of COMPUTER-AIDED MANUFACTURE (CAM), so that programmable machine tools, such as numerically controlled lathes, may work in conjunction with robots and automated storage and retrieval systems. This technology allows for a continuous flow of 'batched' designs with varying specifications, without wasting valuable time and money in lost production. Thus manufacturers can react quickly to changes in design specifications and patterns of market consumption, while still maintaining optimum production levels, thereby keeping product retail prices low.
□ C. Besant and C. Lui, *Computer-Aided Design and Manufacture* (1986)

Bauhaus (1919–33) has been acclaimed for, among many other things, providing the methodological basis for design education in the 20th c.; exemplifying the MODERN MOVEMENT; originating modern typography; and developing a design style which incorporated 'new' materials, such as concrete, glass and steel, and which avoided ornament. Some critics have even credited it with the invention of the modern concept of design. While historians such as Nikolaus PEVSNER and Sigfried GIEDION have perhaps inadvertently inflated the Bauhaus effect, it was an educational institute of considerable force, both in its ideas and in the concentration of important figures among its staff and students. Its posthumous reputation has sometimes obscured the volatile internal history it carried.

Bauhaus is a word made out of a contraction of the German words *bauen* (to build) and *Haus* (house). Originally called the Staatliches Bauhaus Weimar, the name was coined by Walter GROPIUS for the art school that he founded when the fine and applied arts schools in Weimar were merged in 1919.

Despite its radical reputation, the origins of the Bauhaus lay in the growing belief among many, including the German government and educationalists, that reform in art education was vital for economic reasons. Germany was less rich in raw materials than the USA or Britain and therefore relied more on the expertise of its skilled labour force and its ability to export sophisticated and high-quality goods. Designers were needed, therefore, and only a new kind of art education could meet this need. Immediately after World War I, officials in the small town of Weimar were open to Gropius's suggestions for the re-establishment of the School of Arts and Crafts that had been directed by Henry van de VELDE before the War. Its major ideological basis was that artists should be trained to work with industry, 'for the artist possesses the ability to breathe soul into the lifeless product of the machine', Gropius claimed – artists should become the craftsmen of industry. This principle came directly from those who had worked at the DEUTSCHE WERKBUND and who opposed Hermann MUTHESIUS, with his emphasis on the role of the artist as custodian of the avant-garde.

The Bauhaus, then, owed much to the prevailing ideological conditions. However, there has also been a contrasting tendency to link the roots of the Bauhaus to the English ARTS AND CRAFTS movement, via Muthesius and the Werkbund. Certainly, it derived something from the concept of the medieval guild at the beginning: its teachers were called masters

and journeymen, and its ideal was for different craftsmen to collaborate in the most exalted form of expression: the building. The Bauhaus schooling began with a six-month basic course under Johannes ITTEN, which was an exploration of form and materials. This was followed by a simultaneous education in a craft under a craftsman and in formal problems under an artist, with a third stage in the study of architecture and building. Teachers included Paul Klee, Wassily Kandinsky, Lyonel Feininger, László MOHOLY-NAGY, Georg Muche and Gerhard Marcks (one of the few teachers previously to have worked with industry). Little information has survived about the activities of the masters of the craft workshops; this suggests that, despite Gropius's efforts to elevate the status of the crafts, the artists were the stars.

During the early Weimar period, the school was dominated by the mystical approach of Itten (whose views were often diametrically opposed to Gropius's pragmatism) and by Expressionist tendencies. The teaching and criticism of Theo van DOESBURG (1921–23) introduced the influence of DE STIJL, signalling a departure from Expressionism and a move towards a vindication of Gropius's original project to unite art and industry. (This shift away from Expressionism towards a *Neue Sachlichkeit* [new objectivity] is also to be found

Invitation by Herbert Bayer to the final **Bauhaus** *party in Weimar (March 1925).*

in German painting, theatre, cinema, poetry, prose and music at the same time.) As a result, Itten left in 1923 and was replaced by Moholy-Nagy, who brought in a new aesthetic sobriety in graphic and industrial design, seen in the work of his students, Herbert BAYER and Wilhelm Wagenfeld respectively.

After political disagreements with the Nationalist authorities in Weimar, the Bauhaus was moved to Socialist Dessau in 1925, where Gropius designed its building, with interior fittings by other staff and students. It also achieved the official identity of Hochschule für Gestaltung (Institute of Design), and its teachers included Bayer for typography, Josef ALBERS for the basic course, Marcel BREUER for furniture and Gunta Stölzl in the weaving workshop. Hannes Meyer became head of the new department of architecture in 1927. The appointment of this Swiss Marxist architect contributed to the break of the Bauhaus accord with the Social Democratic administration in Dessau, and the following year, Gropius, along with Breuer, Moholy-Nagy and Bayer, resigned his post, mostly from weariness at having constantly to defend the school against ceaseless attack. Certainly, the Bauhaus did not always enjoy a successful public image. Its journal, *Bauhaus* (1926–31), and books did not sell well; many of its product designs, while later providing blueprints for modern taste, remained as prototypes, and its worker housing programme in the Törten district of Dessau (1926–28) suffered severe administrational problems even as it was being constructed. None the less, by the time of the 1927 Stuttgart Exhibition, a particular Bauhaus style was perceived, though its teachers disliked such an idea. Oskar Schlemmer, then master of form in the theatre workshop, noted in 1929: 'The Bauhaus style which sneaked its way into the design of women's underwear; the Bauhaus style as "modern decor", as rejection of yesterday's styles, as determination to be "up-to-the-minute" at all costs – this style can be found everywhere but at the Bauhaus.' Yet it is widely recognized that one of the Bauhaus's major achievements was the formulation of a design language that was free from the HISTORICISM of the previous 50 years.

With Meyer as director (1928–30), the Bauhaus saw considerable commercial success: the company of Emil Rasch of Bramsche manufactured 4.5 million rolls of wallpaper designed by the mural painting department, and other departments secured commissions, including all newspaper advertisements for I-G Farben. Ironically, Meyer's Marxist politics did not suit Dessau, and in 1930 he was replaced by Ludwig MIES VAN DER ROHE. However, the school suffered growing harassment from the National Socialists, the Bauhaus ideology and aesthetic being seen as Socialist, internationalist and, at worst, Jewish. In 1932 it moved to a disused telephone exchange in Berlin before it was closed down in April 1933 by the Nazis.

Many of its refugee staff moved to the USA, via London, where they were welcomed as 'the great white gods', as Tom Wolfe put it. There Moholy-Nagy founded the New Bauhaus in Chicago in 1937, and Gropius became professor of architecture (1937–52) at Harvard University, where Albers also taught. A major retrospective of Bauhaus achievements was mounted at the MUSEUM OF MODERN ART, New York (1938). In 1950 the ULM HOCHSCHULE FÜR GESTALTUNG was founded with Max BILL, a former Bauhaus student, as director. Such initiatives made the Bauhaus a potent force in design thinking and education. Practitioners of POSTMODERNISM have tended to reject its

Bayer*'s* Metamorphosis *(1936) uses photomontage to explore what he called 'Primary Sculpture'.*

teachings, but the combination of the industrialist inheritance of the Werkbund with the medievalist, craft-based tradition embodied in the Arts and Crafts movement generated fundamental and recurring questions in 20th-c. design.

☐ W. Gropius, *Bauhausbauten Dessau* (1974); *Berlin, Paris: Rapports et Contrastes France-Allemagne 1900–1933* (exh. cat., Pompidou Centre, Paris, 1978); H. Wingler, *The Bauhaus: Weimar Dessau Berlin Chicago* (1978); Whitford (1984); Naylor (1985); *Utopias de la Bauhaus – Obra Sobre Papel* (exh. cat., Centro de Arte Reina Sofia, Madrid, 1988); B. Friedman, *The Bauhaus: Masters and Students* (1988); C. Lichtenstein (ed.), *Bauhaus 1919–1933: Meister- und Schülerarbeiten aus Weimar, Dessau, Berlin* (1988)

Bayer, Herbert (1900–85) was born in Haag, Austria, and studied architecture in Linz in 1919 and in Darmstadt the following year before studying wall-painting under Wassily Kandinsky at the BAUHAUS (1921–23). After a period painting, which included a trip to Italy, he returned to the Bauhaus to be master of the print workshop in 1925, teaching visual communication and typography. As a Bauhaus student he had already developed an interest in typography, conceiving the idea of a new alphabet that would simplify the representation of sounds. He designed the cover of the book *Bauhaus 1919–23*. As a master, Bayer established the lower-case SANS-SERIF type as the style for all Bauhaus printing, arguing that the upper case and serifs had only been derived from handwritten forms and were simply perpetuated by tradition. His Universal type was formulated with the hope that it would eventually be developed into a new alphabet; although it was never intended or produced as a functioning typeface, its simple geometric elements marked the character of his work thenceforth. He was also influential in including photography in graphic design and in introducing advertising into Bauhaus teaching.

In 1928 he left the Bauhaus to work independently, becoming head of the Dorland advertising agency in Berlin. The following year he introduced the use of photography, retouch and montage and images of S U R R E A L I S M into advertising and strongly influenced the advertising style of the 1930s.

Having organized and designed the 1938 exhibition of Bauhaus art at the M U S E U M O F M O D E R N A R T, New York, he stayed in the USA, continuing as director of the Dorland International design company until 1945, after which he worked on architectural projects, including buildings for the Aspen Institute of Humanistic Studies. He acted as a visual consultant to many large corporations, among them the General Electric Company and the C O N T A I N E R   C O R P O R A T I O N   O F   A M E R I C A. During his last ten years he moved to California and concentrated more on painting.

□H. Bayer, *herbert bayer visual communication architecture painting* (1967); A. Cohen, *Herbert Bayer the Complete Work* (1984); G. Chanzit, *Herbert Bayer and Modernist Design in America* (1987); *Herbert Bayer − Collection and Archive* (exh. cat., Denver Art Museum, Denver, 1988).

Beck, Henry C. (1903–74) designed the London Underground diagrammatic map. It was innovatory in limiting route lines to horizontal, vertical and 45° diagonal directions, in breaking from a map format to provide a diagram and in enlarging the central section in relation to the outlying areas. He remained responsible for the diagram's development from 1933 to 1959.

Behrens, Peter (1869–1940) studied painting at the Karlsruhe School of Art (1886–89) and then in Düsseldorf (1889). In 1890 he visited the Netherlands, before moving to Munich where he joined the Munich Secession. In 1897 he was one of the founders of the Munich Vereinigte Werkstätte (United Workshops) and later became director of the Düsseldorf School of Applied Arts (1903–7). In 1907 he became a founder-member of the D E U T S C H E   W E R K-

Table lamps by **Behrens** *illustrated in* Deutsche Kunst und Dekoration *(1902–3).*

B U N D, where he and Hermann M U T H E S I U S shared many ideas. It was for his work for A E G (1905–6), however, that Behrens has become best known. His appointment as the company's artistic director marked the emergence of a new phenomenon: C O R P O R A T E   I D E N T I T Y. This involved both a new type of patron (the 'enlightened' industrialist concerned with every aspect of the design of his empire) and a new type of designer (the consultant who is responsible for all the company's concerns, from posters, advertisements and shop-window displays, to the products, the architecture and the housing of the company's workers). Behrens also often autocratically expounded his belief in the necessity of the unification of art and industry.

Soon after his appointment at AEG Walter G R O P I U S and Adolf Meyer joined his studios, followed by Ludwig M I E S   V A N   D E R   R O H E in 1908 and L E   C O R B U S I E R for four months in 1911. Not necessarily a radical designer or thinker, Behrens was none the less a powerful organizer. Gropius wrote of his influence in *The New Architecture and the Bauhaus*, 'It was Behrens who first introduced me to logical and systematical co-ordination in the handling of architectural problems.'

□F. Hoeber, *Peter Behrens* (1913); T. Buddensieg and H. Rogge, *Industriekultur: Peter Behrens and the AEG 1907–1914* (1981); A. Windsor, *Peter Behrens − Architect and Designer* (1981)

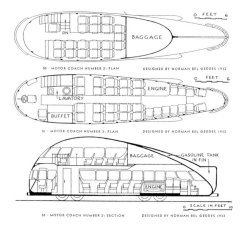

Plans and section for a motor coach, one of **Bel Geddes's** *many speculative designs published in* Horizons *(1932).*

Bel Geddes, Norman (1893–1958) was born in Michigan, USA, and studied briefly at the Art Institute of Chicago. During the early 1920s he worked in theatre design and shop-window display in New York. In 1927 he began working as an industrial designer. His ideas, which were markedly fanciful and futuristic and very few of which ever went into production, included prototype cars for the Graham Paige Company from 1928 as well as coaches, locomotives and aeroplanes (e.g., the Super Airliner 4, 1929). He designed the GENERAL MOTORS pavilion for the NEW YORK WORLD'S FAIR, 1939. However, after World War II his consultancy went into liquidation as a result of his own financial mismanagement and lack of commissions. He was influential in popularizing the notion of STREAMLINING through the publication of his book, *Horizons* (1932). In 1940 he published *Magic Motorways*, which used much material from his General Motors pavilion: the two together are often acknowledged as being influential in the development of the American freeway system.

Bellini, Mario (b.1935) has become one of Italy's leading designers. He was born in Milan and, like many of his well-known contemporaries, studied architecture at Milan Polytechnic, graduating in 1959. Following two years in the design office of Rinascente, Bellini joined OLIVETTI as a consultant. During the 1960s, in his product design for Olivetti as well as in

furniture projects for CASSINA, Bellini treated the objects like skeletons, covering them with a skin that made up an expressive surface. In the 1970s, however, the forms became more rectilinear. ANTHROPOMETRICS is dominant in his theory, as is the ideal of achieving universally accepted design standards.

Beltrán, Félix (b.1938) was born in Concepción, Cuba, and studied advertising design and layout at the School of the Visual Arts, New York (1956–60). He also studied painting and print-making while working as a designer with the American Publishing Company and Cypress Books until 1962. He then returned to revolutionary Cuba, introducing its first basic design course in 1964, before spending a year studying life-drawing at the Círculo de Bellas Artes (Fine Arts Society) in Madrid (1965–66). Back in Havana in 1966, he became the head of design of the Comisión de Orientación Revolucionária (Committee of Revolutionary Direction). He served as a teacher in nearly all of Cuba's higher educational establishments and in 1981 he became professor at the National School of Design in Mexico City. Published and exhibited widely, his work influenced many designers due to its combination of colour, revolutionary content and European form. He thus produced a unique style of Socialist graphic design.
□F. Beltrán, *Desde el Diseño* (1970); S. González, *Símbolos, Símbolos y Más Símbolos* (1970); R. Cabrera, *Los Símbolos de Félix Beltrán* (1983)

Bennett, Ward (b.1917) is an American furniture and interior designer, who was born in

Bellini's *Amanti chair (1967) made for C&B Italia.*

New York but studied painting in Florence (1937), sculpture under Constantin Brancusi in Paris (1937–38) and painting under Hans Hofmann in New York (1943). During the 1940s he worked in jewelry, clothing and shop design and was also apprenticed to LE CORBUSIER (1948–50). From 1950 he worked as a freelance designer in New York. His early furniture design is marked by its conservative elegance that often demanded a high standard of craftsmanship. In the 1970s, however, he was also acknowledged as a pioneer of HIGH-TECH.

Benson's, S.H. (f.1893) was founded by Samuel Herbert Benson, who set up as an advertiser's agent, following the suggestion of the owner of Bovril Ltd, John Johnstone, who had offered him all Bovril's business. The expansion of the agency reflects Benson's dynamic approach: he was not content to remain simply a 'space broker', but led the way in British advertising by offering a full range of services. Among their most important clients, besides Bovril, were Colman's mustard, Guinness and Rowntree's chocolate, all long-standing accounts (Guinness, for example, lasted from 1928 to 1969). Among their best-known artists were John Gilroy, H.H. Harris, John Hassal, Louis Weirter, Tom Purvis, H.M. Bateman, Abram GAMES and Tom ECKERSLEY. Benson's posters were extremely popular – characters such as the cook in Edward's Dessicated Soups and catch-phrases such as 'Guinness is good for you' were instantly recognized and became part of everyday language. In the 1920s and 30s their humour made the images particularly memorable.

Berlage, Hendrikus Petrus (1856–1934) was born in Amsterdam and studied architecture in Zurich (1875–78). After extensive European travel he set up his own architectural practice in Amsterdam. His buildings are characterized by their massive, Romanesque qualities in which materials and construction are exposed – plastering was seen as tantamount to falsification. In his most famous building, the Amsterdam Stock Exchange, completed in 1903, the steel-construction roof was left exposed. He also designed furniture and fittings. A prolific writer, he was responsible for bringing many of the design theories of Frank Lloyd WRIGHT to Europe. In his use of simple, smooth surfaces he was also influential in the development of the MODERN MOVEMENT in the Netherlands,

*S.H. **Benson**'s Guinness poster (1936).*

*The interior of **Berlage**'s Stock Exchange in Amsterdam, built 1898–1903.*

particularly as it affected the DE STIJL movement. In 1928 he attended the first congress of the CONGRÈS INTERNATIONAUX D'ARCHITECTURE MODERNE (CIAM).

☐H.P. Berlage, *Gedanken über den Stil in der Baukunst* (1905); *Grundlagen und Entwicklung der Architektur* (1908); *Studies over Bouwkunst, Stijl en Samenleving* (1910); J. Gratama, *Dr H.P. Berlage Bouwmeester* (1925); J. Havellar, *Dr H.P. Berlage* (1930); P. Singelenberg, *H.P. Berlage* (1969)

Berlewi, Henryk (1894–1967) was a Polish graphic designer who was initiated into the MODERN MOVEMENT through contact with radical Jewish artists and designers, including El LISSITZKY, in the early 1920s. From 1921 he was a member of the *Novembergruppe* (November group), a Berlin-based group of left-wing avant-garde artists. On his return to Warsaw in 1923 he published a booklet entitled *Mechano-Faktur* (Mechanical Production), in which he stressed the social role of art and advocated its 'mechanization' through standard geometric forms. Berlewi's own work at this time concentrated on arrangements of geometric forms in red, black and white, sometimes repeating the same shapes to almost kinetic effect. Mechano-Faktur was applied in the work of Reklama-Mechano (Mechanical Advertisements), a design bureau established in 1924 by Berlewi and two Futurist poets, Aleksander Wat and Stanisław Brucz, which produced brochures for commercial firms, employing the typographic techniques of the 'liberated page' introduced by the Futurists (*see* FUTURISM). In 1928 he left Poland for Paris and took up figurative painting. He returned to the themes of Mechano-Faktur in Poland after World War II.

☐A.K. Olszewski, *Henryk Berlewi* (1958)

Bernhard, Lucian (1883–1972) was born in Vienna and was largely self-taught as a graphic designer. In Berlin from 1905 he designed posters which used rounded, serif (*see* SANS SERIF) letters and eliminated superfluous elements; the posters focused on an illustration of the advertised article, which loomed large in the picture and which was accompanied only by the manufacturer's name in large, clear lettering. He also designed 36 typefaces. In 1920 he became the first professor of poster design at the Berlin Academy of Art. He was involved in establishing the magazine *Das Plakat* (later

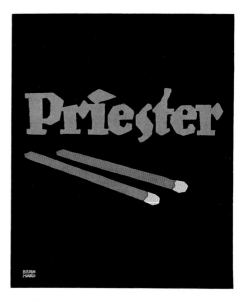

Bernhard's advertisement for 'Priester' (1905) launched his career in Berlin.

renamed *GEBRAUCHSGRAPHIK*). In 1923 he moved to the USA where he was co-founder of the design firm Contempora, with Rockwell Kent, Paul Poiret and Bruno Paul.

Berthold (f.1858) had become the largest producer of metal type in the world by the second decade of the 20th c. and is now one of the world's largest typefounders and manufacturers of PHOTOSETTING equipment. The company was founded by Hermann Berthold as a workshop for the manufacture of brass measuring gauges. In 1878 the German typefounding industry sought to create a standardized system of type measurement. Berthold undertook this task and produced the basis of the Didot System of type measurement, still in use today. By the turn of the century Berthold had added typefounding to its activities and had absorbed several German foundries. Its importance in type design increased following the release of the Akzidenz-Grotesk family – the first unified SANS-SERIF typeface design. For marketing reasons, this face was known as Standard in the English-speaking world. In 50 years time the development of a sans-serif face would result in the production of the Helvetica and Univers families by other main European foundries. After World War II Berthold was the leading company associated with the introduction of photosetting, producing the first commercial photosetting system, Diatype, in 1958. In the late 1970s, Erik Spiekermann (*see* METADESIGN) set about reworking the Berthold typefaces, Berliner Grotesk and Lo-Type, for filmsetting use. These typefaces were first released in 1913 alongside Block and are characterized by a strange, random, wobbly edge to the character. This was to add extra strength to the metal type to withstand the pounding against paper with high print runs. As a result, Block in particular has been a much used type in 20th-c. German printing.

Bertoia, Harry (1915–78) was a sculptor and furniture designer, who was born in Udine, Italy, but emigrated to the USA in 1930. He studied at the CRANBROOK ACADEMY OF ART, Michigan (1937–39), where he then taught metalwork (1939–43). He produced moulded PLYWOOD products for the war effort at the Evans Products Company, Venice, California (1943–46), where he also designed chairs with Charles EAMES. In 1950 he set up his own studio in Pennsylvania with the support of KNOLL International, for whom he designed his most famous piece, the Bertoia chair, launched in 1951. His furniture designs are characterized by a sculptural thinking, lightness and airiness – encouraged by the use of wire mesh in contrast to the plywood and moulded plastic favoured by Eames. Throughout the 1950s and 60s, his chairs were widely perceived as icons of modernity.
□J. Helson, *Harry Bertoia Sculptor* (1970)

Bertone (f.1912) is a Turin coach-building company founded by Giovanni Bertone. His son, Nuccio, joined in 1932, and it was with him that the company moved into car styling during the 1950s. This was seen in particular in its close relationship with ALFA ROMEO, but Bertone has also worked for Ferrari, Lancia, JAGUAR and FIAT, and its apprentices have included Giorgietto GIUGIARO.
□R. de la Rive Box and R. Crump, *The Automotive Art of Bertone* (1984)

Biba was the name of a series of London boutiques dating from the 1960s, and a large department store (1973–75), which became internationally renowned for their style. Devised by the fashion designer Barbara Hulanicki, the 'Biba style', as represented by the

Bertoia's *Diamond chair for Knoll (1952).*

department store's interior, used a mixture of Victoriana, ART NOUVEAU, ART DECO, camp, KITSCH and Hollywood.

Bill, Max (b.1908) is an exhibition, stage, graphic and industrial designer, painter, sculp-

Poster for the **Biba** *shop showing the 1960s revival of the Art Nouveau style.*

tor, architect and theorist, who was born in Winterthur, Switzerland. He studied silversmithing at the School of Arts and Crafts in Zurich (1924–27) and art at the BAUHAUS in Dessau (1927–29). Henceforth, he stalwartly upheld the Bauhaus values of the integration of practical art and design. Returning to Switzerland in 1929 he played a major role in the emergence of a Constructivist ideal in the SWISS SCHOOL of graphic design of the 1930s. In 1931 he embraced the concept of 'concrete art', a term proposed by Theo van DOESBURG in 1930 to describe a universal art of absolute clarity. He expressed this aesthetic in work that used grids, geometric progressions and mathematical formulas. In the early 1950s he designed the starkly a-historicist (*see* HISTORICISM) buildings of the ULM HOCHSCHULE FÜR GESTALTUNG, of which he was rector until 1956. His industrial projects demonstrate his commitment to efficiency of materials and form, beloved of the MODERN MOVEMENT.

☐ *Max Bill: Retrospektive: Skulpturen Gemälde Graphik 1928–1987* (exh. cat., Schirn Kunsthalle, Frankfurt, 1987)

biomorphism is the method of designing objects which imitate the appearance of living things.

bit mapping is a process in COMPUTER-AIDED DESIGN whereby a hard image is converted into (soft) digital form for storage in and retrieval from a computer.

Black, Misha (1910–77) was born in Russia and brought by his parents to Britain, aged 18 months. He studied briefly at the Central School of Arts and Crafts, London, but was largely self-taught in design. From 1928 he worked in the design of exhibition stands, before setting up Studio Z in 1930. In 1933 he joined the Bassett-Gray Group of Artists and Writers, which became the Industrial Design Partnership (1935–40), Britain's first multidisciplinary design studio. During World War II he designed many propaganda exhibitions for the Ministry of Information. In 1945 he was a founder of the DESIGN RESEARCH UNIT, with which he established his international reputation as an exhibition designer for his work on the Festival of Britain (1951). From the 1950s until his death he was extremely active in the DESIGN AND INDUSTRIES ASSOCIATION, the INTERNATIONAL COUNCIL OF SOCIE-

Bill's catalogue cover for the Concrete Art exhibition in Basle (1944).

TIES OF INDUSTRIAL DESIGN and as professor of industrial design at London's ROYAL COLLEGE OF ART (1959–75). As a practitioner and educationalist he was important in the development of ENGINEERING DESIGN in the postwar years.

☐ A. Blake, *Misha Black* (1984)

Black and Decker (f.1910) was founded by S. Duncan Black and Alonzo G. Decker as a small machine shop in Baltimore, Maryland, USA. In 1917 they patented the pistol grip and the trigger switch, innovations that are still standard in electric tools today. The company subsequently became a major multi-national corporation and a world leader in the manufacture of power tools, small household appliances and other labour-saving devices. During the 1960s and 70s, it designed tools for NASA's space programme. In 1979 it put the Dustbuster cordless vacuum cleaner on the market, creating a new category of household appliance.

Black Mountain College (1933–58) was founded by academics who had defected from Rollins College in Florida, USA, following a schism over teaching methods there. Led by

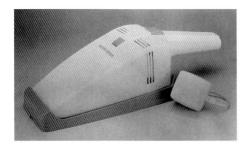

Black and Decker's *cordless vacuum cleaner, Dust Buster, launched in 1979.*

John Rice, they established their alternative 'ideal college' near Asheville, North Carolina. Its basic principles were democratic government and the central role of artistic studies. Its foundation coincided with the New Deal in the USA, but also with the fall of the BAUHAUS in Germany. It was thus saved from conformity by New Deal radicalism and by an influx of Bauhaus refugees. Among its staff, then, figured Walter GROPIUS, Josef ALBERS, Marcel BREUER and Xanti SCHAWINSKY as well as Buckminster FULLER, John Dewey, Carl Jung, Max Lerner, John Cage and Robert Rauschenberg. It was never a credited university and produced only 55 graduates in 25 years, but it none the less served as an important focal point for many successful artists and designers.

BMW (Bayerische Motoren Werke – Bavarian Motor Works) (f.1916) was set up in Munich, Bavaria, and the blue and white of its badge are the colours of the Bavarian flag. Initially it manufactured aero and marine engines and then from 1923 produced motor cycles, following with its first car in 1928. The 1937 BMW 328 was built to aircraft standards and was a lightweight alternative to the Mercedes-Benz. During the more economically stringent period of postwar Germany, BMW produced the Usetta series of bubble cars. However, once the economic miracle of the late 1950s had reached Germany, BMW went on to produce the more luxurious 1500 saloon in 1961. Cars subsequently designed under Wilhelm Hofmeister, Paul Bracq and, since 1974, Claus Luthe gradually became status symbols for young professionals throughout Europe. As a result of this popularity, traditions in BMW's design features could be maintained: these included the quality of production engineering, the res-

trained styling with its distinctive radiator grille and the fighter-plane-like instrumentation.
□P. Simsa, *BMW: La Suprématie Technologique Automobile* (1984)

Bohigas, Oriol (b.1925) is one of Spain's most important design theoreticians and *animateurs*. He qualified as an architect at the Barcelona School of Architecture in 1951, since when he has worked with Josep Martorell, incorporating David Mackay into his studio in 1961 to form MBM, and taking on Lluís Pau in 1974. He was a founder-member of Grup R (1951–58), which was important for its revival of the Modernist proposals of the 1930s GATCPAC group (the Group of Catalan Architects and Technicians for the Promotion of Contemporary Architecture), during a period that was otherwise conservative in its architecture. By the early 1960s, he was a leader of the Realist (*see* REALISM) architecture movement in Catalonia, combining Modernist principles (*see* MODERN MOVEMENT) with local vernacular methods of construction. In his modification of doctrines and styles, he thus laid the theoretical ground for generations of Spanish designers to come. The individualistic scale of projects and the sense of detail (often involving interior and some product design), as well as the interest in history without pastiche, were influential features of his theory and practice. His publications include *Barcelona entre el Pla Cerdà i el Barraquisme* (Barcelona Between the Cerdà Plan and the Shanty Towns; 1963), *Arquitectura Modernista* (Modernista Architecture; 1963), *Contra una Arquitectura Adjetivada* (Against an 'Adjectivized' Architecture; 1968), *Polèmica d'Arquitectura Catalana* (Polemics of Catalan Architecture; 1970) and *Reconstrucció de Barcelona* (Reconstruction of Barcelona; 1985). From 1964 to 1966 he was a lecturer at the Barcelona School of Architecture at the university; however, his political relationship with the university authorities was stormy. The marginalization of members of the radical avant-garde from the School of Architecture meant that their attention was focused on the private design schools, in particular on the art and design school in Barcelona, Eina. In 1970 he regained his position at the School of Architecture, but was sacked within months, the course he had planned to teach being instead transformed into a publication, *Proceso y Erótica del Diseño* (Process and Erotica in Design; 1972). As a leading spokesman of the short-lived School of Barcelona (approximately 1968–71), he crystallized his theories, which included stress on the use of, and sometimes ironic play on, visual languages in design, a position that may be interpreted as typical of POSTMODERNISM. On the other hand, he has also faithfully adhered to some Modernist principles, particularly in drawing attention to the importance of urban planning as the hub of architectural activity. In this respect, his appointment as representative of *l'Area d'Urbanisme* (Town Planning Section) on the new Barcelona city council in 1980 (succeeded by Josep Acebillo in 1984) ensured the urban revitalization of the city. This approach has had important resonances for the conception of town planning in other countries, but more specifically, has brought the concept of design closer to the everyday lives of Catalan and Spanish citizens.

Bonsiepe, Gui (b.1934) is a German product designer and theorist who studied at the ULM HOCHSCHULE FÜR GESTALTUNG (1955–59) and then taught there (1960–68). After the college's closure in 1968 he moved to work freelance in Santiago de Chile in the Dominican Republic (1968–74), Buenos Aires (1974–81) and then in Brasilia from 1981. He has been an important figure in the development of industrial design in South America, and his methodology, seen in his writings, continues the Modernist line (*see* MODERN MOVEMENT) of the Ulm teaching. Set against the backdrop of the fast-growing consumer society of some South American countries, his contribution is significant. He calls for a straightforward approach to design in 'the Periphery', by which he means countries at the edge of Western capitalism such as those of South America, and asserts that neither stylistic gimmicks nor a hankering for 'GOOD DESIGN' are relevant.
□ G. Bonsiepe, *Design im Übergang zum Sozialismus* (1974); *Diseño Industrial: Artefacto y Proyecto* (1975); *Teoria e Pratica del Disegno Industriale* (1975); *Periféria del Diseño* (1984)

Borax was an American slang term dating from the 1920s which was derived from the premiums offered by the Borax soap company. It referred to cheap but ostentatious products, particularly shoddily made furniture. Following the influx of American style into Europe after World War II, it was used in Britain to refer to exaggerated STREAMLINING and surface effects, for example on juke boxes.

Bortnyik, Sándor (1893–1977) was a painter and poster designer who, from 1917, was an active member of MA (Today), the Hungarian avant-garde group led by Lajos KASSÁK. After the collapse of the Hungarian Republic of Councils in 1920, Bortnyik, a Socialist, was forced to flee the country for Vienna and later, Weimar. He returned to Hungary in 1926, where he edited the artistic and literary journal *Uj Föld* (New Earth), and from 1928 he ran 'Workshop', a poster studio in Budapest. His own work as a poster designer in the late 1920s reveals his background as an abstract artist in the period shortly before and after 1920. His advertising poster designs of the late 1920s for products such as Modiano cigarette papers were typically composed from simple, geometric forms using SANS-SERIF display faces. After World War II he taught graphic design at the Budapest School of Applied Arts.
□ *100 + 1 lat Plakatu Wegierskiego* (exh. cat., Muzeum Plakatu w Wilanowie, Warsaw, 1986)

branding is the process through which value and meaning are added to PRODUCTS through a combination of PACKAGING, naming, advertising and MARKETING. The successful branding of a product should lead to what has been termed a 'sustainable, differential advantage' over other, similar goods or services in the same market sector. That is, a well-branded product will be chosen by consumers over palpably identical product ranges on the strength of brand identity, product performance and implications of improved status and lifestyle.

Brandt, Marianne (1893–1983) was born in Chemnitz, Germany, and began studying painting and sculpture in Weimar in 1911. In 1923 she joined the BAUHAUS, working in the metal workshop, then under the direction of László MOHOLY-NAGY. In 1928 she took over the metal workshop for a brief period. In 1929 she moved to Berlin to work as a designer in the studio of Walter GROPIUS. Here she worked chiefly on the design of mass-produced single-piece furniture and the interior decoration of some of the houses of the Building Exhibition at Karlsruhe-Dammerstock. Though all her designs for domesticware were craft prototypes, in their uncompromising geometric purity they marked an aesthetic which was subsequently to be widely employed. One of her most successful designs, a small, metal-

Bedside lamp designed for Körting and Mathiesen by **Brandt** *and Hein Briedendiek in 1928.*

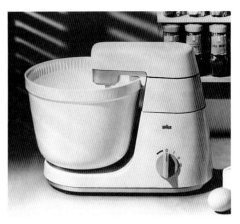

Braun's *Kitchen Machine KM 321 (1957) was an early electric food mixer.*

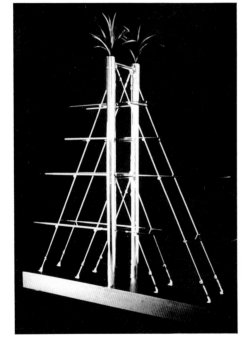

Branzi *designed the Magnolia bookcase for Memphis in 1985.*

shaded bedside lamp set on a flexible stem, was manufactured by Körting and Mathiesen in Leipzig in 1928. Körting and Mathiesen made approximately 50,000 lamps based on prototypes of the Bauhaus metal workshop's students and staff between 1928 and 1932. After World War II Brandt taught at the School of Fine Arts in Dresden (1949–51) and at the Industrial Design School in East Berlin (1951–54) before retiring in 1954. A 1926 Brandt ashtray was re-edited by ALESSI in 1985.

Branzi, Andrea (b.1938) studied architecture in Florence and is a leading intellectual in Italian design. He was a founder member of ARCHI-ZOOM and educational director of the Domus Academy (*see DOMUS*). He also worked with STUDIO ALCHYMIA and MEMPHIS. In his book, *The Hot House: Italian New Wave Design* (1984), he expounded the theory that design is both a practical and a philosophical enterprise, which embraces everything from the practicality of architecture to the philosophy of semiotics. In the 1980s he was a proponent of the NEW DESIGN, and his teaching advocates a recuperation of design for the ordinary individual that is typical of POSTINDUSTRIALISM.
□A. Branzi, *Learning from Milan: Design and the Second Modernity* (1988)

Braun (f.1921) is a German company that makes domestic appliances and scientific instruments and was founded in Frankfurt by Max Braun. The company first produced a patented device for connecting driving belts for machi-

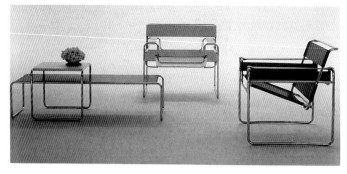

*The Gavina collection, including **Breuer's** Wassily chair, designed in 1925 and now manufactured by Knoll.*

nery, but soon moved into PLASTICS, components for radios and gramophones and then on to whole sets. It was in the context of the reconstruction of Germany following World War II that household appliances and electric shavers were added to this line. When Max Braun died in 1951, his two sons Artur and Erwin took over the company and engaged Dr Fritz Eichler in 1954 to direct its new design programme in collaboration with the ULM HOCHSCHULE FÜR GESTALTUNG. Eichler brought Hans GUGELOT and Otl AICHER from Ulm, and Dieter RAMS later joined in 1955. Henceforth a product style was developed which is synonymous with both Ulm and Braun, based on attention to detail and geometric simplicity. This aesthetic was for many commentators a paradigm of the INTERNATIONAL STYLE and 'GOOD DESIGN'. When, in 1956, Braun set up its own design department, with Rams taking over as chief designer in 1960, almost all appliances and supporting publicity were designed in-house to create a cohesive CORPORATE IDENTITY. Yet despite its excellence in DESIGN MANAGEMENT, the company did not experience great commercial success and was bought by American Gillette in 1967. In the early 1990s it again experienced commercial difficulties as its consistently cold design became outmoded, and it also faced growing international competition in the manufacture of electrical appliances.
□ W. Schmittel, *Design: Concept, Form, Realisation* (1977); F. Burkhardt and I. Franksen, *Design: Dieter Rams &* (1982)

Breuer, Marcel (1902–81) was born in Pécs, Hungary, and studied at the BAUHAUS (1920–24). As a student, his furniture designs were highly influenced by international CONSTRUCTIVISM and the Dutch DE STIJL move-

ment and were thus rather stark. Breuer was one of the few students actually to graduate from the Bauhaus and in 1925 he was appointed head of the carpentry workshop at the school's new site in Dessau. There followed a burst of creative energy until 1930, during which period he developed his most famous contributions to 20th-c. design in the form of TUBULAR-STEEL furniture. When Breuer moved to Dessau he bought his first bicycle, which he worshipped. He was captivated by its strength and lightness, brought about by the tubular-steel frame, and went to its manufacturers, Adler, proposing that they produced furniture in the same material. This initiative met with no interest, so he bought his own tubes and set about producing a prototype for a chair. The end result was the celebrated Wassily chair of 1925. With its cubic shape and tautly stretched planes, it continued to echo the De Stijl-Constructivist aesthetic; none the less it also suggested the idea of the sitter being suspended in space. This concept was continued in his cantilever chair, also known as the B32, designed the following year; with its unbroken length of tubing and panels of wood and caning, it subsequently became the model for countless similar chairs all over the world. He also designed tables and tools in the same materials.

In mid-1928 Breuer moved away from Dessau to work as an architect in Berlin, where he undertook mostly interior work. From 1931 he began to travel more widely, working wherever he could. In Switzerland from 1932 he began to develop ALUMINIUM furniture for retailing by the Wohnbedarf home-furnishings stores. The material had the advantage of being lighter than tubular steel, but it was not as strong. Thus his furniture designs here could not contain the formal clarity of the earlier projects, the construction requiring more complex systems of support. On the other hand, they are also a testimony to Breuer's concern with comfort.

Following his former Bauhaus colleague, Walter GROPIUS, Breuer moved to England in 1935. Via Gropius, he was put in touch with Jack PRITCHARD, who was a founder of the ISOKON Company. Pritchard asked Breuer to produce the company's first PLYWOOD reclining chair, further developing a similar project he had earlier undertaken in Switzerland. Breuer's plywood designs during this English period were highly reminiscent of Alvar AALTO's of a few years earlier; none the less, they were influential in their own right for years to come. Isokon, and the MODERN MOVEMENT in general, was a short-lived adventure and, like Gropius, Breuer found a dearth of architectural commissions in England and subsequently moved to the USA in 1937. There he mostly produced experimental furniture, as well as acting as an associate professor at Harvard University (1937–46). His best-known project undertaken in the USA was his own house at New Canaan, Connecticut, in 1947, which became something of a mecca for aficionados of modern architecture.

With the exception of his tubular-steel chairs, which were nevertheless still expensive in comparison with simple bentwood furniture, few of Breuer's designs achieved commercial success. It was not until the 1960s that his B32 chair became relatively inexpensive (through lower-quality copies). His most densely creative period took place when he was in his twenties and, as Wilk notes: 'Unlike architects already trained in one tradition of design who switched their allegiance to a modern aesthetic, Breuer was of the age where he was able to become completely educated in the precepts of the newly developing modernism.' Concentrating on a narrow range of materials and furniture types, he produced some of the most lasting furniture designs of the 20th c.

☐ C. Wilk, *Marcel Breuer: Furniture and Interiors* (1981)

BrionVega (f.1945) was established in Milan by the Brion family, initially to manufacture radio sets. With the advent of Italy's first television network, the company moved into the production of the first all-Italian television sets in 1952. It was not until the early 1960s that it began to work with designers – Marco ZANUSO, Richard SAPPER, Achille CASTIG-

Brodovitch's poster for Lumière (1928).

LIONI and Mario BELLINI. In 1962 it produced the first fully transistorized Italian television, designed by Zanuso and Sapper, followed in 1964 by the Algol 11 television set, which brought their designs closer to the neo-Modernist box forms that marked the company's style for a decade, and put their products in competition with the Germans.

Brodovitch, Alexey (1898–1971) was art director of *Harper's Bazaar* for 25 years (1934–58) and had a decisive impact on magazine design. He was born in Russia but after World War I and the Russian Revolution moved to Paris in 1920. There he painted houses and later stage sets for Sergei Diaghilev's Ballets Russes. He also began to work as a designer for *Arts et Métiers Graphiques* and *Cahiers d'Art* and won five medals for his design work at the PARIS EXPOSITION DES ARTS DÉCORATIFS ET INDUSTRIELS, 1925. In 1930 he emigrated with his family to Philadelphia, USA, where he was asked to organize the department of advertising

Brody's *cover for the record* James Brown *by Cabaret Voltaire (1984).*

represented. Brodovitch's work was characterized by unconventional cropping of photographs, the use of WHITE SPACE as a design element and classical typefaces. For the photography he hired such innovators as Henri Cartier-Bresson, Man Ray and Richard Avedon and was adept at relating images to typeface and tone. He also established the Design Laboratory at the New York School for Social Research (1941–49), revitalizing it after his retirement in 1958.

☐ A. Grundberg, *Brodovitch* (1989)

Brody, Neville (b.1957) initially studied fine art before turning to graphic design at the London College of Printing (1976–79). His early work – record sleeves for independent record companies – is dominated by imagery: he worked for Rocking Russian, Stiff Records and Fetish Records. When in 1981 he was appointed art director of *The Face*, the style and music magazine, he became increasingly interested in typography as a visual language equalling editorial content. By inventing alphabets, hand drawing and breaking down letter forms and symbols, he freely exploited the facility of typography to influence the editorial message of the text. His other magazine work was for *City Limits* (1983–87), *New Socialist*, *Touch* and, after leaving *The Face* in 1986, *Arena*. He also designs books, posters and logos. Following his 'retrospective' exhibition at the Victoria and Albert Museum and published biography in 1988, Brody has become internationally known. He still chooses to work in a small studio, though in 1990 he joined up with

design at the Pennsylvania Museum School of Industrial Design. His teaching, as well as his appointment as art director at *Harper's Bazaar*, allowed him to introduce many of the ideas he had learnt in the Paris of the 1920s into graphic design. His arrival at the magazine coincided with a change in its direction from a clothes magazine to something more like what is today known as a 'style' magazine; under the directorship of Carmel Snow, it relied less on the endorsement of clothes by rich, 'society' families, than their own merits. The art director thus had to seek other ways to highlight the fashion

Poster by **Burchartz** *for the International Exhibition of Advertising Art in Essen (1931).*

the interior design company, Post. Since 1986, sickened by imitators, he has moved towards a more conventional typography, closer to the traditions of the MODERN MOVEMENT, although freely interpreted using an APPLE Macintosh computer.
☐J. Wozencroft, *The Graphic Language of Neville Brody* (1988)

Bunzlau is a region of Poland which is renowned for its avant-garde ceramics of the interwar years. It formed part of Germany until 1945 and produced some of the most interesting ceramics of the Weimar period (1919–33). The main impetus for this came from the Bunzlau State Ceramic School. Founded in 1897, its first director, Dr Wilhelm Pukall, had previously been head of the technical department of the Königlich Preussische Porzellan Manufaktur (Royal Prussian Porcelain Factory). He instigated a rigorous technical training at the school. Edouard Berdel, who succeeded Pukall in 1925, divided the training equally into two halves: one technical, taught by himself, and the other artistic, taught by Artur Hennig. The resultant works had strongly geometric forms and decorations and exhibited a strong Modernistic spirit which broke from the traditional brownwares of the region. Some of the work that came out of the school was produced by the Friedrich Kaestner and the Krister porcelain factories from 1928. The heyday of Bunzlau ceramics came to an end in 1931 when Hennig left the school, which itself was finally closed in 1945.
☐*Keramik in der Weimarer Republik 1919–1933* (exh. cat., Germanisches Nationalmuseum, Nuremberg, 1985)

Burchartz, Max (1887–1961) was a German graphic designer who studied in Düsseldorf, Munich and Berlin (1908–9). After World War I he lived in Hanover, where he was in contact with Kurt SCHWITTERS and El LISSITZKY; he then moved to Weimar, where he met Theo van DOESBURG, Paul Klee and Wassily Kandinsky. He founded the agency Werbebau in Bochum, Germany, in the 1920s, and it was there that he wrote a number of pamphlets addressing problems of advertising and graphic design. Burchartz was thus an early disseminator of modern advertising principles and is particularly well known for the use of photography in his designs.

Bürolandschaft was a form of office planning developed in Germany by the specialists in office organization, Eberhard und Wolfgang Schnelle, during the late 1950s and early 1960s. *Bürolandschaft* – which means 'office landscape' – explored for the first time the possibility of an open-plan office using screens and potted plants as dividers. This provided a less regimented effect in the office, both managerially and visually, and made office space organization easier. It was a concept adopted and developed in the USA by office furniture specialists such as George NELSON.

C

C&B Italia *see* B&B ITALIA

CAD *see* COMPUTER-AIDED DESIGN

Caflisch's *device for a catalogue cover for the Swiss Booksellers and Publishers (c.1950).*

Caflisch, Max (b.1916) is a Swiss typographic and lettering designer who studied with Jan TSCHICHOLD at the School of Arts and Crafts in Zurich (1936–38), where he later also became an instructor in typography (1962–81). He was subsequently a leading exponent of the SWISS SCHOOL. He translated into German and designed Stanley MORISON's *First Principles of Typography*.

California New Wave was the term given to an internationally influential tendency among graphic designers based in California in the mid-1980s. These designers included April GREIMAN, Lucille Tenazas and the designers of the graphics magazine *ÉMIGRÉ*. Their work generally displayed a loose, intuitive style, often including gaudy colours, the use of older, non-

Carlu's *poster for Cuisine Electrique (1935) extolling the virtues of cooking by electricity.*

Advertisement for the Paris-Brussels-Amsterdam Pullman by **Cassandre** *(1927).*

Modernist typefaces (e.g., Baskerville, Caslon and Garamond) and the mixing and overlay of type, photography and illustration in fragmented compositions. To some extent their work was a more spirited version of design work already developed at the CRANBROOK ACADEMY OF ART, where some of them had studied. It also benefitted from the extensive use of APPLE Macintosh COMPUTER-AIDED DESIGN systems and has been interpreted as being expressive of both DECONSTRUCTION and POSTMODERNISM. A representative exhibition, called Pacific Wave, was shown in Europe at the Museo Fortuny in Venice in 1987.

CAM *see* COMPUTER-AIDED MANUFACTURE

Cappiello, Leonetto (1875–1942) was born in Livorno, Italy, and moved to Paris in 1898. He became known as a caricaturist, but gradually moved into poster design, signing a contract with the printer and publisher Vercasson. For the ensuing two decades, apart from a return to Italy during World War I, he had a considerable influence on French poster design. His advertis-

ing posters were dominated by attention-grabbing motifs, such as wild horses, lions and other exotica. However, by the mid-1920s this approach was seen by Parisian critics as naive and unsophisticated as compared with the work of A.M. CASSANDRE or Jean CARLU. He is reputed to have designed over 3,000 posters during his life and he not only worked for French clients, but also for Italian, Portuguese, Spanish and South American customers.
□ *Cappiello, 1875–1942: Caricatures, Affiches, Peintures et Projets Décoratifs* (exh. cat., Grand Palais, Paris, 1981)

Carlu, Jean (b.1900) was born in Bonnières-sur-Seine, France, and began his training in architecture. On losing his right arm in an accident in 1918, he turned to graphic design. From 1918 to 1923 he was influenced by Cubism and, along with A.M. CASSANDRE, introduced a geometrical treatment of forms into advertising art. Making use of symbols rather than realism, his posters were simple, concentrated and brief in text. He championed an abstractionist – rather than representational or anecdotal – approach to illustration. When

Paris was occupied in 1940, Carlu was in the USA, where he stayed until 1953. There he produced the first US defence poster in 1941. He returned to France in 1953 and continued to design posters there until he retired in 1974.
□ *Jean Carlu* (exh. cat., Musée de l'Affiche, Paris, 1980)

Carter, David (b.1927) is the founder of DCA Design Consultants (f.1958), a large Warwick-based industrial design office specializing in ENGINEERING DESIGN and ERGONOMICS. He was apprenticed in various manufacturing firms from 1943. DCA's clients include Stanley, for whom Carter designed many tools during the 1970s, and London Transport.

Carter, Matthew (b.1937) was born in England and trained as a printer, but moved to the USA in the 1960s. He became a staff designer at Mergenthaler LINOTYPE where he worked on new typefaces and on the conversion of metal faces to PHOTOSETTING. In 1978 he designed the Bell Centennial typeface for AT&T's telephone books; the new face meant that the size of the subsidiary address part of an entry could be reduced, and thus space, money and ultimately paper (and then forests) could be saved. In 1981 he founded Bitstream Inc., the world's first computer 'typefoundry'. While being utterly rigorous in the aesthetic creation of typefaces, he was also a keen promotor of the democratization of printing and graphic design, made possible by the growth of COMPUTER-AIDED DESIGN.

Cassandre, A.M. (1901–68) was born as Adolphe Jean-Marie Mouron and studied painting at the Académie Julian (1918–21). In 1920s Paris he was immersed in avant-garde circles, maintaining friendships with Robert Delaunay, Guillaume Apollinaire, Fernand Léger and Erik Satie. He introduced Modernist painting into poster designs, which he signed as A.M. Cassandre from 1923. The influences of Georges Braque, Pablo Picasso and André Derain are apparent, as well as a debt to Cubism, Purism and machine art, particularly in his transport posters. In 1927 he founded the Alliance Graphique, an advertising and design agency, with Charles Loupot and Maurice Moyrand. He designed three typefaces – Bifur (1929), L'Acier (1930) and Peignot (1937). He also worked for various American companies, including the CONTAINER CORPORATION OF AMERICA and FORD. Like Jean CARLU and E. McKnight KAUFFER, Cassandre was decisive in applying the basic lessons of the MODERN MOVEMENT – the principles of clarity and of the reduction of the message to its essential features – to visual communication. Thus people and objects might be reduced to simple geometric shapes. Unlike the Modernists, however, his typography concentrated on upper-case letters, emphasizing their monumentality.
□ H. Mouron, *Cassandre* (1985)

Cassina (f.1927) was founded by Cesare Cassina and based in the Milanese suburb of Meda. Cassina came from a long line of joiners, and in its early years the firm produced 19th-c. style furniture on a modest scale. In the early 1930s the company expanded rapidly, with the Rinascente store and the Mobilificio di Fogliano as major buyers. Though mechanization increased its production capability, the firm's pre-World War II furniture styles remained conservative. After the War, Cassina was one of the first Italian furniture companies to move into furniture in the modern style for an international market. This development was in part due to a bulk order from the Italian navy, between 1947 and 1952, which forced the company into further rationalization and mass-production. It was also a result of its collaboration with the new generation of architect-designers, such as Franco ALBINI (1946–47) and Gio PONTI (from 1950), the man responsible for the highly successful Superleggera chair. Other designers to work with Cassina include

Gaetano Pesce's Feltri armchair was produced by **Cassina** *(1987).*

Mario BELLINI, Paolo DEGANELLO and Vico MAGISTRETTI. In 1965 it began to produce LE CORBUSIER, Pierre Jeanneret and Charlotte Perriand's chaise longue to its original 1929 design. This alignment with the MODERN MOVEMENT equated the company's contemporary products with the masters of an earlier period. In the 80s the firm extended the manufacture of design CLASSICS by 'name' designers into the work of Gunnar ASPLUND, Marcel BREUER and Charles Rennie MACKINTOSH. This was a polemical move in view of the issue of 'ownership of copyright' of such designs.

Castelli-Ferrieri, Anna (b.1920) was born in Milan, where she studied architecture, graduating in 1943. Marrying into the Castelli family in the same year, she subsequently began a long career designing for their company, KARTELL. She developed many new products with them using PLASTICS as well as POLYURETHANE, polystyrene and polypropylene.
☐A. Castelli-Ferrieri (ed.), *Plastic and Design* (1984)

Castiglioni, Achille (b.1918) has played a particularly important role in the history of Italian design. He was born in Milan, where he studied architecture at the Polytechnic, graduating in 1944. He then collaborated with his

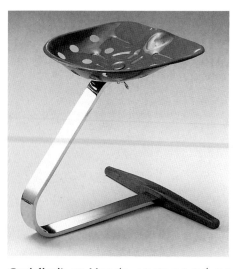

Castiglioni's *220 Mezzadro, a tractor-seat stool, was designed in 1957 and produced by Zanotta from 1971.*

brothers Livio (until 1954) and Pier Giacomo (until 1968) in a range of design disciplines including product, furniture and interior design. While his belief in the reformatory potential of design could be seen as typical of NEO-MODERNISM, his approach has also been 'integral': he designs with a strong awareness of form, production and the user. Equally, the designs themselves have been variable. His lighting (e.g., his projects for Flos) demonstrates a clear 'techno-FUNCTIONALISM' in which nothing is included without an obvious functional meaning. At the same time, he is most famous for his exploration, influenced by artists such as Marcel Duchamp, of readymades; in 1957, for example, he used a tractor seat as the basis for a stool, the Mezzadro, which was eventually manufactured by ZANOTTA from 1971. This stool became very popular for use in HIGH-TECH interiors, though it also expresses a POP design sensibility.
☐A. Castiglioni, *Design e la sua Prospettive Disciplinari* (1977); P. Ferrari, *Achille Castiglioni* (1984)

Centre de Création Industrielle (f.1969) was founded in Paris by the Union Centrale des Arts Décoratifs and moved to the Pompidou Centre in 1972. It acts as an information and communication centre, covering 'spaces, objects and signs', in other words, architecture and urbanism, industrial design and publicity, the media, graphic design and all other forms of visual communication. It has organized thematic exhibitions, including the important Nouvelles Tendances exhibition of 1987, which brought together such avant-garde designers as Phillipe STARCK, Javier MARISCAL and Ron ARAD. None the less, it centres its concerns on the design of everyday objects and therefore holds a considerable documentation centre intended to chronicle the material and visual culture of modern times. It has thus played an important role in focusing theoretical debate in France.

Chermayeff, Ivan (b.1932) is a long-respected American architect, graphic and exhibition designer. He is the son of the celebrated architect Serge CHERMAYEFF and studied at Harvard (1950–52), the Chicago Institute of Design (1952–54) and Yale University School of Art and Architecture (1954–55). In 1957 Brownjohn, Chermayeff and Geismar was formed, becoming Chermayeff & Geismar Inc.

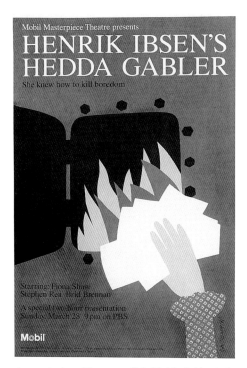

Mobil Masterpiece Theatre presents

HENRIK IBSEN'S HEDDA GABLER

She knew how to kill boredom

Starring: Fiona Shaw
Stephen Rea, Brid Brennan

A special two-hour presentation
Sunday, March 28 9 pm on PBS

Mobil

*A poster by Ivan **Chermayeff** for* Hedda Gabler *in the Mobil Masterpiece Theatre series.*

in 1960. Since 1964 he has also been part of Cambridge Seven Associates, an architectural and multi-disciplinary design firm in Massachusetts. His wide range of work includes record sleeves, posters, CORPORATE IDENTITY, PACKAGING, magazine covers, children's book illustration and art work, particularly collages. Some of the best-known examples of his work are corporate identity schemes for Chase Manhattan Bank (1959), Mobil Oil (1962) and Xerox (1965). He was also responsible for exhibition design for USA displays at Expo '67 and '70, posters for Masterpiece Theatre Television sponsored by Mobil in the 80s and the NBC television symbol (1987). While much of his work remains within the traditions of the MODERN MOVEMENT, exploiting simplicity and directness, there is often also a subtle touch of humour or eccentricity, which ensures the longevity of his designs.
☐ I. Chermayeff, *The Design Necessity* (1973); *Chermayeff and Geismar Associates: Trademarks* (1979)

Chermayeff, Serge (b.1900) was born of a wealthy family in the Caucasus, Russia, and was educated from 1910 in London. As an architect, designer and painter he was largely self-taught, however. He first worked as a journalist at Amalgamated Press (1918–22) and then ran a ballroom in Buenos Aires (1922–24). On his return to London he was employed by the decorating firm E. Williams Ltd (1924–27) and then as director of the Modern Art Studio of the furniture manufacturers, Waring and Gillow. He moved the company away from its HISTORICISM towards a more modern style, influenced to some degree by the PARIS EXPOSITION DES ARTS DÉCORATIFS ET INDUSTRIELS, 1925. From 1929 he was very much influenced by Eric GILL and Erich Mendelsohn, and after a period in private practice as an architect (1931–33), went into partnership with the latter (1933–36). It was during this period that he designed TUBULAR-STEEL chairs for PEL (1931–34) and the highly successful Ekco radio cabinets in BAKELITE (1933). In 1940 he emigrated to the USA, where he taught at Brooklyn College, New York (1942–46), and then took over from László MOHOLY-NAGY as head of the Institute of Design, Chicago, in 1947. From 1951 he taught architecture at MIT, Harvard and Yale universities. He was perhaps Britain's most energetic representative of the MODERN MOVEMENT and was instrumental in bringing Modernism to the USA.
☐ R. Plunz, *Projects and Theories of Serge Chermayeff* (1972); S. Chermayeff, *Design and the Public Good: Selected Writings 1930–1970* (1982)

chrome *see* CHROMIUM

chromium is a silvery metallic element obtained from chrome ironstone by smelting. It was discovered by the French chemist Louis Nicolas Vauquelin in 1798 but was not made commercially available until 1925, after having been used for projectile coverings during World War I. It was quickly adopted as a covering for TUBULAR STEEL by designers such as Marcel BREUER and Ludwig MIES VAN DER ROHE. Its brilliance and resistance to corrosion made it an ideal finish for this material.

Chrysler Corporation (f.1925) was a car manufacturer founded in Detroit by Walter

The **Chrysler Corporation**'s *Airflow (1934).*

The **Citroën** *DS 19, first seen in 1955.*

Chrysler, former vice-president of GENERAL MOTORS (1916–19). The Chrysler Four (1925) represented a new departure in car design, as it isolated the engine from the frame and thus reduced jarring. Chrysler's greatest advance was with the Airflow (1934), which placed the engine over the front axle; this resulted in greater spaciousness throughout the car. Its engineer, Carl Breer, also introduced STREAMLINING and a measure of ERGONO-MICS into the design, but the car had little commercial success, although these new developments were incorporated into many subsequent cars. Chrysler's industrial success, however, was due to its higher profit margins brought about by greater integration – the company made greater use of standardized parts and relied less on subcontracting than its competitors. By 1939 it was the USA's second biggest car manufacturer. It was not until the late 1970s, when Chrysler faced near bankruptcy, that it introduced greater diversification in its models to compete with European and Japanese manufacturers.
☐M. Moritz and B. Seaman, *Going for Broke: Lee Iacocca's Battle to Save Chrysler* (1984)

Chwast, Seymour (b.1931) is an American graphic designer who studied at Cooper Union, New York (1948–51), following which he founded the PUSH PIN STUDIO with Milton Glaser in 1954. His work is visually dense in contrast with the spatial depth of Glaser's designs. He tends unashamedly to acknowledge public advertising's popular origins, using 19th-c. typography, invigorated with bright colour, as demonstrated by his famous anti-Vietnam War poster: 'War is Good Business: Invest your Son' (1967).
☐T. Nishio, *Seymour Chwast* (1974)

CIAM *see* CONGRÈS INTERNATIONAUX D'ARCHITECTURE MODERNE

Cieslewicz, Roman (b.1930) was born in Lvov in the Ukraine, and graduated from the Fine Arts Academy in Cracow in 1955. He first gained prominence as a member of the POLISH SCHOOL of poster design in the late 1950s and early 1960s. In 1963 he moved to Paris where he became art director of *Elle* magazine. He was later art director of *Mafia* (1969–70) and in 1970 founded *Kitsch* magazine. He began to create PHOTOMONTAGES in the early 1960s and started including more surreal elements in the late 1970s. He often used enlarged halftone images and increasingly created disturbing juxtapositions and distortions.

Citroën (f.1913) is responsible for two CLASSIC cars of the 20th c.: the 2CV and the DS. It was established before World War I as an arms factory by André Cirtroën; but when demand dropped at the end of the War, it went into car production. The Type A (1919) was Europe's first mass-produced car – André Citroën had been inspired by the American technique of FORDISM – and the first low-cost car to be sold with an on-board starter and electric lights. Production of this car leapt from 2,000 to 12,000 in its first two years. Citroën soon produced subsequent models and established subsidiary companies through Europe and North Africa during the 1920s. In 1934, despite severe financial difficulties, it launched the Traction Avant, engineered by André Lefevre. The inclusion of front-wheel drive allowed a freer use of passenger space, and the long wheel base gave more comfort. The company's major creditors, Michelin, took over Citroën in 1935. Then in 1936 Citroën conceived the idea of a low-priced car with a very small engine to compete with the VOLKSWAGEN Beetle. The result was architect-engineer Pierre Boulanger's 2CV, launched in 1939. This economic and straightforward car was produced until 1990, when it was superseded by the lightweight AX. The Traction Avant was replaced with the DS19 in 1957. This was the most advanced popular car of all time, its distinctive bodywork designed by Flaminio BERTONE. Unveiled in prototype on 5 October 1955 at the Paris Motor Show, by the end of the day 12,000 people had placed orders. Its streamlined and sculptured body was extremely aerodynamic and looked, as Roland Barthes was to comment, 'as if it has fallen from the sky'. It included a unique hydraulic suspension system, a FIBREGLASS-reinforced plastic roof, disc brakes and semi-automatic transmission.

Although 1.4 million units of the DS were sold, Citroën was not a high profit-making company and in 1975 it was taken over by the more conservative Peugeot Group. Subsequent designs, such as the BX by Bertone (1982), did not achieve the avant-gardism of Citroën's earlier cars.

☐ *Modelfall Citroën – Produktgestaltung und Werbung* (exh. cat., Kunstgewerbemuseum, Zurich, 1967); J. Borge and N. Viasnoff, *L'Album de la DS* (1983)

classic refers to a design which visually or by association sums up the best of its time, and yet whose appeal has surpassed its immediate historical context. One prerequisite for its elevation to 'classic' status is that the design receives the official approval of an institution or individual (e.g., a design historian), and/or that it has become highly popular through its mass production, reproduction or mass publication in photographic form. Posthumously or not, it may also have received the accolade of 'GOOD DESIGN'.

Classics often include automobiles, such as the VOLKSWAGEN Beetle (1945), or even personal effects, such as the Zippo lighter (1932). Increasingly, however, the term has been associated with furniture. The New York MUSEUM OF MODERN ART has been influential in this process, as it has exhibited the furniture of designer heroes such as Ludwig MIES VAN DER ROHE, Marcel BREUER, LE CORBUSIER, Alvar AALTO and Charles EAMES.

Since the late 1970s, demand for reproductions of branded classics has grown, and com-

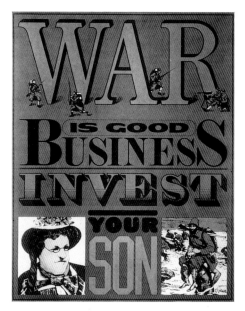

Chwast's *famous anti-Vietnam War poster (1967) for the Push Pin Studio.*

mentators have suggested that this reflects on the one hand a general increase in awareness of design, and therefore of its history, and on the other, a desire to display an alignment with serious, long-lasting, non-gimmicky design. Large companies such as CASSINA and KNOLL, as well as smaller producers such as Aram and B.D. Ediciones de Diseño, have nurtured this demand in bringing out classic re-makes. This has led to some torrid court battles over the intricacies of licences, as well as criticism of the sometimes unfaithful and poor standards of reproduction.

Cliff, Clarice (1899–1972) was the designer of some of the most strikingly original British industrial ceramics. She was born in Tunstall, Staffordshire, and became an apprenticed enameller at the Lingard, Webster & Co. earthenware factory in 1912. She then became an apprentice in lithography at the firm of Hollinshead and Kirkham and took painting classes at the Tunstall School of Art. In 1916 she was taken on as a lithographer at A.J. Wilkinson Ltd, the Royal Staffordshire Pottery in Burslem. She remained with Wilkinson's for the rest

Cliff's boldly decorated table-ware (c.1930) made for the Newport Pottery.

of her working life, and married its managing director, Colley Shorter, in 1941. Around 1925 Shorter allowed Cliff to experiment with the blanks from the Newport Pottery which Wilkinson's had taken over. In 1927 she set up in the Newport Pottery and produced the Bizarre range of pottery: extremely unusual in its bright, almost garish decoration, applied in bold blocks of colour. The pottery itself was often highly geometric, giving it a strong ART DECO feel. These hand-painted ceramics achieved great success between 1929 and 1935; Newport Wilkinson employed about 150 people in its decorating shop to produce them. In 1932 she used contemporary artists as designers, among them Duncan Grant and Vanessa Bell from the OMEGA group; others included Paul Nash and Graham Sutherland. The full range was exhibited at Harrods in London in an exhibition called Modern Art for the Table. Production of the Bizarre pottery stopped during World War II, and demand for it dropped after the War. Cliff continued to work at Newport Wilkinson in an administrative role until her retirement in 1965. The late 1960s saw a revitalization of public interest in her designs which came alongside a general resurgence of interest in Art Deco.

□P. Wentworth-Sheilds and K. Johnson, *Clarice Cliff* (1976); L. Griffin, L. Meisel and S. Meisel, *Clarice Cliff: The Bizarre Affair* (1987)

Coates, Nigel (b. 1949) is a British architect and interior designer who is most noteworthy in design for developing the concept of NARRATIVE ARCHITECTURE. He studied architecture at Nottingham University (1971–74) and then at the Architectural Association, London (1974–77), where he has subsequently taught. Within the Architectural Association he formed the Narrative Architecture Today group (NATO) with students who produced a series of drawings and installations far from the traditional rigours of the architectural profession. In 1985 he formed Branson Coates Architecture with Doug Branson. Coates subsequently embarked on a series of club and bar interiors in Japan, where the finance and desire for Coates's wildly extravagant conceptions was more readily available than in Britain. These included Metropole, Café Bongo and the Bohemia Jazz Club, all in Tokyo. Here rich

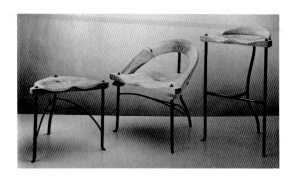

The Noah Collection (1988) designed by Nigel **Coates** for SCP.

textures of images and objects are combined to suggest, in his words, 'a filmic experience of architecture rather than its rational description'. In other words, street culture meets high-minded architectural design to create a style with trend-setting restaurants, bars and shops. He also launched the Jazz and Metropole furniture collections in Japan in 1987, and the Noah collection in Milan in 1988. In London he designed fashion shops for Katherine Hamnett and Jasper Conran. His design practice is supported by an articulate theoretical underpinning in which he discusses the compression of time and experience under POSTMODERNISM.

□N. Coates in Thackara (1988); R. Poyner, *Nigel Coates: The City in Motion* (1990)

Coates, Wells (1895–1958) was one of the leading figures in the short-lived flurry of the MODERN MOVEMENT in England during the 1930s. He was born in Tokyo, where his Canadian father was a missionary. He studied engineering at the University of British Colombia, Vancouver (1914–16 and 1919–21), with his studies broken by service in World War I, firstly as an infantryman and then as a pilot. He took a Ph.D. on 'The Gases of the Diesel Engine' at London University (1922–24). He then worked as a journalist for the *Daily Express* (1923–26), with a short stint in Paris in 1925. He based himself in London thenceforth, and his movement into design work was fired by his scientific and technological interests. At the same time, however, as evidenced by his journalism and many other writings, he had a wider belief in the transformatory role of design on society, driven by a humanistic, radical or even romantic outlook. It must be said, in addition, that by the early 30s, such a view coincided with the liberal aspirations of many middle-class avant-gardists with whom he came into contact. Unlike exponents of the ARTS AND CRAFTS movement before them, however, these designers were distinctly urban and concerned with utilizing and exploring new technologies. In England such avant-garde sentiments were marked by the fact that they were developing in a general context of growing political disillusionment and were spurred on more by influences from abroad.

His first design work was decorating his home in 1927. He then did textile designs for Alec Walker and Tom Heron, whose silk firm, the Crysede Textile Company, was based in St

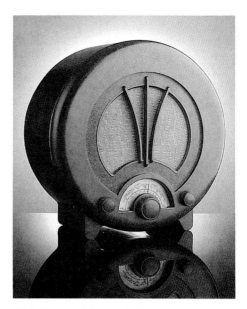

*Wells **Coates**'s Bakelite radio (1934).*

Ives, Cornwall. When Walker set up the Cresta factory in Welwyn Garden City in 1928, Coates designed the interior fittings. Coates had used PLYWOOD here and also in the Crysede shop in Cambridge; and it was through his interests in plywood that he came into contact with Jack PRITCHARD. Pritchard invited him to design the famous Lawn Road Flats in north London, which resulted in the formation of ISOKON. The flats, opened in 1934, were an extraordinary experiment in modern architecture of the calibre of LE CORBUSIER: they were minimal, with built-in furniture and common services such as heating and shoe-polishing. Coates also designed an exhibition stand for Pritchard's Venesta company in 1931. During the 30s he designed radios for Ekco, which were economical in terms of materials and production. After 1945 he branched out into the design of yachts, aircraft interiors and clocks, as well as urban renewal schemes and mass transport systems, but he failed to win much support or backing, and so very few of his later designs were completed. As founder of the MODERN ARCHITECTURAL RESEARCH GROUP (MARS), which was to be a British branch of the CONGRÈS INTERNATIONAUX D'ARCHITECTURE MODERNE (CIAM), as well as in his

Colombo's *Total Furnishing Unit at the exhibition, Italy: The New Domestic Landscape, held at MOMA, New York, in 1972.*

writings and practical design work, Coates was at the cutting edge of bringing the new aesthetic of Modernism into play on the British visual landscape.

☐ S. Cantacuzino, *Wells Coates* (1978)

Colombo, Joe (1930–71) was born in Milan and studied painting at the Brera Academy of Fine Arts and then architecture at Milan Polytechnic. Like many Italian designers of his time, despite his artistic background, he was also concerned with technical problems, an interest that he developed after having taken charge of a firm manufacturing electrical equipment following his father's death in 1959. He established a design studio in 1962, and during the 1960s his designs for furniture and appliances epitomized the concerns of Italian design – his Universale chair (1967) is an uncompromising modern use of plastic. His objects became essays in abstract sculpture, and yet he justified his pieces not in terms of their properties but in terms of their meaning. He wrote, 'I don't think of myself as an artist, nor as a technician, but as an epistemologist'. For Colombo, the designer was the 'creator of the environment of the future', and, to this end, he also produced designs intended to provide an 'integral habitat' – the complete living space. Much of his work was shown at the TRIEN-NALE exhibitions and the New York MUSEUM OF MODERN ART exhibition, Italy: The New Domestic Landscape.

☐ I. Favata, *Joe Colombo and Italian Design of the Sixties* (1988)

Colorcore was launched by FORMICA in 1983 at the Chicago Neocon furniture fair. It is a material formed by the impregnation of approximately 17 layers of compressed kraft paper with melamine resin to form 1.3mm ($c.\frac{1}{20}$in.) thick sheets. Several of these sheets can be bonded together in layers to form a solid, three-dimensional construction material. Its advantage over Formica is that, unlike traditional decorative laminates which only have the expensive melamine on the surface, it has solid colour and resin all the way through. It can be sawed, sanded and finished like a traditional hardwood and yet it is a synthetic plastic. Its properties are well suited to COMPUTER-AIDED DESIGN and COMPUTER-AIDED MANUFACTURE, since colour-coded computer graphics can analyse on-screen different configurations and patterns when working with Colorcore layers. In addition, it does not deteriorate with age. In 1983 and 1984 Formica organized several international competitions in which they invited architects and designers, including Frank Gehry and Oscar TUSQUETS, to design objects using Colorcore. None the less, despite this unusual form of product promotion, the material's expense – it is twice the price of Formica – prevented its subsequent widespread use.

Compasso D'Oro (f.1954), the golden compass, is the oldest and most prestigious design award in Italy. It was founded in Milan to promote new production based on a closer

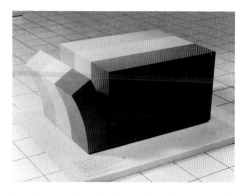

Lee Payne exploits the layers of **Colorcore** *in his Neapolitan coffee table (1984).*

relation with postwar social developments. Originated by the major department store La Rinascente, it was taken over by the ADI (Associazione per il Disegno Industriale – Association for Industrial Design) in 1957. Once a year producers submit products, which are judged by a jury and which subsequently form the basis of an exhibition.

computer-aided design (CAD) is used to replace the designer's conventional drawing tools, such as drawing boards, with a system that can produce higher-quality drawings more quickly. It also has the added advantage that these drawings can be recalled and modified at speed to meet changing design specifications.

CAD originated at the Massachusetts Institute of Technology (MIT) during the 1950s. But the early computers were very expensive and were therefore adopted only in industries where their use in design could justify large capital investments (e.g., the aerospace and automotive industries). However, since these pioneering developments, new and improved hardware has become widely available: computers have increased in processing speed and memory and decreased in cost and size.

The CAD software is a flexible tool that contains both a database of information and all the facilities required to prepare and execute drawings. These facilities include: the option to display the design from any angle; rotate it; perform scaling, panning and zooming; display cross-sections of any part of the design; display the design in line drawing or solid form; remove hidden lines from the structure; and display a selection of standard components. The computer-generated design can then be stored away on disk in the form of files that contain a display list. A hard copy can be obtained using a graphics output device called a pen plotter which will robotically draw the digitally stored information. A list of all components and design specifications used can be 'exported' to input devices in other departments in the factory (e.g., stock control, accounts and COMPUTER-AIDED MANUFACTURE (CAM) equipment.

computer-aided manufacture (CAM) uses the results of COMPUTER-AIDED DESIGN (CAD). These results are fed directly from CAD to CAM, where the information generated on CAD can be read and converted into usable data, usually in the form of a numerical control tape. Numerical control machines, such as lathes, cutting machines, and – increasingly – robots, can read the information supplied to them on the tape and perform the necessary operations to make and assemble the product designed on CAD.

The main aim of the CAD-CAM combination is to achieve a high level of productivity and accuracy. Flexible or BATCH PRODUCTION is also available through CAD-CAM, along with the standardization of sub-assembly components.

☐ C. Besant and C. Lui, *Computer-Aided Design and Manufacture* (1986); N.J. Ford et al., *Computers and Computer Applications* (1991)

Congrès Internationaux d'Architecture Moderne (CIAM) (1928–56) was an international organization of architects whose broad aims coincided with those of the MODERN MOVEMENT. The WEISSENHOF SIEDLUNG exhibition of 1926 had demonstrated the commonality of many modern international architects, and the first 25 CIAM members were brought together by Mme Hélène de Mandrot, a Swiss patron of the arts. She consulted LE CORBUSIER and Sigfried GIEDION on the conference's shape before making her château at La Sarraz, Switzerland, available to the group. It met four more times before World War II and then a further six times before its dissolution in 1956. Of these congresses, the 1932 meeting aboard the *S.S. Patris* between Marseilles and Athens is of note, for under the title of 'The Functional City' it spawned 'The Athens Charter', which followed Le Corbusier's precepts on town planning, including the separation into zones of its functions (residential, work, leisure and traffic). 'The Athens Charter' was itself virtually rejected at the last congress (CIAM X) in 1956, its members calling for a more individualized approach to design and not the blanket imposition of Modernist theory. This tendency can also be found in the Italian shift towards REALISM at the time. CIAM gave rise to various national sub-groups, such as the MODERN ARCHITECTURAL RESEARCH GROUP (MARS) in Britain and the Italian group (also the 1956 congress organizers), Team X, which produced a further meeting in Otterlo, the Netherlands, in 1959. Through these national groups the ideas of CIAM were disseminated throughout the world, CIAM itself providing the focal point by which modern architects and theorists kept in contact through the 30 years spanning World War II.

☐ CIAM, *Die Wohnung für das Existenzminimum* (1930); *Rationelle Behausungsweisen* (1931); *Logis et loisirs* (1938); J.L. Sert and CIAM, *Can Our Cities Survive?* (1942); O. Newman (ed.), *CIAM '59 in Otterlo* (1961)

Conran, Terence (b.1931) is famous in Britain for his championing of 'GOOD DESIGN' and establishment of the HABITAT stores to market it. He studied textile design at the Central School of Arts and Crafts in London (1944–49) and worked as an interior designer in the Dennis Lennon studio (1951–52). He was closely involved in design work for the Festival of Britain (1951) and subsequently opened a coffee-bar, the Soup Kitchen (1953), while running his own design studio. His design work in the 1950s was strongly influenced by the then popular Italian and Scandinavian styles, though he saw his mission as being to design products that were cheaper and more accessible. In 1956 he founded the Conran Design Group and in 1964 he founded Habitat. Henceforward he was often seen as an entrepreneur, with his directorship of such retail chains as Mothercare from 1981 and British Home Stores from 1986, although in reality he was also a lifelong supporter of the Labour party and was active in various institutions to promote design in industry and society. He was a founder-trustee of the Conran Foundation (f.1982), which administered the Boilerhouse Project – a modern design section of London's Victoria and Albert Museum – and the London Design Museum (f.1989), the world's first museum exclusively devoted to mass-produced artefacts.
☐ B. Philips, *Terence Conran and the Habitat Story* (1984)

Constructivism was an artistic movement that emerged in Russia immediately after the Revolution in 1917 and lasted until approximately 1922. It was the product of work, in particular by Vladimir TATLIN, Kasimir MALEVICH, Aleksandr RODCHENKO, El LISSITZKY, Naum Gabo, Antoine Pevsner and Wassily Kandinsky, in line with many contemporary international currents in painting and sculpture dating back to c.1911. It was also influenced by such modern European practices as Cubism and Italian FUTURISM.

The term seems to have appeared in print for the first time in the catalogue for the exhibition,

The Constructivists: K.K. Medunetskii, V.A. Stenberg, G.A. Stenberg, held at the Poets' Café, Moscow, in January 1922. It stated that all artists should now 'go into the factory, where the real body of life is made'. Thus, the traditional concept of art being exalting was to be discarded; instead it was linked with mass production and industry and subsequently identified with a new social and political order. Constructivism therefore had a clear political motivation: it was about putting art to the service of constructing a new society. It is easy in retrospect to interpret their aims as being those of artists wanting to become 'designers'; but coming before the term 'design' in its modern sense had fully emerged, their activities took on different terms, the most common one being 'production art'.

Given its anti-art standpoint, Russian Constructivism avoided the traditional use of art materials (e.g., oil and canvas) or pre-revolutionary iconography. Thus art objects might be constructed out of ready-made materials (e.g., woods, metals, photographs or paper). The artists' work is often viewed as a system of reduction or abstraction, yet in all areas of cultural activity, from graphic design to film and theatre, their aim was to *construct* a reality by bringing different elements together. The development of PHOTOMONTAGE may owe something to this approach: the Constructivist magazine *LEF* stated that 'the photograph is not the drawing of a visual fact but the exact fixation of it.' Thus, within a political poster, photomontage could link a concrete image of the everyday life of the viewer to the wider political aims of the Communist Party.

Constructivists held ambitious plans to put their art into production. Aleksandr Rodchenko designed furniture for the Workers' Club at the PARIS EXPOSITION DES ARTS DÉCORATIFS ET INDUSTRIELS, 1925; El Lissitzky also designed furniture which was exhibited in Leipzig and Dresden (1930); Kasimir Malevich designed porcelain (c.1922) that applied the theory of SUPREMATISM. Nevertheless, these were never put into mass production, and the artists lowered their sights to smaller-scale tasks, such as poster and typographic design – in which Gustav KLUTSIS and Alexei GAN were especially important – and exhibition design. Set against the failure to put its theories fully into practice, from c.1921 Constructivism was progressively superseded in Russia by Social Realism.

Constructivism exerted a strong influence on the MODERN MOVEMENT in the West, however. The art of Malevich, Rodchenko and Tatlin was exhibited in Berlin (1922). El Lissitzky was instrumental in bringing its theories and visual examples to the notice of the practitioners of DADA, to the DE STIJL group and to the BAUHAUS. It is generally argued that its influence was purely aesthetic and lost its holistic political edge upon reception in the West. The term Constructivism was subsequently used to refer to any design that showed geometry, structure, abstraction, logic or order.

□G. Rickey, *Constructivism: Origins and Evolution* (1967); S. Bann (ed.), *The Tradition of Constructivism* (1974); Lodder (1983)

Container Corporation of America (f.1926) is the largest PACKAGING company in the USA, renowned for its support of modern design. Its founder/chairman, Walter Paepcke, pioneered the manufacture of paperboard and corrugated-fibre containers at a time when most products were shipped in wooden containers. In 1936 he employed Egbert Jacobson as the company's design director to produce its CORPORATE IDENTITY. Paepcke sponsored

Constructivism was a focus for debate up to 1922, but Boris Prusakov's 1927 poster, I Hurry to the Khaz Push, *still shows its influence.*

the Chicago Institute of Design in the 1940s and founded the ASPEN INTERNATIONAL DESIGN CONFERENCE in 1951. A.M. CASSANDRE produced advertising for the Container Corporation (1937–38), conducting a campaign that broke with traditional American approaches to advertising (that of using headlines and body copy) to make bolder, simpler visual statements. During World War II Herbert BAYER, Jean CARLU and Herbert MATTER all worked for the design department. Paepcke's design strategy may be interpreted as bringing some of the aims of the MODERN MOVEMENT into corporate culture by mixing notions of collective concern with advertising. Aside from its World War II posters extolling the company's support of the American war effort, the Container Corporation produced advertising in the early 1950s that carried what were called 'Great Ideas of Western Man' – quotations on liberty, justice and human rights. (This polemical strategy was revived in the early 1990s in an advertising campaign by the Benetton clothing company.) It also published

*The **Container Corporation of America** symbol, redesigned by Ralph Eckerstrom in 1957.*

the *World Geo-Graphic Atlas* (1953), a 360-page book incorporating 1,200 diagrams, charts and graphs, all designed by Herbert Bayer. The company logo was redesigned by Ralph Eckerstrom in 1957, and from 1964, under design director John Massey, the corporate identity was brought closer to the International Typographic Style of the SWISS SCHOOL. Massey also founded the Center for Advanced Research in Design in 1966, which undertook experimental projects as well as external commissions.

Contemporary Style is a term used to describe a tendency in art, architecture and design in Britain (1945–56). It is a style that was popularized by the Festival of Britain exposition of 1951 and was therefore also known as the 'Festival Style', the 'South Bank Style' or the 'New English Style'. Aesthetically, it usually involved the use of bright colours together with a mixture of organic and spiky forms. Its furniture often contained a combination of thin metal rods and pale timber, wooden legs which were splayed out and tapered, as well as a profusion of small, coloured, plastic spheres in its fittings. Two-dimensional patterns, as found in upholstery, textiles and wallpaper, incorporated geometric designs. Such a style was also to be found in the sculpture of Barbara Hepworth, the painting of Joan Miró and even in the three-dimensional models of molecular structures used in PLASTICS technology and science laboratories.
☐M. Banham and B. Hillier (eds), *A Tonic to the Nation: The Festival of Britain 1951* (1976)

contract furniture is furniture that is produced as the result of an agreement or contract between an architect or corporation and a furniture manufacturer or supplier. It developed in particular in the post-World War II building boom of large-scale office blocks and institutions. By ordering large quantities of contract furniture, the client may be in a position to demand improvements in it.

Cooper, Susie (b.1902) was born in the heart of Britain's pottery country, Staffordshire, and studied at Burslem School of Art (1918–22). After working as a designer for A.E. Gray and Co. (a pottery decorating firm), she founded her own company (1929). During the 1930s Susie Cooper's earthenware, with its distinctive trademark of a leaping deer, found commercial success and critical recognition in Britain and around the world. She designed the tableware for the Royal Pavilion at the Festival of Britain exhibition in 1951, and in 1956 her firm became a member of the Wedgwood Group (*see* Josiah WEDGWOOD & SONS LTD). Her exuberant ceramic designs again became popular from the 1970s, as they had much in common with the aesthetics of the CRAFTS REVIVAL.
☐A. Woodhouse, *Elegance and Utility 1924 to 1978: The Work of Susie Cooper RDI* (1978); A. Eatwell, *Susie Cooper Production* (1987)

Coray, Hans (b.1907) is a Swiss designer who designed the first ALUMINIUM chair, the Landi, for the Zurich Exposition Nationale (1939). He studied literature and did not begin designing full-time until 1950. None the less his Landi chair caused an international sensation and was in continuous production for 50 years subsequently.

*A sgraffito vase made by Susie **Cooper** for Wedgwood in the early 1930s.*

☐ *Hans Coray: Künstler und Entwerfer* (exh. cat., Museum für Gestaltung, Zurich, 1986)

corporate identity is a system of PACKAGING the visual style of a company and giving it a distinct and unified identity by means of design. Often a company's identity is centred on its logo, though its application, from letterheads to its incorporation in advertising material, is of importance. The concept may be carried through to the company's architecture or even dress. Wally Olins, a pioneer of corporate identity since the 1960s, notes that in small or young companies, the management of identity is intuitive. Large corporations, on the other hand, are more concerned with making a clear statement of their long-term purpose, values and thus identity, bringing cohesion to what might otherwise seem to be a sprawling and complex entity.

It is often argued that Peter BEHRENS's work at AEG (1907–14) created the first corporate identity. It is in the large American corporations that the concept of business identity has been most fully developed.

☐ W. Olins, *The Corporate Personality* (1978); *Corporate Identity* (1989)

Cracow School (*Szkoła Krakowa***)** (f.1902) was initiated by the founding of the Society for Polish Applied Art (*Towarzystwo Polska Sztuka Stosowana*) by leading Polish ARTS AND CRAFTS designers and architects. Their early enthusiasm for protecting a vernacular culture, which they felt to be under threat from the imperial powers denying Polish political and cultural expression before 1918, developed into a complete design practice when many of the Society's members formed the Cracow Workshops (*Warsztaty Krakowskie*). Intellectually close to workshop-based design reform groups across Europe, the Cracow Workshops advocated a 'national' design style derived from peasant decorative and constructional traditions, producing angular, 'carved' forms in furniture, textiles, ceramics and metalwork. After World War I, the influence of these Cracow-based designers (hence 'Cracow School') spread across the newly revived country, as figures such as Józef Czajkowski and Wojciech Jastrzębowski took posts in the State art and design agencies. The postwar Cracow School, for example, master-minded the design and construction of the Polish national pavilion at the PARIS EXPOSITION DES ARTS DÉCOR-

A new **corporate identity** *for British Telecom was launched by Wolff Olins in 1991.*

ATIFS ET INDUSTRIELS, 1925. Members of the Cracow School were the most vociferous critics of the radical Constructivist movement (*see* CONSTRUCTIVISM) in Poland in the 1920s. The formation in 1926 of Ład (Order), a co-operative of designers working within the Warsaw Academy of Fine Art, was a late attempt to revive faltering Cracow School themes in the years when the MODERN MOVEMENT rose to ascendancy in Polish design.

☐ Huml (1973)

Crafts (f.1973) is a monthly magazine produced under the auspices of the Crafts Council of Great Britain. It often distinguishes itself by a high level of academic debate over the nature and meaning of crafts, which frequently also touches on design theory.

crafts revival began in the USA during the 1950s. It was to some degree prompted by the international acclaim which Scandinavian design received at the time, itself exhibiting something of a crafts tradition in its preference for natural finishes and quality workmanship. This, together with craft in general, was seen as an antidote to the growing dominance of the INTERNATIONAL STYLE in the 1960s, and, ironically, the crafts revival owed something to the influx into the USA in the 1930s of BAUHAUS-trained craftspeople, such as the ceramicist Margarete Friedlander.

In Britain the traditions inherited from the ARTS AND CRAFTS movement had been carried through the interwar period by, for example, Gordon RUSSELL and Ambrose HEAL in furniture and Bernard LEACH in ceramics. The establishment in 1971 of Britain's Crafts Advisory Committee and in 1975 of its successor, the Crafts Council, meant that crafts-people benefitted from the support of an official institutional apparatus. This coincided with the rise of the DESIGNER-MAKER and the influence of figures such as David PYE. The meaning of craft also underwent serious recon-sideration at this time. Its definition had pre-viously been restricted to artist-craftsmen con-ceiving, producing, exhibiting and selling their wares on a one-off basis without regard for the market. It was now broadened to represent a direct relationship with the materials and end-product and thus, by extension, a form of material research. Indeed, in the 1980s com-mentator John Thackara went so far as to claim the computer programmer as a craftsperson, as he or she worked directly with the end material without the intervention of models, prototypes or other elements involved in the design process. Another aspect of the craft revival in the 1970s and 80s was the use of materials normally associated with industrial design in a one-off craft mode, as in the work of Ron ARAD, who used reinforced concrete and old Rover car seats. This was countered by some with the rejection of traditional materials, or at least formal and decorative tenets, as in the ceramics of Alison Britton and Janice Tcha-lenko. This blurring of the distinctions between craftsperson and designer has a parallel in Andrea BRANZI's conception of the NEW DESIGN, whereby equally little distinction need be made between designing for series and one-off production. In the minds of many, this is an artificial distinction only upset by a brief period of mass production in the mid-20th c.

☐ *2D/3D: Art and Craft Made and Designed for the Twentieth Century* (exh. cat., Northern Centre for Contemporary Art, Sunderland, 1987); Thackara (1988); J. Freeman, 'The Dis-covery of the Commonplace or Establishment of an Elect: Intellectuals in the Contemporary Craft World', B. Ranson, 'Craftwork, Ideol-ogy and the Craft Life-Cycle', H. Hillman Chartrand, 'The Crafts in the Post-Modern Market' in *Journal of Design History* Vol. 2, Nos 2 and 3 (1989); Dormer (1990)

Cranbrook Academy of Art (f.1925) is an educational community founded by George C. Booth, a Canadian-born newspaper publisher, on his estate 20 miles outside Detroit. Booth had nurtured the idea of a Utopian community, both an American ideal and a re-invigoration of the ARTS AND CRAFTS idea. In 1923 he met the

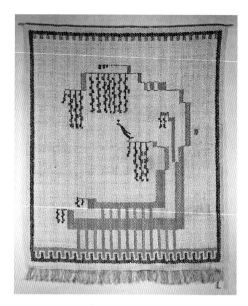

Loja Saarinen's wall hanging with a peacock (c.1932) was made at the **Cranbrook Academy of Art.**

Finnish architect, Eliel SAARINEN, who was teaching at the University of Michigan. Booth had already been impressed by Saarinen's entry for the *Chicago Tribune* architectural compe-tition the previous year. With Saarinen, Booth set up the Cranbrook Academy of Art, where the former was the leading creative force.

Among its graduates have been Eero SAARI-NEN, Niels DIFFRIENT, Charles EAMES, Flor-ence KNOLL, Jack Lenor Larsen and David Rowland. Its spirit was decidedly Anglo-Saxon and Nordic, both in its aesthetic output and in the prominence given to craft activity. George Booth died in 1949 and Eliel Saarinen the year after, thereby signalling the end of its first important phase.

The design department at Cranbrook re-emerged as an important force in the late 1970s, when it had assimilated the theoretical develop-ments of POSTMODERNISM (e.g., the work of Robert VENTURI and Wolfgang WEINGART). Thus, under the direction of Katherine and Michael McCoy from 1971, the department began research taking in linguistic theory, which it applied to design practice. This inevitably led to PRODUCT SEMANTICS. With the inclusion of phenomenology into its design theories, Cranbrook reached its zenith as a leading-edge design centre in the mid-1980s.

☐ *Design in America: The Cranbrook Vision 1925–1950* (exh. cat., Detroit Institute of Arts/ Metropolitan Museum, New York, 1983); H. Aldersey-Williams et al., *Cranbrook Design: The New Discourse* (1991)

Crawford's (f.1914) was a graphic art agency, founded in London by William (later Sir William) Smith Crawford, who was head of the agency until he died in 1951. Crawford was an influential spokesman on advertising, a member of the Empire Marketing Board and was recognized as playing an important part in raising the standard of commercial art. Despite the interruption of World War I, by the 1920s Crawford's had established its reputation as the leading 'modern' agency. Ashley HAVINDEN was an important figure in the agency, as an innovative art director in the 20s and 30s and as vice-chairman in the 1960s. Another important designer was Edward McKnight KAUFFER, who only worked there from 1927 to 1929, but whose working methods and Modernist idiom (*see* MODERN MOVEMENT) had a great impact on the in-house designers. Some of their best-known campaigns were for CHRYSLER CORPORATION cars, the Milk Marketing Board, Eno's, Simpsons Piccadilly and Jaeger.

Crouwel, Wim (b.1928) is a graphic designer who studied at the Institute for Arts and Crafts in Amsterdam (1951–52). He worked as a freelance exhibition designer until 1957, after which he worked with the architect Kho Liang Ie. In 1963 he co-founded TOTAL DESIGN, a design practice with which he was to remain. He was extremely influential from the 1960s in bringing in the lessons of the SWISS SCHOOL and Stanley MORISON to Dutch graphic design. His signage for Amsterdam's Stedelijk Museum (from 1963) and the PTT (1978) is marked by the use of SANS-SERIF typefaces and geometric abstraction with broad flat areas of colour. This highly structured aesthetic underwent criticism for its attempt at political neutrality and was subsequently overturned by studios such as Hard Werken.
☐ W. Crouwel, *Nieuw Alfabet: En Mogelijheid voor de Nieuwe Ontwikkeling* (1967); *Ontwerpen en Drukken* (1974)

Czech Cubism was a short-lived but important design movement in the years immediately preceding World War I. It was centred around the *Skupina Vytvarych Umelcu* (Group of Creative Artists), which was established in Prague in 1911. The Group founded its own magazine, *Umelecky Mesicnik* (Artistic Monthly), in which it proposed the introduction of a new subjectivism and abstraction into design. It rejected the RATIONALISM of existing architectural practice, and opposed the surviving influence of Secessionist (*see* SECESSION) and ARTS AND CRAFTS ideas, which had been introduced into Czech design training by the one-time pupil of Otto WAGNER, Jan Kotera. Once students of Kotera's, the architects Paval Janak, Josef Chocol, Vlastislav Hofmann and Josef Gocar now asserted the need for a new spirituality in architecture. The *Skupina* maintained close links with Parisian Cubism, organizing events like the Third Group Exhibition, which brought works by Pablo Picasso, Georges Braque, André Derain and Juan Gris to Prague. Influenced by developments in the fine arts, the Czech Cubists applied prism-like and crystalline motifs to architecture, furniture, ceramics and jewelry. In architecture, the Cubists proclaimed themselves opposed to the use of applied decoration and instead used facetted, intersecting planes and dynamic forms to adorn a building's facade. The buildings retained the typical house or apartment plan (e.g., Chocol's 1913–14 apartment block in Necklanova Street, Prague) and utilized traditional materials and constructional methods, unlike the Czech FUNCTIONALISM of the interwar years. In 1912 Gocar and Janak established the *Prazske Umemecke Dilny* (the Prague Artistic Workshops), based on the workshop practice of the WIENER WERKSTÄTTE. The furniture designs of this period were highly architectural and sculptural, using traditional materials and production methods. Their designs for ceramics and glass, which were produced by the Artel co-operative in Prague, and which were relatively inexpensive and readily available, to some extent fulfilled the commitment to integrate Cubist principles into everyday design.
☐ I. Margolius, *Cubism in Architecture and the Applied Arts* (1979)

D

*Kurt Schwitters and Theo van Doesburg's poster for a **Dada** recital in The Hague in January 1923.*

Dada was an artistic movement which lasted from about 1916 to 1922. It spread from Zurich to Paris, Hanover, Cologne and New York and was a nihilistic drive against various establishments, including the art world itself. Its exponents used poetry, performance, collage and PHOTOMONTAGE, of which John HEARTFIELD and Kurt SCHWITTERS were notable practitioners. In design terms Dada, like FUTURISM, was influential in its bold use of type, veering towards concrete poetry. Marcel Duchamp produced 'ready-mades', recontextualizing everyday objects to give them different meanings – this was a technique picked up by exponents of ANTI-DESIGN and ADHOCISM in the 1960s and 70s. The nihilism and collage approach of Dada was also adopted in the mid-1970s in the British Punk movement and can be seen in the graphics of Jamie Reid and Barny Bubbles.

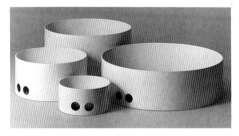

*A set of Tongareva melamine bowls designed by Enzo Mari for **Danese** in 1969.*

Danese (f.1957) was founded by Bruno Danese in Milan. His aim was to produce sample objects that partly reflect an 'anti-industry' belief, initially using small craft workshops to edit pieces which he felt had been ignored either by industrial culture (e.g., children's games), or by the 'universalizing' manifestos of the MODERN MOVEMENT (e.g., flower-vases). To this end he employed many avant-garde designers, notably Enzo MARI and Bruno MUNARI. Danese products often explored simple but effective innovations in manufacture, as well as provocative new forms. In the late 1960s, Danese increasingly moved over to manufacturing rather than EDITING.
☐S. Casciani, *Industrial Art: Objects, Play and Thought in Danese Production* (1988)

Danish Modern is a term used to describe the design achievements of Scandinavian designers such as Finn JUHL, Hans WEGNER and Arne JACOBSEN in the post–World War II period. While Kaare KLINT's prewar design work and teaching introduced FUNCTIONALISM to Danish furniture design, the country's tradition in the applied arts was not subordinated to the zest for new materials found in the work of pioneers of the MODERN MOVEMENT. Thus natural finishes were retained, while pieces were also marked by their sculptural elegance. This softened Modernism was internationally popular in the 1950s and was a style adopted by many manufacturers such as Ercol.

Day, Robin (b.1915) was born in High Wycombe, Britain's major furniture-making town, where he studied at the local art school (1931–33), before attending the ROYAL COLLEGE OF ART (1934–38). He initially worked as a graphic designer and set up a design practice with his wife, the textile designer Lucienne Day, in London (1948). In the same year he gained international recognition when, with Clive Latimer, he won the first prize for storage furniture in the New York MUSEUM OF MODERN ART's Low Cost Furniture Competition. In 1949 he began a long and fruitful relationship with Hille as a design consultant, exploring low-cost production furniture using new materials. The resulting Hillestak chair (1950), which used PLYWOOD with new plastic glues, developed Charles EAMES's concept of considering the shell and base of the chair separately, thus reducing production and assembly costs and allowing the combination of a TUBULAR-STEEL base and a plastic (*see* PLASTICS) or plywood shell. In 1963 production began of a chair range using a polypropylene shell developed by Day, the research product with which he is most associated.

Day's plywood Hillestak chair (1950).

De 8 en opbouw (1932–43) was a magazine covering the work of two groups of progressive architects: 'de 8', which consisted chiefly of Amsterdam architects including Gerrit RIETVELD and Mart STAM; and 'opbouw', which included Piet ZWART and other architects from various Dutch towns. It was highly influential in establishing the graphic design of the MODERN MOVEMENT in the Netherlands. Title pages were largely designed by those architects who were responsible for the publication and were distinguished by their bold use of typography and image.

De Lucchi's Kristall end table designed for Memphis in 1981.

De Lucchi, Michele (b.1951) studied architecture at the University of Florence (1969–75). In 1973 he set up the Gruppo Cavart in Padua, which produced films, documents and seminars on RADICAL DESIGN. He continued at Florence University as a teaching assistant but moved to Milan in 1978 where he worked with Ettore SOTTSASS, Gaetano PESCE, Andrea BRANZI and SUPERSTUDIO. In 1979 he became a consultant to OLIVETTI Synthesis in Massa, was a founder member of MEMPHIS in 1980, thus contributing to the second wave of ANTI-DESIGN in the early 1980s, and was employed in 1984 as a consultant by Olivetti

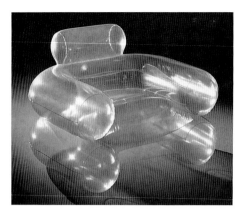

De Pas, D'Urbino e Lomazzi's Blow Chair *was designed in 1967 and manufactured by Zanotta.*

SpA in Ivrea. He has designed more than 50 Fiorucci shops and, with Sottsass, the Olivetti 45CR and Icarus office furniture.
☐ M. De Lucchi, *Architetture Verticali* (1978)

De Pas, D'Urbino e Lomazzi (f.1966) is a Milanese architecture and design studio made up of Jonathan De Pas, Donato D'Urbino and Paolo Lomazzi. They all studied architecture in Milan during the 1960s and they concentrated on the design of furniture and temporary architecture. They designed a series of inflatable housing structures for the Italian Pavilion at the Osaka World's Fair; in 1967 they designed the Blow chair, an inflatable regarded as typical of POP design. They also became known for their Joe armchair (1970), which was in the form of a giant baseball glove. As with many of their Italian contemporaries, the conceptual aspect of their design work dominates, and technical aspects are resolved around this.

De Stijl is the name given to a loose grouping of architects, designers, painters, thinkers and poets who gathered around the eponymous journal first published in the Netherlands in October 1917. Under the nominal leadership of Theo van DOESBURG, the De Stijl group counted among its original number Piet Mondrian, Jacobus Johannes Pieter Oud, Jan Wils, Georges VANTONGERLOO, Vilmos Huszar and Robert Van't Hoff. The aims of De Stijl were set out in the first manifesto published in 1918; this document called for a new culture based upon equivalence between universality and individualism, an abandonment of natural form in art and architecture and the establishment of a new, international unity in culture based upon these revolutionary premises. The same year Gerrit Thomas RIETVELD met some of the members of the group and completed the final, fully painted version of the Red/Blue chair. De Stijl's strengths lay in the multi-disciplinary nature of its membership: the group was able to produce architectural designs, graphics, interiors, paintings and philosophical discourse, all under the De Stijl banner. During its heyday in the 1920s, the group received commissions to design buildings, interiors and furniture and to mount exhibitions, at the same time the journal published work by, among many others, El LISSITZKY. Although the magazine and the group provided a forum for the expression of grand ideas of cultural and social reform in Europe, De Stijl remained marginalized as a small, but influentially vociferous part of the European avant-garde. The death of Theo van Doesburg in 1931 saw the effective end of De Stijl as a going concern, reflecting his central role in the formation and dissemination of its philosophies and ideas.
☐ M. Friedman (ed.), *De Stijl: 1917–1931 Visions of Utopia* (1982); Overy (1991)

deconstruction is a term developed by the French philosopher, Jacques Derrida, from the late 1960s. It was primarily a philosophy of

Gerrit Rietveld's Red/Blue chair (c.1918) became emblematic of **De Stijl**.

literary criticism and described a method of reading in which a text was seen to have numerous interpretations, not just one meaning, and can thus never exactly mean what it says or say what it means. Deconstruction sets out to uncover the 'meaninglessness' of a text by destabilizing the intellectual ground on which it has been founded. By this token, Derrida himself refused to give a straight definition of the term.

The process of deconstruction began to influence architecture and design towards the end of the 70s. In this context it began by viewing the design process as an argument for a solution to a problem. Deconstruction examines the assumptions that the argument is based upon, challenging their right to be assumed. It is thus an *approach* rather than a style. Confusingly, however, DECONSTRUCTIVISM is a style that is often used to represent deconstructionist designs. Architectural critic Charles Jencks has linked deconstructivism with other philosophical practices of POSTMODERNISM. Arguably, however, there is a distinction between them, in that deconstruction rejected any meaningless quotation and the HISTORICISM to be found within Postmodernism. Rather it attempted to challenge and expose what lay beneath the superficial appearance. It is ultimately concerned with meaning, unlike forms of Postmodernism, which negated the concept in the first place. Deconstruction, then, might be seen as the psychoanalysis of architecture and design.

Deconstruction has had most effect in architecture and interior design, as can be seen in projects by Frank Gehry, Peter Eisenman, Hiromi Fujii and Ben Kelly. Here, the traditional layout and functional arrangement of a building might be undermined. In industrial design some of the surrealistic approaches to be found in ANTI-DESIGN may be said to be deconstructionist, although this may not have been the overt intention of the designers. Likewise, Daniel WEIL's famous radio sets held in plastic bags reinterpreted the hitherto accepted forms of this product. Graphic designers associated with the CRANBROOK ACADEMY OF ART from the mid-80s, such as Katherine McCoy and Lucille Tenazas, have made a more conscious effort to apply the ideology of deconstruction to design by the multi-layering of type and images which suggest various interpretations of the message being communicated.

☐C. Norris and A. Benjamin, *What is Deconstruction?* (1988); C. Jencks, *Deconstruction in Architecture* (1988); A. Papadakis, *Reconstruction Deconstruction* (1989)

deconstructivism is a term which emerged in architectural design in the late 1980s. Critics identified it as a tendency towards an aggressive overlapping of forms and a use of geometrically arranged fields of intense colours. It is found in a number of isolated examples, including the architectural work of Frank Gehry, Peter Eisenman and Zaha HADID. An exhibition organized by Philip Johnson at the MUSEUM OF MODERN ART, New York (1988), established the term. While some of the works exhibited may seem like a broken-down form of CONSTRUCTIVISM, any link with the Russian movement of the 1920s is fortuitous. Likewise, while some see deconstructivism as the stylistic end-product of DECONSTRUCTION, this is not necessarily the case. Given that much of it was exhibited in plan or model forms, it was mostly to remain at a fantastical stage and was rarely implemented. Its visual complexity was to be echoed in some Dutch and American graphic design work.

☐P. Johnson and M. Wigley, *Deconstructivist Architecture* (1988)

Deffke, Wilhelm (?–1950) was a German graphic designer. In the 1920s he had a studio in Berlin where he designed trademarks, posters and graphic work for corporations and publishing. With his studio and as director of the Magdeburg Arts and Crafts School, Deffke trained many in the next generation of Modernist designers (*see* MODERN MOVEMENT) during the 1920s, including the Swiss Hermann EIDENBENZ.

Deganello, Paolo (b.1940) was a founder of the Florentine architectural studio ARCHIZOOM together with Andrea BRANZI. He studied architecture in Florence (1961–66) and came to be an important exponent of Italy's RADICAL DESIGN movement, through his involvement in Archizoom. His Torso series of chairs for CASSINA (1982) played on colours and shapes from the 1950s while at the same time allowing interchangeability of parts. This confirmed the theoretical aims of Radical Design in permitting greater user-intervention in determining the form of an object.

A model wearing a coat and hat by **Delaunay** *and standing by a matching roadster (1925).*

DEGW (f.1974) is a British-based architectural and furniture design partnership made up of Francis Duffy, Peter Eley, Luigi Giffone and John Worthington. It has been influential in design and consultancy concerned with INTELLIGENT BUILDING, pointing to the need for greater flexibility in the design of workplaces and their furniture in order to accommodate rapid changes in the use of information technology. In 1982 DEGW was appointed by the British government and British Telecom to work on the Orbit Study on this matter. In May 1983 it launched *Facilities*, a monthly digest for building administration managers, with Duffy as its editor-in-chief. The group also contributes regularly to the *Architect's Journal*, thus placing it in the forefront of writing on the need for new developments in office design.
☐ DEGW, *Planning Office Space* (1979); *Industrial Rehabilitation* (1980); *Information Technology and Office Design* (1983); *The Changing Workplace* (1992)

Delaunay, Sonia (1885–1979) was a pioneer of abstract painting who is best known for her textile and fashion designs. She was born in the Ukraine and studied painting in Karlsruhe (1903–5). In 1905 she moved to Paris, where she worked as a painter. In 1910 she married the painter Robert Delaunay, who was of major influence on her work. Henceforward she worked in bold, abstract, geometric patterns with bright colours. In 1914 she designed several posters and from 1917 worked in textile designs. She and her husband were frequent visitors to Spain, living in Madrid (1914–17). She exhibited ceramics in Bilbao in 1919 and Madrid in 1920.

☐ *Sonia et Robert Delaunay* (exh. cat., Bibliothèque Nationale, Paris, 1977); J. Damase, *Sonia Delaunay: Fashion and Fabrics* (1991)

Den Permanente (f.1931) means 'permanent exhibition' in Danish and is a showroom in Copenhagen dedicated to the display of both craft and industrially produced household wares. It is Denmark's most significant showcase of this important facet of Danish design.

Depero, Fortunato (1892–1960) was an Italian exponent of FUTURISM, who was mostly concerned with painting and poetry. However, like many of his colleagues, he ventured into graphics, either in magazines and books produced to promote Futurism, or in commercial work to pay the bills. He spent a brief, but important, period in New York (1929–31), a city about which the Futurists enthused, as it represented for them the intensity of metropolitan experience which they expounded in their manifestos. There he undertook many advertising commissions for companies, in which he applied bold collage work of startling vitality. He also produced illustrations for *Vogue* and *The New Yorker* among many publications. Aside from advertising he also designed extensively for the theatre, having worked for Diaghilev's Ballets Russes in 1916. There is a museum devoted to him in Rovereto, Italy.
☐ M. Scudiero and D. Leiber, *Depero Futurista & New York: Futurism and the Art of Advertising* (1986)

Design (f.1948) is a monthly magazine produced under the auspices of the Design Council of Great Britain. It covers all aspects of design but has traditionally had a stronger bias towards industrial design. Initially it acted as a mouth-piece for the Design Council, in particular by publishing examples of 'GOOD DESIGN'. However, since its redesign by PENTAGRAM in 1990, its style has loosened up somewhat, and it has become more inventive in its content.

Design and Industries Association (DIA) (f.1915) was an important forerunner in Britain of the Council of Industrial Design (f.1944) and subsequently of the Design Council (f.1960). It was set up by younger members of the ARTS AND CRAFTS Exhibition Society, including Ambrose HEAL and Harry PEACH, following a visit to the Cologne DEUTSCHE WERKBUND Exhibition in 1914. The following year an exhibition of high-quality German and Austrian goods was organized in order to provoke a response from British manufacturers. The Design and Industries Association was subsequently launched with the mission to promote design in industry. It did not follow the line of the Werkbund as a pioneer of the MODERN MOVEMENT, however, and it was not until the 1930s that it began to endorse Modernism with its support for Gordon RUSSELL's increasingly Modernistic approach and, from 1932, the BBC's series of talks on modern design. Its short-lived magazines, *Design in Industry* (1933), *Design for Today* (1933–35) and *Trend* (1936) also promoted Modernism. While the Design and Industries Association provided a gradual break from its Arts and Crafts tradition, its progenies, the Society of Industrial Artists (f.1930), the Council for Art and Industry (f.1933) and the aforementioned Design Council became more important leaders in the development of design in Britain.

design consultancies owe their existence to the period between the wars, when a new form of industrial design emerged as the way to add value, style and meaning to a range of consumer goods which had not previously been exploited to their full potential. The undeniable commercial success of certain consumer goods redesigned by the new breed of American industrial designer meant that industrial design became inextricably linked to ideas of BRANDING, consumer demand and built-in obsolescence. Although the stylistic nuances used by the original designers such as Walter Dorwin TEAGUE, Raymond LOEWY and Henry DREYFUSS are no longer the common

Depero's *poster Coppa 1000 Miglia (1929).*

currency of the designer, the role of the design consultant has not changed a great deal. Modern design consultancies still provide their corporate clients with expertise in a specialist field where an inventive and well-researched design can mean the difference between the success and the failure of a new product.
☐ Heskett (1980)

design for disability involves the design of products and environments that help those described as disabled to overcome their physical problems or limitations. It has become the subject of much attention since the 1960s. Prior to this, products and environments for the disabled were considered primarily in medical terms. This 'medicalization', especially with regard to those products (e.g., wheelchairs) that relate directly to the appearance of people, did (and still does) little to alleviate the social stigma that many disabled people have experienced.

During the 60s, American and European designers began to break away from this medical approach and took steps to bring the large section of the population deemed disabled into the realm of everyday life by making new products and environments accessible to them. One of the first manifestations of this change

A pivoting kettle on a stand showing the adaptations necessary in **design for disability**.

defined constraints on the designer, and many students choose a project of this type for both this reason and for its moral acceptability. On a negative note, only a limited number of new products designed for disability reach the production line, due to their specialized nature and consequent high cost.

Design for Need was the title of an international conference which took place at the ROYAL COLLEGE OF ART, London, in April 1976. The conference focused on design in the context of a range of social and political issues, such as the Third World, the environment (*see* GREEN DESIGN) and DESIGN FOR DISABILITY. The event was the culmination of a surge of interest in such issues which had grown from the late 1960s, and the term 'design for need' subsequently came to represent the wider tendency, as well as the conference itself. In the most general respect, this interest was the result of a reaction against the consumer society, a reaction that was manifested in two ways: by a retreat into the individual – which was expressed in some aspects of hippy culture and in the contemporaneous CRAFTS REVIVAL; and also more directly, by political organization and activity, in which area the interest in design for need was at its strongest. One may even trace a Utopian zeal for non-commercial design, supposedly geared to our real needs, to the 19th c. and the ARTS AND CRAFTS movement. The difference, in the 20 c., however, is that the interest was more often in harnessing existing technologies for human needs than in a return to a medieval ideal of craft production.

Some initiatives prefigure the concerns of design for need. Following a personal crisis in 1927, Buckminster FULLER devoted his life to ways of solving design problems, in order 'to better man's effective survival chances'. Domes, which appeared world-wide from 1952, were originally conceived by Fuller as a form of light, prefabricated shelter, and in 1963 he began his World Resources Inventory at Southern Illinois University – this research project reviewed the distribution of world resources and human resources in order that the former might be used more efficiently. In 1954 Richard Neutra wrote *Survival through Design*, which also exorted a non-commercial, global design strategy.

By the 1960s industrial design was seen by some as supporting the consumerist, capitalist

was the design of an international symbol for disability, developed in the late 60s.

As well as considering the importance of adaptable environments that permitted access for those who relied on various aids to mobility, such as wheelchairs or sticks, designers began to address the function and appearance of products used by disabled people in their everyday lives. By the late 60s it had become a popular and even fashionable theme, and in 1969, a whole issue of *DESIGN* magazine was devoted to the subject, with Selwyn Goldsmith as guest editor.

Since the 60s, activity in the field of design for disability has expanded enormously, and many products specifically designed for those with disabilities have been greatly improved. However, due to the fact that many disabled people have very limited social or political power, in many countries they still rely to a great extent on products and environments provided for them by the State. This means that their choice is still limited and that the style and appearance of these products may come a poor second to their cheapness.

From the designers' point of view, there are a number of problems associated with designing for disability, some positive, some negative. On a positive note, design for disability places very

system, as it was unable to act outside it. In 1971 Victor PAPANEK published *Design for the Real World*. It was translated into 21 languages, making it the world's most widely read book on design. The book's success lay in the way it summed up all the preoccupations facing the alternative designer and advocated 'a return from form to content', shifting away from the traditional concerns with production and external appearance, towards a view of design in use. The moral debate over the end-use of design was subsequently maintained, particularly in northern Europe. Much of it fed into 'green design' debates towards the end of the 1980s. While it never seriously threatened the traditional role of design as part of the industrial complex, it none the less provided a context for ethical discussions beyond the outmoded positions of the MODERN MOVEMENT.
□R. Neutra, *Survival Through Design* (1954); V. Papanek, *Design for the Real World* (1971; rev. 1985); J. Bicknell and L. McQuiston, *Design for Need: The Social Contribution of Design* (1977); R. Hewison, *Too Much: Art and Society in the Sixties 1960–1975* (1986); T. Fry, 'Against an Essentialist Theory of "Need": Some Considerations for Design Theory' in *Design Issues* Vol. 8, No. 2 (1992)

Design Issues (f.1984) is a twice-yearly academic journal of design history, theory and criticism. It is published at the University of Illinois in Chicago under the editorship of the American design historian Victor Margolin. Its aim in part is to establish the practice of critical reflection in design in the USA, bringing it into line with European traditions. Its first two numbers featured articles by the design historian Clive Dilnot mapping out the historiography and contemporary methodological position of design history.

design management is not the process of managing DESIGN CONSULTANCIES. It is, rather, concerned with the organizational place of design in a corporation. Therefore it is concerned with the use of design within a private or public corporate strategy. Design management thus involves such activities as the conscious planning of when a new CORPORATE IDENTITY may be implemented for a company and deciding on priorities when reviewing a city's transport system. The Royal Society of Arts made its first Design Management awards in 1966. Despite this apparent

importance, it has yet to establish itself successfully as a subject for study within education.
□M. Farr, *Design Management* (1966); C. Lorenz, *The Design Dimension: Product Strategy and the Challenge of Global Marketing* (1986); P. Gorb (ed.), *Design Management: Papers from the London Business School* (1990); M. Oakley (ed.), *Design Management: A Handbook of Issues and Methods* (1990)

Milner Gray of **Design Research Unit** *created the Standard Chef symbol for restaurants at the Festival of Britain in 1951.*

Design Research Unit (DRU) (f.1943) is a British design consultancy set up by the Ministry of Information during World War II. It was chaired by Herbert READ with a panel of architects, designers and engineers, including Misha BLACK and Milner GRAY. It was formed with the aim of networking designers and engineers to provide practical advice for industry, equipping it for competition in postwar markets; thus DRU was intended as Britain's first design consultancy. In the event its major commissions in the 1950s were in house-styles and interiors – reflecting its members' backgrounds in graphic and interior design – and never touched on the heavier end of product design.

designer-maker is a term applied to men and women who design and, at least in part, make furniture, and who thus unify the creative and productive processes. Such a concept harks back to the ideology of the ARTS AND CRAFTS movement and the craft tradition in furniture making. Its exponents are motivated by various factors. Some produce their own furniture in order to escape being mere draughtsmen. Others show a more entrepreneurial desire to commercialize their own designs, wishing to shed the traditional, rural-craftsman image which is carried by the term craft, and are involved in serial rather than one-off production of their designs. The term is most commonly applied to activities in the 1970s and 1980s and can thus be seen as part and parcel of the debates which stemmed from the CRAFTS REVIVAL in Britain and the USA at that time.

Deskey, Donald (1894–1989) was a New York exponent of the MODERNE style, known especially for his CHROMIUM-plated steel furniture. He studied fine art in California (1915–20) and then spent two years in Paris, where he came into contact with European Modernists. He is best known for his popularization of the ART DECO style via his interior design for the Radio City Music Hall (1932). After World War II Deskey continued to work in industrial design, including PACKAGING for Procter and Gamble (1949–76) and office furniture for the Globe-Wernicke Company (1948–54).
□D.A. Hanks and J. Toher, *Donald Deskey: Decorative Designs and Interiors* (1985)

Deutsche Werkbund (f.1907) was a coalition of designers and industrialists formed following the 1906 Dresden exhibition of applied art. The Deutsche Werkbund's aims were in response to the idea that the rapid industrialization and modernization of Germany posed a threat to its national culture. In its attempt to reconcile art, craft and industry, however, it did not seek to revive the romantic notion of handicraft, as was advocated by associations spawned by the ARTS AND CRAFTS movement, but rather argued that, 'art is not only an aesthetic, but, at the same time, a moral power, both, however, leading in the final analysis to the most important of powers: economic power.'

This argument was championed by the liberal-democratic politician Friedrich Naumann and elaborated in aesthetic terms by Hermann MUTHESIUS. Muthesius was opposed to the use of ornament to give objects artistic validity and was thus against JUGENDSTIL, believing instead that practicality was the basis for expressing contemporary cultural values. This did not mean a denial of beauty, which was seen as a problem of form. Form became the dominant criterion for aesthetic

Bruno Taut's glass pavilion built for the **Deutsche Werkbund** *exhibition in Cologne (1914).*

judgment; anything 'from the sofa cushion to a city plan' was capable of spiritual value.

The primacy of form, however, could not be left to individual taste; instead, national types were to be distinguished and employed. They, in their turn, Muthesius argued, would have been handed down through tradition, in particular in architecture. In their unification of culture, society and industry, the theories of Naumann and Muthesius corresponded with contemporary middle-class, liberal political ambitions.

The Werkbund's achievements include the production of a yearbook (1912–20), an annual conference and, in 1914, a major exhibition in Cologne. This exhibition clearly demonstrated the stylistic variety of its leading members: Josef HOFFMANN and Muthesius both produced stripped neo-Classical style pavilions; Henry van de VELDE submitted a Jugendstil theatre and Walter GROPIUS designed a model factory, incorporating daring glazed elements into a neo-Classical structure; Bruno Taut created a small pavilion from glass bricks, glazed tiles and mosaics. From 1925 to 1934, the Werkbund published a magazine, *Die Form*, and in 1927 organized an exhibition of housing at Stuttgart, building a model suburb, the WEISSENHOF SIEDLUNG, with Ludwig MIES VAN DER ROHE as its architectural director.

The Werkbund was, however, most characterized by its lack of coherence on a theoretical level. Henry van de Velde, who joined the

Werkbund in 1908, advocated greater artistic freedom than Muthesius. Their debate came to a head at the Cologne exhibition, after which Muthesius's viewpoint to some extent prevailed. None the less, the Werkbund always felt tensions; in reconciling its nationalism with the desire to be modern (and thus internationalist); in acting as an artist in a capitalist society in order to bring art and industry together; and in clarifying the role of the creative minority in a democratic society.

In 1933 the Werkbund sought accommodation within the Nazi regime, despite fierce opposition from Gropius and his ex-BAUHAUS associates Wilhelm Wagenfeld and Martin Wagner, and in 1934 it faded into obscurity. In 1947 it was revived, and while it has failed to achieve a position comparable with that of its first phase, in both its epochs, it has none the less been greatly admired as a promoter of design. □ Campbell (1978); L. Burckhardt, *The Werkbund* (1980); Heskett (1986)

Devetsil Group (1920–31) was the dominant avant-garde group of artists, architects, designers and writers in Czechoslovakia between the wars. Founded on 5 November 1920 in the Café Union in Prague, the group initiated a new approach to international Modernism (*see* MODERN MOVEMENT). It organized theatrical events and exhibitions and published the work of many leading avant-gardists. Members included the architects Josef Chocol, Evzen Linhart and Josef Havlicek, the poet Jaroslav Seifert, the painter Marie Čermínová Toyen and the linguistic theorist Roman Jakobson. Without their knowledge, the American film actors Douglas Fairbanks and Charlie Chaplin were given honorary membership. Devetsil provided a forum for the exchange of ideas, maintaining close links with the Russian Constructivists (*see* CONSTRUCTIVISM), the BAUHAUS, DADA and the Surrealists (*see* SURREALISM). Some Devetsil members, such as Chocol, had been closely involved with CZECH CUBISM before World War I, but had turned their attention more closely to the elimination of decoration in architecture and the expression of the 'machine aesthetic'. Karol Teige, the acknowledged leader of the group, was also editor and art director of the Devetsil journal, *ReD*, published by the progressive Odeon Press. The members of Devetsil experimented with PHOTOMONTAGE, collage and avant-gardist typography, as well as organizing exhibitions of furniture and interior design. Their output, however, remained largely craft-based, and few designers produced designs for mass production. In the 1930s, the group moved away from its early concern with Cubism and Expressionism to a closer interest in FUNCTIONALISM and the INTERNATIONAL STYLE. Czech Modernism then became a strong symbol of national identity for the new Czechoslovakian nation, until its annexation in 1938. □ *Devetsil, Czech Avant-Garde Architecture and Design of the 1920s and 30s* (exh. cat., Museum of Modern Art, Oxford, and Design Museum, London, 1990)

Dexel, Walter (1890–1973) was born in Munich where he studied art history. From 1916 to 1928 he directed the exhibitions of Jena's Art Union. His style of painting was strongly influenced by CONSTRUCTIVISM, but he was also concerned with commercial art and typography. He had contacts with the BAUHAUS (1919–25) and with Theo van DOESBURG (1921–23). His designs never included any illustration, but instead relied on compositions of type and geometric forms. His 1927 exhibition for the Art Union, New Advertising, was one of the earliest attempts to survey developments in 20th-c. commercial design. He also taught at the School of Arts and Crafts in Magdeburg (1928–35) and at the State College of Art Education in Berlin-Schöneberg (1936–42).

DIA *see* DESIGN AND INDUSTRIES ASSOCIATION

Diffrient, Niels (b.1928) studied at the CRANBROOK ACADEMY OF ART (1948–51 and 1952–53), before going on to work with Marco ZANUSO in Milan on a Fulbright Fellowship (1954–55). He was a partner at Henry DREYFUSS Associates (1955–81) before establishing Niels Diffrient Product Design in Connecticut. With Walter Dorwin TEAGUE, Diffrient designed some spectacular products, involving much ENGINEERING DESIGN in his 'from the inside out' approach, whereby the internal workings of a product are given as much dedicated attention as its exterior form. These included high voltage towers for the Edison Electric Institute (1964) and the aeroplane interiors of the Boeing 747, 767, 727, 707 and the Douglas DC-10 for American Airlines

Diffrient's *Helena chair (1984), made in steel and leather for Sunar Hauserman.*

Drawings by **Dillon** *of her Jobber chair for Casas Mobilplast (1982).*

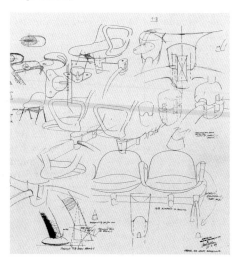

(1968–80). He also undertook investigations in ERGONOMICS for seating for KNOLL in the early 1970s. Since the 1980s he has concentrated on office furniture, designing his acclaimed and highly expensive Jefferson executive office chair for Sunar Hauserman in 1984.

Dillon, Jane (b.1943) studied furniture design at London's ROYAL COLLEGE OF ART (1965–68) and was then employed briefly by KNOLL International (1968–69), where she worked with George NELSON. She then became a consultant to OLIVETTI in Milan, and collaborated there with Ettore SOTTSASS. From 1971 she was based mainly in London, working with her husband Charles Dillon (d.1981). None the less, apart from her consultancy to HABITAT, the Conran Design Group (*see* Terence CONRAN) and WOLFF OLINS, it is noteworthy that she worked with the Spanish companies Casas and Disform through the 1970s. For Disform she designed the simple Cometa lamp (1971), while for Casas she developed the Jobber office chair in the early 1980s, which became one of Spain's biggest exports in furniture.

Diulgheroff, Nicolay (1901–82) was born in Kyustendil, Bulgaria, and was the son of a typographer. He studied at Vienna's School of Arts and Crafts (1920–21), the New School of Art in Dresden (1922) and in 1923 spent a few months under Johannes ITTEN at the BAUHAUS. Moving to Turin in 1926 to study architecture, he in fact began an intense period of activity as a designer, producing lamps, ceramics and glass as well as advertising for Cinzano, Unica and Campari. He took part in the pavilion dedicated to FUTURISM at the Turin International Exhibition in 1929. In the same year his Futurist approach to graphics was introduced in Turin on a wide scale, through the publicity agency of Arturo Tucci. In the second half of the 1930s he turned increasingly towards architectural projects.
☐C. Belioli and M. Pinottini, *Nicolay Diulgheroff Architetto, Graphic e Industrial Designer* (1987).

Dixon, Tom (b.1959) is a London-based designer and small-scale producer of furniture, who became internationally known from the 1980s. Without any formal training, in 1985 he began to weld 'ready-made' objects together in a fashion typical of ADHOCISM, thus creating furniture that had strong overtones of POST-

INDUSTRIALISM. He moved into series production of his furniture in the late 1980s.
□M. Collins, *Tom Dixon* (1990)

Doesburg, Theo van (1883–1931) was born in Utrecht in the Netherlands and was the leading light of the DE STIJL group. His ideas of NEO-PLASTICISM were at the core of the theoretical basis of De Stijl as a visual and tectonic language. Along with Piet Mondrian, with whom he began to correspond in 1915, van Doesburg developed his revolutionary, Utopian ideas and, more importantly, put them into practice. Most important among these was his notion of 'concrete art', developed in 1930, which described an aesthetic of universal clarity and which subsequently influenced Max BILL. It is impossible to overestimate his importance to De Stijl; he was instrumental in disseminating its ideas through lecture tours and through the monthly magazine, the last issue of which commemorated his death.

Domus (f.1928) is a Milanese architecture and design magazine founded by Gio PONTI. During the 1930s it emphasized the aims of the NOVECENTO group, encompassing the work of the WIENER WERKSTÄTTE together with indigenous Italian Classicism. Under the editorship of Ernesto Rogers (1941–47) the magazine veered towards a leftist promotion of RATIONALISM and prefabrication. On Ponti's return, *Domus* reflected a tendency to represent the home in terms of 'the good life'. It was edited by Alessandro MENDINI from 1979. In 1982 the Domus Academy was founded under Andrea BRANZI. This international postgraduate design school aimed to institutionalize many of the concepts of ANTI-DESIGN. Thus, it became supremely conscious of its Postindustrial context (*see* POSTINDUSTRIALISM) and confirmed that Italian design was ultimately conceptual and philosophical by nature.

Dorfsman, Lou (b.1918) is an American graphic designer. He studied at the Cooper Union School for the Advancement of Science and Art in New York, during which time he created exhibition designs for the NEW YORK WORLD'S FAIR, 1939. He joined CBS in 1946 as the radio division's art and creative director, moving on to become creative director of the television network in 1960 following the sudden death of William GOLDEN. He was director of design for the entire CBS Corporation

Van **Doesburg**'s *cover for the book* Klassiek-Barok-Modern (1920).

from 1964 until 1988. His career with CBS spanned a period which saw television's coming of age, the radio coming back from decline and the development of the corporate approach to advertising. Throughout these changes, Dorfsman maintained a classical yet witty approach to design.

Dreyfuss, Henry (1904–72) was among the first generation of American industrial designers. He began his career as a stage designer apprenticed to Norman BEL GEDDES and went freelance in 1927. In 1929 he established his own industrial design office. From the outset he insisted on working on products 'from the inside out' (i.e., paying equal attention to both the internal workings and the external form of a product), and his designs, such as the Mercury diesel locomotive for the New York Central Railroad (1936) and the 300 combined handset desk telephone for Bell Telephones in which the mouth- and earpiece

Driade

*The Traveller's Joy armchair (c.1907) by Benjamin Fletcher was made at Harry Peach's **Dryad** Works in Leicester.*

□ R. De Fusco, *Il 'Gioco' del Design: Vent' Anni di Attività della Driade* (1988)

Dryad (f.1907) was established in Leicester by Harry PEACH. He was motivated by principles inherited from the ARTS AND CRAFTS movement – that production should be a joyous affair without an alienating division of labour. Peach, with the advice of his friend Benjamin Fletcher, who was director of the Leicester School of Art, thus set up a workshop to manufacture quality cane furniture which could compete with that imported from Austria and Germany. Designs were supplied by Fletcher, and Dryad's products competed well with LLOYD LOOM and others into the 1930s, due to their good design and thorough quality control. Dryad was so successful that in 1912 Dryad Metal Works were founded to manufacture interior fittings and tableware. The firm also began to produce handicraft items in 1917, and this was the only branch of the company to survive after World War II.

□ P. Kirkham, *Harry Peach: Dryad and the DIA* (1986)

are combined in a single unit (1937), showed a strong grasp of ENGINEERING DESIGN. Furthermore, at the core of Dreyfuss's success was his belief that machines adapted to people would be the most efficient. In 1959 he published *The Measure of Man*, a book that helped establish ERGONOMICS and ANTHROPOMETRICS as the essential tools of designers. Henry Dreyfuss Associates still continues to function.

□ H. Dreyfuss, *Industrial Design: A Pictorial Accounting* (1929); *Designing for People* (1955); *The Measure of Man: Human Factors in Design* (1959); H. Dreyfuss and D.M. Dreyfuss, *Henry Dreyfuss Symbol Source Book* (1972)

Driade (f.1968) started in Piacenza, Italy, as a small editor of furniture (*see* EDITING). In 1969 it moved to Fossadello di Caorso and by 1972 was undertaking most of the manufacture and assembly of its SYSTEM FURNITURE while at the same time, 'farming out' some processes, mostly in the production of its single-piece furniture. The company was owned by the Astori family and much of the system furniture was designed by Antonia Astori. Its betterknown avant-garde projects include work by Philippe STARCK, Alessandro MENDINI and Paolo DEGANELLO.

Dumbar, Gert (b.1940) studied painting and graphic design at The Hague Academy where he was taught by Paul SCHUITEMA. Schuitema and Piet ZWART, who became a good friend of Dumbar's, were leaders in Dutch modern typography and were enormously influential on Dumbar. In the 60s he was a student at London's ROYAL COLLEGE OF ART. Dumbar worked at the design consultancy, Tel, before setting up Studio Dumbar in 1977. The variety and high quality of the work produced by this small studio is much admired, winning numerous awards and a steady stream of student followers. Of particular interest are Dumbar's fine art approach, his continual search for new ways of communicating, his use of staged photography, and the humour in all areas of his work, from CORPORATE IDENTITY to theatre posters, signage to television graphics. Wellknown projects include award-winning signage for the Rijksmuseum, corporate identities for the Dutch Railway, ANWB (the Dutch Automobile Association) and PTT, and theatre posters for Zeebelt Theatre. Dumbar's influence is widespread, particularly through students in The Hague, the Royal College of Art (where he was professor of graphic design from 1985 to 1987) and the CRANBROOK ACADEMY OF ART, Michigan, as well as the

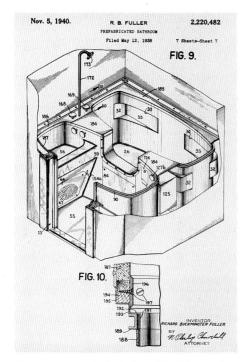

The patent drawing for Buckminster Fuller's **Dymaxion** *bathroom, filed 12 May 1938.*

large number of student placements in his own studio.

Dymaxion is a term created by the combination of the words 'dynamism', 'maximum' and 'ion'. It was coined in 1929 by Waldo Warren, a public relations expert who worked for Marshall Field, a Chicago department store, for which Buckminster FULLER designed a futuristic home to be displayed in the store as a setting for new furniture. Fuller often subsequently used the term to describe designs which he believed to have maximum efficiency in terms of the available technology.

□R. Marks, *The Dymaxion World of Buckminster Fuller* (1960)

E

Eames, Charles (1907–78) studied architecture at Washington University, St Louis (1924–26). He worked with an architectural firm in St Louis (1925–27) and then with his own private practice until he became head of the department of experimental design at the CRANBROOK ACADEMY OF ART (1937–40). In the 40s he worked with Eero SAARINEN, with whom he began to investigate the artistic possibilities of new mid-20th-c. materials, in particular PLASTICS, which enabled die-press stamping of seats. In allowing greater organic expression, plastic – and Eames's exploration of it – also suggested a new aesthetic for seating. Along with his colleague, Harry BERTOIA, Eames was one of the first furniture designers to realize that modern, more open-plan architecture, with its glass walls, would push furniture away from the walls; it would thus have to be seen in the round, like free-standing sculpture.

Eames's *moulded plywood chair (1948).*

Eames and Saarinen won the ORGANIC DESIGN in Home Furnishings competition at New York's MUSEUM OF MODERN ART in 1941, with three PLYWOOD chairs moulded into complex curves. In 1941 Eames married Ray Kaiser, with whom he subsequently shared all design credits; Ray was an abstract painter who had studied under Hans Hofmann in New York (1933–39) and later at the Cranbrook Academy (1940–41). They then moved to Los Angeles, where he designed film sets for MGM film studios. He continued to experiment with plywood, supplying leg splints to the US Navy from 1942. In 1943 the Eames' workshop became the southern California branch of the Evans Products Company and expanded production into laminated glider parts. When the War ended the company turned to the production of Eames's chairs. In 1946 his plywood chairs were exhibited at the Museum of Modern Art in a show entitled New Furniture Designed by Charles Eames. As a result, the right to produce his designs was bought by HERMAN MILLER. Included in the exhibition was the so-called Eames chair or DCM chair, a dining chair that consisted of two pads of moulded body-curved plywood attached to a metal-rod frame with rubber cushions as connectors. The resin that impregnated the plywood laminations of the seat and back units of the chairs was invariably stained with brilliant dyes in shades of red, yellow and blue, which penetrated the wood plies without blurring the natural grain. Also in the exhibition were prototypes for an armchair and an ottoman in laminated rosewood and anodized ALUMINIUM with feather-stuffed hide cushions; these went into production ten years later.

In 1948 the Museum of Modern Art launched an International Competition for Low-Cost Furniture Design. Eames entered in conjunction with the University of California at Los Angeles. The results included stamped steel and aluminium seats with metal or wood bases. None of Eames's metal seats actually went into production, but with a little variation to the designs, Herman Miller produced them in moulded FIBREGLASS and polyester resin from 1950. These were manufactured by Herman Miller in conjunction with Zenith Plastics (later to become Century Plastics): their single-piece organically shaped seat and back, together with the slender rod bases, made them a standard of both domestic and office seating for three decades to follow.

In addition to chairs, Eames also designed tables and screens and magazine covers for *Arts & Architecture* in 1944; towards the end of his life he concentrated more on designing exhibitions and also made films.

☐ *Connections: The Work of Charles and Ray Eames* (exh. cat., S. Wright Gallery, University of California, 1976); A. Drexler, *Charles Eames: Furniture from the Design Collection: Museum of Modern Art, New York* (1981); R. Eames, J. Neuhart and M. Neuhart, *Eames Design: The Office of Charles and Ray Eames 1941–1978* (1989)

Earl, Harley (1893–1969) was a pioneer of STYLING. He was born in Hollywood, California, where his father, a coachbuilder, had founded the Earl Automobile Works in 1908. From 1911 it custom-built bodies for cars and trucks for Hollywood's film stars: significantly, therefore, Harley Earl himself was creating designs that broke the mould of black, standardized cars set by the Model-T FORD. The company was bought by a Cadillac dealer in 1919, which gave Earl direct access to GENERAL MOTORS in Detroit. General Motors was itself in direct competition with Ford and, in line with its policy of developing a more attractive car than the competition, Earl was employed by them from 1925. There he introduced the technique of designing with clay models rather than solely on the drawing board – a more sculptural approach. His first car for General Motors, designed with Larry P. Fisher, was the La Salle (1927). This was based on the exclusive Hispano-Suiza and introduced Hollywood showmanship to Detroit car manufacture. In 1927 he became head of a new department, the Art and Colour Section (known as the Styling Section from 1937), with 50 employees. Between 1927 and 1937 Earl progressively reduced the height and broadened the width of General Motors' cars; he also incorporated the engine and cabin as a visual whole, thus establishing the car's own identity as something more than a mere descendant of the horse and carriage. He also supported a greater degree of standardization throughout General Motors' works. In 1937 Earl designed the Buick 'Y' Job, which was a forerunner of his Buicks and Cadillacs of the post-1945 period. With its exaggerated styling, which was intended to appear glamorous, the 'Y' Job was too expensive to produce. However, during the 1950s, with developments in the stamping of

*Poster by **Eckersley** for the General Post Office, designed in 1952.*

their manufacture. In other words, it carries out the product development, MARKETING and distribution, but subcontracts the manufacture to networks of workshops. The core company often undertakes the assemblage and PACKAGING of the product. This process is more normally carried out by small-sized companies involving short-run production of relatively low-technology products such as furniture, fittings and lighting. As a process it has the advantage of greater flexibility, being able to draw on a range of pre-existing workshops and thus avoiding investment in expensive production plants. But it also has the disadvantage of difficulties on the part of the editor in maintaining quality control when not manufacturing the object in-house.

body parts, Earl's Buick range went into production, each car becoming more extreme in its use of styling, as General Motors relied more and more on stylistic OBSOLESCENCE. Earl retired in 1959.
□ S. Bayley, *Harley Earl and the Dream Machine* (1983); *Harley Earl* (1990)

Eckersley, Tom (b.1914) is a British graphic designer who went to Salford School of Art (1930–34) and then moved to London and set up a partnership with Eric Lombers, designing for clients such as London Transport and Shell Mex. During World War II he worked for the Ministry of Information, the Royal Society for the Prevention of Accidents and the General Post Office, but afterwards he set up as a freelance designer. He was also influential as the head of the department of graphic design at the London College of Printing (1957–75). His early work reflects the influence of Edward McKnight KAUFFER, A.M. CASSANDRE and the modern art movements of Europe in the 1920s and 30s; however, during his long career he developed an increasingly direct way of communicating through simple bold images. This is reflected in his switches in technique from stipple shading to silkscreen and papier collé with bold solid blocks of colour and simple outlines. They convey the essential message often with the extra memorable ingredient of humour.
□ T. Eckersley, *Poster Design* (1953)

editing is a specific term used in Italy and Spain to refer to the production of objects by a company without its actual involvement in

Eidenbenz, Hermann (b.1902) studied at the Art Institute Orell Füssli in Switzerland (1919–22) and continued his studies with Ernst KELLER at the Zurich School of Arts and Crafts until 1923. His working life was split between graphic design, teaching and consultancy in Switzerland and Germany, heading Eidenbenz Studios in Basle from 1932 to 1952. He was

Eidenbenz's poster for the Graphic Technical Exhibition held by Grafa International in Basle (1936).

77

influential in establishing the foundations of the SWISS SCHOOL of graphic design.

Ekuan, Kenji (b.1929) was one of the first Japanese industrial-design consultants to gain international recognition in the 60s. Born in Tokyo, he first trained for the Buddhist priesthood (1947–49) but then studied design at the National University of Fine Arts and Music, Tokyo (1950–55). After a brief spell at the ART CENTER COLLEGE OF DESIGN in Pasadena, California (1955), Ekuan founded GK INDUSTRIAL DESIGN ASSOCIATES in 1957. His international reputation was established through his work with large industrial companies such as Yamaha, as well as his involvement in design institutions – in 1976 he was elected president of the INTERNATIONAL COUNCIL OF SOCIETIES OF INDUSTRIAL DESIGN (ICSID). Despite this strong corporate persona, he is also noted for the deep spiritual element he brings to his practice.
□K. Ekuan, *Dogu Ko* (1967); *Industrial Design: The World of Dogu, its Origins, its Future* (1971); *Design: The Relationship of Man and Technology* (1972); *Ekuan: Dunhill Industrial Design Lecture Series 1973* (1975); *The Philosophy of Tools* (1980); *The Buddhist Automobile and the Automobile* (1986)

Emigré (f.1982) is a twice-yearly, San Francisco based, graphic design magazine, with its founder, Rudy VanderLans, as art editor and Zuzana Licko as typographer. Without an editor, the magazine makes a feature of its innovative graphics. Subtitled, 'the magazine that ignores boundaries', it includes work undertaken specially by various international designers, but was also conceived as a three-dimensional object itself, in its careful treatment of visual narrative from page to page. *Emigré* makes extensive and innovative use of APPLE Macintosh COMPUTER-AIDED DESIGN systems, aligning it with other exponents of the contemporaneous CALIFORNIA NEW WAVE.

engineering design is a term to describe the aspect of three-dimensional design that is concerned purely with the technical workings of an object, rather than its aesthetic or formal characteristics or functions.

environmental psychology is the study of the effects of environments on human behaviour. Since it is concerned with the human user, its data may be of interest to the designer.

Erco (f.1934) is a leading international supplier of architectural lighting. It was established in Germany and grew rapidly during the 'economic miracle' of the late 1950s. It has produced designs by, among many others, Emilio AMBASZ, Terence CONRAN, Ettore SOTTSASS and Roger TALLON.

ergonomics is the systematic study of the characteristics of human users and their relationships with environments, systems and/or objects. The ergonomist's aim is to avoid any mismatch by the application of scientific information concerning human beings to the problems of design. In the USA it is generally known as 'human factors'. It is closely related to ANTHROPOMETRICS, the branch of ergonomics that deals with body size, shape and strength.

Ergonomi Design Gruppen (f.1979) is a Swedish industrial design consultancy which specializes, as its name suggests, in ERGONOMICS. Its founders, Maria Benktzon and Sven-Eric Juhlin, are known in particular for their research into DESIGN FOR DISABILITY.

Ermilov, Vasilii (1894–1968) was trained primarily in fine art in his native Ukrainian town of Kharkov and then at the Moscow Institute of Painting, Sculpture and Architecture from 1913. During his time in Moscow he met the Cubo-Futurists Burliuk and Mayakovsky, leading figures in the Russian avant-garde. In 1917 Ermilov returned to Kharkov, taking with him the style and ideology of CONSTRUCTIVISM. In 1919 and 1920 he designed and produced agitprop posters and murals, and painted the exterior of trains with simple images intended to convey messages of the Revolution to outlying areas of Russia.

F

Fantasy Furniture was the title of an exhibition held at the Museum of Contemporary Crafts, New York, in 1966. As the title suggests, the pieces exhibited displayed elaborate ornamentation and colouring which challenged a strictly Functionalist conception of furniture (*see* FUNCTIONALISM).
☐ T. Simpson, *Fantasy Furniture: Design and Decoration* (1968)

Fast Moving Consumer Goods (FMCG) are the opposite of consumer durables and include foodstuffs and any goods that are subject to repeated re-purchase.

feminism is a political position which seeks to implement change in the interests of women. A feminist analysis of design provides a range of historical and critical methods which challenge mainstream definitions of design practice and encourage access to the often anonymous and traditional design activity of women. It raises questions regarding the values that are given priority in assessing design, the types of designed objects that are examined and the people who are accorded the status of designer. It thus discusses those aspects of design that are omitted from conventional studies.

The dominant conception of design history, resulting from the discipline's roots in the MODERN MOVEMENT, still considers form the effect of function, the product of professional designers, industrial production and the division of labour. This view of design historically assumes that a woman's place is in the home, assigning men to the determining, functional areas of design (industrial production) and women to the private, domestic realm (decorative arts). The belief that women belong in the domestic area (normally seen as subordinate) is thereby reinforced.

This hierarchy of disciplines is implicit in any object-based study of design. It follows that, although such a methodology allows the historian to address ANONYMOUS DESIGN (often resulting from the work of a number of people) and examine it in the light of contemporary social, cultural, economic and technological conditions, it is not objective. In contrast, feminist historians have developed a range of methodologies, drawing on models derived from cultural studies, social history, psychoanalysis and anthropology, in order to address the effect of material goods in forming our sexual and gender identities.

The biographical monograph, a form particularly favoured by 19th-c. art historians and sometimes carried over to design history, has been greatly criticized by feminists. The point is made that a discipline celebrating art as the achievement of the individual creative personality, the result of individual 'greatness' or 'genius', cannot accommodate those outside its ideological parameters of class, race and gender. While recognizing the importance of retrieving women's design work from obscurity (not least to provide role models for young women embarking on design careers), a feminist process of historical enquiry, practice or critique of design challenges traditional hierarchies in order to establish a broader cultural landscape.

Feminist historians have examined those areas of production rarely covered by traditional design histories: the crafts (particularly traditional domestic crafts such as quilting), fashion, film, ephemera and popular culture. Historically, the crafts provided middle-class women with 'respectable' employment through creative activities that were considered suitably domestic. Work in the crafts (ceramics, metalwork, book-binding, embroidery, etc.) enabled women to achieve economic independence and even status within the professional world.

The relationship between design and lived experience as seen from the female point of view has been explored by feminists examining women in a man-made environment – how the designed environment gives material form to assumptions about women's place in terms of buildings, public spaces and transport. Much study in the areas of consumption and representation has taken place. The former has been examined as a positive rather than a passive activity (shopping as a form of power), while the complex subject of the representation of an idealized femininity through media images of fashion and beauty have initiated controversial debates around issues of pornography and how we construct our identities through interacting with the world of objects and images that surrounds us.
☐ J. Williamson, *Consuming Passions* (1978); *Decoding Advertisements* (1978); A. Callen, *The Angel in the Studio: Women in the Arts and Crafts*

Giacomo Matté-Trucco's 1923 **Fiat** *works in Turin with the test track on the roof.*

Movement (1979); J. Winship, *Woman Becomes an 'Individual': Femininity and Consumption in Women's Magazines* (1981); J. Boys, 'Is There a Feminist Analysis of Architecture' in *Built Environment* Vol. 10, No. 1 (1984); L. Walker, *Women Architects: Their Work* (1984); T. Gronberg and J. Attfield (eds), *A Resource Book on Women Working in Design* (1986); C. Buckley 'Made in Patriarchy: Towards a Feminist Analysis of Women and Design' in *Design Issues* Vol. 3, No. 2 (1987); J. Attfield in Walker (1989); Attfield and Kirkham (1989); C. Buckley, *Potters and Paintresses – Women Designers in the Pottery Industry 1870–1955* (1990); J. Burkhauser (ed.), *Glasgow Girls – Women in Art and Design 1880–1920* (1990)

Festival Style *see* CONTEMPORARY STYLE

Fiat (f.1899) stands for 'Fabbrica Italiana Automobili Torino' (Italian Car Factory, Turin). It is Europe's leading car manufacturer and Italy's largest industrial undertaking. It was formed in Turin on the second wave of Italy's comparatively late industrial revolution, which saw the establishment of an engineering industry. Fiat started out manufacturing sports cars – the automobile was still a luxury item and Fiat was just one among many craft-production-based automobile manufacturers at the turn of the century. However, under the guidance, in particular, of its founder, Giovanni Agnelli, who steered the company towards an American model of mass production, by 1905 Fiat had become a leading automobile factory. In the face of competition from the USA, where much cheaper vehicles were being made, Fiat quickly reorganized itself to achieve volume production and in 1912 launched a small capacity car, the Tipo Zero. By 1914, with its adoption of a Fordist model of manufacture (*see* FORDISM), 16,000 cars were appearing on the Italian roads every year, and the company's subsequent success led it to be perceived almost as an 'American island' in the engineering sector – something, which has changed little since in terms of industrial organization. This shift was further reinforced as demand grew during World War I. By 1919 Fiat's famous Lingotto factory, designed by Giacomo Matté-Trucco, was in action – this building consisted of a spiral of five floors, the finished vehicles emerging on its test track on the roof.

During the last three years of the 1920s, the transition from wood-framed to totally metal-framed car-bodies took place. The era of the hand-finished car was over and automobile manufacturers experimented with new methods of making vehicles lighter. Fiat's chief engineer from 1928 was Dante GIACOSA. Following a severe economic crisis, Fiat launched the 508 Balilla in 1932. This car and its successor of 1935, the 1500, used the new design features of STREAMLINING. In 1936 the smallest production car in the world was launched, the Fiat 500.

By the end of the 1930s Fiat had up to 24 international sales outlets. To cope with the higher demand for Fiat's cars among middle-class consumers, the company established the Mirafiori factory in the late 1930s. In 1956 and 1957 two cars appeared which became emblematic both of Fiat and of Italy's postwar economic recovery: these were the Fiat 600 and the Nuova 500. With its two-cylinder rear air-cooled engine, over 3 million examples of the 600 appeared all over the world. This car continued the compactness and streamlining already seen in the earlier 500. However, the Fiat 1800 introduced in 1959 was characterized by its angular shape and straight lines, in complete contrast to previous styles, perhaps making a faint echo of the Detroit mode of STYLING then current in the USA. It was not until the 1980s that greater attention was given to aerodynamics; in the meantime, successive models demonstrated a marked contrast between the window section of the cabin and the main body of the vehicle. This change of direction took place under the consultancy of PININFARINA. Other consultants who worked for Fiat were GHIA and Giorgietto GIUGIARO.

Fiat commanded about 80 per cent of the Italian market in automobiles through most of the 20th c. Alongside its strident designs for small cars, particularly in the 1930s and 50s, its publicity included the work of Marcello NIZ-ZOLI, Fortunato DEPERO and Marcello Dudovich. The Lingotto plant was closed in 1982 and converted into a residential and exhibition centre. Its first exhibition was on FUTURISM in 1986, an apt recognition of a movement that reflected a crucial step in social adjustment to the motor vehicle.

□ A. Anselmi, *Automobili Fiat* (1986); *Las Formas de la Industria: Arte Diseños y Productos de una Empresa* (exh. cat., Museo Español de Arte Contemporáneo, Madrid, 1987); A. Friedman, *Agnelli and the Network of Italian Power* (1988); *Fiat 1899–1989: An Italian Industrial Revolution (exh. cat., Fiat, Milan, 1989); Design Automobile: Les Maitres de la Carrosserie Italienne* (exh. cat., Rome, Istituto Nazionale per il Commercio Estero, 1990)

fibreglass is the trade-name of the glassfibre products made by Fibreglass Ltd. It is also called spun glass and is a fibrous form of glass, often used as a reinforcing ingredient of PLASTICS. Combined with layers of resin, fibreglass is a popular medium for car bodies, for instance, the roof of the CITROËN DS (1955) was made from fibreglass-reinforced plastic, which was left unpainted and translucent on some early models. Weight for weight, fibreglass is stronger than steel and it resists corrosion.

Fleckhaus, Willy (1925–83) was probably the most influential book and magazine designer in

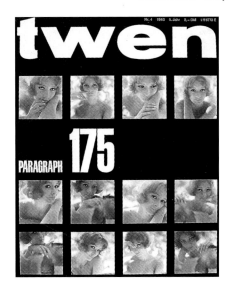

Cover for the magazine Twen *in 1963 by its art director,* **Fleckhaus**.

postwar Germany. He trained as a journalist but soon discovered a dislike for writing. Instead, he was more influenced by American magazines such as those designed by Alexey BRO-DOVITCH and in 1952 he took over the design of *Aufwärts*, the youth magazine of the German trades union movement. Here he made heavy use of images rather than text, incorporating photography and text on the page and adding full-bleed pictures. *Aufwärts* became one of Germany's first lifestyle magazines.

In 1959 the Munich-based magazine *Twen* (a cropping of the word 'twenty') was launched with Fleckhaus as its art director. He had a thorough knowledge of the teachings of the ULM HOCHSCHULE FÜR GESTALTUNG and the BAUHAUS. He was also a close friend of Max BILL, and the grid format of *Twen* owed something to the influence of the SWISS SCHOOL. This grid was, however, only a starting point for a spectacular combination of words and images. He made a strong use of black and white space, cropping photographs and changing their scale into either striking or tantalizing views. Dubbed, in fact, the 'super-cropper', he often manipulated articles on the page, sometimes even adjusting their editorial emphasis in the process. Unsurprisingly, this often undermined the editorial role, and *Twen* went through six editors during Fleckhaus's contract with the magazine. Ultimately, after twelve years with the magazine, he was sacked for that very reason. From 1974 he was a professor at the Folkwangschule of the University of Essen and then professor at the University of Wuppertal from 1981.

Fletcher, Alan (b.1931) is a British graphic designer and founder-partner of PENTAGRAM. He studied at the Central School of Arts and Crafts, London (1950–51), and the ROYAL COLLEGE OF ART (1953–56), before spending a year at Yale University, where the USA's advanced state of consumerism made a big impression on him. He began his career in New York, where he worked for *Fortune* magazine, the CONTAINER CORPORATION OF AMERICA and IBM. Moving back to London in 1962 he co-founded Fletcher/Forbes/Gill before the foundation of Pentagram in 1972. He left Pentagram to open his own studio in 1992. His work is distinguished by its clarity and sometimes by its humour. It includes the symbol and signage for the Victoria and Albert Museum (1988).

Eric Gill's illustration for the final issue of The **Fleuron** *(1930).*

Fleuron, The (1923–30) was a typographic journal founded by Oliver Simon, who edited it until 1925. He was succeeded as editor by Stanley MORISON (1926–30). Oliver Simon went on to found *The Signature* (1935–54).

flexible production *see* BATCH PRODUCTION

FMCG *see* FAST MOVING CONSUMER GOODS

Ford (f.1901) was established as the Ford Motor Company in Detroit, Michigan, by Henry Ford. He had been chief engineer of the Edison Illuminating Company, but resigned in 1899 to build the forerunners of automobiles, firstly with the Detroit Automobile Company, which had been valued at $150,000, the most solid amalgamation of assets placed behind any American horseless-carriage business to date. This company failed within two years, mostly because Ford was unable at the time to overcome the technical and commercial difficulties connected with manufacturing his models in series. In partnership with Alex Malcolmson, Ford got backing to set up the Ford Motor Company, which was to commercialize the Model A car, though not necessarily to manufacture it, for early automobile makers were essentially designers, assemblers and marketers – the manufacture of its parts would be 'farmed out'.

Ford's cars were progressively more successful, and in 1908 he brought out the Model T, of which 16 million were produced before 1927. Its success was primarily due to its competitive price resulting from the economies of scale afforded by the use of the manufacturing system later to receive the denomination of FORDISM. This was chiefly brought about by the perfection of the moving production line in 1913. While the Model T underwent nearly 20 years of consistent development, Ford's second most celebrated car, the V8, was launched in 1932. It was only then that Ford's cars took on a more streamlined shape, and, subsequently, that STYLING began.

Separate manufacture of the Model T began in Berlin (1926), Cologne (1931) and Dagenham, England (1931). In 1950 the Consul, Zephyr and Zodiac ranges were introduced to Britain, thus bringing the pazzazz of American styling to Europe. In 1962 Ford in Britain brought out the Cortina, designed by the Canadian Roy Brown. This car was extremely successful, as it was marketed as both a family and business car.

In 1967 Ford in Germany and Britain joined to create Ford of Europe, and their MARKETING became much more Europe-orientated. The Ford Capri (1971), manufactured in Germany, Britain and Spain, was heralded as the first Euro-car. Uwe Bahnsen's Sierra (1982) established a new standard in the engineering and design of cars. Indeed, such was the success of Ford of Europe during the 1980s, that it

*Henry **Ford**'s Model T (1908), first manufactured on the production line in 1913.*

propped up the ailing Ford Motor Company in the USA during that decade.

☐ F. Ford and S. Crowther, *My Life and Work* (1924); S. Bayley, *The Car Programme: Fifty-Two Months to Job One, or How They Designed the Ford Sierra* (1982); R. Lacey, *Ford: The Men and the Machine* (1986)

Fordism is a term used to describe a method of manufacture that has dominated economics in much of the developed world during the 20th c., namely mass production. As its name suggests, it is derived from the manufacturing system for the Model-T FORD, first produced in Michigan, USA, in 1908, a technique that was the fruit of industrial developments that stretch back to the mid-19th c. Its major feature was the use of the production line to replace nodal assembly, so that rather than workers moving, the product flowed past them. It owes a certain amount to Taylorism, a science developed by Frederick Winslow Taylor from 1900, which studied time and motion in order to make scientific decisions about the most efficient use of labour. This required the codifying of craft knowledge: tasks were broken down to their most simple forms and machines replaced handwork wherever possible. Higher wages compensated for the resultant de-skilling and monotony. The standardization of parts for assembly also became necessary.

The ramifications of Fordism for design are enormous. It was decisive in increasing the volume of production and decreasing the unit cost, as the initial investment in development and machinery would be soon offset by the lower production costs. In 1910 20,000 Model Ts were produced using nodal assembly, each costing $850; in 1916 600,000 were built, each

costing $360; by 1927 a total of 15 million had rolled off the production lines. Final assembly time was cut from 12.5 to 5.8 hours. Standardized, easy-to-assemble parts were important in the design stage, as was an overall design that was stylistically durable. However, such mass production presupposes mass consumption: customers must be willing to buy standard products. This requires the complete domination of the market by the manufacturer. Thus, accompanying Fordism we find the development of advertising and CORPORATE IDENTITY. Although markets may be dominated by other means (e.g., government legislation or the creation of monopolies), to ensure that the road system dominated railways, for example, GENERAL MOTORS, Standard Oil and Firestone Tyres bought up and dismantled railways in 44 urban areas in the USA.

During World War II Fordism transformed many sectors beyond automobile manufacture, especially food, furniture, clothes and shipbuilding. It has come to be associated with other forms of 'mass' organization: the corporation, the mass party, factory farming, American football, classical ballet and even a barbershop in Moscow with 120 seats. Indeed, it is not confined solely to Western capitalism. It was equally associated with the planned economies of many Communist countries until the 1990s. Obliquely, the MODERN MOVEMENT, with its prescriptive solutions for design in mass society, is often seen to go hand-in-hand with Fordism. Some historians have argued that it is a system that has dominated perceptions of manufacture and subsequently decision-making, rather than providing the most rational means of production in different economies.

Wherever a Fordist method is applied, it is invariably supported by a halo of smaller industries – some parts for FIAT cars are cast in factories no bigger than shacks. Where entities in this halo have intervened in product development and design, the HIGH-TECHNOLOGY COTTAGE INDUSTRY phenomenon has developed. Since the 1960s the Fordist monopoly has also slowed down with the break-up of the mass market, so that it cannot serve particular demands. In turn, competition from industries in developing countries in the Far East and Central and South America which have either copied Fordism or relied on distinctly 'un-Fordist' production methods have ensured this break-up. At a most sophisticated technological level, the development of BATCH PRODUC-

Fornasetti's *Palladiana vase.*

TION has meant that manufacturers can now address specific demands much more effectively than with Fordist methods. At a cultural level, the NEW DESIGN, POSTMODERNISM, ANTI-DESIGN and the CRAFTS REVIVAL may also be seen in part as rejections of Fordism.
☐ C. Maier in *Journal of Contemporary History* 5 (1970); C. Sabel, *Work and Politics: The Division of Labor in Industry* (1982); D. Hounshell, *From the American System to Mass Production, 1800–1932* (1984); C. Tolliday and J. Zeitlin, *The Automobile Industry and its Workers* (1986)

Formica is the trademark for a plastic material used to make various laminated plastic products, such as tabletops and wallboards. Layers of paper are impregnated with synthetic resins (e.g., melamine) and then bonded together under heat and pressure. Approximately seven sheets are used to form a hard and durable surfacing material. The top sheet is usually patterned and coloured, for instance, wood grain is commonly used. The surface can be shiny or matt.

Fornasetti, Piero (1923–88) was a prolific Italian designer, known mostly for his Surrealist (*see* SURREALISM) *trompe l'oeil* application

of motifs to ceramics, furniture and textiles. He often used images derived from old engravings, especially architectural prints. His decorative work, which in total numbered over 11,000 designs, became very fashionable in the 1950s. Although Gio PONTI commissioned him to work on interiors, he essentially remained an independent designer throughout his life. His designs regained their popularity in the late 1980s.

Foster, Norman (b.1935) is primarily known as a HIGH-TECH architect. He studied with Buckminster FULLER at Yale University in the 1960s and founded the Team 4 office in London with his wife, Wendy Foster, and Richard and Su Rogers. In 1967 he founded Foster Associates. Among his important buildings figure the Sainsbury Centre (1978) and the Hongkong and Shanghai Bank headquarters (1986). He has also designed a set of office furniture for the Italian manufacturer Tecno (1985).

Franck, Kaj (b.1911) studied furniture design at the Helsinki Central School of Industrial Design (1929–32) and is a Finnish designer of ceramics, glass and other decorative objects. He worked for various Finnish glass manufacturers before World War II and after hostilities ended became head of design at ARABIA (1945–73). Through his work there he was influential in promoting a potently utilitarian aesthetic in Scandinavia. He also designed tableware in PLASTICS for Servis from 1979.

Frogdesign (f.1969) is an international product design consultancy with offices in Tokyo and California as well as in Altensteig, Germany, where it was founded by Hartmut Esslinger. It was not until 1982 that it took the name of Frogdesign. Its clients include AEG, ERCO, SONY and APPLE – its best-known design is the Apple IIC computer (1982). Frogdesign's work is characterized by the introduction of colourful, organic and sometimes whimsical features into electronic hardware.
☐ V. Brandes, *Hartmut Esslinger & Frogdesign* (1992)

Froshaug, Anthony (1920–84) was a British typographer and graphic designer influenced initially by Jan TSCHICHOLD. His studies included drawing, medicine and architecture, and he taught at the Central School of Art and Design in London (1952–54 and 1970–84) as well as at the ULM HOCHSCHULE FÜR GE-STALTUNG (1957–60). His design work combined the 'craft' approaches of a print workshop with a strong Modernist (*see* MODERN MOVE-MENT) understanding of typography.

☐A. Froshaug, *Typographic Norms* (1964); *Typography 1945–65* (1965)

Frutiger, Adrian (b.1928) was born and educated in Switzerland but spent all his working life in France. While serving his four-year apprenticeship with a printer, he attended the Zurich School of Arts and Crafts, and his early successes brought him to the notice of the Paris foundry, Deberny et Peignot, who invited him to France in 1952. There he worked on typefaces for both foundry metal and film. He designed four faces before 1957, including Univers (1954), with which his international reputation became established. A SANS-SERIF face reduced to its most basic and rational form, its success was immediate. It was quickly taken up by the MONOTYPE CORPORATION and led to commissions such as the signage for Orly airport in Paris. Although primarily a typographer, Frutiger has also worked on lettering, signage, book design and symbols, particularly since setting up his own studio with Bruno Pfäffli, first in Paris in 1962 and from 1965 at Arceuil. Another well-known typeface was Frutiger (1976), developed from his designs for the 1975 signage of Paris's Charles de Gaulle airport. He has worked for most of the major type foundries and has also done important work as a consultant for IBM, designing typewriter faces since 1965 and later computer faces. His success as a typographer is based on his ability to combine artistic vision with a full understanding of technical processes and mathematics, enabling him to design faces for metal, film and digitized systems.

☐A. Frutiger, *Type, Sign, Symbol* (1980); *The Development of the Roman Alphabet* (1981)

Fry, Edwin Maxwell (b.1899) is an English architect who was closely associated with Jack PRITCHARD and Wells COATES in the attempts to establish the MODERN MOVEMENT in Britain during the 1930s.

☐M. Fry, *Maxwell Fry: Autobiographical Sketches* (1975)

Fukuda, Shigeo (b.1932) is a Japanese graphic designer, sculptor and thinker who studied design at the Tokyo National University of

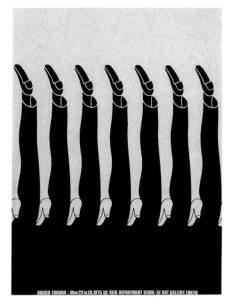

Fukuda's *advertisement for his exhibition at the Keio Department Store, Tokyo (1975).*

Fine Arts and Music until 1956. His graphic designs first achieved international recognition at the Expo '70 in Osaka. Mixing eastern and western imagery, his posters display a strong sense of humour. He uses juxtaposition, visual puns and touches of SURREALISM. He has taught in Tokyo and at Yale University, USA.

Fuller, Richard Buckminster (1895–1983) was one of the USA's most radical 20th-c. inventor-designers. He studied mathematics at Harvard University (1913–15), from which he was sent down twice, and then served in the US Navy (1917–19) before working for a meat company, Armour and Company, until 1922. He then became president of a company formed to promote the Stockade Building System, a method of building walls out of cement and compressed wood shavings. In 1927 he was forced to resign, the system having repeatedly come up against resistance from building-control officers. He then went into a year of recluse, during which he established himself as an independent inventor and created 4-D, a company to develop his inventions, which were driven, apparently, more by a humanistic concern than by the desire for personal gain. The fruit of this period of investigation and reflection was the ambition to develop a 'design science' that would obtain maximum human advantage from the minimum use of energy and materials. In 1929 this concept was named DYMAXION, though it was also called 4-D for some years. Fuller's Dymaxion house was developed from 1927 through to 1946; it was an easily movable and totally self-contained structure which hung from a central mast. He also invented the Dymaxion car in 1933, a streamlined automobile inspired by aeroplane design, which Fuller claimed should accelerate from 0 to 60 miles per hour in three seconds and achieve a fuel consumption of 30 miles per gallon. With financial backing from a stockbroker named Philip Pearson, who believed that the motor industry could draw the USA out of the Depression if only it could make another major design breakthrough (as Henry FORD had done), prototypes of the car were produced by a labour force of 28, headed by Fuller. While this car was revolutionary in concept and attracted international interest, it carried many dangerous design faults and was thus destined to failure as a serious alternative to conventional cars. Likewise, Fuller's transformation of the Dymaxion house into the more commercial Wichita house (1945) saw a similar fate. This metal pre-fabricated house, weighing just four tonnes, was to be built by the Beech Aircraft Company using redundant wartime bomber production lines, adapting the technology of the B-29 bomber to peacetime demands for housing. Within months of its press launch, Fuller's company, Fuller Houses Inc., had received 37,000 orders. However, perhaps with the Dymaxion car experience in mind, Fuller insisted on perfecting the design to the point where its backers lost patience, and the whole scheme collapsed.

Fuller continued mixing a visionary humanistic view of design with scientific and mathematical research, eventually achieving success with the development of the GEODESIC DOME from 1949. This structure could be transported easily and assembled with little technological know-how. It was a radical proposal for architecture and design, suggesting temporality and thus, perhaps, undermining the idea of property ownership (Fuller himself believed that housing should be regarded as a service rather than a product), as well as providing an ecologically sound building method with its 'more for less' attitude. It is not surprising that it was subsequently adopted both conceptually

Fuller *sitting in his Dymaxion car in 1934.*

and technically by members of ARCHIGRAM, Norman FOSTER (who studied with Fuller) and proponents of GREEN DESIGN, and was also extensively used for exhibition design.

The artefacts of Fuller's radical alternatives in design were supported by an impressive number of publications which appeared from 1960 and also by the relentless and lengthy lecturing which he continued right up to his death.

☐ R.W. Marks, *The Dymaxion World of Buckminster Fuller* (1959); S. Rosen, *Wizard of the Dome: R. Buckminster Fuller, Designer of the Future* (1969); E.J. Applewhite, *Cosmic Fishing: An Account of Writing Synergetics with Buckminster Fuller* (1977); M. Vance, *Richard Buckminster Fuller: A Bibliography* (1980); M. Pawley, *Buckminster Fuller* (1990)

Functionalism is a term that has been applied broadly so that it tends not to represent a particular style, though it does reveal a particular way of design thinking. The American architect Louis Sullivan is invariably noted as the founder of Functionalism. In 1896 he published an essay in which he coined the maxim, 'form follows function'. He was referring to an object's appearance and the ways in which it was governed by external factors, particularly physical or climatic ones. However, its definition soon altered, referring to the object itself and leaving out any consideration of the influence of its context. Through its use within the MODERN MOVEMENT, particularly by LE CORBUSIER, the term became interchangeable with RATIONALISM. Furthermore, in the arena of design theory, it was often misused or its value exaggerated: Reyner BANHAM and Tim Benton have both argued persuasively that the term has dominated perceptions of Le Corbusier's theories – yet he was equally enthusiastic about the expressive character of objects of the machine age, as he was about their functional value.

☐ E. de Zurko, *Origins of Functionalist Theory* (1957); Banham (1960); T. Benton 'The Myth of Function' in Greenhalgh (1990)

Futurism was an Italian fine arts movement launched in 1909 by Filippo Tommaso Marinetti and was the first cultural movement of the 20th c. to be directed deliberately at a mass audience. The Futurists' aims were to celebrate the dynamic power of the mass market, the machine and global communication which – they argued – was changing the nature of the world and culture. Thus typical Futurist imagery used a geometric means to represent motion or the juddering of movement. They organized evenings and wrote manifestos, poems and music. In its aggressive, individualistic attitudes, the movement has frequently been aligned with Fascism. Marinetti and Ardengo Soffici produced 'concrete' or 'pattern' poetry in which the meaning was expressed in typography and layout, casting aside traditional horizontal and vertical conventions in type printing. Futurism's vigorous formal and ideological components were employed in the subsequent graphic design of Fortunato DEPERO, Lucio VENNA and Nicolay DIULGHEROFF during the 1920s and 30s, which celebrated the activities of the Futurists themselves. It was also expressed in advertising, and in 1928 a pavilion representing Futurist poster design was included in the Esposizione Nazionale del Decennale della Vittoria (Decennial National Exposition of Victory) in Turin.

Futurism was essentially an urban expression, and it was with some relief that the architect Antonio Sant'Elia joined the movement in 1914, bringing it academic respectability. In his drawings for 'The New City', exhibited in Milan in 1914, and in his broadsheet *Manifesto of Futurist Architecture*, Sant'Elia proposed a massive architecture in which lines were to be dynamic, oblique and elliptical, and whose decoration was not to be like the 'absurd encrustations of the past' (Sant'Elia), but would come from the 'use and disposition of materials left raw or bare or violently coloured'. Elements should also be interchangeable. His architecture was thus to express the virulent dynamism of Futurism. Sant'Elia died in 1916, but his manifesto reached members of DE STIJL in 1917.

An architectural interpretation of **Futurism** *in Antonio Sant'Elia's drawings for his 'New City' (1914).*

It is customary to link the death of Futurism to the death of Sant'Elia, claiming that, despite all its aggressive posturing, Futurism did not survive the ravages of World War I. This dating represents the important first phase of Futurism and fits the movement's anticipation of Russian CONSTRUCTIVISM and the beginnings of the MODERN MOVEMENT. Such a view ignores, however, the fact that most of its members vigorously maintained Futurist activities in publications, exhibitions (participating, for instance, in the PARIS EXPOSITION DES ARTS DÉCORATIFS ET INDUSTRIELS, 1925) and commercial work until after World War II. It fell out of favour with the Italian public in the postwar period because it was perceived as having been close to Fascism.

☐ F. Marinetti, *La Cucina Futurista* (1932), trans. L. Chamberlain (ed.), *The Futurist Cookbook* (1989); C. Tisdall and A. Bozzolla, *Futurism* (1977); E. Crispolti, *Il Futurismo e la Moda: Balla e gli Altri* (1986); P. Hulten, *Futurismo & Futurismi* (1986); D. Leiber and M. Scudiero, *Depero Futurista & New York: Il Futurismo e l'Arte Pubblicitaria/Futurism and the Art of Advertising* (1987); A. Tanchis, *Bruno Munari: From Futurism to Post-Industrial Design* (1987); A. Fanelli, G. and E. Godoli, *Il Futurismo e la Grafica* (1988); E. Crispolti and M. Scudiero, *Balla/Depero: Recostruzione Futurista dell'Universo* (1989).

G

Games, Abram (b.1914) studied for two terms at St Martin's School of Art, London, on their 'commerical art' course, only returning for evening classes in life drawing and painting while he worked at a commercial art studio. From his student days he reacted against traditional commercial art methods, in which several designers worked on one master poster that would subsequently be touted around by printers, changing lettering according to the client with whom they were dealing. Games himself was inspired by the work of such men as Tom Purvis, Edward McKnight KAUFFER and Continental poster artists of the 1920s and 30s such as A.M. CASSANDRE. These men were artists who designed posters for specific clients. Games therefore set up as an independent graphic designer in 1935 and, working in the technique of chromolithography, soon had clients such as the Post Office and London Transport. His reputation, however, was made during World War II, when he was appointed official War Office poster artist (1941–46) and produced almost 100 posters. During this period he refined his visual language to fit his maxim 'maximum meaning, minimum means'. After the War he had an increasing number of commercial clients, such as Guinness, Orient Line and the *Financial Times*, and took on book design, symbols and postage stamps as well as posters. Perhaps his most famous work was the symbol for the Festival of Britain. However, by the late 50s posters were generally being produced by advertising teams who favoured colour photography.
□A. Games, *Over My Shoulder* (exh. cat., Camden Arts Centre, London, 1990)

Gan, Alexei (1893–1940) was a graphic artist. Little is known of his early life, but he began his association with exponents of Russian CONSTRUCTIVISM in 1917 and was closely associated with Kasimir MALEVICH. It is suggested that he experimented with PHOTOMONTAGE as early as 1918. He was involved in the First Working Group of Constructivists and published a treatise in 1922, aimed at defining the ideology of Constructivism, which had striking typography to back up its iconoclastic message. His poster for the First Exhibition of Contemporary Architecture, held in Moscow in 1927, shows his characteristic use of various typographic sizes and asymmetrical layout. He was art director of *Sovremennaya Arkhitektura*, journal of the Association of Contemporary Architects, and also designed film posters and kiosks. He died in a labour camp.

Gandini, Marcello (b.1938) had no formal training in engineering or design and yet was the designer responsible for the most exotic sports car of the POP era – the Lamborghini Muira (1962). He also designed the Lamborghini Countach (1971) and the Lancia Stratos (1973). He worked for BERTONE (1965–78) – with whom he designed the CITROËN BX – and then spent five freelance years working exclusively for Renault. Gandini sees the car as 'the fruit of a dream that has lasted a thousand years', and is noted for his insistence on bringing a touch of exoticism to automobile design.

Garland, Ken (b.1929) studied at the Central School of Arts and Crafts, London (1952–54), under Herbert Spencer and Anthony FROSHAUG. He was art editor of *DESIGN* magazine (1956–62), where a combination of the influences of the MODERN MOVEMENT – from

A propaganda kiosk by **Gan** *(1923).*

László MOHOLY-NAGY to the SWISS SCHOOL – and the more illustrative American graphic design (e.g., that of Saul BASS) was evident. His work thus displays a clear attention to typographic detail while losing no visual excitement. In 1962 he founded the design consultancy Ken Garland Associates. Aside from his own design work, he has consistently put forward an intelligent critique of commercial graphic design in his writing and teaching.

☐ *Ken Garland and Associates: 20 Years of Work and Play 1962–1982* (1982)

Garrett, Malcolm (b.1956) is a British graphic designer who studied typography, graphic communication and psychology at Reading University, and then graphic design at Manchester Polytechnic. Much of his early work was for independent record companies and magazines, which allowed him the freedom to explore innovative ideas and led him to establish his reputation early. While at college he was involved in the Manchester Punk/New Wave music scene through his work for the Buzzcocks. Some of his most influential record sleeves were the Buzzcocks' *Orgasm Addict* (1979) and *UAG30159* (1980). He later worked for such groups as Simple Minds, Duran Duran, The Culture Club and Phil Collins. In 1981 he began designing the short-lived style magazine *New Sounds, New Styles*; his approach inspired many, including Neville BRODY. Garrett's design studio, Assorted Images (set up in 1978), is based on a collective ethic whereby individuals can work independently and it is therefore able to cope with a wide range of projects. Although best known for his music work, Garrett has worked on book design, CORPORATE IDENTITY, exhibitions and VIDEO GRAPHICS. This flexibility is part of his style. He is primarily concerned with typography as opposed to images, but he is not bound by rules or theory. With his eclectic borrowings from a wide range of symbols and innovative rearrangements, his work is not stamped by a conspicuously personal style but is very diverse.

Gaudí, Antoni (1852–1926) studied architecture at Barcelona University (1873–78). His training and early commissions took place in the cultural climate of a region that was undergoing a renaissance of its own identity. Thus Catalonia's medieval roots, including its architecture and language, were reinvoked. Gaudí worked in the Catalan ART NOUVEAU

A bench designed by **Gaudí** *for Santa Coloma de Cervelló, built 1908–15.*

style of MODERNISME, which included medievalism, romanticism and inspiration from nature for both decorative and structural elements. Broadly speaking this was in line with ARTS AND CRAFTS sensibilities, but he was also influenced by the eclectic Parisian architect Eugène Emmanuel Viollet-le-Duc. In addition to these leanings towards HISTORICISM, Gaudí also expressed the Catalan desire for technological advancement. Thus his curvilinear, naturalistic forms also explored new structural possibilities. Spanning almost the entire period of his career, his best-known work is the Church of the Sagrada Familia in Barcelona (1883–1926). This vast project remains unfinished and somewhat overshadows many of his less famous works, including furniture and fittings for many of his private commissions. His Calvet chair (1902), designed for a house of the same name, was brought back into manufacture in the 1970s by the Spanish company B.D. Ediciones de Diseño. Its revival symbolized a revitalization of interest in craft-produced organic forms.

Gavina (f.1949) was established in Bologna by Dino Gavina to manufacture and retail experimental modern chairs by unknown local designers. However, in the early 1950s Gavina was introduced to Carlo MOLLINO and Pier Giacomo CASTIGLIONI. The firm subsequently manufactured Castiglioni's well-known trestle table, the Cavaletto. In 1960 it became Gavina SpA with Carlo Scarpa as its

Advertisement of the 1920s for **General Motors'** *Cadillac V-16.*

president, and during the ensuing decade the designers Tobia SCARPA, Mario BELLINI and Vico MAGISTRETTI worked with the company. In the mid-1960s Gavina acquired the rights to manufacture Marcel BREUER's side chair. As was the case with CASSINA, this re-edition of a CLASSIC established the company's international reputation. Gavina was acquired by KNOLL International in 1968. Dino Gavina also set up the lighting company Flos in the early 1960s.

Gebrauchsgraphik (Commercial Graphics) (f.1925) is a magazine published in Berlin and subtitled (in English), *International Advertising Art: Monthly Magazine for Promoting Art in Advertising*. It has always included articles on both German and international graphic design in advertising. It appeared in English and German until after World War II, when a French translation was added. It moved to Munich after the partition of Berlin in 1945. From 1959 it included a Spanish translation and became *Novum Gebrauchsgraphik* in 1972. Its international character, longevity and representation of the avant-garde in commercial art make it a journal of significant influence.

☐J. Aynsley, '*Gebrauchsgraphik* as an Early Graphic Design Journal, 1924–1938' in *Journal of Design History* Vol. 5, No. 1 (1992)

General Motors (f.1908) was founded in Detroit, Michigan, by William C. Durant as a company that bought up various motor-vehicle manufacturers (e.g., Chevrolet in 1918). Under Alfred Sloan its car division soon became a strong rival of FORD, a rivalry that was made more acute by the appointment of Harley EARL as chief stylist (1925–59). Earl's major contributions were to rationalize the production processes within General Motors and to make the car more squat and a more visually integrated whole. Thus perhaps the first mass-market car to undergo thorough STYLING, the 1933 Chevrolet, was General Motors' creation. During the 1950s General Motors' Chevrolets and Cadillacs represented the zenith of the Detroit style – tail fins, big bumpers and plenty of CHROMIUM. When William Mitchell took over from Earl in 1959 this trend was becoming outmoded, due to the increased popularity of smaller European cars such as the VOLKSWAGEN Beetle. The Chevrolet Corvair (1960) was a European-looking response, signalling the end of General Motors' more fantastical line of cars. Design was carried out by Turin's PININFARINA from 1986.
☐A. Sloan, *My Years with General Motors* (1963); S. Bayley, *Harley Earl and the Dream Machine* (1983)

geodesic dome is a structure developed by Buckminster FULLER in 1949 with students at BLACK MOUNTAIN COLLEGE. Following his 'more for less' approach to designing, a dome made up of high tensile ribs, arranged geometrically and covered with a plastic skin, created a strong structure which was capable of spanning large areas. This was commercialized via his company, Geodesic Inc. (f.1949), and was also developed with the US Air Force and the Marine Corps. The use of such domes ranged from shelters for Antarctic expeditions to the giant United States Pavilion at the Montreal Expo of 1967, and between 1954 and 1984 no fewer than 300,000 were built throughout the world. Although the geodesic dome may be perceived as an architectural structure, it is also of importance as physical evidence of a design approach that incorporates a scientific, if not mathematical, method alongside a visionary approach.

Georg Jensen (f.1904) was begun in Copenhagen by a silversmith of the same name to retail and manufacture his wares. Jensen was heavily influenced by the British ARTS AND CRAFTS movement, and he was soon joined by Harald Nielsen and Johan Rohde. Jensen's output drew on a repertory of natural forms typical of the ART NOUVEAU style, while adding greater solidity to those forms. Rohde in particular developed a strong sculptural, yet Functionalist approach (*see* FUNCTIONALISM). In 1909 Jensen opened a retail outlet on the Kurfürstendamm in Berlin. The workshop expanded in 1912 with the silverware being partly machine-produced and hand-finished in large quantities. In 1935 Jensen and Rohde both died, but the shop was continued by Nielsen, and several prominent Danish silversmiths and sculptors such as Henning Koppel and Count Sigvard Bernadotte joined the firm. In 1922 Frederik Lunning established an American branch of Georg Jensen in New York, and the firm has continued to manufacture household metalware of the highest standards in design and finish.

Stirling silver coffee pot designed by Johan Rohde for **Georg Jensen** *(1906).*

Gerstner, Karl (b.1930) was an internationally influential member of the second generation of the SWISS SCHOOL of graphic design, having studied under Armin HOFMANN at the School of Arts and Crafts in Basle (1946–49). He turned the theoretical basis in Modernist graphic design (*see* MODERN MOVEMENT) – on which he also wrote prolifically – into commercial work through the multinational agency GGK, which he co-founded in 1962. He retired from GGK in 1970 to pursue painting and typographic design.
□K. Gerstner, *Kalte Kunst?* (1957); *The New Graphic Design* (1959); *Designing Programmes* (1963); *Mit dem Computer Kunst Produzieren* (1968); *Typographisches Memorandum* (1972); *Andre Thomkins: Inspiration und Methode* (1974); *The Forms of Color* (1986)

Ghia (f.1915) was founded as Carrozzeria Ghia by Giacinto Ghia in Turin. As an engineering and car-styling firm, it mostly designed luxury cars such as the Maserati Ghibli (1968). In 1972 Ghia was taken over by FORD; it was subsequently responsible for the Capri Ghia (1974) and the Mark II Escort (1975).
□D. Burgess-Wise, *Ghia: Ford's Carrozzeria* (1985)

Giacosa, Dante (b.1905) is an Italian car designer who studied mechanical engineering at the Polytechnic in Turin. He worked as a draughtsman before joining FIAT in 1930, for whom he designed the 500A. He went on to design the Fiat Nuova 500 (1957) and later the 124 (1966), the 128 (1969) and the 127 (1971).
□D. Giacosa, *Motori Endotermici* (1938); *Forty Years of Design with Fiat* (1981)

Giedion, Sigfried (1888–1968) was born in Prague and studied mechanical engineering in Vienna, graduating in 1913. At the same time, however, he studied history of art in Munich with Heinrich Wölfflin, the author of the seminal book *The Principles of Art History* and a pioneer in establishing new categories in the subject. Giedion met members of the BAUHAUS in 1923, was strongly influenced by LE CORBUSIER's *Vers une Architecture* and in 1928 he was a co-founder of the CONGRÈS INTERNATIONAUX D'ARCHITECTURE MODERNE. In 1938 Walter GROPIUS invited him to lecture at Harvard University, his lectures being published in 1941 as *Space, Time and Architecture*. In 1948 Giedion published *Mechanization Takes Command* which places him alongside Nikolaus PEVSNER and Reyner BANHAM as one of the most important figures in the study of 20th-c. design history. His thesis was that of technological determinism, meaning that issues of design are controlled by scientific advance. Thus it shifted design history away from Pevsner's doctrine of dominant designer-heroes towards a broader, contextually-driven analysis. Equally, his analysis is clearly influenced by the Modernist attack on tradition (*see* MODERN MOVEMENT). From 1948 he taught in Zurich.
□D. Watkin, *Morality and Architecture* (1977)

St George, an illustration by **Gill** *for* Nisi Dominus, *printed by the St Dominic Press in 1919.*

Gill, Arthur Eric Rowton (1882–1940) worked in the architectural office of W.D. Caröe in London (1899–1903). He became a close friend of Edward JOHNSTON at this time and also studied letter-carving at the Central School of Arts and Crafts in London. From 1904 he worked as a letter-cutter but also designed title pages for Insel Verlag in Leipzig. From 1907 he achieved considerable fame as a stone-carver and from 1913 was a devout Catholic. Henceforward he was also known as a religious and sociological thinker, although many of his essays are regarded as dogmatic or even cranky. In the 20s he illustrated books for the Cranach Press in Weimar and the Golden Cockerel Press in Berkshire, and later in London, where he combined a medieval re-vivalism, redolent of the ARTS AND CRAFTS movement, with a distinctly modern page layout, through the integration of illustrations, capitals, headings and text. In 1925 he was persuaded by Stanley MORISON to design typefaces for the MONOTYPE CORPORATION. He subsequently produced the roman and italic types Perpetua and Felicity (1925–29) and Gill Sans (1928), his most used typeface. His book entitled *An Essay on Typography* (1931)

extended his views on industrialism, religion, legibility and politics.

☐E. Gill, *A Bibliography of Eric Gill* (1953); F. McCarthy, *Eric Gill* (1991)

Girard, Alexander (b.1907) is noted as the American architect who continued to bring colour and pattern to interiors and products regardless of the dominance of the INTER-NATIONAL STYLE during the 1950s and 60s. From 1952 he was design director of upholstery for HERMAN MILLER, developing new weaves and colour lines. His CORPORATE IDENTITY programme for Braniff International Airlines (1964) made each of its aircraft a different colour, appearing to some viewers like racing cars or even Easter eggs.

Gispen, W.H. (1890–1981) was a designer-manufacturer of considerable influence in the Netherlands. He founded Gispen in 1916 as a small smithy in Rotterdam supplying the building industry. His readings of the ARTS AND CRAFTS, DE STIJL and then LE CORBU-SIER gradually led to an interest in standardized machine-made products. In 1927 he began to manufacture the Giso lamp in large series and developed a modernistic 'house style' around this product. This house style was extended into his furniture projects, manufactured from 1929 using TUBULAR STEEL. Subsequent furniture was important, due to its combination of materials and of both FUNCTIONALISM and comfort. After Gispen's retirement in 1949, Gispen International continued as an important manufacturer of office furniture.

Giugiaro's *Nikon F4 camera (1988).*

Giugiaro, Giorgietto (b.1938) is perhaps the world's most influential automobile designer. He was born in Garessio, Italy, and studied at the Turin Academy of Fine Arts before joining the FIAT styling centre at the age of 17. During his four years there, he also studied mechanical design at a Turin engineering technical college. In 1959 he became head of the styling department at Carrozzeria BERTONE. His work there included the BMW 3200 CS (1961), ALFA ROMEO Giulia GT (1963) and the Fiat 850 Spider (1965). In 1965 he was appointed director of the GHIA styling and prototype centre where he designed the Fiat Dino Coupé (1967). In 1968 he left Ghia to found Italdesign with Aldo Mantovani and Luciano Bosio. The firm was organized on a new basis, whereby expanded pre-production services beyond straightforward design were offered to the automotive and related transportation industries. These included: STYLING; the construction of models and prototypes; feasibility studies; body and chassis engineering; manufacturing process auditing; automation and die design. Among designs figure the Alfa Romeo Alfasud (1971), the VOLKSWAGEN Golf (1974) and the Fiat Panda (1980). The so-called 'two-box' solution of the Golf – with its sharp edged contours and vigorous break between the engine compartment and the passenger area – was subsequently much copied.

In 1981 Giugiaro Design was created and its achievements included the Nikon F4 camera (1988) and sewing machines for Necchi. In 1987 Giugiaro SpA was formed to work in the field of clothing and accessories. By the late 1980s Italdesign, which had been undertaking industrial design since 1974, included some 400 employees.

GK Industrial Design Associates (f.1957), GK standing for Group Koike, is led by Kenji EKUAN and was formed when industrial design began to take shape in Japan during its economic boom of the 1950s. Just as American and British designers had taken their first steps through PACKAGING design, so did those in Japan, and GK's first big success was in the design of a soy sauce bottle for the Kikkoman Soyu Company (from 1958). It designed urban furniture and signage for the 1970 Osaka Expo, thus spreading the consultancy's work into a large number of different areas.
□GK, *A Design Declaration: GK's 30 Year History* (1987)

Glaser, Milton see PUSH PIN STUDIO

glassfibre see FIBREGLASS

Gödöllő Workshops (1902–21) were formed when the medievalist painter Aladár Körösfői-Kriesch and his family moved to a village of that name just outside Budapest. By the following year an artists' colony had formed with Körösfői-Kriesch joined by the Swedish craftsman/designer Leo Belmonte and the architect István Medgyaszay among others. These artists and designers built and furnished their own homes with vernacular-style furniture and weavings, becoming a living embodiment of the ARTS AND CRAFTS ideal. In 1904 Körösfői-Kriesch established a weaving workshop in the village for local peasant girls to revive ancient techniques and the use of natural vegetable dyes. These workshops received State support from 1907 (becoming part of the National School of Applied Art with Körösfői-Kriesch as professor) and achieved great success at international exhibitions and competitions such as the St Louis World Fair in 1904. Other members of the colony worked in other fields: Sandor Nagy, regarded as the most successful member, produced works, usually on moral or 'national' themes, in a number of graphic media, including illustration and stained-glass windows. The high point in the history of the Gödöllő School came in 1909 in a group exhibition at the National Salon in Budapest (although the critical response was scathing). The Gödöllő experiment survived World War I, only to collapse in 1921.
□J. Szabadi, *Art Nouveau in Hungary* (1989)

Golden, William (1911–59) was a pioneering art director at CBS who had joined the company in New York in 1937, after working under Mehemed Fehmy AGHA. At CBS he gave the network a distinctive and pervasive house style. He created CBS's classic 'eye' symbol (1950).
□C. Golden, K. Weiks and R. Strunsky (eds), *The Visual Craft of William Golden* (1962)

'good design' is a concept that emerged in Northern European countries and the USA during the period immediately following World War II. Particular centres for design championed it: in 1952 at the ULM HOCHSCHULE FÜR GESTALTUNG Max BILL called for 'Forms linked to the quality and function of the object, honest forms, no inventions to increase sales . . .' in his vindication of the BAUHAUS. Similarly the Design Council in London and the MUSEUM OF MODERN ART in New York espoused the cause of good modern design through articles, exhibitions, lectures and seals of approval for selected products. Much of the value of good design was upheld in opposition to STYLING, which was seen as the application of superficial effects, and the simple product design of BRAUN and OLIVETTI was acclaimed in many countries as the zenith of integrity in design. In its turn, good design became synonymous with the INTERNATIONAL STYLE, and was therefore judged as aesthetically unadventurous. It was also felt that the concept did not question the basic existence of the object and its symbolic value. This criticism led in the late 1960s to some designers turning to ANTI-DESIGN, a deliberate rejection of the values of good design by various means, sometimes making a cult of the ugly. Subsequently good design has become a term of abuse in many cases, though it remains as a term of praise when considering the functional and ergonomic success of an object.

Graeff, Werner (1901–78) studied at the BAUHAUS (1921–23) and was a member of the DE STIJL group (1922–30). He followed a career as an artist, arts writer, film-script writer and teacher. He was notable for his motorcycle and car designs of the 1920s which, though never used in industry, captured the spirit of CONSTRUCTIVISM and De Stijl.

Grange, Kenneth (b.1929) is a British product designer who was a founder-partner of the design consultancy PENTAGRAM in 1972. Before then he had worked in various design firms, including his own Kenneth Grange Design (1958–71). His seminal designs include the Chef food-mixer for Kenwood (1960), the power car exterior of British Rail's 125 high-speed train (1976), the Parker 25 fountain pen (1979) and a new bus shelter for London Transport (1990). He consistently argued the case that product design should be an integral part of the manufacturing process and that the designer should be as much an innovator as a stylist. Much of his work from the 1970s has been in Japan, where he is of considerable influence.

Graphisme Actuel see NEW GRAPHIC DESIGN

Grapus (f.1970) is a Parisian graphic design studio founded by Pierre Bernard, Gérard Paris-Clavel and François Miehe. Bernard studied in Paris with Jean WIDMER, before he and Paris-Clavel travelled to Warsaw in 1962 to study under Henryk TOMASZEWSKI. This brought a vigorous, painterly quality into their work, influenced by the POLISH SCHOOL. It also opened up to them the notion of poster design for cultural and political means rather than for advertising. The Grapus studio was formed in the wake of the events of 1968 in Paris, a pinnacle of student unrest in the 60s. The studio's members joined the French Communist Party, and during its first decade the studio lent its creative abilities exclusively to political struggles. Its posters were informed by a semiological analysis of the meaning of imagery. They often included subversive imagery, even questioning the ideologies of the clients themselves. The work of Grapus is unusual in its integration of image and typography – although France is perhaps not renowned for any typographic strengths – which derives in part from the calligraphic influence of the Polish School but primarily from the New York PUSH PIN STUDIO of Milton Glaser. Grapus developed this integration, often placing typography and image in tension with one another. From 1980 its work has encompassed more commercial designs, including the CORPORATE IDENTITY of the Paris science park, the Parc de la Villette, and the Louvre. In 1991 it split into three parallel collectives, but its members remain committed to avant-garde, socially-charged design activity.

Gray, Eileen (1879–1976) was born in Ireland and studied drawing and lacquerwork in London (1892–1902) but moved to Paris in 1902, first studying drawing and then working with the Japanese lacquer-worker and cabinet-maker, Sugawara. Her early pieces were one-off decorative arts objects for private patrons, but from 1922 she had a workshop and shop to produce and sell her furniture and textile designs. These included her famous black lacquer screens (c.1923) which, like many of her furniture designs, were visually and technically sophisticated and had a strong ART DECO emphasis. From 1926 she worked on architectural projects with Jean Badovici, and her work subsequently came closer to that of LE CORBUSIER and other pioneers of the MODERN MOVEMENT.

Tubular ceiling light designed by Eileen **Gray** *(1928).*

☐ J.S. Johnson, *Eileen Gray, Designer* (1979); B. Loye, *Eileen Gray* (1985); P. Adam, *Eileen Gray* (1987)

Gray, Milner (b.1889) was a founder of the Bassett-Gray Group of Artists and Writers, which described itself as 'the distributing organization of a body of artists who design for industrial and commercial purposes' and which was the first multi-disciplinary design practice of its kind in England. In 1935 it became the Industrial Design Partnership and its work extended from graphic design to product design. During World War II Gray organized exhibitions for the Ministry of Information alongside his colleague Misha BLACK, with whom he founded the DESIGN RESEARCH UNIT in 1945. Gray specialized mostly in PACKAGING and CORPORATE IDENTITY, and although his design work was not stylistically revolutionary, he was an outstanding pioneer of DESIGN MANAGEMENT in Britain.

☐ A. Blake, *Milner Gray* (1986)

green design is a general design term that emerged in the late 1980s. An international surge of interest in ecological issues resulted from various man-made disasters (e.g., the leaks of radiation at Chernobyl and crude oil in Alaska) combined with the growing awareness of the accumulating effects on the environment of the industrial world (e.g., global warming).

The role of the designer as a protagonist in turning production and consumption towards a more 'environmentally friendly' process had already been considered by Buckminster FULLER, Richard Neutra and many others in the 1950s. In the late 1960s and early 70s this was picked up by the DESIGN FOR NEED tendency, in particular by Victor PAPANEK.

By the 1980s, however, it had shed its 'alternative' tinge. This was due to the mass appeal of ecological issues and the belief that change might be effected through consuming 'green' products. Thus, for instance, it was taken up by the MICHAEL PETERS GROUP – a design consultancy normally associated with ecologically unfriendly design practices such as PACKAGING – as a central focus of the company. The group looked into the use of recyclable materials and developed concepts for a 'green' lifestyle. Some commentators have seen such moves as a cynical ploy to differentiate one design consultancy from its competitors (the word, 'bandwagon' has often been used in parallel with 'green'). Elsewhere, the growth of green design has had lasting effects in raising consciousness regarding the use of materials, attitudes to OBSOLESCENCE and the energy efficiency of products and processes. By the 1990s it was clear that green design was not a passing fad, as it had been seen in the 1970s; the need for taking issues such as energy consumption into account was constantly reinforced by events such as the 1990 Gulf crisis with the consequent loss of oil and environmental destruction. Green design, however, was to work as an adjustment to pre-existing structures of industry and consumption; it was not to embrace the more radical recommendations of Papanek or Mollison.

☐ A. Fox and R. Murrell, *Green Design: A Guide to the Environmental Impact of Building Materials* (1989); B. Mollison, *Permaculture: A Designer's Manual* (1989); D. Mackenzie, *Green Design* (1991)

Greiman, April (b.1948) is an American graphic designer. She graduated in fine art from Kansas City Art Institute in 1970 and then studied at the Basle School of Arts and Crafts for a year under Armin HOFMANN and Wolf-

Greiman's *poster for the presentation* Snow White and the Seven Pixels *(1986)*.

gang WEINGART. She then established herself in New York and Connecticut and taught at the Philadelphia College of Art. In 1976 she moved to Los Angeles, where she combined her Swiss training with West Coast POSTMODERNISM. Type was sandwiched and layered, but also made to float in space along with geometric shapes, exaggerated letter spacing and eccentric colours. She also created a sense of depth and dynamic, in particular by combining graphic elements with the work of the photographer Jayme Odgers, making extensive use of APPLE Macintosh technology. Her work was acclaimed as representative of the CALIFORNIA NEW WAVE of graphics in the 1980s. In 1982 she was appointed head of design at the California Institute of the Arts.
□ A. Greiman, *Hybrid Imagery: The Fusion of Technology and Graphic Design* (1990)

Gronowski, Tadeusz (1894–1989) was a graduate of the faculty of architecture at the Warsaw Polytechnic. He practised in all fields of graphic, interior and set design. In 1924 he established a graphic and advertising studio with other Modernist designers (*see* MODERN MOVEMENT), which they called 'Plakat' (Pos-

ter). In the interwar years he travelled frequently between Poland and Paris and worked for a number of modish shops, including Au Printemps in Paris and an exclusive confectioner, Wedel, in Warsaw. His witty poster designs of the 1920s and 1930s (e.g., his advertisements for the Pluto confectionery manufacturer) played off silhouette, shadow and line through skilled use of airbrushing techniques. He was renowned for his highly creative hand-drawn letterforms, though he owed much to French designers such as A.M. CASSANDRE. Gronowski enjoyed a great international success in the 1930s and was awarded a gold medal at the Exposition Internationale des Arts et Techniques Appliquées in Paris in 1937. After World War II Gronowski held the role of an *éminence grise* within the POLISH SCHOOL. □ Bojko (1971)

Gropius, Walter (1883–1969) came from an established family of architects and studied architecture in Munich and Berlin (1903–7). In 1906 he designed farm-worker housing for his uncle Erich, which probably began his interest in the mass production of housing through prefabrication. He then worked in the office of Peter BEHRENS (1908–10) in Berlin before starting his own practice. He joined the DEUTSCHE WERKBUND in 1910 and was a strong opponent of Hermann MUTHESIUS, supporting Henry van de VELDE on the primacy of the creative individual over standardization. His Fagus shoe factory facade (1911) saw the first use of a curtain wall, with the cantilevered steel-frame construction creating a screen across the upright columns of the building's structure. After serving in World War I, he became director of both the applied arts school and the fine art school in Weimar, merging them to form the BAUHAUS. Here he proposed the unity of the arts, something which had been a preoccupation of reformers since before the War. His skill as director of the Bauhaus was in maintaining a relentless momentum of educational experimentation, often employing staff of widely differing ideological standpoints, while justifying or defending his decisions in the face of the officialdom of Weimar and then Dessau. However, tired of this constant struggle, he resigned in 1928.

In 1929 he became vice-president of the CONGRÈS INTERNATIONAUX D'ARCHITECTURE MODERNE. Increasingly aware that the German National Socialist Party would not

*The Bauhaus school in Dessau, designed by **Gropius** in 1925 and completed in 1926.*

tolerate his internationalist and modern ideas on architecture and design, he moved to London in 1934, where he worked in partnership with Maxwell FRY from 1936 to 1937. He also designed for ISOKON, becoming its controller of design in 1936. In 1937 he moved to the USA to become professor at the graduate school of design at Harvard. He also worked in partnership with Marcel BREUER from 1938 to 1941 and founded The Architects Collaborative (TAC) in 1945. While his architecture and design was important, his influence on the promotion of the MODERN MOVEMENT was even greater: as a spokesman, writer and educationalist he took with him the lessons of the Bauhaus first to Britain and then to the USA.

☐J. Fitch and I. Gropius, *Walter Gropius: Buildings, Plans, Projects 1906–1969* (exh. cat., MIT, Cambridge, Mass., 1973); D. Sharp (ed.), *The Rationalists: Theory and Design in the Modern Movement* (1978); H. Probst and C. Schädlich, *Walter Gropius* (2 vols, 1986, 1987)

Gugelot, Hans (1920–65) was born in Indonesia, studied at the technical college in Zurich and then worked with Max BILL (1948–50). He was head of industrial design at the ULM HOCHSCHULE FÜR GESTALTUNG (1955–65),

during which time he also designed for BRAUN along with his former pupil, Dieter RAMS. His designs are distinguished by their lack of decorative detail, and include the Braun SK4 record player (1956) and the Kodak Carousel slide projector (1962).

Gustavsberg (f.1640) was originally founded as a brickworks at Värmdö near Stockholm. It was established as a ceramics factory in 1825, adopting English industrial methods by 1839. It expanded steadily with Gunnar Wennerberg as art director from *c*.1900. In 1917 Wilhelm KÅGE joined as art director, and by the early 1930s Gustavsberg was producing much simpler kitchen and tableware, which showed the influences of the MODERN MOVEMENT. This simplicity also satisfied local demands for more space-saving designs. By 1937 Gustavsberg's line moved into a softer form of Modernism, using more organic shapes. In that year it was sold to Kooperativa Förbundet (the Swedish Consumer Co-operative and Wholesale Society) and the company continued to produce reasonably priced utilitarian ware. In 1987 it was bought by the Finnish company ARABIA and in 1988 it was combined with RÖRSTRAND as Rörstrand-Gustavsberg AB.

H

Habitat (f.1964) was founded in London by Terence CONRAN as a result of his frustration with British retailers. They had consistently failed to show interest in selling modern furniture, and, indeed, his designs. From the outset he avoided the minimalism of a traditional modern furnishings showroom, instead creating a kind of 'warehouse of good design' atmosphere. By 1968 a further four branches of Habitat had opened and it was also selling by mail order. During the 1970s Habitat opened branches in Paris and New York, and by the early 1980s branches were also established in Belgium, Iceland and Japan. This globalization was accompanied by a consolidation of its MARKETING approach, whereby sets of interiors were designed to conform to different lifestyles. Whereas in the 1960s the shop was heralded for making modern design more accessible, by the late 1980s it was criticized by some for its growing conservatism – its catalogue became increasingly classical. This coincided with Habitat's merger with Mothercare (1981), a major retailer of children's clothes and equipment, and with Heal's (see Ambrose HEAL) (1983). None the less, Habitat had a major global influence on the retailing of design, particularly on Spain's Vinçon and France's Prisunic.

☐ B. Philips, *Conran and the Habitat Story* (1984)

Hadid, Zaha (b.1950) was born in Baghdad, Iraq, and studied mathematics at the American University in Beirut, Lebanon (1968–71). She then went on to the Architectural Association in London (1972–77), where other students and tutors included Ron ARAD and Nigel COATES. She taught there (1977–86) and also worked with the Office of Metropolitan Architecture before setting up her own architectural practice in 1979. Her research interests have included Kasimir MALEVICH and SUPREMATISM, and this has served as a design basis for her own work, which includes the Irish Prime Minister's house in Dublin (1979) and an office building on the Kurfürstendamm in Berlin (1986). The latter is an interesting example of DECONSTRUCTION, in that the standard uses and perceptions of the building are challenged. Designs are developed through paintings,

WE ARE COMING IN THE CHRYSLER!

Poster advertising Chrysler by **Havinden** *(1929).*

drawings or diagrams, stressing the conceptual aspect. Many of her projects thus exist as Utopian investigations.

Havinden, Ashley (1903–73) was a British graphic designer who had no formal training except for evening classes in drawing and design at London's Central School of Arts and Crafts (1922–23). In 1922 he joined CRAWFORD'S, the advertising agency, and worked his way up from junior trainee layout man to art director by 1929, and finally vice-chairman (1960–67). He was also director and then chairman of Design International, Crawford's industrial design firm (1946–67). In the 1920s he very much admired Edward McKnight KAUFFER, whom he persuaded Crawford to employ in 1927, and was also influenced by the BAUHAUS and CONSTRUCTIVISM. This was reflected in his CHRYSLER CORPORATION car campaign of 1925, with its Constructivist-inspired layout, bold simplified images and dynamically designed lettering: this campaign in fact established Crawford's as Britain's leading, most 'modern' agency. During his career he made use of a wide variety of approaches, such as layouts that were inspired by the new typography (see Jan TSCHICHOLD) or that were given an abstract painterly treatment (e.g., his Milk Marketing Board advertisements). He worked in all forms of publicity work, including CORPORATE IDENTITY and PACKAGING for Simpsons, LIBERTY & CO.,

Richard Shops and Pretty Polly. He also exhibited his paintings and worked on textile designs.

☐ A. Havinden, *Advertising and the Artist* (1956)

Heal, Ambrose (1872–1959) served an apprenticeship as a cabinet-maker before joining Heal's, his family's firm of furniture manufacturers and retailers based in London. His first catalogue, *Plain Oak Furniture*, was issued in 1898, and contained designs that were stark in comparison to much of the reproduction 'Queen Anne' furniture that Heal's normally sold. He became chairman of Heal's in 1913 and transformed the company into one of the most progressive businesses in England. He also helped found the DESIGN AND INDUSTRIES ASSOCIATION in 1915. In the 1930s his designs, and the company's production in general, went into a more Modernistic mode (*see* MODERN MOVEMENT) with the use of TUBULAR STEEL and laminated woods.

☐ T. Benton, *Up and Down at Heal's: 1929–35* (1978)

Heartfield, John (1891–1968) was born Helmut Herzfeld in Berlin but changed his name in 1916 to an anglicized version in a protest against an anti-British hate campaign. He was apprenticed to a bookseller in Wiesbaden in 1905, but undertook studies at Munich's School of Arts and Crafts in 1909, continuing them at Berlin's School of Arts and Crafts in 1916. He and his brother, a radical poet, formed the Malik Verlag publishing house in 1917. He was also a founding member of the Berlin DADA group in 1919. In 1918 he joined the German Communist Party and from 1924 to 1933 he produced illustrations and literature for its magazine, *AIZ*. He was an early experimentalist with typography and PHOTOMONTAGE, as was seen in his work for both his publishing house and *AIZ*. During the 30s his political critique was directed especially at the Nazi party. In 1933 he went into exile in Prague and then moved to England in 1938, where he designed book covers for Penguin Books. In 1950 he returned to Leipzig and subsequently worked as a stage designer in East Berlin with Bertolt Brecht, among others.

Henrion, Frederick Henri Kay (1914–90) was born in Nuremberg, but trained in Paris, first as a textile designer (1933–34), and then as a graphic designer, in the studio of Paul Colin.

A page from a 1913 **Heal**'*s catalogue,* A Book of Bedroom Furniture.

He worked in Paris and London (1936–39) before emigrating to England in 1939, where he soon found eager clients such as the General Post Office. During the War he designed posters for the Ministry of Information and exhibitions for the American Office of War Information. Many of his posters from the 1930s and 40s reflect the influence of SURREALISM and the PHOTOMONTAGE of the BAUHAUS and John HEARTFIELD. After a short spell working for ADVERTISING AGENCIES he set up Henrion Design Associates (1951), a design consultancy embracing product and exhibition design as well as graphics. It worked in particular on some early CORPORATE IDENTITY schemes, such as KLM (Royal Dutch Airlines); other later examples include the National Theatre in London, the London Electricity Board, Tate and Lyle, British European Airways and Girobank. Many of his schemes of the late 1950s and 60s reflect the impact of the SWISS SCHOOL and its use of abstract symbols to illustrate the rationalization

Poster by **Henrion** *for Super National petrol (1960).*

Herman Miller

An Ethospace office interior designed by Bill Stumpf and a team from **Herman Miller** *(c.1987).*

of a company's structure. His internationalist approach existed before he changed his company's name to HDA International in 1973. In 1982 he took on two younger partners to form Henrion, Ludlow & Schmidt.

☐F.H.K. Henrion, *Design Co-Ordination and Corporate Images* (1967); *Top Graphic Design* (1983); *AGI Annals 1989* (1989); *Henrion: 5 Decades a Designer* (exh. cat., N. Staffordshire Polytechnic, Stoke, 1989)

Herman Miller (f.1923), with KNOLL, became the USA's leading manufacturer of modern furniture during the 20th c. Its forerunner was the Michigan Star Furniture Company (f.1905), a producer of traditional furniture situated in Zeeland in the state of Michigan, near the centre of American furniture manufacturing at Grand Rapids. This company was set up by Herman Miller and other local businessmen. D.J. De Pree joined the company in 1909 and in 1914 married Miller's daughter. In 1923 he and Herman Miller bought up 51 per cent of the company's stock and renamed it Herman Miller.

It was not until the 1930s that Herman Miller moved away from traditional furniture to produce modern designs, thereby differentiating the company in the, by then, saturated market. This was largely brought about by the arrival of Gilbert Rohde in 1930 as the company's designer: he had previously worked in advertising and as a display illustrator. He was responsible for the idea of designing furniture for changing lifestyles; in the contemporary context, he anticipated smaller houses with lower ceilings. Accordingly, furniture would be simpler, coinciding with De Pree's own Christian belief in sincerity, or austerity. During the 1930s the company's production was still dominated by traditional pieces, but it had begun to be design led.

When Rohde died in 1944, George NELSON was appointed as director of design, though his role extended to corporate tutor and teacher of design and marketing within Herman Miller. He recommended greater standardization and the move towards the architectural market, abandoning the lines of reproduction furniture. Herman Miller moved increasingly in the direction of office furniture, distinguishing the company for the first time from its roots in domestic furniture. In 1945 Nelson designed the Storage Wall, from which both domestic and office SYSTEM FURNITURE was developed. Alongside this he developed the Comprehensive Storage System (CSS), which included cabinets, desk and shelves, could be assembled by the customer and was therefore highly flexible. His Executive Office Group of 1947 included the L-shaped desk, which was a forerunner of the work station. Nelson also introduced Charles EAMES as a consultant to Herman Miller, his PLYWOOD and steel chair going into production in 1948, having been seen by De Pree at the MUSEUM OF MODERN ART, New York, in 1946. At the same time, the company brought out the Eames Storage Units.

Herman Miller's most important breakthrough in office furniture was the development from 1958 of the Action Office under Robert PROPST, whom De Pree had met at the ASPEN INTERNATIONAL DESIGN CONFERENCE in 1958. Propst had been a sculptor, artist, teacher and inventor, and his brief was to find problems outside the furniture industry and then to find solutions for them. He applied himself to office design, seeing the need for solutions that addressed the non-hierarchical, individual or group-orientated management system. With George Nelson, Propst produced the Action Office in 1964; it included built-in electrical outlets to avoid clutter, as well as storage for other electrical hardware, now integral to the office environment. The modifications made for the Action Office 2, brought out in 1968, made the line a much greater commercial success. These improvements involved a shift away from the free-standing desk towards 'screen-mounted' furniture, using panels which supported work surfaces and storage units. This redefined the layout of offices, suggesting the creation of mini-environments within the larger open-plan office space.

Eames's further contributions in furniture were the Aluminium group of seating (1958) and the Soft Pad version of it (1969). In 1985 Ethospace by Bill Stumpf was launched. It includes snap-together elements which the user can assemble, creating his or her own personal environment and offering greater privacy. Unusual fabrics and fittings were incorporated to emphasize this sense of individuality.
□R. Caplan, *The Design of Herman Miller* (1976); L. Knobel, *Office Furniture* (1987)

high-tech is a term that has been used mostly in architecture to describe the work since the mid-1960s of a small group of architects, which includes Norman FOSTER and Richard Rogers. Their ideas stem in part from the RADICAL DESIGN proposals of Buckminster FULLER, with whom both had worked, and were reinforced by the theories of the ARCHIGRAM group. High-tech should not be confused with its meaning in industry – electronics, computers, robotics etc. In architecture it includes the rejection of traditional 'cumbersome' building materials (e.g., stone, brick and wood) in favour of non-traditional synthetic components and materials (e.g., asbestos tiles, FIBREGLASS insulation, steel joist hangers and plastic windows). The resulting forms appear to be mass produced and are sometimes starkly machine-like, with elements that may at times quite literally be 'bolted-on'. In design much the same applies, except that it also includes the use of prefabricated elements such as wire mesh, plastic tubing, galvanized steel or slip-resistant rubber in furnishings and interior design. It sometimes makes idiosyncratic use of such elements in a design process bordering on ADHOCISM.
□J. Kron and S. Slesin, *High-Tech: The Industrial Style and Source Book for the Home* (1978); C. Davies, *High Tech Architecture* (1988)

high-technology cottage industry is a term used by the American economic historian Charles Sabel to describe the cluster effect of small workshops in many towns of central and northern Italy. Since the 1970s these workshops have taken on work subcontracted by large manufacturers of domestic and industrial machinery in major cities. As a result they have become progressively more sophisticated in their level of technological output until, through a process of 'tinkering' in the workshop whereby tools are developed to cope with complex technical demands, they have become innovators themselves. This has important ramifications for design, since, as networks of workshops are formed to produce single items, the production process is decentralized and may also become much more flexible. Thus objects of varying technical sophistication may be produced on short runs, responding quickly to market demands. This is in effect a non-computer-based version of BATCH PRODUCTION. It is not exclusive to Italy, though hitherto it has not been exploited to the same degree elsewhere.
□C. Sabel, *Work and Politics: The Division of Labor in Industry* (1982)

High Touch is a concept invented in the early 1980s by the American John Naisbitt as a counterbalance to HIGH-TECH. Thus it is a design trend in which colours, forms, patterns, textures and materials combine to make a visually rich and meaningful object. Invariably it includes the use of unconventional materials; thus raw, untreated metals, plastic, rubber, laminates and cement replace the conventional wood, glass and steel. COLORCORE is a favourite material of High-Touch designers. High Touch's roots may be traced back to the first uses of BAKELITE, through Charles EAMES's use of PLASTICS, to Italian ANTI-DESIGN and its use of plastics-based materials in the 1960s. As an approach to design it is most evident in the work of some American designers of the 1980s and 90s (e.g., Jay Adams, Don Ruddy and Robert Robinson) and is to be found in ART FURNITURE and one-off pieces, rather than applied to objects manufactured in series.
□J. Naisbitt, *Megatrends: Ten New Directions Transforming Our Lives* (1982); R. Janjigian, *High Touch: The New Materialism in Design* (1987)

historicism is a term used to describe the reuse of earlier historical styles in art, design and architecture. The MODERN MOVEMENT advocated the rejection of historicism and the

Palais Stoclet in Brussels by
Hoffmann, *built 1905–11.*

forging of a new style to reflect the modern world. POSTMODERNISM, on the other hand, reincorporated historical styles into its designs.

Hoffmann, Josef (1870–1956) was born in Moravia and studied architecture in Munich and Vienna. He worked with Otto WAGNER (1895–99) and became involved in the SECESSION in 1897. He was professor at the Viennese School of Applied Arts (1899–1941). From 1900 his design work was strongly rectilinear in style, owing something to the influence of Charles Rennie MACKINTOSH, whom he visited in 1903. This represented a Secessionist shift away from the dominant curvilinear ART NOUVEAU style. Along with Koloman MOSER he founded the WIENER WERKSTÄTTE in 1903, inspired by C.R. ASHBEE's Guild of Handicraft. Hoffmann produced designs for the Wiener Werkstätte until 1931 and also designed some chairs manufactured by THONET. His *magnum opus* was the Palais Stoclet (1905–11), a large villa on the outskirts of Brussels, which sums up the approaches and attitudes of the Wiener Werkstätte at that time – in everything there is a self-conscious emphasis on simple geometric forms, and a unity between architecture and design is sought. From 1905 he also turned to classicism and Biedermeier styles but by the 1920s Hoffmann had returned to a more curvilinear style in his metalwork. There was a strong revival of interest in his work among designers and architects in the 1980s. ALESSI reproduced his metalwork designs in the early 1980s.

☐ W. Neuwirth, *Josef Hoffmann: Bestecke für die Wiener Werkstätte* (1982); E.F. Sekler, *Josef Hoffmann* (1982); D. Baroni and A. D'Auria, *Josef Hoffmann und die Wiener Werkstätte* (1984); P. Noever and O. Oberhuber, *Josef Hoffmann (1870–1956): Ornament zwischen Hoffnung und Verbrechen* (exh. cat., Österreichisches Museum für Angewandte Kunst, 1987)

Hofmann, Armin (b.1920) trained at the Zurich School of Arts and Crafts and taught at the School of Arts and Crafts in Basle from 1947 as well as at Yale University. Having worked as a lithographer and graphic designer, his graphic work displays a control akin to that of the SWISS SCHOOL but it none the less includes a strong photographic presence.

Hollein, Hans (b.1934) is a Viennese architect and interior designer noted as a prominent exponent of POSTMODERNISM. He has also made forays into industrial design: he collaborated with the MEMPHIS group in the early 1980s and designed a tea and coffee set for ALESSI (1983).

Holwein, Ludwig (1874–1949) was born in Wiesbaden and studied architecture in Munich

An advertisement by **Holwein** *for a sporting tailor, Hermann Scherrer (1911).*

but was self-taught in graphic design, on which he concentrated from 1904. His posters were characterized by a strong painterly approach initially influenced by the Beggarstaff Brothers. Holwein's use of form and colour retained a flat, decorative quality. Between 1910 and 1920 his work developed into a combination of symbolic and naturalistic imagery. From 1920 onwards much of his output was dedicated to propaganda for the Nazi party.

Honda (f.1948) is the biggest motorcycle manufacturer in the world and the fourth largest Japanese motor-vehicle company. At the small Hamamatsu factory, Soichiro Honda made a bicycle equipped with a two-stroke 50cc engine, thus creating the Dream (1948). The following year came his first complete motorcycle. But it was not until the Super Cub (1958) that Honda began to make its mark. In 1959 the American Honda Motor Co. was established, and the Honda 100cc and 50cc Super Cub became the world's most popular motorcycles. Honda moved into car production in 1962, and with the new economy car, the N360 (1966), somewhat similar to Alec ISSIGONIS's Mini, sales took a marked upturn. The 1300 (1968) was particularly advanced for its time, with the first two-way air-cooling system, and following the launch of the Civic (1972) Honda's automobile sales exceeded its motorcycle sales.

Horta, Victor (1861–1947) was a Belgian architect and is renowned for developing the visual language of ART NOUVEAU. He studied drawing and architecture at the Ghent Academy (1874–77) and then at the Académie des Beaux-Arts in Brussels (1881–84). In his Hôtel Tassel (1892–93) he used ironwork for decorative purposes, introducing the 'Horta line' or 'whiplash line', derived from natural forms. His Hôtel Solvay (1895–1900) represents the zenith in his eclectically rich style. From 1912 he was a professor at the Académie des Beaux-Arts in Brussels and was its head from 1927 to 1931.
□P. Ortoghesi, *Victor Horta* (1969)

Huber, Max (b.1919) studied at the Zurich School of Arts and Crafts, where he experimented in PHOTOMONTAGE and the formal ideas of the BAUHAUS. He then moved to Milan, returning to Switzerland during World War II. From 1946 he based himself in Milan, working there as a graphic designer. His work

Gilt-bronze chandelier by **Horta** *in the Hôtel Solvay, Brussels (1903).*

subverted the traditional austerity of the SWISS SCHOOL, overlapping images in complex compositions that sometimes verged on chaos. In this way it anticipated much design work produced from the 1980s onwards with the aid of COMPUTER–AIDED DESIGN, in particular that of April GREIMAN.

human factors *see* ERGONOMICS

The logo for La Rinascente created by **Huber** *(1951–52).*

I

Selectric typewriter (1961) designed by Eliot Noyes for **IBM**.

IBM (f.1914) was founded in the USA by Charles R. Flint and Thomas J. Watson as the Computing Tabulating and Recording Company (CTR), becoming International Business Machines (IBM) in 1924. It developed steadily in the manufacture of office equipment and during the 1930s pioneered the punched card system of recording tabulated information. Its use in controlling supply was important to the American military during World War II, and revenue leapt from $34.8 million (1939) to $143.3 million (1944). IBM was also involved in the development of computers for the military's nuclear programme. It was, however, after World War II that IBM moved to world dominance in office equipment, and that its distinctive corporate style was consolidated. This was marked by 'intrapreneurship' – sections within the company competed with each other – as well as an aggressive MARKETING policy and after-sales service. The company's success is also due to its DESIGN MANAGEMENT. Influenced in part by OLIVETTI, IBM built up a strong sense of CORPORATE IDENTITY. Most important in this was the work of Eliot NOYES and Paul RAND. Noyes brought to IBM a pervasive INTERNATIONAL STYLE, which dominated not just the company but also its competitors henceforward. Although IBM was not the first company to develop personal computers (PCs) in the late 1970s, its world-wide marketing ensured that it set the agenda on them: on the day that it launched its PC in 1981, 30,000 were bought by IBM employees. They in turn wrote programmes that were reinvested into the company's sales. By the early 1990s, IBM's market dominance had begun to wane as rival computer companies developed.

□N. Foy, *The IBM World* (1974); T. Schutte (ed.), *The Uneasy Coalition: Design in Corporate America* (1975); R. Sobel, *IBM: Colossus in Transition* (1981); B. Rodgers and R. Shook, *The IBM Way: Insights into the World's Most Successful Marketing Organization* (1986); D. Mercer, *IBM: How the World's Most Successful Corporation is Managed* (1987); P. Rand, *The IBM Logo* (1990)

Icograda *see* INTERNATIONAL COUNCIL OF GRAPHIC DESIGN ASSOCIATIONS

Icsid *see* INTERNATIONAL COUNCIL OF SOCIETIES OF INDUSTRIAL DESIGN

ID Magazine of Industrial Design *see* INDUSTRIAL DESIGN

Ikea (f.1943) was founded by Ingmar Kamprad and is a Swedish furniture company whose simple, knockdown furniture is designed to appeal to a large section of the market. By the 1990s it had become the world's largest furniture chain store with a total of 75 outlets in every part of the world except South America. Some 45 million copies of the 1987 Ikea catalogue were printed in ten languages, and over 40 per cent of Swedish furniture production was for Ikea.

Imprint (1913) was a London-based printing journal published just nine times in 1913. It was important in consolidating the status of typographic design and therefore of the typographer him or herself within the printing industry.

Independent Group (f.1952) was a group of artists, architects and critics – including Reyner BANHAM – who met at London's Institute of Contemporary Arts during the 1950s, chiefly from 1955, to discuss the relationship between the fine arts and popular culture. They put on three exhibitions there: Parallel of Life and Art (1953), Man, Machine and Motion (1955) and This is Tomorrow (1956). The architects Alison and Peter Smithson, who were also members, wrote revealingly in the ROYAL COLLEGE OF ART magazine, *Ark*, 'GROPIUS wrote a book on grain silos, / LE CORBUSIER one on aeroplanes, / And Charlotte Perriand brought a new object to the office every morning; / But today we collect ads.' By embracing the symbols of popular culture, its members were in fact, it may be argued, reverting to a form of the earlier MODERN MOVEMENT. They were celebrating the icons of modern life, rather than making a critical statement about KITSCH. Their response may also be interpreted as a rejection of the puritanical values of 'GOOD DESIGN', which were being advocated at that time by the Design Council of Great Britain. While being associated more often with POP art, the Independent Group was also important in the development of design theory in Britain. ☐ A. Massey and P. Sparke, 'The Myth of the Independent Group' in *Block* No. 10 (1985); K. Varanedoe in *High and Low: Modern Art and Popular Culture* (exh. cat., Museum of Modern Art, New York, 1990); D. Robbins, *The Independent Group: Postwar Britain and the Aesthetics of Plenty* (1990)

Industrial Design (f.1954) is the USA's leading magazine for industrial designers. Its coverage is broad, taking in New York ART FURNITURE as well as theoretical discussions. Since 1980 it has been called *ID Magazine of Industrial Design*.

intelligent buildings are buildings that make extensive use of information technology for their running and for the use of their occupants. No building, however, may be classified as intelligent unless it can adapt to changing needs. In practice this may mean that an office building requires centralized information technology services (as well as others, such as heating, air-conditioning and telephones) which are linked by a cabling system that is integrated into the building. Sections of the building may be rented out, the information technology system being available as part of the deal.

The development of this system has been partly in response to the fact that, as computer technology needs developed during the 1970s, office buildings were unable to cope with the unforeseen quantities of cabling required, making them prematurely obsolete. This was the conclusion of the 1983 ORBIT report (Office Research on Buildings and Information Technology). The development of high-capacity cable networks, which were integrated into the building, meant that they could be seen as part of the building services, as if they were a 'fourth utility' on tap like water, gas and electricity. Thus, small offices and companies, by renting space in an intelligent building, may have access to powerful information technology systems – which may in turn influence their activities.

Companies such as AT&T, OLIVETTI, Pilkington, Honeywell and IBM responded with a new generation of 'universal' or 'structured' cabling schemes. Beyond these advances, the development of intelligent buildings in the 1980s has had other ramifications in design: an intelligent building requires a design that takes into account the inclusion of the cable systems, while the flexibility it offers may eventually affect office and office furniture design.

International Council of Graphic Design Associations (Icograda) (f.1963) holds an international congress every two years and its archive is held by the Design Museum in London.

International Council of Societies of Industrial Design (Icsid) (f.1957) holds its international congress every two years at a different location. Its secretariat is in Brussels, and it publishes a quarterly information bulletin made up of contributions from several international design organizations.

International Style is a term that was coined in the 1930s to describe the aesthetics of the MODERN MOVEMENT, focusing on simple, utilitarian, undecorated designs. For some design historians it represents the second phase of Modernism following that of Pioneer Modernism, which developed between 1900 and 1930. Pioneer Modernism underwent a demise between 1929 and 1933, in particular with the closure of the BAUHAUS. When its key figures such as Walter GROPIUS and Ludwig MIES VAN DER ROHE then emigrated to Britain, and from there to the USA, the stylistic canons of abstraction, truth to materials, anti-HISTORICISM, FUNCTIONALISM and technology were disseminated with their movement. At the same time, many of the designs that they had developed during the 1920s and which expressed their aesthetic aims went into wider mass production during the 1930s – THONET, PEL, KNOLL, HERMAN MILLER and ISOKON were all important producers of furniture by torchbearers of Pioneer Modernism – thus disseminating its style.

International Typeface Corporation

An exhibition entitled The International Style and organized by Philip Johnson and Henry-Russell Hitchcock was held at the MUSEUM OF MODERN ART, New York, in 1932. The style was also mediated internationally in the architecture and in exhibits seen at expositions such as those held in Antwerp (1930), Chicago (1933–34), Paris (1937) and Glasgow (1938). In the late 1940s and 50s, Modernist aesthetics, with their connotations of technology, efficiency and truth, began to be used in much corporate architecture and furnishings, led by examples such as Mies van der Rohe and Johnson's Seagram Building in New York (1956–59). Enthusiasm for the International Style peaked in the 1960s when town centres were reshaped, offices were refitted and products of all kinds were subjected to radical restyling. The sleek, functionalist product design of Dieter RAMS for BRAUN in particular was a strong expression of this 'look' which, with its clean STREAMLINING facilitated by the use of PLASTICS, was particularly applicable to electrical appliances.

International Typeface Corporation (f.1970) was founded by Aaron Burns, Ed Rondthaler and Herb LUBALIN. Its aim was to license and distribute original typestyles to manufacturers of typesetting equipment, thus ensuring royalties for their originators. It has had many popular traditional typefaces reworked into a digital format. It also began a journal, U & lc, with Lubalin as design director, to publicize and demonstrate its designs.

International Typographic Style *see* SWISS SCHOOL

Isokon (1932–39) was a company founded by Jack PRITCHARD and Wells COATES related closely to their Lawn Road building project. Its name is derived from 'Isometric Unit Construction', which is itself based on Coates's preference for drawing isometric views. In a company memo of March 1932, its aims were spelt out, calling for standardized units, use of new materials, movable interior walls and large, ribbon windows: in other words, it was an English restatement of the architectural aspirations of the MODERN MOVEMENT. At the time, Pritchard had commissioned Coates to design the Lawn Road Flats in north London – a truly Corbusian set of 'machines for living in' – and Isokon was to be the building's

Isotype *chart devised by Otto Neurath. It shows the number of marriages in Vienna between 1911 and 1926.*

controlling company. The foundation of Isokon also had much to do with Pritchard's nervousness regarding Coates's domination of its predecessor, Wells Coates and Partners. Partly to create furnishings for Lawn Road and partly to promote the use of PLYWOOD as a modern material, Isokon went on to commission and edit furniture (*see* EDITING) by designers such as Egon Risse, Marcel BREUER and Walter GROPIUS, all of whom lived in the Lawn Road Flats at some time. The advent of World War II cut off the company's hitherto significant supply of furniture from Estonia and it ceased production. In the 1960s, when Pritchard retired, the production of Breuer's Long Chair and Gropius's nesting tables was undertaken by John Alan Designs.
☐C. Buckley, *Isokon* (1980)

Isotype (International System of Typographic Picture Education) was a system of conveying statistical information by means of repeated unit-symbols, and was used in graph form to convey comparative statistics of different elements. It was formulated by Otto NEURATH and his colleagues, including Marie Reidemeister, at the Vienna Gesellschafts- und Wirtschaftsmuseum in 1925. It was originally called the 'Wiener Methode der Bildstatistik' (Vienna method of pictorial statistics) but became Isotype in 1935 after the group moved to The Hague. The concept of 'transforming' ideas and information into visual forms, as pioneered within Isotype, was an important breakthrough for the role of graphic designers.

Issigonis, Alec (1906–88) was born in Turkey but emigrated to Britain in 1922. He studied engineering in London (1924–27) and then worked in the Edward Gillett design office

(1928–30) and at Rootes Motors, Coventry (1934–36), before settling at Morris Motors, Oxford (1937–52). There he designed the Morris Minor (1948) and then the Mini (1959). The Morris Minor was quite unlike previous Morris small cars with its rather American lines. The Mini, however, showed no concession to STYLING. 'If you style a car it goes out of date,' Issigonis asserted; and a 30-year production run seems to have proved his point. The innovatory use of the same oil supply to serve both the engine and the gearbox as well as the space-saving transverse placement of the engine was highly original. This economy of space gave the car a nippiness, and thus cheekiness, which made it a symbol of POP in the 1960s. Issigonis was rare in his insistence on working alone as an automobile designer rather than with a team of specialists.
☐A. Nahum, *Alec Issigonis* (1988); R. Golding, *Mini: 30 Years On* (1989)

Itten, Johannes (1888–1967) was born in Switzerland in the Bernese Alps. He trained as a primary school teacher in Berne and began teaching in 1908. In 1910 he studied art in Geneva but rejected the academic tradition – as he had done in teaching. From 1913 to 1916 he studied at the Stuttgart Academy under Adolf Hölzel, with whom he developed his a-historicist (*see* HISTORICISM) approach to painting. In 1916 he moved to Vienna, where he taught and painted; in 1919 he exhibited abstract paintings. He also met Franz Cizek, then famous for his work in art education for children. Through meeting Walter GROPIUS, Itten came to teach at the Weimar BAUHAUS, where he was in charge of its preliminary course from 1921. His influence there, and in art and design education in general, was important. He believed that students should learn through interaction with materials; he also carried a strong mystical and experiential element into the school, embracing the religion of Mazdaznan. This put him at odds with Gropius, and in 1923 he resigned and returned to Switzerland to study oriental philosophy. In 1926 he opened his own design school in Berlin and then directed a textile design school in Krefeld (1931–38). He fled the Nazis to the Netherlands and then to Zurich where he ran the Museum and School of Applied Arts until 1953.
☐J. Itten, *Mein Vorkurs am Bauhaus: Gestaltung und Formlehre* (1963); *Design and Form: The Basic Course at the Bauhaus* (1964)

J

Jacobsen, Arne (1902–71) is one of Denmark's most renowned architect-designers. He studied architecture (1924–28) and did not explore any significant design projects until the 1950s, when he became interested in Charles EAMES's experiments in PLYWOOD. His three-legged chair for Fritz Hansen (1953) and the subsequent four-legged version (1957) offer greater refinement in the shaping of the material. This was followed by his equally famous Egg and Swan chairs, both produced in 1958.
☐T. Faber, *Arne Jacobsen* (1964); P. Shriver, *Arne Jacobsen: A Danish Architect* (1972); L. Rubino, *Arne Jacobsen: Opera Completa* (1980)

Jaguar (f.1935) was established in Coventry by William Lyons, who had previously manufactured the popular motor car, the SS1, from 1931. He chose the name of Jaguar to symbolize grace and speed. From the launch of the AK120 (1948) Jaguar specialized in the production of powerful and elegant automobiles. Typically its cars have a curvaceous, low-slung body mounted on large wheels; an unbroken coach-line stretching from headlamp to rear-light cluster; a plush wood-and-leather cabin and sports-car handling.

Jacobsen's *Swan chair (1958).*

The record player of the Beogram 4000 hi-fi system designed by **Jensen** *for Bang & Olufsen (1972).*

Jensen, Jacob (b.1926) is a Danish product designer known for his work for Bang & Olufsen (B&O), the audio manufacturer. With B&O he developed the tangential pick-up arm first seen in the Beogram 4000 (1972); the design is also notable for its uncluttered, almost minimalist layout.

Johnston, Edward (1874–1944) was a British calligrapher and type-designer who is best known for his design of the London Underground typeface in 1915. It was commissioned by Frank PICK and formed the basis of Eric GILL's Gill Sans typeface (1927–28). Virtually self-taught, Johnston taught calligraphy at the Central School of Arts and Crafts, London, from 1899 (Gill was a student of his in 1901), and during the first decade of the 20th c. he was closely associated with the private presses of the ARTS AND CRAFTS movement. In 1906 he published *Writing & Illuminating & Lettering*, which was of great influence on British and German calligraphy. He was also a founder of *IMPRINT* in 1913. He worked with London Underground until 1933, when Henry C. BECK completed his famous underground map.

Jones, Terry (b.1945) studied graphic design at the West of England College of Art (1962–66). He was the art director of *Vogue* (1972–77) before designing and editing *Not Another Punk Book* (1978). In this publication Jones used what he later called 'instant design': this included the rapid collaging of typewriter lettering, cut-out newspaper print, handwriting and photographs to put over a sense of energy and immediacy. This technique was based to some extent on punk fanzines, and its roots stretch back to DADA. Its principal design tool was the photocopier. In 1980 he founded *i-D*, where he extended this approach to a monthly style magazine.
□T. Jones, *Instant Design: A Manual of Graphic Techniques* (1990)

Journal of Typographic Research (f.1967) was a quarterly academic journal published from the Cleveland Museum of Art, Ohio. With an international editorial board, its initial aims were to report and to encourage the scientific investigation of alphabetic and related symbols. In 1971 it changed its name to *Visible Language* but continued its articles on calligraphy, typography and other forms in which linguistic and graphic communication meet. The basic premise of the journal is that writing and reading form an autonomous system of language expression that is defined and developed in its own terms. Broad ranging in its historical, geographical and thematic parameters, it is of

Josef Rudolf Witzel's poster (c.1900) for the journal Jugend *which gave its name to the German Art Nouveau style,* **Jugendstil**.

great relevance to graphic designers and indeed to anyone involved in visual communication. Special issues dealing with particular subjects, such as bi-lingualism and visible language (Winter, 1987), are often published.

Jugendstil was the German and Scandinavian term for ART NOUVEAU. Its name comes from the decorative arts magazine *Jugend* (1896–1914).

Juhl, Finn (1912–89) studied architecture in Copenhagen (1930–34) but was mainly self-taught in industrial design. He worked in the architectural office of Vilhelm Lauritzen (1934–45) before establishing his own design office. In the 1950s, along with Erik Herlow, Arne JACOBSEN and Hans WEGNER, he was responsible for making Danish design internationally influential. His designs relied on the high-quality local craft skills, particularly in the use of wood, but also gave the object a greater expressive quality than had been seen in the pioneering work of Kaare KLINT. His inspiration came from primitive African sculpture as well as the work of abstract artists. He was also influential as a lecturer at the Frediksberg Technical School in Denmark (1944–54).

just in time is a term used to describe a manufacturing and distribution system whereby goods are produced and delivered to order rather than held in stock. This requires much greater flexibility in terms of the workforce and manufacturing technique, as a continuous production line is not assured. As a result COMPUTER-AIDED MANUFACTURE supported by a sophisticated information technology system is often a feature of it. Data concerning demand can be fed efficiently into the system, and computer-aided tooling can respond to it, incorporating any specific customer requirements. It is a system that has become increasingly prominent with the need in a highly competitive world market to cut costs (e.g., in the holding of stock). It goes hand-in-hand with BATCH PRODUCTION and other aspects of industry that break the mould of FORDISM. While computer technologies are nearly always used, they might be coupled with low-technology production, as may be seen in the phenomenon of the HIGH-TECHNOLOGY COTTAGE INDUSTRY. In design terms, this has important ramifications when assessing the market and manufacture of an object.

K

*Argenta ceramic vase with silver ornamentation, made by Wilhelm **Kåge** for Gustavsberg in the 1930s.*

Kåge, Wilhelm (1889–1960) was a Swedish painter, graphic designer and ceramicist who was art director of the ceramics manufacturer GUSTAVSBERG (1917–49). He is notable for the introduction of a line of ceramics there in the early 1930s that was stark in its FUNCTION-ALISM (e.g., a stackable, heat-treated dinner service called Pyro). From 1937, with the Praktika range, he designed a softer, more organic style which was to mark Sweden's famous design style in the 1950s.
□N. Palmgren, *Wilhelm Kåge* (1953)

Kalman, Tibor (b.1949) was born in Budapest but emigrated to New York in 1956. He studied journalism in the late 1960s, and worked in window display before founding the M&Co. graphic design studio in 1979. Not strictly a graphic designer, his aim was to develop a method rather than a style. This entailed a rejection of MARKETING while foregrounding the communication of ideas that engaged the client's audience, resulting in visual solutions that may be quirky or provocative in concept. M&Co. is best known for its collaborations with composer-performer David Byrne and the Talking Heads.

Kartell (f.1949) began in Milan as a manufacturer of car accessories, but under Giulio

Plastic children's chair designed by Richard Sapper and Marco Zanuso in 1961 and produced by **Kartell** *from 1964.*

Castelli, its main objective after 1951 became that of introducing PLASTICS into the home, thereby giving new images to familiar products. With this in mind Gino Columbini, a young designer who had already worked for ten years in the studio of Franco ALBINI, was made head of Kartell's technical office. Its first products in 1953 were small, simple objects – lemon squeezers, buckets, dustpans – which aimed to be superior to traditional non-plastic ones, and thus the products were redesigned rather than simply reproduced in the new material. In 1964 Kartell also manufactured Marco ZANUSO and Richard SAPPER's children's chair, thus launching the company into furniture production. Subsequently, Kartell has produced important designs in plastic by Joe COLOMBO, Gae AULENTI and Anna CASTELLI-FERRIERI. Since the early 1980s, Kartell has concentrated on furnishings and plastic articles for use in laboratories.
□ A. Morell, 'Material Culture and the Culture of Materials' and A. Castelli-Ferrieri, 'Planning and Reality at Kartell' in *Plastic and Design* (1988)

Kassák, Lajos (1887–1967), the editor of a number of radical literary and artistic journals, was a central figure in Hungarian Modernism (*see* MODERN MOVEMENT) in the late 1920s. His graphic designs for these publications were crucial visual catalysts for Modernist design theory in Hungary, from the Expressionist anarchy of the early covers of *MA* (Today) to the FUNCTIONALISM of *Munka* (Work), akin to the designs of Herbert BAYER at the BAUHAUS. Following the collapse of the Budapest Republic of Councils in 1920 he emigrated

to Vienna, where he produced a series of paintings, together with schematic architectural designs, entitled *Bildarchitektur* (Image Architecture). These were shown at his solo exhibition at the Der Sturm gallery in Berlin in May 1924 and reveal a strong understanding of Russian CONSTRUCTIVISM. Following his return to Budapest in October 1926 Kassák concentrated his activities on popularist literary and political works. After World War II he continued to produce abstract paintings and PHOTOMONTAGES (bar a period of six years from 1950 when the official aesthetics of Stalinism forced him into 'internal emigration').
□ *Kassák Lajos 1887–1967* (exh. cat., National Gallery, Budapest, 1987)

Kauffer, Edward McKnight (1890–1954) was born in Great Falls, Montana. He began formal art studies at the Mark Hopkins Institute in San Francisco, and in 1913 spent six months at the Chicago Art Institute. Having seen the famous Armory Show there, he decided to study in Europe and travelled to Paris. His studies were cut short by the onset of World War I, and he moved to London in 1914. In 1915 he received his first commission from London Underground, the company for which

Poster by **Kassák** *(1922).*

he was to produce his most celebrated posters for the next 25 years. His early works reflect the influence of Cubism and the English Vorticist movement. McKnight Kauffer was, in fact, involved in a short-lived attempt to revive Vorticism, the Group X of 1920. Consistent characteristics are his simplification of form, his bold and legible composition, and the symbolic imagery used to convey the essence of his subject matter. The 1930s marked the height of his success, when his posters were common sights in the 'subterranean picture galleries' of the London Underground. This exposure is significant, for his work helped to familiarize a large public with the conventions of modern painting. The MUSEUM OF MODERN ART, New York, held a one-man show of his work in 1937. He returned to the USA in 1940.

□ *E. McKnight Kauffer* (exh. cat., Victoria and Albert Museum, London, 1955); M. Haworth-Booth, *E. McKnight Kauffer: A Designer and His Public* (1979)

Keller, Ernst (1891–1968) is generally seen as the progenitor of the SWISS SCHOOL. He was born in Aarau, Switzerland, and worked for a time as a lithographic draughtsman. Keller became fascinated with typography while a student in Leipzig (1912–14), and in 1918 he joined the faculty of the Zurich School of Arts and Crafts, where he transformed a course for advertising draughtsmanship into a complete training programme in design and typography. During nearly four decades of teaching Keller exerted a lasting influence on design trends in Switzerland. His own work encompassed poster design and sculpture. He advocated a return to legibility and simplicity of design in poster art as well as a unique solution for each design problem.

□ *Ernst Keller Graphiker 1891–1968 Gesamtwerk* (exh. cat., Kunstgewerbemuseum, Zurich, 1976)

Kepes, Gyorgy (b.1906) was born in Hungary and studied at the Royal Academy of Arts, Budapest (1924–28), before working as an independent film-maker and painter. He worked as a graphic, exhibition and stage designer for two periods (1930–32 and 1934–36) in Berlin before joining the studio of László MOHOLY-NAGY in London (1936–37). As with many avant-garde émigrés in London, he moved on to the USA in 1937, where he taught at the New Bauhaus and then at the Chicago

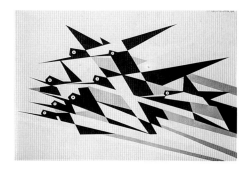

Kauffer's Flight of Birds *poster for the* Daily Herald *(1919).*

Institute of Design (1938–43). He was heavily influenced by pioneers of the BAUHAUS, particularly in his experimental approach and interest in links between design and architecture. In 1944 he published *Language of Vision*, which remained a basic text in design schools for nearly 40 years. In 1967 he founded the Center for Advanced Visual Studies at the Massachusetts Institute of Technology, where his strong belief in interdisciplinary collaboration was given priority.

□ G. Kepes, *Language of Vision* (1944); *Graphic*

Keller'*s poster for the* Zurich Press Ball at Hotel Baur au Lac *on 19 November 1932.*

Forms: The Art as Related to the Book (1949); *The New Landscape in Art and Science* (1956); J. Wechsler and J. Van der Marck, *Gyorgy Kepes: The MIT Years 1945–77* (1978)

Kilkenny Design Workshops (KDW) (f.1965) was set up by the government of the Republic of Ireland in order to foster industrial design, following a report by an invited group of Scandinavian designers on the state of design there. Drawing on the similarity in scale between Scandinavian and Irish industries, the KDW set out initially to exploit and develop design in Ireland's craft-based industries: woven and printed textiles, ceramics, metalwork and wood-turning. It developed many products for export as well as for its own retail outlets. Through the 1970s it also did some work in ENGINEERING DESIGN, though this did not develop rapidly due to the economic recession. In these ways, it served as an active 'design centre'. In 1989, however, most of its non-profit activities folded.
□N. Marchant and J. Addis, *Kilkenny Design: Twenty-One Years of Design in Ireland* (1985)

King-Miranda (f.1977) is a Milanese industrial design studio comprising an Englishman, Perry King, and a Spaniard, Santiago Miranda. King had worked (1965–71) with Ettore SOTTSASS, collaborating on the design of his famous Valentine typewriter. King-Miranda has designed lighting for Flos and Arteluce and furniture for the Spanish companies Akaba, Andreu World and Disform. The firm is perhaps best known for its research projects with OLIVETTI, in particular for its innovatory development of interfaces for photocopiers.
□H. Aldersey-Williams, *King and Miranda: The Poetry of the Machine* (1991)

kitsch is a term used in art and design criticism to describe artefacts that are cheap, ugly, shoddy and overly decorative or sentimental. It is seen as the reverse of 'GOOD DESIGN' and, indeed, academic interest in it has burgeoned since the rejection of the MODERN MOVEMENT by some designers from the late 1960s, and in particular since the publication of Gillo Dorfles's seminal book, *Kitsch: An Anthology of Bad Taste*. Since then, some exponents of POSTMODERNISM, such as Robert VENTURI, have almost deliberately incorporated the visual language of kitsch into their work in recognition of its popular roots. Italian design

groups, such as ARCHIZOOM, SUPERSTUDIO and MEMPHIS, were particularly interested in this 'reversal' of taste.

The term's linguistic roots are unclear: most writers on kitsch point out its derivation from the German *verkitschen* (to make cheap or sentimentalize); it may also derive from the Russian *Kichit'sya* (meaning to be haughty and puffed up). Interestingly, a word used in the North East of England, 'kets', is used by adults to describe cheap, rubbishy things, and by children to mean sweets. If there is a linguistic connection here, then it all goes to show that kitsch is a matter of taste . . .
□G. Dorfles, *Kitsch: An Anthology of Bad Taste* (1969); *Kitsch: The Grotesque Around Us* (1970); L. Giesz, *Phänomenologie des Kitsches* (1971); J. Sternberg, *Les Chefs d'Oeuvre du Kitsch* (1971; English trans., 1972); A. Moles, *Le Kitsch: L'Art du Bonheur* (1971); R. Steinberg (ed.), *Nazi-Kitsch* (1975); C.F. Brown, *Star-Spangled Kitsch* (1976)

Kjaerholm, Poul (1929–80) studied cabinet-making and furniture-design at the School of Arts and Crafts in Copenhagen (1949–52) and was noted in the late 1950s for breaking with the traditional Danish use of natural materials. He thus used more INTERNATIONAL STYLE-type materials, particularly CHROMIUM and TUBULAR STEEL. Many of his furniture designs combined soft forms with stark geometry and were manufactured by companies such as E. Kold Christiensen, P.P. Furniture and Fritz Hansen.

Klint, Kaare (1888–1954) started out as a painter, but studied architecture under his father, P.V. Jensen Klint, in Copenhagen. From 1920 he worked as an architect and designer, becoming a lecturer in furniture at the Copenhagen Academy of Art in 1924 where he was made professor of architecture in 1944. He was important in moving Danish furniture design forward in the interwar period and undertook research into real needs, employing ANTHROPOMETRICS. While he greatly admired the cabinet-making of Chippendale for its faultless sense of proportion, he was anti-historicist (*see* HISTORICISM) and believed that painted or varnished wood was absurd, preferring materials to be kept in their natural state. His Safari chair (1933) clearly demonstrates this. Through his teaching these beliefs had a profound effect on the course of Danish design.

Kjaerholm's stainless steel and cane chair (1965).

Klint's folding wicker deckchair (1933) produced by Rud. Rasmussen.

Klutsis, Gustav (1895–1944) was born in Latvia and attended the Riga Art Institute (1913–15) and art school in Petrograd (1915–17). In 1918 he attended the Second State Free Art Studios, where he came into contact with Kasimir MALEVICH and Antoine Pevsner. Influenced by SUPREMATISM and CONSTRUCTIVISM, from the early 1920s he was involved in designing utilitarian objects, such as propagandist stands in the service of the Revolution. He was a founder-member of the October group, a group of artists dedicated to serving the needs of the proletariat, and he was responsible for extending the group's scope to architecture, film, photography and festivals. He produced posters reflecting the group's aims, which demonstrated a mastery of PHOTOMONTAGE. October was disbanded in 1932 by the Communist Party, and Klutsis was arrested during the Stalinist purges and died in a labour camp.

Kner, Imre (1890–1945) led the reform of book design in Hungary from his print shop in Gyoma. Initially working in an ART NOUVEAU idiom, from 1908 he began to develop a more formal typographical style in publications, such as the 1912 *Könyv a könyvről* (A Book on Books), following the ideas of English ARTS AND CRAFTS designers. After World War I, Kner, with the artist and designer Lajos Kozma, sought to revive the traditions of Hungarian printing, which resulted in the *Kner Almanach* (Yearbook, from 1919) using Kozma's 'naive' woodcuts for headpieces. By the end of the 1920s, Kner came to advocate undecorated, classical typefaces (e.g., Bodoni) and balanced symmetrical page composition in publications such as the three volumes of *As örök Goethe* (Eternal Goethe, 1932). He was an intellectual who promoted the cause of design reform through his publications and membership of design societies in Hungary; his designs also secured much acclaim in Europe (in 1927 he was made an honorary member of the German Book Designers' Association). In 1938 Kner was forced out of public life by anti-Semitic legislation and in 1945 was murdered by the Nazis in Mauthausen.
□György Haiman (ed.), *Kner Imre Emléke* (1989)

Knoll (f.1946), along with HERMAN MILLER, was the USA's principal design-led manufacturer of furniture. Hans Knoll was born in Stuttgart, the son of a cabinet-maker. He attempted to set up a modern furniture company in England, where his cousin, Willi Knoll, had already established a business, based on a new system of sprung chairs that he had devised. In partnership with Tom Parker, Parker-Knoll produced well sprung armchairs and sofas. Meanwhile, Hans Knoll's avant-garde leanings were not sufficiently well accepted in Britain to be a commercial success, and in 1937 he moved to the USA. There he founded the Hans G. Knoll Furniture Company in New York. In 1946, with his second wife, Florence Schust, he set up Knoll Associates. She had been a student at the CRANBROOK ACADEMY OF ART, where she met Eero SAARINEN and Harry BERTOIA, and then at the Illinois Institute of Technology, where she knew Ludwig MIES VAN DER ROHE. Later she worked with Walter GROPIUS and Marcel BREUER. Mostly, then, through Florence's contacts, the company had links with leading figures in architecture and design, and Knoll became instrumental in introducing European work into the USA. The Knolls' idea was to create a 'collection', promoting designers by name and paying them royalties on pieces sold. The company's most famous products are the Mies designs. In 1948 Mies granted the production rights to his BAUHAUS era work, and the Barcelona, Tugendhat and Brno chairs became widely disseminated CLASSICS. Knoll also became the exclusive manufacturer of Breuer's furniture designs. Although originally intended for office use, they were absorbed into corporate America, furnishing reception areas and executive suites. In this way, Knoll became a leader in defining modern standards of good taste. It also commissioned designs, such as work by the sculptor Isamu NOGUCHI and Eero Saarinen's most famous chair, the 1948 Womb chair.

Hans Knoll was killed in a car accident in 1955 in Havana, Cuba, but Florence Knoll continued to run the company. It maintained its high artistic standards but was not financially successful. In 1959 it was taken over by Art Metal, and then in 1977 by General Felt.
□E. Larrabee and M. Vignelli, *Knoll Design* (1981)

Koch, Rudolf (1876–1934) was an important figure in Germany, both in the renaissance of handlettering for books and in the establishment of typography. Most noteworthy was his insistence that type design was a drawing activity: types would be designed by a calligrapher to perfection before being cut. As a result, high standards in design were maintained.

Born in Nuremberg, he was apprenticed to a metal foundry in Hanau in 1896. He worked in Leipzig (1898–1906), where he developed his lettering in the JUGENDSTIL style. He then moved to Offenbach am Main to join the Rudhardsche Giesserei typefoundry, later to become known as Klingspor. His first typeface was Deutsche Schrift (1910). After service during World War I he returned to Offenbach. In the mid-1920s he established the Offenbach Werkstatt, a creative community of an ARTS AND CRAFTS mode. His dedication as an educator was matched by a devout Christianity. He is thus often regarded as Germany's Eric GILL.

Kurumata's *Sally 87 side table (1987) designed for Memphis.*

□R. Koch, *The Little ABC Book of Rudolf Koch* (1976)

Komenda, Erwin (1904–66) was a German automotive engineer. He worked for Daimler-Benz before joining Ferdinand PORSCHE in 1934. Komenda was responsible for the STYLING of the original VOLKSWAGEN Beetle. After World War II he designed the Porsche 356, again employing the aerodynamic principles previously developed by Wunibald Kamm at Daimler-Benz.

Kurumata, Shiro (1934–91) studied architecture and then cabinet-making in Tokyo before turning full-time to furniture design in 1965. His use of distortion and optical illusion since 1970 has brought him close to contemporary avant-garde movements in Europe. His Drawers in Irregular Forms chest (1970) was influenced by traditional Japanese storage furniture, yet in its conceits it comes close to the aims of many a Western DESIGNER-MAKER of its time. Kurumata collaborated with the Italian MEMPHIS group (1981–83).

L

Lalique, René (1860–1945) was a highly influential craftsman in glass. He was apprenticed to a goldsmith in 1876 and lived in London between 1878 and 1880 before returning to France to set up as a goldsmith. In the mid-1880s he began to build up a jewelry manufacturing firm, and by the turn of the century his jewelry and accroutrements were much in demand among the wealthy elite. From 1905 he also began to manufacture other luxury items, such as textiles and mirrors. His designs combined oriental, classical and symbolist sources. In 1909 he established Cristal Lalique, with a glass factory near Paris and another in Alsace in 1921. He had his own pavilion at the PARIS EXPOSITION DES ARTS DÉCORATIFS ET INDUSTRIELS 1925 and also designed and manufactured furniture for the Sèvres porcelain pavilion at the same exhibition. His son, from 1945, and then granddaughter, from 1977, continued as principal designers for Cristal Lalique.

Corsage ornament of gold, plique à jour enamel, chrysoprase and moonstones by **Lalique** *(c.1897–98).*

Landor Associates (f.1941) was founded by Walter Landor in San Francisco. Walter Landor was born in Munich in 1913 and was a founder-partner of the Industrial Design Partnership in London (1935–39). Landor Associates rose to be the world's largest strategic design firm with regional headquarters in New York, London and Tokyo and supporting offices in many different capitals. It specializes mostly in CORPORATE IDENTITY, BRANDING and PACKAGING, its impressive portfolio of designs including the Bank of America, 7-Up and Levi's.

Le Corbusier (1887–1965) is the pseudonym of Charles-Edouard Jeanneret, who was perhaps the most influential figure in modern architecture from 1920 to 1960. He was born in La Chaux-de-Fonds in the Swiss Jura, the son of a watch-case engraver. His earliest training was in his father's trade at the civic art school. Here his design work exhibited many traits of the late ARTS AND CRAFTS movement, with its combination of naturalistic and geometric ornament.

Pavillon de l'Esprit Nouveau which **Le Corbusier** *designed for the Paris Exposition des Arts Décoratifs et Industriels, 1925.*

Le Corbusier

It is commonly thought that the break from this approach dated from 1907, when he began to travel to Italy, Istanbul, Athens and Central Europe, meeting Josef HOFFMANN in Vienna. From 1908 to 1909 he worked in Paris in the office of the architect Auguste Perret, noted for his promotion of the use of steel-reinforced concrete. He later went to the office of Peter BEHRENS in Berlin (1910–11), where he encountered modern production engineering. While in Berlin he came into contact with leaders of the DEUTSCHE WERKBUND as well as, through publications, the work of Frank Lloyd WRIGHT.

During these years of wandering Jeanneret developed two fundamentally important architectural ideas: one was the *Villes Pilotis*, a concept of cities elevated on piles; the other was the *Maison Domino* construction unit (both 1914). This was a building type adapted to industrial production, whereby concrete floors were supported by steel pillars, with no need for load-bearing walls; subsequently, elements could be added in any direction to this basic cube with little technical difficulty.

In 1917 he settled in Paris, taking the name of Le Corbusier in 1920. During the 1920s he became firmly established among the Parisian avant-garde, in particular with painters as a proponent of a form of post-Cubism, which he named Purism. He also edited the successful reforming art journal, *L'Esprit Nouveau* (1920–25), publishing essays that later appeared in *Vers une Architecture* (1923). Here he expounded several theories of modern design which were to have a lasting international effect. One was his definition of architecture as 'the masterly, correct and magnificent play of masses brought together in light' which resonated with his Purist approach to painting. Another suggested the universality that underpinned the aims of the MODERN MOVEMENT, namely that in art and architecture one could distinguish between 'primary' and 'secondary' sensations. The latter was culturally determined while the former was a universal human experience. Accordingly, by stripping away the secondary element of aesthetic practice and experience – that determined by local influences – one was left with forms, colours and effects as readable, acceptable and appropriate in India as in Iceland.

Such objective rationality followed on into another famous claim of his, that 'the house is a machine for living in'. Thus, internal living

Le Corbusier's *Grand Confort armchair (1928) made in stainless steel with leather cushions.*

areas could be grouped according to their function, and, by extension, the layout of a town could be zoned according to different activities: home, leisure, work and travel. This precept, basic to modern town planning, was disseminated internationally through the CONGRÈS INTERNATIONAUX D'ARCHITEC-TURE MODERNE (CIAM) from 1928.

These theories were demonstrated in model form (e.g., the Maison Citrohan, 1922) carried out in collaboration with his brother, Pierre Jeanneret. In addition to the *Domino* and *Pilotis* conceptions, he added three other major facets to his architectural design approach: free composition in the vertical plane; ribbon windows; and the roof garden restoring green space otherwise covered by the house itself. These tenets were published in his *Les 5 Points d'une Architecture Nouvelle* (1926); his Villa Savoye in Poissy-sur-Seine (1929–31) clearly carries them out. At the same time, in collaboration with Charlotte Perriand, Le Corbusier began to design a range of modern furniture which was shown at the 1929 Salon d'Automne in Paris. These pieces included the Fauteuil Grand Comfort armchair and the Chaise Longue, both of which have since become established as design CLASSICS.

During the 1930s, Le Corbusier was largely involved in urban planning projects for several North African and South American cities, which followed the conclusions of CIAM's Athens Charter from the 1933 congress. Le Corbusier had little direct involvement in the reconstruction of European cities after World War II, due more, it is often argued, to the loss in visionary belief dear to the 1920s than any conscious rejection of his theories.

His architecture in this period took on a much more obviously expressive character. His seminal block of flats in Marseilles, the Unité d'Habitation, is as noteworthy for the rough textural effect left on the concrete (part of what was described as a 'brutalist' tendency) and the use of colour and the expressive forms in the *pilotis* (piles) and roof terrace, as it is for its brilliant combination of living space and service elements. At the end of his career he placed less emphasis on function than on expression. Accompanying this shift was the tendency to treat each architectural element with a rich regard for its immediate context and use, as seen in his pilgrimage church of Notre Dame-du-Haut at Ronchamp (1950–54).

Both the main phases of Le Corbusier's work have in common a rejection of historical precedent. At the same time, while his design theories and some of his architecture are motivated by a stark RATIONALISM, he also produced enduring, poetic forms. It may be argued that he adopted the 'machine aesthetic' as much for its expressive as for its rationalistic potential. Thus, for later architects and designers he has served equally as an inspiration and as a warning.

☐A. Ozenfant and C.-E. Jeanneret, *Après le Cubisme* (1918); Le Corbusier, *Vers une Architecture* (1923), trans. as *Towards a New Architecture* (1937); *Urbanisme* (1925), trans. as *The City of Tomorrow and its Planning* (1929); *Précisions sur un Etat Présent de l'Architecture et de l'Urbanisme* (1930); *La Ville Radieuse* (1935), trans. as *The Radiant City* (1967); *Quand les Cathédrales étaient Blanches. Voyage au Pays des Timides* (1937), trans. as *When the Cathedrals were White* (1947); *Sur les Quatre Routes* (1946), trans. as *The Four Routes* (1947); *Les Trois Etablissements Humains* (1945); *Propos d'Urbanisme* (1946); Le Corbusier and F. de Pierrefeu, *La Maison des Hommes* (1942); W. Boesinger (ed.), *Le Corbusier. Oeuvre Complète* (8 vols, 1930–65), trans. as *Le Corbusier: Complete Architectural Works* (8 vols, 1966–70); S. Papadaki, *Le Corbusier. Architect, Painter, Writer* (1948); F. Choay, *Le Corbusier* (1960); M. Besset, *Qui était Le Corbusier?* (1968); S. von Moos, *Le Corbusier: Elemente einer Synthese* (1968); C. Jencks, *Le Corbusier and the Tragic View of Architecture* (1973); *Le Corbusier Sketchbooks* (4 vols, 1981–82).

Leach, Bernard (1887–1979) studied pottery in Japan under Ogata Kenzan (1909–20), the last in a long line of potters. On his return to England in 1920 he founded the Leach pottery in St Ives. Through his writings he established in Europe the Japanese concept of the artist-potter, breaking the mould of the ceramicist as either a designer or an artisan for industrial production. None the less, his simple pottery has also had some stylistic influence on industrial ceramics since World War II.

☐B. Leach, *A Potter's Book* (1940); *A Potter's Work* (1967); *Beyond East and West* (1978); C. Hogben, *The Art of Bernard Leach* (1978)

Stoneware pot by **Leach** *decorated with sgraffito through black slip (1965).*

Lenica, Jan (b.1928) belongs to the second generation of the POLISH SCHOOL of poster design. He studied architecture in Warsaw (1947–52), but from 1950 directed his energies towards poster design for theatre and cinema. He was a teaching assistant to Henryk TOMASZEWSKI from 1954, but in 1963 he emigrated to Paris. From 1979 he was a professor at the Polytechnic Art Academy in Kassel, Germany. Also famous for his experimental animated films, he moved away from the collage style of the Polish School towards a more subjective interpretation of themes, employing into the 1960s, for instance, contoured bands of colour to express the metaphysical elements present in his films.

☐Z. Kaluzynski, *Jan Lenica* (1963)

Lesser, Gilbert (b.1935) is an American graphic designer who is best-known for his theatre posters. Among the very large number of posters he has designed, the most famous was for Peter Shaffer's *Equus* (1974); during the 1970s in particular his posters dominated Broadway. They are generally composed of bold simplified shapes, often silhouettes or semi-abstract outlines, and are always printed in primary colours. He works in a variety of areas: devising corporate logos, acting as special promotion director of *Life* magazine and staging operas. He has studios in New York and Paris.

Lethaby, William Richard (1857–1931) was born in Barnstaple, Devon, the son of a carver and gilder. He trained locally as an architect and in 1879 entered the office of Richard Norman Shaw. Ten years later he left Shaw's office and joined up with Ernest Gimson to found Kenton and Co., a short-lived furniture company. His designs were distinctly rustic, and unsurprisingly he was influential in the ARTS AND CRAFTS movement. He was professor of design at London's ROYAL COLLEGE OF ART from 1900 and was a master of the Art Workers' Guild from 1911. In 1915 he was also involved in the creation of the DESIGN AND INDUSTRIES ASSOCIATION, which was important in introducing Arts and Crafts values into design theory in Britain.
☐ S. Backemeyer and T. Gronberg (eds), *W.R. Lethaby, 1857–1931: Architecture, Design and Education* (1984); G. Rubens, *W.R. Lethaby: His Life and Work 1857–1931* (1986)

Liberman, Alexander (b.1912) was born in Kiev, Russia, but grew up in Paris, where he

A collection of furniture commissioned from Hélène Tiederman by **Liberty & Co**. *(1991).*

worked briefly with A.M. CASSANDRE before becoming art director of the news magazine *VU* in 1933. Escaping World War II, he moved to New York in 1940, where he worked in the art department of Condé Nast Publications. Liberman brought his news magazine experience from *VU* to Condé Nast's *Vogue*, which was subsequently marked by its clarity as against the prevailing decorative tendencies of other similar magazines. From 1942 through to the 1980s he was art director of *Vogue* and in 1947 he changed its masthead to Franklin Gothic, a typeface which until then had been used only in newspapers. While less WHITE SPACE was used from the 1960s, Liberman brought in bolder type to make for more visual power and faster communication.

Liberty & Co. (f.1875) was founded in London by Arthur Lasenby Liberty and was conceived as an Oriental warehouse, dealing in Eastern goods and fabrics. This coincided with the then highly fashionable 'aesthetic' taste, and the shop was immensely successful in these early years. It soon moved into furniture, much of which was designed by George Walton from 1903. Liberty's carried a strict policy of anonymity for its designers and while it disseminated much work by members of the ARTS AND CRAFTS exhibition society, its value to that society was equivocal. The company's ventures into contemporary furniture were extremely successful, however, and STILE LIBERTY, the Italian version of ART NOUVEAU, and its 1960s revival, NEO-LIBERTY, owe their names to the company's influence abroad. In 1991 it began issuing own-label furniture for the first time in 60 years.
☐ A. Adburgham, *Liberty's: A Biography of a Shop* (1975)

Linotype (f.1890) is a company whose name is generally associated with advances in mechanical type composition during the 20th c. The first fully automated hot-metal typesetting machine was invented by Ottmar Mergenthaler and was installed at the *New York Tribune* in 1886.

Linotype was first founded in the USA to develop and market this technology in response to the growing demand for printed material; it was established in Britain in 1895. In competition with the MONOTYPE CORPORATION, whose machine produced the single letterform rather than lines of words, Linotype developed

Proun 99 by El **Lissitzky** (1941).

or revised many typefaces, including Ionic in 1925 for newspaper composition. Among its advisors have been Stanley MORISON and Hermann ZAPF.

Lissitzky, El (Eleazar Markevich) (1890–1941) was born of a Jewish, middle-class family in Polschinok, Russia. He studied architecture under Joseph Maria OLBRICH at the Technical College in Darmstadt (1909–14). From 1914, when he returned to Russia, he continued architectural practice but also worked in fine art and illustration. In 1919 the painter Marc Chagall invited him to teach architecture and graphics at the Vitebsk Institute of Art and Practical Work. There, he soon came under the influence of Kasimir MALEVICH and adopted SUPREMATISM. He subsequently developed his concept of PROUN (an acronym based on the Russian for Project for the Affirmation of the New), a form of art using constructions placed on the flat surface of a wall, which he described as, 'a half-way station between architecture and painting'. While at Vitebsk he also designed his famous poster, *Beat the Whites with the Red Wedge*, which used abstract shapes to make a revolutionary point. While teaching at the

Moscow VKHUTEMAS from 1921 he also published the journal *Veshch* (Object) in Berlin, in which he explored the possibility of extending the concept of art into production, a view which differed from Constructivists who believed more in the suppression of art in favour of 'production art', conceptually a forerunner of design. Between 1920 and 1925 he travelled regularly between Russia and Western Europe, establishing close relationships with the avant-garde: with DADA artists in Düsseldorf, with DE STIJL in the Netherlands (for whose magazine he published articles on PROUN which were of considerable influence on its members) and with the BAUHAUS in Weimar. From 1925 he stayed in Russia and resumed a teaching post at the Moscow VkHUTEMAS where, in his teaching of furniture design, he expounded much of the fundamentalism of the MODERN MOVEMENT. During this period he moved more towards CONSTRUCTIVISM, while in the 1930s he concentrated increasingly on photography and PHOTOMONTAGE. Of all Russian avant-garde artist-designers, through his European contacts and extensive writings, Lissitzky was perhaps the most influential on the development of Modernism in Western Europe.

☐ E. Lissitzky, *Russland: Die Rekonstruktion der Architektur in der Sowjetunion* (1930); O.A. Shvidkovsky (ed.), *Building in the USSR 1917–1932* (1971); *El Lissitzky 1890–1941* (exh. cat., Yale University School of Architecture, New Haven, 1977); Lodder (1983)

Lloyd Loom (f.1919) was an American furniture-manufacturing company that used imitation cane work invented by an American, Marshall B. Lloyd. It was made of twisted paper, woven on mechanized looms and later strengthened by the addition of steel wire in the warp. The fabric was attached to a steam-bent wooden frame with staples which were covered up by braiding before the whole piece was spray painted. British manufacturing rights were taken over by Lusty and Sons in 1922 and the material swamped the British and American markets during the 1920s and 30s. It was found, however, that it did not stand up to heavy use and that cane was ultimately preferred by many users.

☐ L. Curtis, *Lloyd Loom* (1991)

Lluscà, Josep (b.1948) was a prodigy from the first student intake of Barcelona's Eina School.

He learnt very early on that one's conceptual dexterity came first and the technical aspects of design came later. As with many young designers, economic necessity caused him to work in a wide range of design disciplines during the 1970s. In the 1980s he produced many splendid pieces of product design, but as the decade progressed he concentrated more exclusively on furniture for Enea and Andreu World and lighting for Metalarte. Likening his approach to that of a sculptor, he none the less considers both the expressive and ergonomic (*see* ERGONOMICS) aspects of design with scientific rigour. In order to realize these ideals, he makes use of wide-ranging research, sometimes incorporating both Antoni GAUDí and 1950s RATIONALISM into the same piece.

Loewy, Raymond (1893–1986) is invariably recognized as having done for design what Elvis Presley did for music. He gave style, razzmatazz and sex to machinery and consumer products. By the end of his life, Raymond Loewy International, which had offices in New York, Chicago, Los Angeles, London, Paris, Milan, Geneva, San Juan and Saõ Paulo, had over 2,200 clients. His portfolio includes the S-I steam locomotive for the Pennsylvania Railroad (1933); the Coldspot Super Six refrigerator for Sears, Roebuck and Company (1934), sales of which jumped 400 per cent following his redesign; packaging for Lucky Strike cigarettes (1941); the Scenicruiser coach for the Greyhound Bus Company (1946); logotypes for the Exxon Oil Corporation (1966) and the Shell Oil Company (1967) as well as the interiors of Skylab for NASA (1967–73).

Born in Paris, he studied engineering there (1910–14) and then served as an engineer in the French army during World War I. In search of the American dream, he followed his brothers to New York in 1919. Capitalizing on his status as a Frenchman in New York, he suppressed his title of engineer and instead infiltrated high society as an artist and illustrator. His skill in public relations and self-promotion brought him work as a fashion illustrator for *Vogue* and *Harper's Bazaar* magazines and as a window-display artist for Macy's department store. In the late 1920s he moved into industrial design and in 1929, coinciding with the establishment of Raymond Loewy Associates, had his first major success with the Gestetner duplicating machine company in Britain. The design commentator Peter Dormer writing in *The Times* notes that Loewy's Gestetner duplicating machine is one of the touchstones of design history, because it is a good example of the extension of a product's life and the expansion of its market penetration by restyling rather than the more expensive means of technical innovation. This was typical of Loewy's approach to design – it was not sophisticated in any technical sense, nor was it aesthetically avant-garde. Instead, he looked to style products so that they appeared more attractive – hence the subsequently much debated term, STYLING. Loewy's next big success, the Coldspot refrigerator, clearly demonstrates the stylist coming into his own: the overall curved form draws on recent developments in metal stamping which allowed shallow curves, thus giving the form a streamlined edge; beyond this, he hid the door hinges, gave it a jewel-like name plate and installed rust-proof ALUMINIUM shelving. Thus the fridge was turned into a desirable object, and such self-advertisement in the product was important for sales in the depressed consumer market of the 1930s USA.

After World War II Loewy became famous. In 1949 he was on the cover of *Time* magazine, which captioned his portrait, 'he streamlines the sales curve'. His studio grew with his fame: in 1938 it numbered 18 designers; in 1941 there were 56 and between 1947 and the mid-1960s, it expanded from 150 to 180 employees. His professional lifespan thus followed a general trend in the USA: from individual freelancer in the 1920s, through being the head of a studio in the 1930s – which drew on the greater opportunities for design consultancy created by increasing competition between manufacturers and in turn received high media attention itself – and then to a postwar emergence as an almost mythical figure, capable of redesigning (or restyling) anything from cigarette packets to airports. By the economic boom years of the 1950s and 1960s, Loewy's studio, like many others, was so large as to make its own designers anonymous. By contrast, Loewy maintained his up-front public persona, even encouraging myths, such as that of his authorship of the 1916 Coca-Cola bottle.

Yet Loewy was essentially a stylist, and did not bring his engineering background to his design. For example, insisting on installing a window for Skylab, thus allowing the astronauts to give excited descriptions of their view of the world, was a brilliant piece of public relations for NASA; but at the same time, his

Loewy's *Silversides Greyhound motor coach (1940–54)*.

design methodology was not up to the highly technical problem-solving NASA required. Indeed, while Loewy himself never personally suffered, the demise of styling, which he represented, may be connected with the questioning of the American dream and the subsequent moral debate within industrial design felt in the USA and Europe in the 1960s. As articulated in his no-nonsense book, *Never Leave Well Enough Alone* (1951), Loewy clearly positioned the role of design at the service of the corporation and consumerism – something which underwent criticism from many more socially-concerned designers. None the less, Loewy's great achievement is that he showed that product design was about capturing the public's imagination and recognizing what they regarded as modern and exciting – he himself used the acronym MAYA for his design philosophy, meaning 'most advanced, yet acceptable'. It is significant that he was retained as a major industrial design consultant by the Soviet Union in the 1970s.

□R. Loewy, *The Locomotive: Its Esthetics* (1937); *Never Leave Well Enough Alone* (1951); *Industrial Design* (1979); *The Designs of Raymond Loewy* (exh. cat., Smithsonian Institute, Washington, 1975); Schönberger, Angela (ed.), *Raymond Loewy: Pioneer of American Industrial Design* (exh. cat., Internationales Design Zentrum, Berlin, 1990)

Loos, Adolf (1870–1933) was born in Brno, Czechoslovakia, and studied building at Liberec (1887–88) and then at the Dresden Institute of Technology. He was in the USA (1893–96), where he did a variety of architectural jobs. Returning to Vienna, he set up an architectural practice, also designing furniture

for his projects. His greatest influence, however, was in his writings, in particular with an article 'Ornament und Verbrechen' (Ornament and Crime), published in *Der Sturm* in 1908 and in LE CORBUSIER's journal *L'Esprit Nouveau* in 1920. In this article, he linked cultural evolution to the removal of ornament. This, together with his usually simple designs, led to his being seen as a pioneer of the MODERN MOVEMENT. It must be added, however, that his buildings in Vienna, Paris and Prague demonstrated distinct neo-classical tendencies. In 1903 he founded the review *Das Andere* (The Other), in which he wrote of his admiration for British and American simplicity.

□B. Gravagnuolo, *Adolf Loos: Theory and Works* (1982)

Louis Vuitton (f.1854) is a Paris-based manufacturer of luxury travel products. It began life producing flat trunks, but now, as part of the Louis Vuitton-Moët-Hennessy conglomerate, its famous initials are applied to a range of objects from silk scarves, featuring architectural drawings by Arata Isozaki, to watches and pens by Gae AULENTI. In the 1980s its design director, Françoise Jollant-Kneebone, had to resolve the dilemma created by increased demand, which in turn led to the need for production on an industrial scale – this would undermine the exclusivity on which luxury items depend. This was to some extent achieved through maintaining high production standards and carefully controlling the product's retailing.

Lubalin, Herb (1918–81) studied at Cooper Union, New York, and then worked freelance as a graphic designer and typographer (1939–

41). After working as art director of various ADVERTISING AGENCIES he set up his own design firm in 1964. His design activities spanned the entire range of graphic communications, but he is most acclaimed for his original typographic work from the 1950s. Lubalin understood the potential of PHOTOSETTING, which during the 1960s rapidly replaced hand-set metal type for display material and machine-set metal type for text matter. Thus he explored the facility this allowed to overlap characters, distort, play with large sizes and employ tight line-, word- or letter-spacing. Such developments were carried out through design work in the 1960s for the magazines *Eros*, *Fact* and *Avant Garde* and later in the typographic design magazine he founded in 1973, *U&lc* (Upper and Lower Case). In 1970 he co-founded the INTERNATIONAL TYPEFACE CORPORATION, an organization established with the aim of licensing and distributing original typestyles to manufacturers of typesetting equipment. This ensured royalties for typeface designers (typefaces cannot be copyrighted), which resulted in the subsequent expansion in the production of original type.

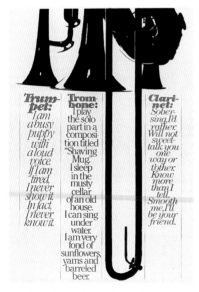

Poster by **Lubalin** *(1978),* Come Home to Jazz.

M

Mackintosh, Charles Rennie (1868–1928) was the foremost exponent of ART NOUVEAU in Britain and was of considerable influence abroad among SECESSION artists and designers. He undertook an apprenticeship in an architectural office (1884–89) in his native Glasgow and travelled extensively in Europe during the 1890s. Departing from a classical revivalist tradition in Scotland he used a more stylized, elongated vocabulary based in part on Celtic designs. He designed posters from the mid-1890s and exhibited at the 1896 ARTS AND CRAFTS Exhibition, although his work was not positively received by the movement. He also designed furniture from that time onwards. His best-known work is his Glasgow School of Art building, for which he won a competition in 1897, and the second, and better known, stage of which he designed in 1906. He moved to London in 1913, after which he limited his work to a few private interior commissions and printed fabrics. Some of his furniture was manufactured by the Italian company CASSINA from 1975.
□N. Pevsner, *Charles Rennie Mackintosh* (1950); T. Howarth, *Charles Rennie Mackintosh and the Modern Movement* (1952); R. Billcliffe, *Charles Rennie Mackintosh: The Complete Furniture, Furniture Drawings and Interior Designs* (1978)

Maclaren, Denham (1903–89) was a British artist and designer who designed some interesting pieces during the 1930s. He was from a talented family – his brother Owen designed the Maclaren pushchair in the 1950s – and after studying painting at the Académie Julienne in Paris he went up to Cambridge in 1922. In 1930 he opened his own studio showroom in London and in 1936 he began to retail through the Duncan Miller shop. His furniture falls into two categories: firstly, the pure Modernist pieces, using glass, TUBULAR STEEL and CHROMIUM, veering towards the style of LE CORBUSIER; and secondly, a more 'Hollywood' style, using glass and exotic textural effects such as zebra skin, echoing the style of Eileen GRAY.

Magistretti, Vico (b. 1920) trained in architecture at the Polytechnic in Milan (1940–45) like

The main bedroom of Hill House, Helensburgh, Dumbarton, with decoration and furniture by **Mackintosh** *(1902–5).*

many important Italian designers and turned to design during Italy's postwar *recostruzione* period. He gained an international reputation in the 1960s for his designs such as the Selene chair of 1966, made by ARTEMIDE. He had begun work on it in 1961, originally conceiving it in reinforced polyester, only later changing it to ABS PLASTICS. In this design Magistretti took into account the problems of production and strength, and its curved forms helped to establish a new Italian aesthetic for plastic goods. He continued to produce technically and aestheti-

cally innovative furniture designs for 20 years, in particular for CASSINA. His 1981 Sinbad armchair was inspired by the image of a horse blanket thrown loosely over an upholstered base and was his boldest attempt at sculptural form in lounge seating.

Maldonado, Tomás (b.1922) is an industrial designer and design theorist. He was born in Buenos Aires and studied at the Academy of Fine Arts there (1938–43). He worked freelance as a painter and designer in Argentina (1944–54) before becoming, on the invitation of Max BILL, a professor at the ULM HOCHSCHULE FÜR GESTALTUNG (1954–64) and then Rector until 1966. His design work was mostly in high-technology products such as medical and office equipment. However, his greatest impact was as a theorist: at Ulm he steered the school away from its heavily formalist approach, inherited from the BAUHAUS, towards a broader humanistic emphasis. This meant that the social sciences, mathematics and semiology were to be studied, though in a way which was to be highly scientific and directed towards the fulfilment of universal needs. In 1967 he became professor of environmental planning at the University of Bologna, and has continued to publish and lecture internationally.
□ T. Maldonado, *Ambiente Humano e Ideologia* (1959); *Vanguardia y Racionalidad* (1977); *El Diseño Industrial Reconsiderado* (1977)

Malevich, Kasimir (1878–1935) studied at the Kiev Drawing School (1895–96) and the Mos-

Malevich's paintings exhibited at the 0.10 Gallery, Petrograd, in 1915.

Malmsten, Carl

cow School of Art (1904–5). Between 1910 and 1920 he was influenced by Cubism and FUTURISM. In 1915 at the 0.10 Gallery in Petrograd he launched SUPREMATISM, which consisted of paintings of primary Euclidean geometric forms in pure colours against a white background; he described them as 'the supremacy of pure emotion'. To explain his ideas he published a leaflet entitled *From Cubism to Suprematism: The New Painterly Realism* (1915). After the Revolution, in 1918 he began teaching at the First State Free Art Studios in Moscow, a forerunner of the VKHUTEMAS, and he gained prominence as an artist and theoretician. He then replaced the ousted Marc Chagall as director of the Vitebsk Institute of Art and Practical Work in 1919. The following year he founded the UNOVIS group which included El LISSITZKY and Nikolai SUETIN. After 1919 he turned away from painting and began to design cities and individual dwelling units, creating small-scale architectural models in plaster. Following his return to Petrograd in 1922, where he became professor at the Academy of Arts, he designed Suprematist-inspired ceramics which were manufactured there at the Lomonossov state porcelain factory. In 1927 he went to Berlin and also visited the BAUHAUS in Dessau. His ideas were revived and disseminated internationally by a Bauhaus book, *The Non-Objective World* (1927).
K. Malevich, *Essays on Art 1915–1933* (2 vols, 1968); *Soviet Union/Union Soviétique: Special Issue, Kasimir Malevich* (1978); *Malevich* (exh. cat., Pompidou Centre, Paris, 1978); L.A. Zhadova, *Malevich: Suprematism and Revolution in Russian Art, 1910–1930* (1978); *Kasimir Malevich* (exh. cat., Stedelijk Museum, Amsterdam, 1981)

Malmsten, Carl (1888–1972) was a Swedish furniture designer and teacher who came to national prominence when he won a competition for decorating the Stockholm Town Hall. He was a promoter of better design in ordinary objects, partly influenced by the ARTS AND CRAFTS movement, and he thus extolled national romanticism. In his design work this meant seeking forms inspired by peasant craftsmanship, described as 'rural rococo' due to its 18th-c. roots. He was a staunch adversary of FUNCTIONALISM, refusing to exhibit in Gunnar ASPLUND's steel and glass pavilion for the Stockholm Exposition (1930). As a result he somewhat hindered the development of the MODERN MOVEMENT in Sweden and helped maintain craft values in its national design. He ran his own production units and retail outlets and was also influential as a teacher and critic of crafts.

Mangiarotti, Angelo (b.1921) is an Italian industrial designer. He was born in Milan where he studied architecture at the Polytechnic (1944–48). Until 1960 he worked in collaboration with the architect Bruno Morassutti and has worked in architecture, urban planning and industrial design. His major interest in design is in the problem of achieving efficient industrial production and prefabrication while aiming at high-quality finishes. His client companies have included CASSINA, KNOLL and DANESE.

Manzù, Pio (1939–69) studied at the ULM HOCHSCHULE FÜR GESTALTUNG (1960–64) and, despite his tragically short life, subsequently worked at the FIAT styling centre, where he developed their 127 car range. He was also important in bringing the Ulm lessons to his native Italy, developing the 1968 City Taxi and designing projects in lighting and three 1968 clocks for Italora.

Mari, Enzo (b.1932) was born in Novara, Italy. He studied at the Academy of Fine Arts in Milan and since the 1950s has been very active artistically. In 1963 he co-ordinated the Italian group Nuove Tendenze (New Tendencies). At the same time he began his work as a designer of graphics, products and exhibitions. A characteristic of his work is the constant experimentation and research into new forms and meanings of the products, many of which were developed with DANESE.
E. Mari, *Funzione della Ricerca Estetica* (1970); R. Pedio, *Enzo Mari Designer* (1980); A.C. Quintavalle (ed.), *Enzo Mari* (1983)

Mariscal, Javier (b.1950) was born in Valencia, Spain, and had little formal training as a designer apart from a brief stint at the Elisava School in 1970. From the early 1970s he was closely associated with the 'underground' comics which circulated around Barcelona's Plaça Real, and this sketchy and irreverent style of comic drawing by chance found its way into various design projects in the 1980s. Via design work on a bar with Fernando Salas in Valencia in 1980 and an exhibition of *Muebles Amorales*

*Duplex stool in black, white and primary colours designed by **Mariscal** in 1981.*

Mathsson's *webbing chair, Eva, originally designed in 1934.*

(amoral furniture) at the Sala Vinçon in Barcelona with Pepe Cortés in the following year, Mariscal came to the attention of Ettore SOTTSASS, who invited him to take part in the MEMPHIS show of 1981. Thus he shot to international fame and has since been in high demand, applying his skills to projects ranging from sofas to textile designs and the Olympic mascot for 1992.
□ E. Dent-Coad, *Javier Mariscal: Designing the New Spain* (1991); G. Julier, *Mariscal Design* (1992); J. Busquets, *Cobi al Descobert* (1992)

market research is part of the armoury of techniques at the disposal of modern business. It is the collection and analysis of data from a sample of individuals or organizations relating to such information as their characteristics, behaviour, attitudes, opinions or professions. It includes all forms of MARKETING and social research, such as consumer and industrial surveys, psychological investigations, observational and panel studies.

marketing is the name given to the process by which all of the elements of selling products by a consumer-oriented company are co-ordinated. Advertising, PACKAGING, new product development, MARKET RESEARCH and point-of-sale material are all juggled and analysed to decide upon the marketing mix, which will determine the position of the brand in its market sector (*see* BRANDING).

MARS *see* MODERN ARCHITECTURAL RESEARCH GROUP

Mathsson, Bruno (1907–88) was Sweden's pioneering modern furniture designer. He was apprenticed in his father's woodworking firm, Karl Mathsson, in Värnamo (1923–31) and began experimenting with bentwood in the early 1930s. This brought him into line with other designers connected with the MODERN MOVEMENT, such as Marcel BREUER, an association made clear in his exhibits at the Stockholm Exposition (1930), which broke from the traditional decorative arts leanings of Carl MALMSTEN. He made analyses of proportion and weight-bearing stresses, and found new ways of bending and laminating, using industrial processes. His designs, produced mostly by the furniture manufacturer Dux Moebel or Karl Mathsson, are distinguished by their lightness and simplicity and often include an innovatory constructional feature. A good example of this is the inclusion of a table leg which splits and spreads into a Y in his tables developed with Piet Hein in 1964, giving added supportive stability while maintaining an elegant form.

Travel poster for the Swiss National Tourist Office by **Matter** *(1935).*

Matsushita (f. 1918) is the largest manufacturer of electrical consumer goods in the world, but outside of Japan the name is relatively unknown to consumers. The Matsushita Electric Industrial Company owns a range of familiar brand names (e.g., National, Panasonic, Technics and Quasar) and has a half share in one of its major rivals – the Japanese Victor Company (JVC). Founded by Kanosuke Matsushita to manufacture plugs and sockets, the company was incorporated as Matsushita Denki Sangyo in 1935. Such is the corporate strength of the company that it was Matsushita, along with JVC, who forced SONY to abandon the Betamax video format in the early 1980s in favour of the Video Home System (VHS), now the standard international format.

Matter, Herbert (1907–84) studied painting in Geneva (1925–27) and then in Paris (1928–29) under Fernand Léger. His interest in photography and design led to his employment in the Deberny et Peignot type foundry (1929–32) where he worked with A.M. CASSANDRE and LE CORBUSIER. In 1932 he returned to Swit-

zerland, where he produced posters for the Swiss National Tourist Office (1932–36) using the bold collage and montage techniques developed within the MODERN MOVEMENT. He also pioneered the dynamic use of strong contrasts of scale and the mixture of black and white photography and colour planes. In 1936 he moved to New York, where he worked as a photographer for *Vogue* and *Harper's Bazaar* before joining the staff of Condé Nast Publications (1946–57). He also designed advertisements for KNOLL (1946–66) which were more abstract than his earlier work, but retained a bold, playful effect that was highly influential. He was professor of photography at Yale University (1952–76).
☐ P. Rand, *Herbert Matter* (exh. cat., Yale University, New Haven, 1978)

Maurer, Ingo (b. 1932) began his career proper in Munich in 1963, when he founded Design M and began designing and making ornaments and lamps. This firm was notable for its desire to astonish and provoke the spectator, using such devices in its work as outsize objects and decoration and recontextualization influenced by POP culture and avant-garde movements of that period. The materials used were 'poor', suited to projecting a simple, craft image. At the beginning of the 1980s, however, Maurer moved away from craft products towards technological 'quality' experimentation. Thanks to the scope afforded by low-tension cabling and Design M's own development of a smaller transformer, lights could be stripped down until they were reduced to mere points of light. Henceforth, products could be assemblages of components offering varieties of minimal forms and lighting effects. Maurer came to the attention of the general public when he exhibited in the Lumière je Pense à Vous exhibition at the Pompidou Centre, Paris, in June 1985.

Medium Density Fibreboard (MDF) was developed and first produced in the USA in the mid-1960s by the Celotex Corporation. It is a wood-based sheet material manufactured from fibres bonded together with a synthetic resin adhesive. This tight fibre distribution makes it possible for intricate machining operations to be carried out on the edges without disturbing the centre of the board. Its smooth and stable surface provides a good area for painting, spraying and applying decorative foils, laminates and wood veneers. It shares similarities with both hardboard and wood chipboard in that it is made from fibres like hardboard and, like chipboard, has a high internal bond strength derived from its resin binder. Additionally, it shows many of the mechanical and physical characteristics associated with solid wood. Though it is at least 80 per cent more expensive than chipboard, it is considerably cheaper than softwood or hardwood and has greater stability. Its strength, inexpensiveness and ability to be worked easily have made it a popular choice.

MDF may have encouraged the use of spray finishes and decorative laminates in contemporary furniture. This tendency has also been stimulated by the MEMPHIS group; though its designers used chipboards and not MDF, they treated the furniture carcass as a blank canvas upon which the designer could make his or her own mark. Often the appeal of MDF furniture is visual rather than tactile.

□ A.J. Sparkes in *The Furniture Manufacturer* (1983); FIRA (Furniture Industries Research Association), *MDF Handbook* (1985)

Thrift Cutlery by **Mellor** *(1965).*

Mellor, David (b.1930) is famous as a designer and retailer of modern kitchen- and tableware. He studied at Sheffield College of Art (1946–48), London's ROYAL COLLEGE OF ART (1950–54) and the British School in Rome (1953–54). He then set up a silversmithing workshop in Sheffield. Some of his early design

consultancy work was in street furniture, but he specialized in cutlery from the late 1950s. He opened his first shop in London in 1966 and established a cutlery workshop in Sheffield in 1975, expanding into a factory near Hathersage in 1988. Mellor is perhaps uncharacteristic of British craftsmen in bringing his work into industrial production.

Memphis (f.1981) originated in Milan as the successor of STUDIO ALCHYMIA when Ettore SOTTSASS left the latter, due mainly to disagreements with Alessandro MENDINI. The direction of 're-design' which Alchymia was taking at that time was not conducive to innovation, and with Memphis Sottsass hoped to break new ground. He enlisted the support of Renzo Brugola, the owner of a carpentry shop, and Mario and Brunella Godani, who had a furniture showroom, and planned Memphis with Michele DE LUCCHI and others as a design group. It is widely reported that Memphis got its name because Bob Dylan's 'Memphis Blues' was playing on the record player during the group's first meeting. Having found backing from the Italian industrialist, Fausto Celati, and Ernesto Gismondi, the president of Artemide (which Memphis joined as a partner in 1982), Memphis had its first show in September 1981. The group never formulated any central design philosophy or methodology. Aesthetically, however, their objects (which included fabrics, furniture, lighting, silverware, ceramics and glassware) are very much a commercial extension of work instigated at Alchymia and by other individual contributors during the 1970s. This is marked by the breaking of the traditional canons of FUNCTIONALISM governing typologies – thus a set of bookshelves rarely looks as if it might support books – and, by extension, an emphasis laid on the decorative function of the created object, particularly by the bold use of colour. Memphis created new plastic-laminate designs which were used extensively: thus greater emphasis was placed on surface decoration than on material structure. In doing this Memphis acknowledged the use of styles found in popular culture (e.g., in punk hairstyles).

Memphis's contributors include Andrea BRANZI, Aldo Cibic, Michael Graves, Hans HOLLEIN, Shiro KURUMATA, Javier MARISCAL, George Sowden, Matteo Thun and Daniel WEIL among many. Its art director is Barbara Radice. Memphis exhibited in many world capitals during the 1980s. Its commercial success and worldwide exposure made it of enormous influence in most subsequent disciplines of design, and it thus spearheaded the so-called NEW DESIGN.

□B. Radice, *Memphis: Research, Experiences, Results, Failures and Successes of New Design* (1984); R. Horn, *Memphis: Objects, Furniture and Patterns* (1986); P. ter Hofstede, *Memphis 1981–1988* (exh. cat., Groninger Museum, Groningen, 1989)

Mendini, Alessandro (b.1930) is an Italian designer and writer who worked as an architect for Marcello NIZZOLI until 1970. He was a leading spokesman for STUDIO ALCHYMIA and was active in the growth of RADICAL DESIGN and ANTI-DESIGN, particularly as editor of *Casabella* (1970–76). He was editor of the fashion numbers of *DOMUS* (1976–85) and since 1979 has been editor of *MODO*. His furniture for Alchymia, which was exhibited at the 1981 Milan Furniture Fair and subsequently through the 1980s, tussled with the problems of consumerism and the mass media. He also produced silverware designs for ALESSI.
□*Alessandro Mendini* (exh. cat., Groninger Museum, Groningen, 1988)

MetaDesign (f.1983) is Germany's leading graphic design studio. It was established in Berlin by Erik Spiekermann and while never expanding beyond 20 members is renowned for its innovatory typographic work. Spiekermann studied art history at the Free University in Berlin and then spent most of the 1970s in London, working first as a typographer and as a teacher at the London College of Printing and later as a consultant to WOLFF OLINS and HENRION Design Associates. His interest in typography – with a background in traditional metal type – was thus combined with a more public and commercial application. This was brought to MetaDesign, whose activities include a redesign of the literature for the Deutsche Bundespost (German postal service) and a strong working relationship with the German typefoundry and machinery company, BERTHOLD. MetaDesign is also a member of EDEN (the European designers network) along with such companies as BRS Premsela Vonk in Amsterdam, Eleven Design in Copenhagen and Stockholm and KING-MIRANDA Associati in Milan. The network was formed in 1991 to link studios together in the context of the Single European Market.
□E. Spiekermann, *Ursache & Wirkung: Ein Typografischer Roman*, trans. as *Rhyme & Reason: A Typographic Novel* (1987)

Metz & Co. (f.c.1800) is a Dutch furniture producer and retailing company that is notable for its remarkable policy on design and its extensive co-operation with artists in the 20th c. Its owner-director from about 1900 was Joseph de Leeuw who, in 1902, acquired the general agency for the Netherlands of the British department store LIBERTY & CO. To some extent the Liberty style – rooted in the ARTS AND CRAFTS movement and ART NOUVEAU – marked Metz's line subsequently. However, the firm also began its own production in 1918 with designs by Paul Bromberg. He was replaced as furniture designer by W. Penaat, whose aesthetic was allied to the rationalistic design of H.P. BERLAGE and K.P.C. de Bazel. It was also during the late 1920s that Metz employed avant-garde artists such as Sonia DELAUNAY to do its textile designs. During the early 1930s it produced work by Gerrit RIETVELD, J.J.P. Oud and Mart STAM. As that decade progressed, Metz's severe FUNCTIONALISM gave way to a more playful line, allowing room for decoration. Jean CARLU and A.M. CASSANDRE figure among its advertising designers during the 1930s.
□P. Timmer in *Het Nieuwe Bouwen Amsterdam: 1920–1960* (exh. cat., Stedelijk Museum, Amsterdam, 1983)

Michael Peters Group (MPG) (1970–90) was initially founded as Michael Peters & Partners by Michael Peters, who had studied at the London College of Printing and at Yale University and later worked at CBS Television and at the advertising agency Collett, Dickenson & Pearce. The company specialized in PACKAGING design for a decade and became the Michael Peters Group in 1981. In 1983 it was floated on the Unlisted Securities Market at 85p per share. This was to finance a move to bigger premises which Peters dubbed 'the new commercial Bauhaus', and in 1986 the MPG tied up a deal with the PA Consulting Group to give the MPG access to high-technology product design skills. Then came a programme of diversification across countries and design disciplines in which the MPG bought up several other large design companies and opened

Mies van der Rohe's *Cantilever chair (1926).*

offices in various European countries and Canada. Its full-year pre-tax profits peaked at £2.1 million in 1986.

During its steady growth, the company won many international awards for design work, particularly for its application of an eclectic style to packaging, though it also worked on much larger projects (e.g., the £60 million Eurohub passenger terminal at Birmingham International Airport). By 1989, however, many of the large international design groups had begun to feel the effect of a recession in the design industry, and the Michael Peters Group itself went into receivership in 1990; at the time it had some 150 workers in London and another 150 in Europe and North America.

The story of Michael Peters is a dramatic illustration of more general trends in the design industry, particularly the London-based design industry. The company weathered the recession of the 1970s to emerge in the 1980s as a leading and expanding force. It was floated on the Stock Market along with several other design companies in the early 1980s, but by the end of decade appeared to have outgrown itself, begging the question as to whether the Stock Exchange and design mix successfully.

Michelotti, Giovanni (1921–80) was born in Turin and worked for the company that later became PININFARINA (1937–49). He then set up on his own as a car designer. He is most noteworthy for his work for non-Italian com-panies. He designed, for example, the Japanese Datsun Prince Skyline (1961) and the British Triumph Herald (1959).

Mies van der Rohe, Ludwig (1886–1969) was born in Aachen, where he worked as a draughtsman in various architectural offices (1902–5). He then moved to Berlin, where he worked in the office of Bruno Paul before joining Peter BEHRENS's office (1908–11), where he met Walter GROPIUS. From 1912 he had his own architectural practice in Berlin, which he maintained until 1938, save for World War I service. Mies was comparatively late in coming to the postwar groups that advocated Modernism: he was a member of the DEUTSCHE WERKBUND from 1921, the Novembergruppe (November Group) from 1922 and then director of the BAUHAUS in Dessau (1930–33). Much of his architecture in Germany was of a conceptual and experimental nature; for instance, he developed several designs for high-rise steel and glass structures during the 1920s. These concepts became buildings after he moved to the USA in 1938, where he became director of the department of architecture at the Illinois Institute of Technology, Chicago. Otherwise, in architecture he was best known for his design of exhibition pavilions, especially the German contribution to the Barcelona International Exhibition (1929). Here his preference for lavish materials, colour and texture is evident. His furniture design, however, did go into production. He designed furniture for all his early houses, but his first furniture for mass production appeared at the WEISSENHOF SIEDLUNG, where he collaborated with Lily Reich. The two pro-duced TUBULAR-STEEL cantilever chairs, already developed by Marcel BREUER and Mart STAM. Ironically it is Mies's Barcelona chair (1929) that has sold most and reached CLASSIC status. The chair was conceived mere-ly as a ceremonial seat for the king of Spain and is neither comfortable, light nor appropriately designed for mass production – the welding of the joints and the polishing of the frame is still mostly done by hand. Its success lies, perhaps, in its appropriateness for the office-block entrance halls typical of the post-1945 INTERNATIONAL STYLE (as seen, for instance, in Mies's own Chicago office-block of 1951, Lake Shore Drive). It is modernistic yet classical in its curved X-frame and is hard-wearing. A small locksmith's shop, called Berliner Metall-

Minale Tattersfield

gewerbe, manufactured his furniture until 1931, when Mies signed a contract with THONET-Mundus of Zurich which brought him a substantial income. From 1947 KNOLL manufactured his Barcelona chair.
☐ L. Glaeser, *Ludwig Mies van der Rohe: Furniture and Furniture Drawings from the Design Collection and the Mies van der Rohe Archive* (1977); P. Johnson, *Mies van der Rohe* (1978); W. Blaser, *Mies van der Rohe: Furniture and Interiors* (1982); J. Zukowsky, *Mies Reconsidered: His Career, Legacy and Disciples* (1986); F. Schulze, *Mies van der Rohe: Critical Essays* (1989)

Minale Tattersfield (f.1964) was founded in London by Marcello Minale and Brian Tattersfield who had both previously worked at the Young and Rubicam agency. They are noted for bringing to mainstream commercial design highly creative and often witty design solutions using the minimum means necessary. The majority of their work is in graphic design but they have also undertaken work in interior, retail premises, exhibition and furniture design. During the 1980s they rapidly internationalized their operations through a process of mergers and acquisitions, establishing studios in Paris, Brisbane and Barcelona with marketing offices in Milan, Brussels, Cologne, Casablanca, Hong Kong, Sydney, Osaka and New York.
☐ M. Minale and B. Tattersfield, *Minale Tattersfield* (4 vols, 1965–72); E. Booth-Clibborn, *Design à la Minale Tattersfield* (1986); J. Myerson, *The World of Minale Tattersfield* (1990)

Modern Architectural Research Group (MARS) (f.1932) was the British branch of the CONGRÈS INTERNATIONAUX D'ARCHITECTURE MODERNE (CIAM). Under the leadership of Wells COATES, it provided a focus for Modernists such as Maxwell FRY, Colin Lucas and Berthold Lubetkin. It put on a major exhibition of modern work in London in 1938, which influenced post-1945 planning. It disbanded in the late 1950s.

Modern Movement is far from being a closed book since the advent of POSTMODERNISM, for the debates over its origins, meaning and future have continued. It was not represented by a particular group of people with a single manifesto, and thus is also often known simply as Modernism, suggesting a shared aesthetic or ideological tendency. And Modernism itself as an interpretive concept may be applied beyond design, to analyses of music, art, literature and many other cultural or scientific expressions. It has dominated these phenomena and their interpretation for much of the 20th c.

Many design historians have laid stress on the moral debates that formed a background to Modernism towards the end of the 19th c. Nikolaus PEVSNER's *Pioneers of the Modern Movement*, first published in 1936, had a great influence on understandings of the development of Modernism. The revised edition of 1960 was subtitled *from William Morris to Walter Gropius*. The book traces the development of Modernism via the architectural feats of individuals. That this development is illustrated within architecture may be understandable given architecture's historical dominance in theoretical debates over craft or design. The central thesis of the book is that the development of Modernism was a response to the growth in industrialization from the 19th c. into the 20th c. William Morris opened the debate, objecting to the idea that machine production slavishly copied typologies and, in particular, ornamentations that were originally planned for hand production. Beyond this aesthetic response to machine production, there was also an ideological response: this was essentially to the alienation brought about by industrialism – man had become a 'mere appendage to the machine' as Marx had argued. However, while Morris and the ARTS AND CRAFTS movement solved these problems with a return to a medieval ideal of craft production, outside England at the turn of the century the debate was taken up and resolved differently.

Pevsner and many of his followers consistently linked the ideology of William Morris directly through to Hermann MUTHESIUS and on to the DEUTSCHE WERKBUND from 1907. But in recent years design historians, particularly John Heskett, have linked the establishment of a moral debate over commodity production to the development of bourgeois liberalism towards the end of the 19th c. The Werkbund was important in trying to bring clarity to a melange of activity in design between 1880 and 1914. Its two main tenets were firstly that artistic endeavour and technical and mechanical practice were not mutually exclusive, but instead were reconcilable, and secondly that architecture, and by extension design, was expressive of national culture – national types therefore subsequently provided the basis for accepted cultural standards.

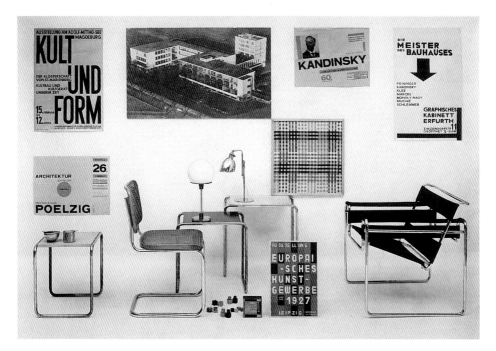

Following World War I the tenets of Modernism were mature in the Netherlands, Germany, France and the new Soviet Union, though at the same time the national boundaries between their individual contributions were breaking down, so that by the 1930s, Modernism came to be known as the INTERNATIONAL STYLE. The period from 1914 to 1930 is also referred to as Pioneer Modernism by Paul Greenhalgh.

Each strand of Pioneer Modernism had a focus: this could be a journal, institution or gallery which allowed designers and artists to come together to formulate a position and ultimately a movement. In Russia CONSTRUCTIVISM and SUPREMATISM came to the fore in the wake of the Revolution. It is generally felt that while champions of these movements such as Kasimir MALEVICH, El LISSITZKY and Vladimir TATLIN aimed to break free of traditional conceptions of the fine arts to involve themselves in what they saw as a more democratic and less elitist cultural production, which might include theatre, posters, monuments and constructions, their material contributions to Modernism did not reach far into the field of design. None the less, their politics and examples provided significant

A major influence in the **Modern Movement** *was the Bauhaus, as is clearly shown by these works produced there in the mid 1920s. Works displayed include furniture by Marcel Breuer, posters by Walter Dexel and Herbert Bayer and ashtrays by Marianne Brandt. In the centre is an aerial view of Walter Gropius's Dessau Bauhaus building.*

models for succeeding generations. Of particular importance in their work was the suggestion of the universalism of experience; that we all share a common vocabulary of both natural and abstract symbolism.

It has been argued that Russian Constructivism was largely received in the West stripped of its political vigour, it having been reduced to a constructive aesthetic. Yet the Dutch DE STIJL movement was influenced by the Constructivists, in particular by El Lissitzky. While they also considered the 'universality' of their aesthetic ideology, they made a more forceful contribution to Modernism with their exploration of space which was based on NEO-PLASTICISM. Drawing from a range of philosophical backgrounds, including Neo-Platonism and *Gestalt*, the *De Stijl* magazine advocated the reduction of the conception of space to systems of co-ordinates which did not suggest enclosure and made a minimum distinction between the interior and exterior of a construction, be it a building or a chair. Thus the ideas of pure, harmonic design were enshrined in Modernist ideology.

Partly due to the influence of Theo van DOESBURG, this was picked up at the BAUHAUS in Germany, which remains perhaps the most potent symbol of Modernism. During its existence from 1919 to 1933, particularly under the influence of Walter GROPIUS, Modernist canons were brought together. At the Bauhaus the idea of breaking down barriers between the various disciplines of art, design, craft and architecture was propagated and explored in the context of the school, to produce objects, paintings and buildings as *Gesamtkunstwerke* – 'total art works'. The school itself acted as an important centre and launch pad for Modernism. Many of the prototypes of furniture that later became the CLASSICS of the movement were created there. In France, LE CORBUSIER made explicit through his publications, in particular *Vers une Architecture* (1923), the importance of the extension of Modernism to town planning and beyond to the whole ideological destiny of society.

The general aesthetic, which through the activities of these centres has come to be understood as representing the Modern Movement could be described as follows: the use of steel frames with concrete and glass infillings in architecture; the use of new industrial materials such as TUBULAR STEEL and PLYWOOD in furniture; the use of abstraction and suppression of ornament and colour; the exposure of structure. However, beyond these stylistic features, there are also several ideological facets by which the movement may be identified: decompartmentalization, social morality, truth, technology, function, progress, anti-HISTORICISM, internationalism, universality, transformation of consciousness and theology.

The dominant concern of the Modern Movement was to break down barriers between aesthetics, technology and society so that an appropriate design of the highest visual and practical quality could be produced for the mass of the population. The movement was concerned with social morality because its exponents hoped to improve the conditions of society. Many Modernists felt that in industrial society the masses had been brutalized by the economic and political processes that shaped their lives. In response to this alienation, they proposed that truth should be given primacy. In aesthetic terms this meant, for instance, that decoration should not mask the way a product was made, its constructional basis or spatial honesty. Objects had to express what they were. The total work of art implied that there should be no hierarchy between the arts. Embracing technology meant that products could be mass produced and in turn reach the masses on the streets. By stressing the functional, objects would first of all work well, but also attain a high aesthetic value in their honesty. This may seem to reflect Louis Sullivan's notion that 'form follows function'; on the other hand, it has been seen as a negation of expressive qualities in design. A reading of Le Corbusier, however, would suggest that this was not exactly the case – expressive values were part of aesthetic progress. Additionally, progress encompassed the evolution of political structures, technology and aesthetics. A natural progression from democracy to Socialism was part of this. Historical styles and technologies had to be eliminated if the human race was to progress. This anti-historicism did not mean that ideas of great artists of the past were not used; the past could be reused, but not to evoke memory. Abstraction avoided the use of any narrative or symbolism in design, thus avoiding historicism. If historicism was referential in terms of time, then nationalism was in terms of place. Thus internationalism and universality were important in overcoming divisions in the same way, and Modernists sought to break down divisions between disciplines and classes of consumer. To seek an internationalist style of design was not new; practitioners associated with ART NOUVEAU had first suggested it, nature being their universal language. In their pure abstraction, Modernist aesthetics also pertained to an almost Platonic belief in the existence of a universal, timeless beauty. At the same time, design was believed to have the ability to transform the consciousness, in that by improving environmental conditions through design, one could also affect the psychological condition of those who experienced them. This cause and effect outlook may be rooted in the ascendancy of *Gestalt* psychology in the first two decades of the 20th c. as well as in the growth of behaviourism.

Such tenets of Modernism may appear restrictive by comparison with Modernism in the fine arts. As a timeless morality, these beliefs were not to refer to the immediate historical

Decorative ironwork by Antoni Gaudí at the Casa Vicéns in Barcelona (c.1880), typical of **Modernisme**.

context within which they were generated. None the less, the extreme claims made by the Modern Movement were only part of the wild changes that took place on the visual and social landscape of Europe between 1900 and 1930. Alongside the rapid urbanization and industrialization of Europe and the advent of electricity, motor cars, telephones, cinema and skyscrapers, there were also the effects of the thinkers Marx, Nietzsche and Freud, whose secular materialism brought new world views. Everywhere there was the thought that the world was capable of fundamental change.

Part of the failure of Modernism to be carried through to its logical universal end was caused by the discrepancy between the belief in a stable, all-pervasive truth and the dynamic flux of the industrialized world. Following its transition into the International Style, Modernism was perceived by some to be 'selling out to capitalism', becoming merely a sleek style rather than a holistic and radical programme for society. Echoes of Modernism, in the sense of creating a centrally controlled cultural production, were appropriated in varying degrees either by the rising Fascist forces in Germany, Italy, Spain and Portugal in the 1930s or by Soviet-dominated regimes in Central and Eastern Europe. The radical Spanish architect, Oriol BOHIGAS, reflecting on this situation commented in 1968, 'We no longer consider the possibility of a "total design" . . . because we are now aware of the fact that this is also the method of all despotisms that often attempt to create such a world in which one expresses the formal order of objects and one ignores, on the other hand, the disorder of men.'

Finally, with the growing dissatisfaction with the claims of Modernists in the post-1945 period, it was argued, particularly in the arena of semiotics, that there was a difference between intended meaning and perceived meaning – that the reading and interpretation of objects was invariably different from the meaning which the producer intended. Furthermore, the producer had no control over the consumer. Often the claims of the Modernists have been exaggerated (for instance by Tom Wolfe in *From Bauhaus to Our House*) in order to ridicule them. If these claims have caused a rejection of Modernism by many designers and commentators, then it is remembered by many others that they were generated along with 'the same wave of protest that made the dignity of all human beings the absolute prerequisite for cultural activity' (Greenhalgh, 1990).

☐ P. Johnson, *The Machine Age* (1934); Pevsner (1936); J.M. Richards, *An Introduction to Modern Architecture* (1940); S. Giedion, *Space, Time and Architecture* (1941); Banham (1960); C. Jencks, *Le Corbusier and the Tragic View of Architecture* (1973); M. Berman, *All That is Solid Melts into Air: The Experience of Modernity* (1983); Thackara (1988); Greenhalgh (1990)

Moderne is a term that was used in the USA during the 1920s and 30s to describe a style which lies somewhere between ART DECO and the MODERN MOVEMENT, with influences from the WIENER WERKSTÄTTE. It thus featured the heavy use of CHROMIUM and other new materials, while not necessarily eschewing a decorative feel. The designs of Donald DESKEY are often considered the zenith of Moderne.

Modernism *see* MODERN MOVEMENT

Modernisme or Modernismo is often a confusing term, for, despite its name, it refers to an ART NOUVEAU-type movement in Spain, and more specifically in Catalonia, from approximately 1880 to 1910 and not to the MODERN MOVEMENT. Its principal exponents were Antoni GAUDÍ, Lluís Domènech i Muntaner and Josep Puig i Cadalfach. While it embraced the national romanticism of the ARTS AND CRAFTS movement, it also carried a progressive belief in science and technology. This was an attractive prospect to the Catalan liberal bourgeoisie and, unlike the Arts and Crafts, it became a popular movement. The style thus

The Law of Series *(1925), a photomontage created by* **Moholy-Nagy**.

pervades many of Catalonia's major towns. Due in part to Spain's relative cultural isolation from the rest of Europe in this period, it was a particularly extreme version of Art Nouveau, with bulbous, exaggerated forms. Modernisme was notable, in design terms, for the architect's desire to design everything from tiling to fittings and furniture.

☐J. Marfany, *Aspectes del Modernisme* (1975)

Modernismo *see* MODERNISME

Modo (f.1977) is an architecture and design magazine. Its first director was Alessandro MENDINI and its editorial policy is to link the problems of planning to those pertaining to anthropology, social customs, industrial techniques and craftsmanship. In 1984 Andrea BRANZI became its director.

Moholy-Nagy, László (1895–1946) was born in southern Hungary. His legal studies in Budapest were curtailed by World War I, in which he was wounded while serving as an artillery officer. During his convalescence he rekindled his childhood interest in drawing. After a short and uninspiring stay in Vienna in

1920, he was exposed to the cosmopolitan, avant-garde ambience of Berlin. There he took up painting and experimental photography with his wife Lucia. He had already come into contact in Hungary with the *Ma* (Today) group, young Russian-inspired art-activists who were convinced of the role art had to play in a revolutionary society. First in Vienna and then in Berlin he became the representative for their magazine of the same name. He soon moved into CONSTRUCTIVISM in his painting, using found objects and embracing the machine aesthetic. Despite his obvious lack of experience as a designer and his poor German, in 1923 he was invited by Walter GROPIUS to teach at the BAUHAUS, mainly on the strength of Gropius's enthusiasm at their first meeting in 1921 for 'the character and direction of his work'. Largely because of his linguistic difficulties, he avoided any mysticism or intricate philosophies in his teaching at the Bauhaus, unlike his predecessor, Johannes ITTEN. He was put in charge of the metal workshop and the preliminary course alongside Josef ALBERS. In 1929 he outlined this foundation course in a book, *Von Material zu Architektur (The New Vision)*, and co-edited with Gropius the Bauhaus books, which he also designed. He was influential in moving the Bauhaus away from what Albers described as 'personal expression and individualistic graphic and pictorial representation of material, to a more rational, economic and structural use of the material itself.'

On leaving the Bauhaus in 1928, Moholy-Nagy worked as a designer, photographer, film-maker and exhibition designer in Berlin, Amsterdam and London. In Berlin he designed sets for the Kroll Opera. In London he designed a mobile exhibit for Imperial Airways, posters for London Transport and made a film for an association of lobster catchers.

At Gropius's invitation, in 1937, Moholy-Nagy moved to the USA, where he became a director of the school of design at the Association of Arts and Industries in Chicago. Hoping to recreate the Bauhaus ideology, he named the school 'The New Bauhaus: American School of Design'. At the same time he founded the Chicago Institute of Design Research with Sigfried GIEDION as its director. In 1944 this became the Institute of Design, and in 1949, three years after Moholy-Nagy's death, it became part of the Illinois Institute of Technology. His influence, then, was both as an educator and as a designer and artist.

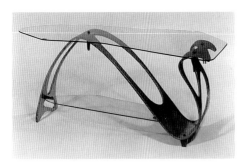

The maple plywood base of **Mollino**'s *table (c.1950) shows his interest in biomorphism.*

□L. Moholy-Nagy, *Von Material zu Architektur* (1929), trans. as *The New Vision* (1932); *Vision in Motion* (1946); S. Moholy-Nagy, *Moholy-Nagy: Experiment in Totality* (1950); R. Kostelanetz, *Moholy-Nagy* (1972); H. Spencer, *Pioneers of Modern Typography* (1982); K. Passuth, *Moholy-Nagy* (1985)

Mollino, Carlo (1905–73) was born in Turin where he studied architecture, graduating in 1931. He worked with his father, an engineer (1930–36), and his architectural projects include the Fascist headquarters in Voghera (1934). Even when Mollino began to work independently in 1936, his design method continued to be based on that inherited from his father, using accepted practices of construction and referring to catalogues of building and decorating materials available on the market. Thus his architecture, interior designs and furnishings became a collage of materials that were easy to obtain. A man of flamboyant character, motor-racing, skiing, aeronautics, fashion, the occult and erotica figured among Mollino's interests. His architectural and design projects were frequently characterized by a fluid, curvilinear feel which, to some extent, reflects the influence of Belgian ART NOUVEAU and also of Antoni GAUDÍ (indeed in 1949 he designed a chair called Gaudí; Oscar TUSQUETS in turn designed a chair in 1986 combining the influences of Mollino and Gaudí). In the late 1940s, his strongly biomorphic furniture designs (*see* BIOMORPHISM) made use of bent PLYWOOD.

Like Gaudí, Mollino combined daring distortions of visual idioms with technical developments. During the 40s he patented several constructional inventions; these included a lightweight concrete construction system, a solid wooden construction system for wooden panels that used no glue and prevented warping, and quick-lock joints for tubular scaffolding. From the 50s, Mollino was attracted to the idea of working as a designer for mass production and in 1960 he took designs for cutlery for Reed and Barton to prototype stage. None the less, his drawings showed infinite variations which were at odds with the very notion of mass production. From 1952 he taught in the faculty of architecture at the Turin Polytechnic, becoming the faculty's director in 1962. Many of his architectural projects, such as an equestrian centre, the Ippica (1937), have subsequently been demolished or were never carried out. Likewise, his interior decorations and furnishings are mostly known through photographs. Mollino's work re-emerged in the early 80s with the general interest at the time in design of the 50s. Much of his exquisite detailing which never reached production was emulated in contemporary furniture designs, translating forms, for instance from wood to ALUMINIUM.

□G. Brino, *Carlo Mollino: Architecture as Autobiography* (1987)

Monguzzi, Bruno (b.1941) was born in Ticino, Switzerland, and studied at the Ecole des Arts Décoratifs, Geneva, St Martin's School of Art, London, and the London College of Printing (1956–61). While Swiss typography provided a strong formalist element in his work, as a student he was equally inspired by American work, such as that of Gene Federico, Herb LUBALIN and Lou DORFSMAN, and then from 1961 by the approach of Antonio Boggeri. In 1961 he moved to Milan and joined STUDIO BOGGERI. While he was there he worked for Pirelli and Roche, among other clients. Since 1963 he has mostly worked as a freelance designer based in Milan but has also worked in London, New York and Montreal. He has done a considerable amount of work designing exhibitions (e.g., nine pavilions for the Expo '67 in Montreal). Perhaps his best-known poster is that designed in 1980 to raise aid for the Irpinia earthquake victims.

□B. Monguzzi, *Note per una Tipografia Informativa* (1964); *Lo Studio Boggeri 1933–1981* (1981)

Monotype Corporation (1887–1992) was founded by Tolbert Lanston as the Lanston

Monotype Company. This American inventor had devised a type-composing machine after inspecting a Hollerith Tabulator (a machine for presenting figures in tabular form) and set out to develop it with backers. Due to a shortage of capital for its development the company sought backing in England, and the Lanston Monotype Corporation was founded there in 1897. A factory was built at Salfords in Surrey in 1902, and the company became the Monotype Corporation Ltd in 1931.

The Monotype machine differed from that of its main competitor, LINOTYPE, in that each piece of type was individually produced as a letter, and not as a line. It suffered from a lack of fine typefaces, and Imprint, which was produced for the journal of the same name (*see* IMPRINT) in 1912, was the first original type design to be cut for mechanical composition. It showed that Monotype could compete in quality with traditional typefoundries. In 1922 Stanley MORISON was appointed as typographical advisor. Through the 20s and 30s, Monotype advanced rapidly in the production of new typefaces: Morison brought Baskerville, Fournier, Garamond, GILL Sans and Times New Roman into Monotype use, in turn promoting their use or revival.

After World War II Monotype moved into filmsetting (*see* PHOTOSETTING). Through the 60s it also developed its computer-aided typesetting capabilities and introduced the world's first laser typesetting system, the Lasercomp, in 1976. In 1992 the corporation went into liquidation, though its typeface section continued on its own.

Morison, Stanley (1889–1967) worked for a string of publishers until he was appointed typographical adviser to the British MONO-TYPE CORPORATION in 1922. He also launched the scholarly typographic magazine *The FLEURON* in the same year. For Monotype, Morison revived the typefaces Garamond (1922), Baskerville (1923) and Fournier (1924) and commissioned a number of new typefaces from Eric GILL, including Gill Sans (1928). In 1931 he was commissioned by the London newspaper, *The Times*, to supervise a new design; he thus produced the Times New Roman typeface, one of the most widely used typefaces of the 20th c. He was also typographical adviser to the Cambridge University Press from 1925 and designed book jackets for Victor Gollancz in 1929. He was a prolific writer on

Moser's *poster for the thirteenth Vienna Secession exhibition of 1903.*

the history and theory of typography, his best-known works being *First Principles of Typography* (1929) and *Pioneers of Modern Typography* (1969).

☐F. Baudin, *Stanley Morison et la Tradition Typographique* (exh. cat., Bibliothèque Albert 1er, Brussels, 1966); J. Moran, *Stanley Morison: His Typographic Achievement* (1971); H. Jones, *Morison Displayed: An Examination of his Early Typographic Work* (1976)

Moser, Koloman (1868–1918) studied in Vienna at the Academy (1886–92) and at the School of Arts and Crafts (1892–95), where he taught from 1899. His graphic design showed a progressive shift from an organic to a more geometric style, typical of the SECESSION, of which he was a founder. With Josef HOFF-MANN he established the WIENER WERK-STÄTTE in 1903, and his furniture designs for the Werkstätte were similarly rectilinear and refined.

☐D. Baroni and A. D'Auria, *Kolo Moser: Graphic Artist and Designer* (1984)

Moulton, Alex (b.1920) is best known as the British man who reinvented the bicycle. He studied engineering at Cambridge (1938–39 and 1947–49) and worked in the research department of the Bristol Aeroplane Company during World War II. However, on joining his family's rubber-manufacturing business, he set out to design, develop and perfect innovative forms of rubber suspension for automobiles after the War. In conjunction with Alec ISSI-GONIS he developed the suspension for the Mini (1959). Three years later he designed the cycling equivalent of the Mini, the Moulton Compact Bicycle. This revolutionary bicycle with its small wheels and rubber suspension sold well initially, but was quickly superseded by cheap, thick-tyred imitations. He produced two more versions of the bicycle (in 1983 and 1990), which were highly expensive but superb in their handling.

Mourgue, Olivier (b.1939) was one of France's foremost designers during the 1960s. He studied at the Ecole Boulle (1954–58) and the Ecole Nationale Supérieure des Arts Décoratifs (1958–60) in Paris. He subsequently produced a series of furniture for Airborne, which was distinguished by its anthropomorphic suggestions and sculptural qualities, achieved using a polyester shell.

Poster by **Müller-Brockmann** *for a concert in the Zurich Tonhalle (1960).*

Müller-Brockmann, Josef (b.1914) was born at Rapperswil, Switzerland, and attended the School of Arts and Crafts in Zurich, opening his studio there in 1936. In 1957 he was made a professor of graphic design at the School of Arts and Crafts and in 1958 he became a founder and co-editor of NEW GRAPHIC DESIGN, a tri-lingual journal propagating the aims of the SWISS SCHOOL of graphic design. He was most famed in the late 1950s for a series of concert posters for the Zurich Tonhalle, in which the structural harmony of music was reflected in the typographic layout. He was also a design consultant to IBM Europe from 1966. Apart from his articles for *New Graphic Design*, he also published *The Graphic Artist and his Design Problems* (1961), *A History of Visual Communication* (1971) and, with Shizuko Müller-Yoshikawa, *A History of the Poster* (1971).

Munari, Bruno (b.1907) was born in Milan, and his early artistic work was strongly influenced by FUTURISM. In the 1930s he gradually moved away from this tendency and by 1945 was designing products, lay-outs and above all, toys for children, collaborating on such projects with DANESE from 1957. In 1962 he co-ordinated the first large exhibition of kinetic art for OLIVETTI. His major concern has been in working in non-elitist communication: he writes extensively and has centred much of his work around art and design education for children.

☐ A. Tanchis, *Bruno Munari: From Futurism to Post-Industrial Design* (1987)

Murray, Keith (1892–1981) was born in Auckland, New Zealand, but travelled to England in 1906 and, after service in World War I, studied at the Architectural Association in London. He found little architectural work in the depressed climate of the 1920s and was therefore driven to seek work in design. He began designing glass in the early 1930s and then ceramics for Josiah WEDGWOOD & SONS LTD from 1933. The clear, functional simplicity of his designs of the 1930s combined a style suggestive of the aims of the MODERN MOVEMENT with a traditional 18th-c. classicist approach to style. A survey of *The ARCHITECTURAL REVIEW* would suggest that there was a wider acceptance of the Georgian within Modernist canons in 1930s Britain. After World War II Murray himself returned to architecture as a partner at Murray, Ward and Partners.

☐ M. Batkin, *Wedgwood Ceramics 1846–1959* (1982)

Museum of Modern Art (MOMA) (f.1929) in New York was chartered by the State of New York 'to encourage and develop the study of the modern arts and the application of such arts to manufacture and practical life.' Under its first director, Alfred H. Barr, it was therefore the first museum to include a curatorial department devoted to architecture and industrial design. Industrial design became a separate department in 1940 with Eliot NOYES as its director. The museum was a strong supporter of the MODERN MOVEMENT, and its first exhibitions included: The INTERNATIONAL STYLE (1932), which gave rise to the term of the same name, Machine Art (1932) and ORGANIC DESIGN in Home Furnishings (1940), which firmly established the softened Modernism of Charles EAMES and Eero SAARINEN in the 1940s. It also held annual exhibitions of 'GOOD DESIGN' (1950–55), under the direction of Edgar Kaufmann. In 1966 it was host to Robert VENTURI's import-

ant series of lectures which formed the basis of his seminal book, *Complexity and Contradiction in Modern Architecture* (1966), and in 1972 to the important exhibition of Italian RADICAL DESIGN, Italy: The New Domestic Landscape, mounted by Emilio AMBASZ. Thus MOMA has consistently been a pioneer in the introduction of new trends and theories into design in the USA.

Muthesius, Hermann (1861–1927) read philosophy (1881–83) and then architecture in Berlin (1883–87), following which he travelled widely in China, Thailand, India and Egypt as well as working for a German architectural firm in Tokyo (1887–91). In 1893 he became a civil servant to the Prussian government, editing its official architectural journal. Then in 1896 he was appointed to the German embassy in London. While in Britain, he became friendly with Charles Rennie MACKINTOSH, Walter Crane and Herbert MacNair as well as publishing numerous articles in *Dekorative Kunst* on the ARTS AND CRAFTS movement. The most influential of his books were *Stilarchitektur und Baukunst* (Architectural Styles and the Art of Building, 1903) and the three-volume *Das Englische Haus* (The English House, 1904 and 1905). The latter is in part a celebration of the English way of life and an ideal of the home. Muthesius was writing mostly about houses commissioned by the upper middle classes, who were creating a past for themselves; English taste did not draw on its industrial culture, in which, as Muthesius realized, lay the future. He championed 'modernity' as lying in 'reason and practicality'.

As an official in the Prussian trade ministry (1904–26), he helped to reform Prussian schools of design. He was also important in the foundation of the DEUTSCHE WERKBUND in 1907, within which his *bête noire* was that he saw JUGENDSTIL as containing the death throes of HISTORICISM, rather than the seeds of regeneration. Industry, rather than art, with its potential for producing standardized designs which themselves fell within national stylistic boundaries, had the vigour and energy to inspire a new cultural revolution. In the Werkbund, Muthesius came into conflict with Henry van de VELDE in 1914 due to this opinion, which was to become a fundamental point of conflict in the subsequent development of design.

N

Narrative Architecture is an expression that was developed by the architect and interior designer Nigel COATES in the mid-1980s and was used for his group, Narrative Architecture Today (NATO), founded in London in 1983. Coates insists that the term refers to an 'attitude' rather than a style. He noted that the function of a building has less to do with its architectonic structure and more to do with aspects that are virtually invisible – modern environments are largely dependent on electric cables, telephone lines and radio waves. Thus architecture is open to redefinition. Realizing that the symbolic function of a building could be multi-layered, 'so that a restaurant might become a stage', he claims that they should be allowed a mental dimension, a time dimension and, therefore, a narrative dimension. In other words, he looked at the interior as providing a scenario which goes beyond being a space to inhabit: it also invokes psychological responses by being read like a story. Thus, if the outside world involves energy, volatility, chaos and conflict, then these things should be reflected and exaggerated in interiors. Furthermore, the layering of references to the past and the future might also accentuate the present. If such notions come close to a filmic, televisual world view, in which time is distorted, stories with an array of sub-plots are woven and conflicting images are 'banged together', then Narrative Architecture deliberately uses the language of film and television. Thus, in developing a project, the architect should create a picture of the environment in action, highlighting the experiences of being in that space rather than the space on its own – drawing is thus an important activity of the designer. Interestingly he likens this approach to that of film-directors, in particular Eisenstein, who investigate the combination and juxtaposition of images to evoke a general impression in the viewer. In the manipulation of visual information Narrative Architecture therefore draws on a wide range of intellectual sources outside architecture, such as linguistics, art theory and structuralism.

Such an approach may fall under the general umbrella of POSTMODERNISM alongside RADICAL DESIGN or ANTI-DESIGN, except that it discards their Utopianism. Equally, while Robert VENTURI tended to suggest the application of the signs and symbols of the commercial world to architecture, Narrative Architecture looked to a more subtle use and reuse of modern imagery in which its sensuous, experiential aspects played an important role. Narrative Architecture as a working concept was confined to Coates's own designs. None the less, similar approaches may be recognized in the design work of the Spaniards Alfredo Arribas and Javier MARISCAL during the 80s, as well as close colleagues of Coates in Britain

Narrative Architecture *demonstrated by the work of Nigel Coates and Shi Yu Chen in the Caffè Bongo, Tokyo, in 1986.*

ranging from Tom DIXON to Daniel WEIL.
□N. Coates in Thackara (1988)

National Institute of Design (f.1961) is
India's only design college and was established
in the Gujarati city of Ahmadabad on the
recommendation of a report by Ray and
Charles EAMES which had been commissioned
by the Indian government. The government
was seeking advice on a programme of design
training that would help India's nascent small
industries develop and prosper against a background of deteriorating quality of goods. By
the 1990s the Institute had a teaching staff of 45
and up to 300 students. It offers its own
consultancy service in product design, furniture, ceramics, textiles, visual communication
and environmental projects. While it attempted
to maintain a national craft tradition, the
growing middle-class demand for consumer
products in India undermined this initiative
somewhat, and by the 1980s the institute's
alumni were beginning to form design consultancies to work in a market economy.

Nelson, George (1908–86) was one of the
most influential figures in the development of
design in the USA. After studying architecture
at Yale University he was awarded the Rome
Prize and went to study at the American
Academy in Rome (1932–34). While in Rome
he prepared himself for returning to unemploy-
ment in the Depression years in the USA by
writing a series of articles on leading European
architects. Subsequently he not only brought
back to the USA a strong modern European
influence, but also found his way into writing
about design. He became co-managing editor
with the designer Henry Wright of *Architectural
Forum* – a magazine dedicated to corporate
interests and, like Britain's *ARCHITECTURAL
REVIEW*, to the promotion of the MODERN
MOVEMENT. In 1944 he created the Storage
Wall, with which he established his reputation
as a furniture designer, and two years later he
and Henry Wright wrote *Tomorrow's House*,
which stimulated investigations in design.

He worked for HERMAN MILLER as director
of design from 1946. There he developed the
Action Office system (1964) with Robert
PROPST, which revolutionized the design of
office space, in particular with its subsequent
development, the Action Office 2 (1968). The
Action Office introduced the concept of storage
panels as space dividers, thus avoiding central

The ball and spoke clock designed by **Nelson** *in the 1950s.*

focus on the office desk. Nelson also designed
the Editor 2 typewriter for OLIVETTI.
□G. Nelson and H. Wright, *Tomorrow's House*
(1946); G. Nelson, *The Problems of Design* (1957)

neo-liberty was the term, used initially in Italy
and subsequently in Spain, for the revival of the
ART NOUVEAU style. The term was first used
by Paolo Portoghese in 1958 and was derived
from STILE LIBERTY, the Italian name for Art
Nouveau. Neo-liberty presented a POP version
of stile liberty and applied the style to mass-
produced objects, while at the same time
reviving a craft tradition to undercut the
machine aesthetic of the MODERN MOVE-
MENT. It was mostly applied to furniture,
lighting and interior design. Exponents of this
essentially curvilinear style included Franco
ALBINI, Gae AULENTI, Vittorio Gregotti and
Carlo MOLLINO.
□R. Banham 'Neo-Liberty: The Italian
Retreat from Modern Architecture' in *Architectural Review*, No. 747, 1959; *Neoliberty e Din-
torni* (exh. cat., Salone del Mobile di Milano,
Milan, 1989)

neo-Modernism is a term whose name alone
would seem to suggest a return to some of the
avant-garde intent of the MODERN MOVE-
MENT following the vagaries and excesses of
POSTMODERNISM. It was a position advocated
in 1981 by Franco Raggi, then editor of *MODO*,

Between 1926 and 1928 Theo van Doesburg translated De Stijl forms into three-dimensional **neo-Plasticism** *at the Aubette bar, Strasburg.*

and Gaetano PESCE at the ASPEN INTER-NATIONAL DESIGN CONFERENCE and rejected the universalism of the INTER-NATIONAL STYLE, claiming it to be, 'one solution for thousands of problems'. Thus, unlike Modernism, neo-Modernism argued for pluralism – meeting design problems with specific, localized responses. (Such a position may be seen as a revitalization of Italian REALISM.) However, within it the motif of 'form follows function' that was central to FUNCTIONALISM is extended to include the user's *aesthetic* needs. (This also bears some similarity to Andrea BRANZI's notion of NEW DESIGN.) Stylistically, neo-Modernism has been used since 1980 to describe objects or graphic imagery that express the anti-HISTORICISM of the Modern Movement, but it also has a more sensuous side to it. A revitalization of interest in DANISH MODERN in the early 90s might be seen as part of this. Equally, much of the public spaces programme promoted in Spain by Oriol BOHIGAS during the 80s also safeguarded the incorporation of provocatively avant-garde projects while maintaining a sense of place and expression.

neo-Plasticism is an aesthetic approach closely aligned with the DE STIJL movement. The term is a direct translation from the French, *néo-plasticisme*, itself a vague translation of the Dutch, *nieuwe beelding*, meaning something like 'new image creation' or perhaps 'new structure', though many of its nuances are lost in translation. *Nieuwe beelding* itself is a term used by Piet Mondrian, a leading member of the De Stijl group before 1920. Mondrian himself borrowed it from Matthieu Schoenmaekers, a former Catholic priest and theosophist philosopher. In their writings, Theo van DOESBURG and Mondrian combined Schoenmaekers's theosophist writings with a Hegelian philosophical tradition, though Mondrian also incorporated the anthroposophic writings of Rudolf Steiner. The outcome was a world view couched in oppositions of universal/individual, horizontal/vertical, masculine/feminine and so on. They believed that the history of art was the history of a gradual evolution from the Italian 14th-c. painter, Giotto, through to pure abstraction. Mondrian saw *nieuwe beelding* as a perfect, modern resolution of the tensions in that history. This was seen as a development from 'naturalistic' representations in painting to the expression of spiritual values. Furthermore, this resolution was seen as an extension of the German art historian Heinrich Wölfflin's view of art history whereby its development involved the constant swing between the Classical and the Baroque, or order and expression. *Nieuwe beelding* harmonized this tension. This may be seen in Mondrian's own paintings of the 1920s, where form was progressively broken down to a harmony of horizontal and vertical black lines on a white background and geometric planes of primary colours. Van Doesburg, however, refuted the claim that art had thus reached its highest plane. He believed that the developmental process continued indefinitely. Thus, believing that Mondrian's horizontals and verticals were a return to Classicism, van Doesburg introduced the diagonal to his paintings, rupturing the assumed harmony and providing another Hegelian 'antithesis' to Mondrian's 'thesis'. This was his own 'Baroque', which he called 'Elementarism' or 'Counter-Composition'.

Van Doesburg, along with Hans Arp and Sophie Taeuber-Arp, carried these notions through to the design work in his Aubette bar in Strasburg (1926–28). This extensive commission – including the design of several multifunctional rooms as well as virtually every piece of equipment – was treated as a vast painting within which the user participated. His Elementarist style was employed in the interior decoration, with rectangular colour planes of varying intensity to suit the use and architectural prerequisites of each room. The Aubette was undoubtedly a visual manifesto of the design application of *nieuwe beelding*, though it met with little public enthusiasm, and most of the decorations were soon dismantled. It was none the less well recorded and reconstructed in several exhibitions from 1960. In the early 90s the bar was restored to van Doesburg's designs.

The origins and fate of neo-Plasticism (and, by extension, the Aubette) may be indicative of those of the MODERN MOVEMENT as a whole. Originating from an ideological or philosophical standpoint, both developed from painting into design and architecture. They were both generally unpopular, but were revered by critics and those who followed in their tradition. The term neo-Plasticism itself has been open to misunderstandings, and the varying interpretations, even among its practitioners, also testify to the complexity and subtlety of Modernism.

□ Overy (1991)

Neue Grafik see NEW GRAPHIC DESIGN

Neurath, Otto (1882–1945) was the Viennese sociologist who developed the ISOTYPE visual information system. In 1925, with the support of the city council and several trade unions and other bodies, he founded the Gesellschafts- und Wirtschaftsmuseum (Social and Economic Museum), whose aim was to explain the council's programme of social reform. It was thus concerned with the presentation of information, and Neurath put together a team (including his future wife, Marie Reidemeister) to develop graphic methods for this purpose. It displayed statistics in pictorial form, thus quantified information on education, health provision and especially the large-scale Viennese housing programme was translated into a series of repeated images or unit-symbols. This system acquired the title 'Wiener Methode der Bildstatistik' (Vienna method of pictorial statistics). Marie Reidemeister – a graduate in mathematics and physics with some art-school training – took on the role of 'transformer', translating verbal or numerical information into a visual statement.

Both with an eye on the worsening political situation in Vienna and a desire to distribute the group's ideas internationally, Neurath set up a network of bases in Amsterdam (1932) and in London and New York (both in 1933). These bases were among sympathetic organizations; for instance in London, an arrangement was made with the World Association for Adult Education. In 1934, after civil war broke out briefly in Austria, Neurath and his colleagues left Vienna for The Hague. In 1935 they changed the name of their system to Isotype (International System of Typographic Picture Education). Much of their work during this period came from the USA (e.g., exhibition charts for the New York City Department of Health). Upon the German invasion of the Netherlands in 1940, Neurath and Reidemeister fled to Britain. They were briefly interned before resuming their Isotype work in 1941 and establishing the Isotype Institute in Oxford the following year. During World War II much of their work came from Adprint Ltd, a book-packaging firm, which conceived, designed and saw books through to production on behalf of publishers. These were normally complex, fully illustrated publications: among them were such government pamphlets as one designed to popularize the Beveridge Report on social security of 1943.

The Isotype Institute continued to function under Marie Neurath's direction after Neurath's death in 1945. Indeed, in the postwar reconstruction period its work flourished. The Neuraths' work provided a breakthrough in visual representation.

□ O. Neurath, *Empiricism and Sociology* (eds M. Neurath with O.S. Cohen, 1973)

New Design is a term that was in widespread use during the 1980s to describe much design of that decade, though it was more often qualified by place or discipline: hence 'New Italian

Design' or 'New Graphics'. Of course, the notion of 'the New' had often been invoked within the MODERN MOVEMENT, for example in Jan TSCHICHOLD's *Das Neue Typographie* (The New Typography, 1928), in the English version of LE CORBUSIER's *Vers une Architecture* (1923), published in 1937 as *Towards a New Architecture*, or in NEW GRAPHIC DESIGN (1958–64), the journal of the SWISS SCHOOL.

In the 1980s, however, it was used to refer to any style that broke from the formal tenets of RATIONALISM, FUNCTIONALISM or the INTERNATIONAL STYLE. This effectively includes all of POSTMODERNISM. A more precise definition may be found in the statements of the Italian philosopher and designer, Andrea BRANZI. In his 1984 book, *The Hot House: Italian New Wave Design*, he argues that the New Design broke away from the former homogenization of mass markets (which underpinned FORDISM, and by extension the International Style). He defends the intervention of the applied arts in design, 'full of signs and quotations, of metaphors and ornament'. He also sees the New Design as expressing the paradoxes and contradictions of postindustrial society (*see* POSTINDUSTRIALISM). In an exhibition that he organized in 1991 at the Pompidou Centre, Paris, entitled European Capitals of the New Design, he extended this notion beyond the Italian context to claim that New Design was the prevailing international style of the age, even though it was generated in specific centres such as Paris and Barcelona. Perhaps this concept is too broad to be of any critical use. For some, the term refers to tendencies that appeared after Postmodernism, while for others it describes a part of Postmodernism itself.

In the 'New Graphics' of the 1980s (sometimes referred to as 'New Wave') it is possible to detect the same tendency to move away from the anonymity of design for the mass market, towards greater emphasis on the authorial voice. If this implied less reliance on the single statement and on the use of clear, unambiguous typography (as seen in the work of Alan FLETCHER, for instance), then it also included a more complex use of colour, image and type. The use of COMPUTER-AIDED DESIGN was influential in this development. Thus the advances of László MOHOLY-NAGY's graphic design in the 1920s and 30s were extended through the complex interplay of photographic image and type. The SANS SERIF of the Swiss

School was also continued. This was an international tendency, as seen in the work of April GREIMAN and the CALIFORNIA NEW WAVE, as well as in work from the CRANBROOK ACADEMY OF ART in the USA, the studio of Gert DUMBAR in the Netherlands and Why Not Associates in London.

□ Branzi (1984); P. Dormer, *The New Furniture* (1987); H. Aldersey-Williams et al., *Cranbrook Design: The New Discourse* (1991)

New Graphic Design (1958–64) was issued in German (as *Neue Grafik*), French (as *Graphisme actuel*) and English from Zurich and was founded by pioneers of the SWISS SCHOOL of graphic design, Richard Lohse, Josef MÜLLER-BROCKMANN, Hans Neuburg and Carlo Vivarelli. It was one of the principal international promoters of the 'New International Style' which emanated from Zurich and Basle. Its first editorial recorded that its founders 'did not prize modernity for its own sake or applaud boldness and originality at all costs, but they value the attempt at a solution by constructive methods, not an illusory solution based on emotional, representational effects.' Regular articles either by or on figures such as Max BILL, Max HUBER, Anton STANKOWSKI and Ernst KELLER appeared, as well as features on other international designers with similar aims, such as STUDIO BOGGERI.

new typography *see* Jan TSCHICHOLD

New York World's Fair, 1939 was the last in a series of great international exhibitions stretching back to the Great Exhibition held in London in 1851. It was staged to celebrate the 150th anniversary of the inauguration of George Washington as first president of the USA, and democracy was central to the whole event. Its motto was 'Building the World of Tomorrow', and the exhibition included a model of the Utopian city of the future called 'Democracity'. The overall visual language employed in the scheme was that of the MODERN MOVEMENT, although of a form closer in style to the film *Metropolis* (1926) by Fritz Lang, László MOHOLY-NAGY's montage in the film *Things to Come* (1936) by Alexander Korda, or even *Flash Gordon* (1936) than to the strict tenets of LE CORBUSIER or Walter GROPIUS. The organizer's insistence on modernity as the overall design idiom – as had happened at the PARIS EXPOSITION DES ARTS

The Norman Bel Geddes Futurama exhibit at the **New York World's Fair, 1939.**

DÉCORATIFS ET INDUSTRIELS, 1925 – was taken up by the new generation of American industrial designers who dominated the Fair site. These included Raymond LOEWY, Norman BEL GEDDES, Walter Dorwin TEAGUE, and Henry DREYFUSS. The major decorative element in the show was STREAMFORM, and its overwhelming presence on the 1,200 acre site was important in establishing it as a visual feature of the marketing virtues of expendability and mass consumerism in the USA. The version of Modernism found in the highly-charged commercial arena of this exhibition contrasts strongly with that seen at the PARIS EXPOSITION UNIVERSELLE, 1937.

☐H. Harrison (ed.), *Dawn of a New Day: The New York World's Fair, 1939–40* (1980); P. Greenhalgh, *Ephemeral Vistas: The Expositions Universelles, Great Exhibitions and World's Fairs, 1851–1939* (1988)

Nissan (f.1911) started out in Tokyo as the Kwaishinsha Co. It was founded by Masujiro Hashiumoto, and its first car was the DAT (1914), the Japanese for 'hare'. In 1925 it merged with another car producer in Osaka, the Jitsuyo Jidosha Co., and in 1930 they produced a new car, the Datson – 'son of DAT'. Since 'son' in Japanese means 'ruin', it was changed to Datsun in the following year. In 1934 the company took on the name of Nissan and in 1936 made an agreement for technical co-operation with the car manufacturer Graham-Paige in the USA. This resulted in the prestigious new 70 series of

cars, which appeared in 1937 and was based on Graham-Paige's Crusador. Production of Nissan cars was interrupted by World War II, being resumed in 1947. An agreement with Austin in 1952 resulted in the first Anglo-Japanese car, the A40. In the face of competition from TOYOTA in the 1950s Nissan gained a reputation for mechanical excellence. Through the 1960s Nissan underwent a steady internationalization, with worldwide distribution. Research and development of new technology are undertaken by Nissan in Japan, in five plants specializing in different areas, at the Nissan Design International Center in San Diego, California, and at a European design centre in Brussels.

Nizzoli, Marcello (1887–1969) was born in Boretto, Reggio Emilia, Italy, and studied painting, architecture and graphics at the Acad-

Nissan *S-Cargo (1991).*

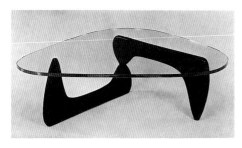

Table designed by **Noguchi** *(c.1940) and manufactured by Herman Miller from 1947.*

emy of Fine Arts in Parma (1910–13). He subsequently worked as a freelance painter and designer and became associated with exponents of FUTURISM in Milan and Rome. In 1918 he established a design studio in Milan, working with Giuseppe Terragni (1931–36). Until 1936 he worked on many exhibition design projects, including some with Edoardo Persico, the editor of the progressive architectural magazine *Casabella*, such as the 1934 Italian Aeronautical Exhibition in Milan, an event that proved a dramatic testimony to Italy's commitment to the modern age. He also produced graphic design work in the modern idiom. In 1936 he became chief consultant designer to OLIVETTI, working on its office machines. His greatest projects for Olivetti did not emerge until after World War II; these included the Lettera 22 typewriter (1950).
☐ G. Celant, *Marcello Nizzoli* (1968)

Noguchi, Isamu (1904–88) was a sculptor and designer celebrated in the USA for his organic-style furniture (*see* ORGANIC DESIGN) and wire and paper lampshades during the 1940s. He was born in Los Angeles and, after a childhood in Japan, returned to the USA to study medicine in 1918. He then studied sculpture in Paris (1927–28), where he knew the sculptors Constantin Brancusi and Alberto Giacometti, before making pottery in Kyoto. In 1931 he returned to the USA via Europe. After World War II he continued to work as a freelance designer and sculptor. Among his most important designs figure his glass-topped sculptural coffee table for HERMAN MILLER (c.1940) and a lamp – known in Japan as an Akari lamp – with three slender legs supporting a paper cylinder for KNOLL (1948).
☐ *Isamu Noguchi* (exh. cat., Whitney Museum, New York, 1968)

Noorda, Bob (b.1927) studied at the Institute of Industrial Arts and Crafts, Amsterdam (1944–47), but has worked as a graphic designer in Milan since 1952. In 1965 he co-founded UNIMARK INTERNATIONAL. His earlier work (e.g., his 1956 advertisement for Pirelli) is noteworthy for its bold use of imagery, but his most famous design is the signage for the Milan Metropolitan subway system (1964) which demonstrates his facility for restraint and clarity.

Noucentisme was the name given to a revival of Mediterranean classicism seen in Catalonia just before World War I. It superseded MODERNISME and remained in place primarily as an architectural style for 20 years.

Novecento emerged as an architecture and design movement in Italy in the 1920s. The Novecento group, formed in 1926, included Gio PONTI and Emilio Lancia. Unlike RATIONALISM, the impact of Novecento was stronger in the area of the traditional applied arts than in the products of the new, technological industries. It drew its aesthetic inspiration from the decorative arts of France and Austria, and in its stripped-down classicism it might be regarded as an Italian form of ART DECO. It exhibited influences of the Austrian designers Josef HOFFMANN, Dagobert Peche and other members of the WIENER WERKSTÄTTE, as well as the French cabinet-maker, Jacques-Emile RUHLMANN. While Alfonso and Renato Bialetti's Moka Express coffee-maker might be seen as a descendent of the Novecento idiom, as a style it was implemented more in architecture. Indeed, it superseded Rationalism as the major architectural style of Italian Fascism during the 1930s.

Noyes, Eliot (1910–77) studied architecture at Harvard University (1932–34, 1937–38), where he met Marcel BREUER and Walter GROPIUS. He then worked in their office in Cambridge, Massachusetts (1930–40). He was also director of the department of industrial design at New York's MUSEUM OF MODERN ART (1940–42, 1945–46) and was responsible for its important exhibition, ORGANIC DESIGN in Home Furnishings (1941–42). After World War II he was design director in the office of Norman BEL GEDDES (1946–47), who had a consultancy contract with IBM. Noyes set up his own practice in 1947 and also began transforming

IBM, becoming its corporate design consultant in 1956. He brought the lessons learnt from European Modernism, plus the influence of OLIVETTI'S DESIGN MANAGEMENT policy to the corporation, employing graphic designer Paul RAND to work on its CORPORATE IDENTITY and Marcel Breuer to design its buildings. The refinement of design brought the INTERNATIONAL STYLE to IBM's products such as the Selectric typewriter (1961). He was also design consultant to Westinghouse Electric from 1960, Mobil Oil from 1964 and PanAm (1969–72).

O

obsolescence often lies at the fulcrum of moral debates on consumerism and, thence, design. Planned obsolescence emerged in the USA in the 1950s as part of the strategies of large corporations. It meant that a product would have a limited life, either through its lack of physical durability or because it quickly became stylistically unfashionable. The second of these relied on the strategy of STYLING. Consumer loyalty to a brand would be created through advertising, CORPORATE IDENTITY strategies and after-sales service, so that the customer would continue to buy within the range of products offered by the same manufacturer. Ranges of products would then be planned and designed to serve this 'ladder' of consumerism. For supporters of such a system, work was thus guaranteed for all involved in the industry, including designers. Opponents such as Vance Packard saw this as an insidious manipulation of consumers, as well as being environmentally unjustifiable. In response some manufacturers, particularly in Germany and Scandinavia, have in their advertising and product planning emphasized the durability of their wares. In the 1980s, car manufacturers, notably BMW and VOLKSWAGEN, even began to develop the possibility of recycling parts.
☐ V. Packard, *The Waste Makers* (1960)

Odeon Style was a term given to a popular mixture of ART DECO and MODERNE seen in Britain in the 1930s. Its name originates from the Odeon cinemas which were opening at a

rate of an estimated two a week by 1935. They usually occupied prominent positions in the townscape and their lavish colours and use of CHROMIUM provided a significant visual counterpoint to the Depression of the decade. This helped to popularize the style, so that it became acceptable in domestic objects, particularly those representing modernity (e.g., radios).

Odermatt & Tissi (f.1968) is a Zurich-based graphic design studio which from its formation broke the rigid typographic rules of the SWISS SCHOOL. Rosemarie Tissi (b.1937) studied design at the School of Arts and Crafts, Zurich (1954–55), and joined Siegfried Odermatt's studio as an apprentice thereafter. In 1964 she designed a poster for E. Lutz & Co., in which letters, symbols and text are layered on one another. Odermatt had also studied at the School of Arts and Crafts (1942–44) but was largely self-taught. He mostly worked freelance until he established his studio in 1950. From *c.*1966 he began experimenting with type, bending and juxtaposing letter forms. After Tissi became a partner in the studio, they continued these experiments and also introduced strong colour fields from *c.*1980.

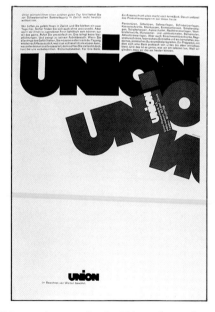

Odermatt's poster for the Union safe manufacturer (1968).

*Poster by **Olbrich** for an exhibition of the work of the artists' colony in Darmstadt (1901).*

Olbrich, Joseph Maria (1867–1908) was an Austrian architect who, along with Josef HOFFMANN, was the best-known designer to come out of the Viennese SECESSION. He worked under Otto WAGNER (1893–95) and in 1899 moved to Darmstadt at the invitation of the Grand Duke of Hesse, who was establishing an artists' colony there. His design work there for furniture and metalwork progressively broke away from the ART NOUVEAU obsession with naturalistic forms and moved towards abstract patterns and rounded geometric forms. At Darmstadt he was also influential on Peter BEHRENS.

Olivetti (f.1908) was founded in Ivrea, Italy, by Camillo Olivetti, following his studies of manufacturing in the USA. It succeeded CGS (Centimetro Grammo Secondo), a precision electrical instruments plant, which Olivetti had founded in 1896. Italy's first typewriter, the M I, was put into production in 1910. The company expanded steadily through World War I and during the 1920s, establishing its first allied foreign company, Hispano Olivetti SA in Barcelona, in 1929. Olivetti brought out Italy's first portable typewriter, the MP1, in 1932. It was designed by Aldon Magnelli with his brother, the abstract painter, Alberto Magnelli, and was the first typewriter to undergo STYLING. The Studio 42, created by Xanti SCHAWINSKY and the architects Luigi Figini and Gino Pollini, appeared in 1935, and was to mark the form of the modern typewriter for 40 years to come. Camillo's son Adriano took over as director-general in 1933, by which time Olivetti's distribution was world-wide. The following year, the factory's day nursery was opened as part of Adriano's visionary approach to commerce. This move was in keeping with the firm's programme of social welfare for its employees, which had existed since its beginnings. Adriano was not only important in the consolidation of Italian style, but was also an important social thinker; he joined the *Movimento Comunità* (Community Movement) and wrote widely on social issues; he also founded the journals *Zodiac* and *Urbanisticà*.

In 1936 Marcello NIZZOLI was employed as chief consultant designer, and his appointment confirmed the company's commitment to evolving a modern image for the whole of its production, from publicity to the machines themselves. Olivetti had thus established itself as a major international presence in office-

*Giovanni Pintori's poster for the **Olivetti** 82 Diaspron (1952).*

machine manufacture and had continued to expand through World War II, but it was not until after the War that it became known as an innovator in design. The company established itself more firmly in the international market by opening in the USA in 1946; accordingly, its research and development was increased by, for example, bringing in major designers on projects – a policy maintained ever since. Apart from the interventions of Nizzoli, Olivetti has acted almost as a godfather or umbrella company for many Milan-based designers: these include Franco ALBINI, Gae AULENTI, Mario BELLINI, Rodolfo Bonetto, Michele DE LUCCHI, Vico MAGISTRETTI, Carlo SCARPA and Marco ZANUSO. Ettore SOTTSASS's appointment as consultant to Olivetti in 1958 was important for both. Sottsass remained as an independent consultant, avoiding becoming ensnared in what he himself called the 'hierarchic-bureaucratic structures of industry'. He headed a team of designers, engineers and draughtsmen who were employed directly by Olivetti, dividing it into two groups, one based inside the company and the other in his office in Milan. This dual system of design input continued, allowing for the contributions of many important designers in Milan.

The MUSEUM OF MODERN ART, New York, organized an Olivetti Exhibition in 1952, the first time a European company had been invited by the Museum to show its products and graphic work.

In 1964 Olivetti's electronics division was sold off to the American General Electric Company, which became part of Honeywell in 1970. Olivetti returned to electronics in 1968, this time concentrating on small to medium-sized computers, though during the 1970s the company passed through a low patch until Carlo De Benedetti was appointed chief executive manager in 1978. As a result of his reorganizations, by 1983 the company had increased its profits by 40 per cent. His changes included an increase in expenditure and development – an agreement was signed with American Telephone and Telegraph (AT&T) in 1984 which gave 25 per cent of the company over to AT&T in return for access to their research laboratories. Through the 1980s, therefore, Olivetti continued to develop as a supplier of office automation while maintaining its excellence in DESIGN MANAGEMENT.

□M. Labo, *L'Aspetto Esterico dell'Opera Sociale di Adriano Olivetti* (1957); F.H.K. Henrion and

Portable electronic typewriter, ET 55 P, designed by Mario Bellini and Alessandro Chiarato *for* **Olivetti** *in 1987.*

A. Parkin, *Design Coordination and Corporate Image* (1967); L. Soria, *Informatica: Un'Occasione Perduta. La Divisione Elettronica dell'Olivetti nei Primi Anni del Centrosinistra* (1979); Olivetti, *Design Process Olivetti 1908–1983* (1983); G. Barbacetto, *Design Interface: How Man and Machine Communicate: Olivetti Design Research by King and Miranda* (1987)

Omega (1913–20) was founded by the artist, critic and writer Roger Fry in London's Bloomsbury and inherited the craft tradition of the ARTS AND CRAFTS movement, though without the social purpose of John Ruskin and William Morris. The Omega Workshops are noteworthy for their decorative tendencies and for their lack of professionalism. Many of its members worked on the decoration of each other's homes, including Roger Fry's own home near Guildford (1914) and Charleston, Duncan Grant and Vanessa Bell's home in Sussex (1916). Fry insisted on charging unrealistically low prices for work and many of the decorative effects were sub-Postimpressionist – appearing as a crude version of the work of the French painter Paul Cézanne. The venture folded in 1920 but its legacy as one of the first attempts to apply Fauvist and Cubist styles to objects was important. A strong revival of interest in the Omega Workshops took place in the early 1980s.

□I. Anscombe, *Omega and After: Bloomsbury and the Decorative Arts* (1981); J. Colling, *The Omega Workshop* (1983)

OMK Design (f.1966) was founded by Jerzy Olejinik, Bryan Morrison and Rodney Kinsman, who had all just graduated from the Central School of Art, London. The company produced and marketed furniture, lighting and interior and exterior design, almost all of which was designed by Kinsman. From the mid-1970s much of its furniture was manufactured by Bieffeplast of Padua, Italy, and it gradually came to specialize in public seating, its products including the Omkstack chair (1971) and the Trax seating unit for concourse areas (1989), which was evocative of an aircraft wing, thus implying high speed.

organic design is a term which, through misuse, has come to mean any form that exhibits a curvilinearity or even BIOMOR-PHISM. Its roots lie in the concept of organic architecture, itself developed by Frank Lloyd WRIGHT. His one-time master, Louis Sullivan, claimed that, 'it is really the essence of every problem that it contains and suggests the solution.' Thus form need not necessarily be based on traditional aesthetic values, but is present in the design task itself. This would appear to come close to FUNCTIONALISM, though in design the visual end-product may seem far removed from any organic look. Wright thus developed Sullivan's notion of 'form follows function' by claiming that they must be one and the same thing. Thus his architectonic vision meant that while every part of a building should have its own identity, it should also express its relationship to the whole. Furthermore, the building itself should express a special relationship with its immediate environment. This may be expressed in its harmony with nature, through the use of materials, distribution of forms in relation to the surrounding landscape, colour and so on.

In terms of design, however, this approach has been somewhat perverted. This is partly as the result of a 1942 competition and exhibition at the MUSEUM OF MODERN ART, New York, called Organic Design for Home Furnishings. Its stated aim was to highlight furnishings that were of an organic nature in terms of their material and design approach. However, the competition winners, Charles EAMES and Eero SAARINEN, interpreted the theme purely in formal terms. Their moulded PLYWOOD chairs were 'organic' in the sense that they expressed the curvilinearity of natural forms. Since then, this more general definition has mostly been applied. Organic design, in this sense, has thus been helped by the development of PLASTICS, but also by developments in the 80s in computer-controlled wood-cutting and -shaping and an increase in the use of moulded ALUMINIUM due to its drop in raw-material price. In 1991 London's Design Museum held an exhibition entitled Organic Design.

Ottagono (f.1966) is a Milanese design magazine supported by the companies Arflex, Artemide, Bernini, Boffi, CASSINA, Flos, ICF De Padova and Tecno.

P

packaging is the method by which branded goods are prepared for display both in advertisements and on the shelves in shops. Pack design is a highly important part of BRANDING and of the development and maintenance of a successful brand identity. The process of designing the packaging for new products is most often carried out by specialist design agencies who, through the use of carefully considered materials and graphic design, will attempt to present the product in a pack which is eye-catching and suggestive of the perceived qualities of the brand. This is done with a view to communicating specific values to clearly defined target groups. A great deal of emphasis is placed on packaging design, particularly in the world of FAST MOVING CONSUMER GOODS, to the extent that new designs will often be subjected to extensive MARKET RESEARCH and testing before reaching the shops.

Papanek, Victor (b.1925) was born in Vienna, but emigrated to the USA in 1939. He graduated with a diploma in architecture and industrial design from Cooper Union, New York, in 1948 and then continued studies in such diverse subjects as ethnology and biology through the 50s. From 1964 he ran an independent design consultancy, but he also taught widely and began to develop his pioneering ideas in the realm of DESIGN FOR NEED. In 1971 he published a summation of these ideas in *Design for the Real World*. Subsequently published in 21 languages, it became one of the world's most widely read books on design. In it he vigorously attacked design's subservience to commercialism and its lack of social responsibility; he offered alternative approaches to design, stressing the need to consider the use of the object before the more traditional preoccupations with form or production. Subsequent publications, *Nomadic Furniture* (1973–74) and *How Things Don't Work* (with James Hennessey, 1977), advocated the manufacture of products for assembly by the user, thus allowing greater customization of the product to meet the user's actual needs. Papanek and Hennessey also went to the extent of suggesting that some products, particularly specialized tools, could be more efficiently used if they were pooled among various users. Thus his vision extended from the simple design solution through to the wider social context in which it was implemented. During the 70s and 80s, Papanek worked increasingly in Third World countries, developing solutions for specific local problems. In doing this, he demonstrated that designers could play a vital role in the betterment of humankind, and did not have to become doctors to help remedy the world's problems.

☐ V. Papanek, *Design for the Real World* (1971, rev. 1985); *Nomadic Furniture*, 2 vols (1973 and 1974); V. Papanek and J. Hennessey, *How Things Don't Work* (1977); V. Papanek, *Design for Human Scale* (1983); *Viewing the World Whole* (1983)

Paris Exposition des Arts Décoratifs et Industriels, 1925

was the penultimate of the Parisian expositions that had a major focus on design and the decorative arts, the last being in 1937. It had been planned by the Société des Artistes-Décorateurs for 1915, but with the interruption of World War I was postponed until 1925. As with all the expositions, its aim was partly to show off and partly to improve the standards of French design. The 1925 exhibition represented the zenith of the ART DECO style (the name deriving from the selfsame exhibition, in fact), with prominence given to the work of Jacques-Emile RUHLMANN and René LALIQUE. The Exposition was criticized for its grand opulence, the cost of objects being far beyond the reach of the average consumer. Also to be seen was LE CORBUSIER's Pavillon de l'Esprit Nouveau (Pavilion of the New Spirit).

Paris Exposition Universelle, 1937

was an international exhibition that saw the meeting of the INTERNATIONAL STYLE and the various national design styles prevalent in the period immediately before World War II. As such it represents an important case study in the expression of national ideologies through the design of respective pavilions. These included the German pavilion designed by Hitler's architect-in-chief, Albert Speer, which displayed the stripped-down monumental classicism also to be seen in the Italian NOVECENTO-style pavilion – in their combination of ancient and modern visual languages, both were expressive of their political regimes. Facing the German pavilion was the equally monumental pavilion of the USSR, which had by then left the heady days of CONSTRUCTIVISM and SUPREMATISM behind. Meanwhile national variants on Modernism (*see* MODERN MOVEMENT) were displayed in Alvar AALTO's Finnish pavilion and Josep Luis Sert and Luis La Casa's Spanish pavilion, which housed Pablo Picasso's famous painting, *Guernica*. The CONGRÈS INTERNATIONAUX D'ARCHITECTURE MODERNE also had a pavilion, designed by LE CORBUSIER. Thus this exhibition represented divergent strands in Modernism – one was in its partial appropriation by totalitarian regimes to be seen in Germany and Italy; another was in the development of regional variants. In either case, the moral and ideological nature of Modernism was maintained. A third destiny was to be seen two years later in the NEW YORK WORLD'S FAIR, 1939, where Modernism was combined with ART DECO (subsequently creating STREAMFORM) to suggest its infusion into mass consumerism.

Paulin, Pierre

(b.1927) is a French designer who is most noted for his organic furniture of the late 1960s. He was mostly self-taught in design and produced designs for THONET from 1954 and for Artifort from 1958. His Ruban chair (1969) showed an intelligent manipulation of POLYURETHANE foam. In 1975 he formed ADSA + Partners, a design consultancy, which took on Roger TALLON in 1984. In 1983 Paulin also designed products for Calor and furniture for the presidential office at the Elysée Palace.

Pawłowski, Andrzej

(1925–86) was a design theorist and educationalist in postwar Poland. His output as a designer, for companies such as Prozamet, an engineering works, in the early 1960s, was relatively small. As a theorist, by stressing that it was the consumer who largely

The pavilion built to display work by Jacques-Emile Ruhlmann at the **Paris Exposition des Arts Décoratifs et Industriels, 1925**.

defined the meaning and function of the designed object, he developed a sophisticated notion of design as an activity that echoed the contemporary literary philosophy of 'Reception Theory'. He held a number of official positions within the design profession in Poland and between 1967 and 1969 was vice-president of the INTERNATIONAL COUNCIL OF SOCIETIES OF INDUSTRIAL DESIGN (Icsid), although, intellectually, he was far closer to the growing radical wing of design theory in the late 1960s. His experimental film, *Professor Morpheo Cracoviensis*, for example, was shown at Icsid in Ottawa in 1967.

□A. Pawłowski (collected writings, ed. J. Krupiński), *Initiations on Art, Design and Design Education* (1989)

Peach, Harry (1874–1936) was born in Canada but grew up in Leicester, England. He was a committed Socialist, influenced by the writings of John Ruskin, William Morris and subsequently W.R. LETHABY. He ran a book-shop (1902–6) but due to his failing sight switched to the manufacture of cane chairs, setting up DRYAD with Benjamin Fletcher, Headmaster of Leicester School of Art and Dryad's chief designer, in 1907. Through furniture manufacture he became involved in the DESIGN AND INDUSTRIES ASSOCIATION from 1915 and was instrumental in moving it away from its ARTS AND CRAFTS background, bringing its aims closer to those of the DEUTSCHE WERKBUND.

□P. Kirkham, *Harry Peach, Dryad and the DIA* (1986)

Pel (f.1931) was a British furniture company which became famous for its manufacture of TUBULAR-STEEL furniture in the 1930s. It was founded as Practical Equipment Limited, changing its name to Pel a year later. Its parent company, Tube Investments, had manufactured seamless tubular steel, and an offshoot, Accles and Pollock, in its search for new trade outlets in the worsening economic climate,

A tubular-steel table produced by **Pel** *in the 1930s.*

began manufacturing tubular-steel furniture. Another company, Cox and Co., had made a similar move from motor-car components to tubular-steel furniture the year before, having seen the furniture of THONET. Neither company had, however, solved the particular problems associated with the material. Pel's directors, also inspired by Thonet furniture, set out to market tubular-steel furniture as a high-quality, prestige product. They had the advantage of connections with designers such as Serge CHERMAYEFF and Wells COATES, and a technical edge due to the firm's easy access to high-quality materials through its parent company. Some of Pel's pieces were eventually made under licence from Thonet, including designs by Marcel BREUER. Pel was thus instrumental in the diffusion of the MODERNE style in Britain. It continued to manufacture after World War II.

□D. Sharp, T. Benton and B. Campbell Cole, *Pel and Tubular-Steel Furniture of the Thirties* (1977); B. Campbell Cole in *Tubular-Steel Furniture* (1979)

Penrose Annual, The (f.1895) is published by Lund Humphries in London. It began as *Penrose's Pictorial Annual* and was a review of the graphic arts, incorporating articles about technological developments in printing with visual examples (it was subtitled 'The Process Yearbook'). In 1915 it became *Penrose's Annual* and began to admit a few articles reviewing more general aspects of the graphic arts industry, either covering developments in its business structure, or aesthetic developments. It was not until the mid-1930s, however, that the annual took on a balance of technological and general articles. It assumed its present name in 1936. For the ensuing decade, publication was irregular. It was only in 1950 that it resumed its truly annual character, by which time it was almost entirely devoted to international issues and examples of graphic design. These shifts, set against its unchanging format through the 20th c., make *The Penrose Annual* a fascinating survey for anyone tracing the development of graphic design in Britain.

Pentagram (f.1972) was formed in London as a multi-disciplinary design studio which was to act on a loose 'federal' basis, within which up to 50 members came together to work on projects in varying coalitions – taking on commissions

A selection of work by **Pentagram**.

as a group and then dividing the work up between teams according to its nature. Its precursor was Fletcher/Forbes/Gill (f.1962) which was made up of graphic designers Alan FLETCHER, Colin Forbes and Bob Gill. Architect Theo Crosby joined in 1965 when Gill left. When graphic designer Mervyn Kurlansky and industrial designer Kenneth GRANGE joined Pentagram was born. It thus shifted from small group practice to big office, responding to the bigger and more complex design demands of the large corporation then beginning to establish itself in Britain. Among its extensive design portfolio figure: the CORPORATE IDENTITY for Reuters (1973), the British Rail 125 High Speed Train (1976), products for Kenwood, Ronson and the Parker Pen Company and several exhibitions. It has also published several important books on design as well as a series of monographic pamphlets from 1975, which aim to bring to public notice examples of 'curious, entertaining, stimulating, provocative and occasionally controversial points of view'. A 1981 monograph featured six ingenious ways to fold a table napkin, for example. Indeed, much of Pentagram's work in graphic design clearly shows a sense of humour that has allowed freshness into the visual results. Lord Reilly, when he was director of the British Design Council, said that the Pentagram members, 'have many times saved me from putting my head in a gas oven when contemplating the state of design in Britain'.

In 1978 Pentagram opened an office in New

York and another in San Francisco in 1986, yet the company did not undergo the global expansion that other groups such as MICHAEL PETERS or Fitch-RS underwent in the 1980s. Instead it continued to be led by designers rather than account executives, allowing them a closer involvement in the management of design projects.

☐Pentagram, *Living by Design* (1978); Pentagram, *Ideas on Design* (1986); *The Compendium* (1993)

Peret (b.1945) was born as Pere Torrent and began his career working in Barcelona as an illustrator and graphic designer for various advertising agencies and publishing firms in 1965. In 1970 he moved to Paris, where he became art director of Prisunic and Delpire-Advico, before working freelance with, among others, *Marie-Claire*, Air France and CITROËN. He returned to Barcelona in 1978. Much of his graphic style is influenced by studies in fine art, taking in movements such as CONSTRUCTI-VISM, Cubism and Expressionism, while at the same time including provocative, or even explicit features.

Perspex is the trade name for Polymethyl-methacrylate. It is a colourless solid plastic and is widely used as a substitute for glass, though it can also be tinted or rendered opaque. Its chief properties are its high flexibility and good resistance to weathering. Developed by the German chemist Dr Otto Röhm (1901–2), it took on the trade name of Perspex in 1936. It was widely used in aircraft during World War II. It also has the unusual property of keeping a beam of light reflected within its surfaces and thus carrying the beam around bends and corners or inside sheets, and reflecting it out through the ends or edges. These qualities make it an ideal material for use in the lenses of

*Part of the visual identity created by **Peret** for the restaurant at the Reial Club Marítim, Barcelona, in 1989.*

cameras. Perspex, however, was also very popular with the professional jewelers Wendy Ramshaw and David Watkins, whose early Optik Art Jewellery made use of this material's optical qualities. Perspex is usually fabricated by moulding it into solid articles or casting it into sheets.

Pesce, Gaetano (b.1939) is best known as an exponent of RADICAL DESIGN. He studied architecture in Venice (1959–65) during which period he was a founder-member of the Gruppo N art group in Padua. He also worked as an independent artist and film-maker on projects involving programmed, kinetic, performance and serial art. His first venture into design was with his Up series of chairs (1969) manufactured by C&B Italia (*see* B&B ITALIA) and presented at the 1969 Milan Furniture Show. The chairs were moulded out of expanded POLYURETHANE foam, compressed under vacuum to a tenth of their volume and then packaged in flat, compact boxes. When the 'envelope' was opened the chairs automatically

Pesce's imaginative sofa, Sunset in New York (1980).

regained their normal dimensions. Further-more, the series was made for a variety of users, from adults to children. As the forms unfolded they suggested the rotundity of the human body, thus giving the object an anthropo-morphic connotation. This, combined with the active role of the user in determining the form, brought Pesce's thinking into line with avant-garde design in Italy at that time. Subsequent furniture projects, mostly for CASSINA, conti-nued to use PLASTICS-based materials to explore 'soft' shapes. The Sansone table (1980) was conceived so that the industrial worker determined the shape of the top and the colour combination to be used for each table, depend-ing on his or her taste or mood. Thus each one was unique, although it was also mass pro-duced. The Dalila chairs to accompany it were made in rigid polyurethane and, in their rock-like form and Old Testament subject matter, added to the monumentality of the overall concept. His architecture, design and art work (he does not recognize any boundaries between these disciplines) have consistently investigated meaning rather than function, with the result that Pesce can also be seen as an exponent of ANTI-DESIGN.

□G. Ranalli, *Gaetano Pesce* (1983); F. Van-laethem, *Gaetano Pesce: Architecture, Design, Art* (1989)

Pevsner, Nikolaus (1902–83) was the found-ing-father of the academic discipline of the history of design. He was born and educated in Leipzig, where he took a Ph.D. on German Baroque architecture in 1924. He was on the staff of the Dresden Gallery (1924–29) and then became a lecturer specializing in the history of British art at Göttingen University (1929–33). In 1933 he moved to Britain, where he became Slade professor of fine art (1949–55) and professor of the history of art at Birkbeck College, University of London (1959–69). Besides his teaching, he was a prolific writer; his books include: *An Enquiry into Industrial Art in England* (1937), *An Outline of European Architec-ture* (1943), *High Victorian Design* (1951) and his vast survey, *The Buildings of England* (1951ff). He was also on the editorial board of *The* ARCHITECTURAL REVIEW. However, it is his *Pioneers of the Modern Movement* (1936, reissued in 1949 by the MUSEUM OF MODERN ART, New York, as *Pioneers of Modern Design: From William Morris to Walter Gropius*) by which he has become most known in design history. In

this book he traced a more-or-less straight line of theoretical and stylistic influence from Wil-liam Morris and the ARTS AND CRAFTS movement, through Louis Sullivan, Victor HORTA and ART NOUVEAU to the SECESSION and the DEUTSCHE WERKBUND and culmi-nating in Walter GROPIUS and the BAUHAUS. His thesis is driven by a determinism that sees the MODERN MOVEMENT as the logical end whereby design emancipates itself from orna-ment and historical precedent and becomes a machine art with an accompanying belief in honesty, technology and the spirit of youth. He combined this attempt to define styles in art and architecture in terms of 'the spirit of the age' with an emphasis on the contribution of individuals. His reputation as an art historian (editor of the *Pelican History of Art*, author of *Building Types*, etc.) gave weight to his justifica-tion of the Modern Movement as the only orthodox style for our time. His work estab-lished design as the object of serious historical study but also perhaps limited the investigations of the design historian. The work of Sigfried GIEDION and Reyner BANHAM somewhat broke this mould. Pevsner was knighted in 1969.

□D. Watkin, *Morality and Architecture* (1978); P. Madge, 'An Enquiry into Pevsner's *Enquiry*' in *Journal of Design History* Vol. 1, No. 2 (1988)

Philips (f.1891) was founded by Gerard Philips in the Netherlands to manufacture light bulbs. The company rapidly expanded its market into the Rhineland-Westphalia region of Germany, a huge industrial centre, and by 1901 Philips was the third largest producer of light bulbs in Europe. The Netherlands' neutrality during World War I helped the company further increase its market share and from 1918 it began a process of diversification, producing radio receivers (from 1928), gramophones (from 1929) and later televisions (from 1937) and electric shavers (from 1939). Many of these new products used BAKELITE components.

In 1925 Louis Kalff joined its advertising section with responsibility for the artistic aspects of publicity, products and some archi-tecture. The following year he produced a design for a radio which included the stars and waves that later evolved into the company emblem. Kalff remained with Philips for 35 years, during which time he undertook many different design tasks (e.g., lighting plans for International Expositions), and had a profound

*A **photomontage** of photos, prints and postcards by Paul Citroën (1923).*

effect on the company's design policy. He was heavily influenced by the DEUTSCHE WERK-BUND and was a founder-member of the KIO (the Dutch designers' association). In 1954 an apparatus design group was formed within Philips taking on young graduates from the Academy of Industrial Design in Eindhoven, where evening courses in industrial design had commenced in 1950. None the less Kalff's personal style of leadership did not include a coherent DESIGN MANAGEMENT policy, with the result that new developments took place in an ad hoc manner.

This problem was largely solved in 1960 by the establishment of the Industrial Design Bureau which was concerned with all aspects of industrial design within the company. Henceforward, under Rine Veersema, Frans van der Put and then Knut Yran, the design department and its management went from strength to strength. In the 1970s the company experienced growing competition from Japanese manufacturers. In response, a process of restructuring began and the company's design policy became markedly more global, projecting series of products rather than targetting goods at specific markets. By the 1980s it had outlets in more than 100 countries and factories in more than 60

of them. With an ever increasing variety of electrical appliances being marketed, Philips became important in the field of research into new product design.

☐ K. Yran, . . . *A Joy Forever* (1980); Akademie voor Industriele Vormgeving, Eindhoeven, *Industrial Design in Practice* (1987); J. Heskett, *Philips: A Study of the Corporate Management of Design* (1989)

photomontage is a term invented by Berlin exponents of DADA. It derives from the French word *montage*, meaning 'fitting' or 'assembly'. Thus photomontage implies the assemblage of photographs or photo-negatives to create new images. It is not restricted to the use of photographs, but also includes the addition of texts, colour or drawing to photographs. In terms of graphic design, the technique allows for the interplay of images and type. At times this not only means that separate images may be included in a design but also that they may be contrasted or distorted, creating different layers of reading. In turn, the result may encourage a particular subversive strategy whereby the juxtaposition of images may, sometimes humorously, break down their traditionally accepted semantic effect or significance. Furthermore, the mere introduction of photography into graphic design enables images hitherto unconsidered to enter the realm of two-dimensional design.

The application of photomontage in graphic design has been extensive. It received most widespread usage during the 1920s and 30s, particularly in the work of some of the practitioners of Russian CONSTRUCTIVISM, and then at the BAUHAUS, with Herbert BAYER and László MOHOLY-NAGY. Designers of Italian FUTURISM also employed photomontage extensively, as did pioneers of the SWISS SCHOOL, and it was used in the propagandist REPUBLICAN POSTERS OF THE SPANISH CIVIL WAR. In the late 1960s, when the 'subversion of the sign' – whereby the meanings of images were changed, often to bring a political slant to them – was at its most modish, photomontage was a particularly effective tool. Milton Glaser (*see* PUSH PIN STUDIO), Roman CIESLEWICZ and Enric Satué were effective exponents of this approach. The use of photomontage had been facilitated by the possibility of screen-printing photographs. It received another impetus from the advent of COMPUTER-AIDED DESIGN and VIDEO

A publicity still for Roman Holiday *(1953) featured Eddie Albert, Gregory Peck, Audrey Hepburn and* **Piaggio**'s *Vespa.*

GRAPHICS, in which photographs could be fed onto computer software and subsequently manipulated with ease.
☐ D. Ades, *Photomontage* (1986)

photosetting is the broadest term used in the graphic process and incorporates filmsetting, photocomposition and phototypesetting. It covers all processes by which type images are reproduced on light-sensitive film or photographic paper.

Piaggio (f.1884) was founded in Pontedera, Italy, as an engineering firm. From 1928 it operated as Piaggio Air and during World War II produced Italy's only heavy bomber, the P108B. In 1943 the works were destroyed by Allied bombing. After the War they were converted to peacetime production, and in 1946 the company launched the Vespa motor scooter. Originally the idea of Enrico Piaggio, its designer was Corradino D'Ascanio, who had previously specialized in helicopter design. D'Ascanio incorporated into the scooter various features derived from aircraft production: an air-cooled engine, a stressed panel structure and stub-axles, said to have been based on aircraft landing-gear. Its biggest departure from traditional motor-cycle design, of course, was the sheet-metal frame concealing the engine which gave a generally streamlined appearance. It had a simple, 98cc, two-stroke engine, giving it a top speed of only 30mph but a fuel consumption of 120mpg. As well as presenting a clean, uncomplicated image and being relatively easy to maintain, its controls were intended to be quickly mastered, with handlebar gear controls rather than the traditional foot-pedals. Thus the Vespa provided a 'new transport category' aimed at both sexes for cheap, easy, local travel (FIAT imitated this concept in 1957 with their small car, the Fiat 500).

The Vespa remained in production until 1987. By 1960, 1 million had been sold and in 1980, 450,000 a year were being produced. Despite this success it did have competitors, especially the Lambretta, launched in 1947. Manufactured by Innocenti in Milan, the latter had a larger (125cc) engine and a pillion seat, although its engine remained fully exposed until 1951. During the 1950s Piaggio and Innocenti carried out aggressive international advertising campaigns, vying for market share. It was, however, the Vespa was that 'the victor in the race to find a metaphor for *ricostruzione*, to develop a "popular" commodity capable of translating the more inchoate desire for mobility and change . . . into a single object, a single image' (Hebdige). The Vespa also starred alongside Audrey Hepburn and Gregory Peck in *Roman Holiday* (1953) and thus mediated the notion of 'Italian style' at a popular level.
☐ D. Hebdige, *Hiding in the Light* (1988)

Pick, Frank (1878–1941) was commercial manager of London Underground from 1909. He was responsible for commissioning Edward JOHNSTON to design a typeface for the Underground in 1916. Johnston's Railway Type, a classically proportioned SANS SERIF, has been used ever since on the London Underground system and was part of an early CORPORATE IDENTITY programme. Pick also commissioned posters from Edward McKnight KAUFFER and was a founder of the DESIGN AND INDUSTRIES ASSOCIATION.

Pininfarina (f.1930) is an automobile design firm founded in Turin by Battista 'Pinin' Farina. It took on the name of Pininfarina in 1961, two years after Farina's son Sergio had taken it over. It is notable for its concern with research in design and housed the first COMPUTER-AIDED DESIGN centre in Italy. Among its designs figure the Lancia Aurela B20 (1952), the Austin A40 (1958) and the Peugeot 504 (1968).
☐ M. Frostick, *Pininfarina: Master Coachbuilder/*

Pininfarina's *Cisitalia Coupé (1947)*.

Architect of Cars (1977); D. Merlin, *Pininfarina 1930–1980: Prestige and Tradition* (1980); A. Alfieri, *Pininfarina* (1982); T. Anselmi, *Le Ferrari di Pininfarina* (1988); G. Rogliatti, *Ferrari e Pininfarina* (1988)

pixel is an acronym for 'picture element' and describes the small units that make up a complete picture on a video display screen. When magnified they create a 'stepped' edge to a curve – a visual effect exploited by designers such as April GREIMAN.

Plan Créatif (f.1985) was founded by Charles Braunstein and Clement Rousseau when PA Design, a subsidiary of the international advertising, branding and design consultancy, PA Consulting Group, closed its Paris office. It benefitted from the French government's high investment in nuclear power, telecommunications, aerospace and trains in the late 1980s, producing projects for the Paris public transport system (RATP) and the French railway system (SNCF) as well as the cockpit of Aerospatiale's Airbus plane in 1990.

plastics have been among the 20th c.'s most widely used synthetic materials. Their use and look have revolutionized mass consumption, from intricate gearbox components to jewelry, furniture and clothing. It is indeed safe to say that no other 20th-c. material has done more to shape the Western world than plastics.

Although natural plastics such as shellac, ivory and tortoiseshell have been available for centuries, their use was once mainly confined to the luxury goods market. Around the mid-19th c., the plastics market expanded, taking in machinery as well. As a direct result of this expansion, supplies of natural plastics began to diminish. In 1869 Alexander Parkes developed and patented the first alternative to natural

plastic, namely Celluloid (cellulose nitrate), a semi-synthetic plastic made from a naturally occurring polymer. It was this material that formed the basis for the future development of the plastics industry.

Around 1907 the first completely synthetic plastic was developed by Leo H. Baekeland and marketed under the trade name BAKELITE. Bakelite was the first of the thermosetting plastics – that is, plastics that set hard on heating and cannot be remelted without decomposing (more recent thermosetting plastics include urea and melamine). These early plastics continued as little more than an imitative replacement for natural and expensive materials (e.g., Bakelite replaced wood in the production of ART DECO radio cabinets). Walter GROPIUS even described plastics as having no intrinsic qualities of their own. By the 1930s, however, plastics were increasingly accepted as a material in their own right. Wells COATES, for instance, redesigned the Ekco radio cabinet using Bakelite, and Walter Dorwin TEAGUE used plastic for the case of his new Eastman Kodak. The use of this new cheaper material by industrial designers added a further dimension to the social meaning of plastics; indeed, plastics

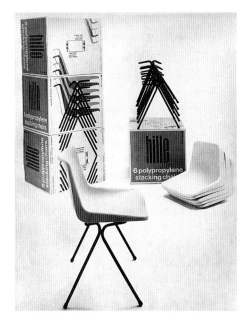

Robin Day's stacking chairs (1962) exploited the lightness and toughness of **plastics**.

proved to be an appropriate material for use with modern technologies that had yet to establish visual identities of their own.

World War I had witnessed an increase in the demand for plastics – in fireproof dopes and lacquers, for instance – and, as in the case of so many other innovations, it created a much needed impetus for their development. As a result, yet another large group of plastics was created, the thermoplastics (so called because they soften on heating). By the end of World War II, PVC (polyvinyl chloride), polystyrene, polythene and PERSPEX had all been developed. The 'miracle materials of war', as they were known, became available commercially to industry and to industrial designers. The possibilities for these plastics were thought to be almost endless: die casting, injection moulding and vacuum forming were just some of the manufacturing processes open to companies adopting thermoplastics. Companies such as British Industrial Plastics (BIP) and Runconlite in Britain and KARTELL in Italy made use of their pliable properties, employing innovative designers, including David Harmen-Powell, Gaby Schreiber and Gino Columbini. A variety of colours was also available, adding to the many possibilities open to designers wishing to use plastics.

The postwar period also saw further advances made in the development of other new plastics, such as glass reinforced plastics, POLYURETHANE, polypropylene, polytetrafluoroethylene and the polycarbonates. Polyurethane foam, for instance, replaced foamrubber and allowed more flexibility in the design of soft furnishings, while Robin DAY used polypropylene in his famous polyproplene chair for Hille.

□ S. Katz, *Plastics: Design and Materials* (1978); A. DiNoto, *Art Plastic: Designed for Living* (1984); E. Manzini, *The Material of Invention: Materials and Design* (1986); D. Cleminshaw, *Design in Plastics: Successful Product Design in Plastics* (1989); P. Sparke (ed.), *The Plastics Age* (1990)

plywood consists of three or more layers or veneers of wood plied together with the grain running crosswise to give strength and resilience. It has been used in furniture-making since the 18th c. if not earlier. In the 19th c. THONET exploited the material extensively. Plywood was explored in the 20th c. by Alvar AALTO and Marcel BREUER before World War

Jan Mlodozeniec's advertisement for an exhibition of the **Polish School** *of posters (1990).*

II and by Charles EAMES, Harry BERTOIA and Eero SAARINEN during the War for both military and medical purposes (e.g., splints and aircraft), as well as for furniture. The later designers began to bend the material in three dimensions, exploring its plastic potential.

□ A. Wood and T. Linn, *Plywoods of the World, their Development, Manufacture and Application* (1963)

Polish School of poster design came to international recognition in the 1950s. In the context of postwar Poland, a country which had suffered particularly heavy devastation, the growing poster design movement served as an important reinstatement and revitalization of the Polish national identity. It was centred around the Warsaw Academy of Fine Arts, initially with Tadeusz Trepkowski and then with Henryk TOMASZEWSKI as its leader. Around them also worked Eryk Lipinski and Olga Siemaszko. Their work was often characterized by bold collage work with the simple use of symbols. In the 1960s a more Surrealistic (*see* SURREALISM) tendency was developed, expressed by Franciszek STAROWIEYSKI and Roman CIESLEWICZ, who took his experience to Paris. Many foreign students studied under and were influenced by Tomaszewski, in particular members of the GRAPUS studio. From 1964 Warsaw hosted an International Poster Biennial, which has in turn strengthened the impact of the Polish poster.

polyurethane is created by the polymerization of urethanes by the reaction of isocyanates and poly-oils. The process was invented in 1937 by Otto Bayer but began to be used industrially only in the mid-1950s, in the production of both flexible and rigid foams. The reaction occurs between liquid components, requiring no heat or pressure; the compound expands and forms a foam that settles and solidifies, coating itself with an external film. In the early 1970s Bayer developed the injection-moulding process which produces thin walls (4–5mm, *c.* ⅙in.) that are quite strong. The material has the added advantage of being able to encapsulate and hold rigid any insert, such as a chair leg, unlike other thermoplastics (*see* PLASTICS), which shrink when removed from the mould. It has been used on nearly all types of object, from clothing to automobiles.

Ponti, Gio (1891–1979) studied architecture at the Polytechnic in Milan (1918–21) and went on to be a designer for the ceramics firm, Richard Ginori, before setting up an architectural firm with Emilio Lancia in 1927. The following year he became the founder-editor of the *DOMUS* magazine, which was to act as a mouthpiece for the NOVECENTO group founded by Ponti in 1926. As a writer, educator and practising designer and architect, he was in a position of great influence on future Italian design. Besides the indigenous classical idiom, Ponti brought to Novecento the influence of the Austrian WIENER WERKSTÄTTE. He believed that craft should continue as the true basis of design, but also aimed at enabling designers to work across a wide spectrum of projects. He himself designed mainly for craft-based industries (e.g., Richard Ginori and Fontana Arte) but also designed an interior for a locomotive, which was manufactured by the Breda company and exhibited at the TRIENNALE of 1933. In the postwar *ricostruzione* (reconstruction) period, Ponti, having returned to the editorship of *Domus* in 1947 after seven years editing *Stile*, ignored the attempts made during his absence under the editorship of Ernesto Rogers to return to the ideas of RATIONALISM. Instead he expounded a more

individualistic craft approach, and also took some inspiration from the USA. *Domus* focused on the need for a renewed visual language for modern design, looking to sources outside modern architecture. He turned the Italian concept of the 'good life' – popularly known as *La Vita Dolce*, an expression which implied post-World War II social and economic comfort and stability – towards the home and life style.

He was a professor at the Polytechnic in Milan (1936–61). During the 1950s he created some seminal pieces of Italian architecture and design. These include the Distex armchair of 1953, an aggressively modern design produced by CASSINA, the Superleggera chair, also designed for Cassina in 1956 and the Pirelli building, completed in 1958. The Superleggera chair was based on traditional furniture from the fishing villages of Chiavari, and was subsequently to be found throughout Italy.
□ *Gio Ponti* (exh. cat., Seibu Museum of Art, Tokyo, 1986); L. Ponti, *Gio Ponti: The Complete Work* (1990)

pop is a word that emerged in the 1950s as an abbreviation for popular, referring to popular culture. Pop culture is the output of the mass

Ponti's *influential 699 Superleggera chair (1956) was inspired by traditional design.*

media including film, television and high-circulation glossy magazines. Pop design is a phenomenon that emerged in the 1960s following on from the pop art of Andy Warhol, the INDEPENDENT GROUP et al. and that made a conscious use of imagery or ideas from pop culture in design. Thus it might include the deliberate highlighting of expendability (e.g., Peter Murdoch's disposable paper chair of 1964) or the reuse of ephemera (e.g., Peter Blake and Jan Howarth's 1967 album cover design for the Beatles' 'Sgt. Pepper's Lonely Hearts Club Band'). Indeed the artist Richard Hamilton's famous statement of 1957 that pop culture was 'Popular . . . transient . . . Expendable . . . Low Cost, Mass Produced, Young . . . Witty, Sexy, Gimmicky, Glamorous, Big Business' could equally be applied to pop design. In Britain the Independent Group, which included Reyner BANHAM, was an important mover in the break from the Council for Industrial Design's official version of the MODERN MOVEMENT, which championed 'GOOD DESIGN'. This rift led to an enthusiastic embracing of the machine aesthetic which incorporated American STYLING and was more akin to the outlook of Italian exponents of FUTURISM. Pop design of the 1960s could, however, extend to bulbous typefaces and the use of fluorescent, gaudy colours – the exact antithesis of Modernism. Furthermore, by the end of the 1960s pop design incorporated a strong revival of ART NOUVEAU and ART DECO, as seen in the logos for BIBA. Pop design might be seen as the product of the economic boom years in many Western countries during the 1960s, both optimistic and expendable. The following economic depression of the 70s perhaps dampened its spirit. Its most important legacy, however, is that henceforward the notion of 'good design' had to be qualified.
□ Whiteley (1987)

Porsche (f.1949) is a car and engine manufacturer that was founded by Ferdinand Porsche, who had been largely responsible for the design of the VOLKSWAGEN Beetle. Since 1908 he had been involved in the development of engines for airships and aeroplanes. However, he and his son, Ferdinand Porsche II, wanted to build a sports car. They used Volkswagen parts for their first car, the 356 (1947–64), and its basic body shape echoed that of the Beetle, as both had been designed by Erwin KOMENDA. Subsequent stylists included BERTONE, who

Milton Glaser's Dylan poster (1967) used strong colouring that is typical of **pop** *design.*

designed the 911 Cabriolet (1967), and PININFARINA, who built the 911 four-seater (1969). Porsche also designed numerous racing cars, and many of the lessons learnt there were brought to its production vehicles.
□ L. Boschen and J. Barth, *Porsche* (1983); *Porsche Specials* (1986)

postindustrialism, like POSTMODERNISM, is a term that takes on a broad framework of meanings. At its most general it represents the state of Western society following the end of the dominance of FORDISM or monopoly capitalism in the 1960s and 70s and the shift from an industrial to a service-based economy. In design terms, postindustrialism provides the cue for an aesthetic response. The demise of heavy industries in the West is thus a feature ironically alluded to in the work of some designers, such as Tom DIXON, whose furniture contained reused, fragmentary, 'found' objects, which had reference to an industrial past. Equally, a postindustrial response may also imply an approach to production whereby the Fordist styles of mass manufacture, producing objects in long runs for a mass consumer market, are overturned. Thus goods are produced for determined sectors or individuals within the market on much shorter runs, which obviously affects the design approach. BATCH PRODUCTION using HIGH-TECHNOLOGY COTTAGE INDUSTRY, COMPUTER-AIDED DESIGN and COMPUTER-AIDED MANUFAC-TURE are ways by which this may be achieved.

Postmodernism is, like Modernism, a term which may be applied to many aspects of cultural and economic activity. It may equally be understood as a particular style and as a conceptual tool for interpreting phenomena. The simplest way of understanding the term is to see it as a rejection of Modernism and all that entails. Postmodernists maintain that the unrestrained avant-gardism of the MODERN MOVEMENT led to paintings and books no one understands, buildings no one can live in or bear to look at, and faceless, alienating products with little sensuous appeal. Their response, which gained increasing momentum from the late 1960s, is to mix the highbrow and the populist, as seen in the work of POP artists and designers and the architectural theories of Robert VENTURI. It includes the use of colour, decoration and texture, as found in the work of Ettore SOTTSASS, MEMPHIS and STUDIO ALCHYMIA but also to be seen in various examples of

Michael Graves's pendulum mantel clock (1986) combines the classical motifs of **Postmodernism**.

Aldo Rossi's silver service for Alessi (1981). The classical pediment of its architectural setting is a sign of **Postmodernism**.

the CRAFTS REVIVAL and HIGH-TOUCH design. This may sometimes presume that a common visual language is shared by the perceivers of objects: thus in architecture in particular there is a reversion to the visual language of classicism – pedimented entrances, for instance – though the architect may not adhere to the strict rules of classicism inherited from the Renaissance and may verge on ART DECO. Other visual languages may be used however, and so a vital ingredient of Postmodernism is the 'sampling' of elements of different styles and eras: HISTORICISM and eclecticism, in other words.

These formal characteristics are part and parcel of a broader philosophical definition of the term. Postmodernism also refers to a loss of faith in the entire project of modernity, with its belief in progress, reason and the power of human consciousness. Freudian psychology has shown that we are governed by the 'hidden iceberg' of our uncontrollable unconsciousness. Linguistics scholars have suggested that we are created by language rather than the creators of it. As such there is a loss of belief in absolute truths, rather, we are constituted by and constantly interact with a series of signs, symbols, images and/or metaphors. For some

Postmodernism

this shift away from absolutes and identities signifies freedom. Now one can reinvent oneself, occupying different subject positions according to one's personal needs and desires. For others this signifies the metamorphosis of society into a schizophrenic condition, manipulated by the mass media. Furthermore, Postmodernism, as understood in an extreme form by the French philosopher Jean Baudrillard, creates an 'ecstasy of communication', as he termed it, meaning that we loll around in a Bacchanal orgy of signs, concerned only with surface and not with substance. STYLING, OBSOLESCENCE, CORPORATE IDENTITY and the activities of ADVERTISING AGENCIES are all causes and effects of this.

Indeed, the rise of design since World War II, and particularly since the 1980s, has played a vital role in Postmodernism. The term is invariably explained through the example of shifts in architectural practice and theory: Charles Jencks's publications on Postmodern architecture in the early 1970s were important steps in the popular establishment of the term (though instances of its usage predate his writings as far back as the 1930s). At the same time Postmodernism may at times suggest a loss of faith in the architect and the town planner. This no doubt stems from a rejection of the Modern Movement and the primacy it gave to the architect in the planning and building of the modern world. Modernist architects had failed to deliver their radical aims: Modernism had either ended up in an empty INTERNATIONAL STYLE or had been appropriated by both extreme right- and left-wing despotisms. Thus the Postmodern architect 'came indoors', metaphorically speaking, and joined the designer to work for the individual, private user of consumer goods rather than mass use of public space. Indeed one might go so far in architecture as to say that Postmodernism represented a shift in interest from public architecture (schools, hospitals, housing schemes) to private commissions (offices, shopping malls, houses).

The Postmodern shift from public to private also carries a key shift from production to consumption. The most important prerequisite for this has been the slow death of FORDISM. Since World War II the development of flexible manufacturing systems has gone hand-in-glove with the break up of mass markets. Thus manufacturers and retailers have targeted much smaller groups in society or even individual needs. This has important ramifications for

John Outram's pumping station, Blackwall (1988), is an example of **Postmodernism** *in architecture.*

design: customization and flexibility have had to be included as design features and approaches. Equally, MARKETING in the Postmodern labyrinth has become increasingly sophisticated. Many manufacturers, notably SONY, have relied less on market surveys and consumer response than on a broader culturalist reading, taking in user habits and psychology and even a reading of socio-political trends to predict market opportunities.

Postmodernism, both as a style and as a means of interpretation, has been much criticized, in particular by those who have continued to hold some belief in all or part of Modernism's aims. Ultimately, given the wide variety of the term's connotations, some elements of its meaning may be taken up in preference to others; and as such, it is a useful tool for the design historian and designer in re-evaluating the past and acting on the present.

□ C. Jencks, *The Language of Postmodern Architecture* (1973); *Post-Modern Classicism* (1980); Foster (1983); H. Klotz, *Moderne und Postmoderne: Architektur der Gegenwart 1960–1980* (1984); C. Ritchie and L. Calzolari (eds), *Phoenix: New Attitudes in Design* (1984); B.C. Brolin, *Flight of Fancy: The Banishment and Return of Ornament* (1985); J.-F. Lyotard, *The Postmodern Condition: A Report on Knowledge* (1986); J. Habermas, *The Philosophical Discourse of Modernity: Twelve Lectures* (1987); A. Papadakis (ed.), *The Post-Modern Object* (1987); D. Hebdige, *Hiding in the Light: On Images and Things* (1988); A. Huyssen, *After the Great Divide: Modernism, Mass Culture and Postmodernism* (1988); Thackara (1988); L. Appignanesi, *Postmodernism* (1989); J. Collins, *Uncommon Cultures: Popular Culture and Post-modernism*

(1989); M. Collins and A. Papadakis, *Postmodern Design* (1989); L. Hutcheon, *The Politics of Postmodernism* (1989); C. Jencks, *What is Postmodernism?* (1989); M. Miyoshi and H.D. Harootunian, *Postmodernism and Japan* (1989); R. Boyne and A. Rattansi, *Postmodernism and Society* (1990); D. Harvey, *The Condition of Postmodernity: An Enquiry into the Origins of Cultural Change* (1990)

Praesens (f.1926) was a group founded by leading Modernist (*see* MODERN MOVEMENT) architects, designers and artists in Poland in the interwar period. Its members displayed a wide range of attitudes towards Modernism in the late 1920s: the painter Władysław Strzemiński, a colleague of Kasimir MALEVICH in revolutionary Russia, took a Suprematist stance (*see* SUPREMATISM), arguing for the independence of art from design, whereas Szymon Syrkus's advocacy of the mechanization of design and housing was close to the theories of LE CORBUSIER. The group's journal, also named *Praesens*, was published in 1926 and 1930 and was the primary medium through which the collective promoted its ideas. Praesens's members were active outside Poland as delegates to the CONGRÈS INTERNATIONAUX D'ARCHITECTURE MODERNE (CIAM) and as exhibitors at the Machine Age exhibition in New York in 1927. The group survived a major schism in 1929 when its painter members, led by Strzemiński, left to form a.r. (Revolutionary Artists). After this split Praesens was dominated by architects and planners and concentrated on major urban schemes such as *Warszawa Funkcjonalna* (Functional Warsaw), which was presented to CIAM in 1937.
□ *Constructivism in Poland* (exh. cat., Museum Folkwang, Essen, 1973)

Priestman, Jane (b.1930) studied at Liverpool College of Art, following which she ran her own design practice (1955–75). She then spent ten years managing design for the British Airports Authority before being appointed director of architecture, design and environment for British Rail (BR), reputedly one of the world's most complex and intensive transport networks. Before her retirement from BR in 1991, she was instrumental in bringing a new design awareness into action on the system.

Pritchard, Jack (b.1899) was at the centre of attempts to introduce the MODERN MOVEMENT to England during the 1930s. Until his retirement he was a furniture manufacturer and entrepreneur. After a brief spell in the navy during World War I he went to Cambridge, where he studied economics and engineering, graduating in 1922. On graduation he worked with Michelin and then from 1925 with the Venesta Plywood Company, a large building-materials supplier. This experience allowed him to travel abroad and brought him into contact with many architects. In 1930 he commissioned LE CORBUSIER to design a stand for Venesta at Olympia. László MOHOLY-NAGY was also commissioned to design advertisements for the firm. While continuing to work at Venesta, Pritchard commissioned the Lawn Road Flats in north London, which opened in 1934; this development was designed by Wells COATES and was heavily influenced by Le Corbusier's notion of the house as a 'machine for living in', with minimalist flats devised around common services. The furnishings were made by ISOKON, a company set up by Pritchard and Coates to oversee Lawn Road as well as to manufacture modern PLYWOOD furniture. The flats subsequently became a focus for avant-garde designers, artists and writers. Among their residents from 1934 to 1937 was Walter GROPIUS, whom Pritchard had invited to England. Pritchard was also responsible for the completion of Gropius's only major public commission in England, the Village College at Impington, Cambridgeshire, in 1939.
□ J. Pritchard, *View from the Long Chair* (1984)

product semantics is a term that was widely used by industrial designers from the mid-1980s. It is derived from the semiological discussions developed by philosophers such as the Frenchman, Roland Barthes. Itself a development from the early 20th-c. philosophical writings of Ferdinand de Saussure, Barthes's writing from the 1950s extended the notion of meaning from written and spoken language to the language of objects and images. He argued that such objects and images not only signify their basic function, but also carry a 'meta-' meaning; in addition they operate, due to their wider associations, as signs. Thus, for instance, he argued that the CITROËN DS motor car could be likened to a cathedral: not only may its name (*déese*) be read as the French word for 'goddess', but the lightness of its STYLING gives it a celestial quality, destined to be treated with religiosity. The car was a modern point of worship. In essence, then, he was attempting to uncover the socio-psychological function of objects, environments and events, assuming that they carried a greater power and significance than immediately hit the eyes.

Such a process is called 'semiology' (or 'semiotics' in the USA) – the study of signs. It was used from the early 70s by left-wing observers as a conceptual tool for a critique of Western society. None the less it was also absorbed into commercial activity. Judith Williamson's seminal critique of advertising, *Decoding Advertisements* (1978), is widely read within advertising agencies, and advertising itself has subsequently become more sophisticated. Implicit signs in advertising are now made explicit; the associations that were suggested are now made more visible. This might be achieved sometimes by cross-referencing (called 'intertextuality' by Barthes) between advertisements. Williamson wrote in the preface to the 1982 edition of the book, 'Today, Silk Cut can make a similar reference by using the colour and typography of a Cadbury's Dairy Milk ad (purple swirls) thereby evoking, *through form alone*, the famous "glass and a half of full-cream dairy milk" which, *another* ad has told us, go into Cadbury's chocolate.'

In product semantics the same shift applies. Often the term is misused by designers when they really mean styling. However, when properly applied it refers to the conscious inclusion of certain features in an object – colour, form, texture, size – which make wider suggestions beyond the product. Such associative value would in turn de-alienate it for the user, bringing a layering of connotations to it, but may also communicate its use and status more clearly. This might be seen as the decoding process of semiotics taken in reverse, so that one works from concept to detail. Thus the potential frivolous fun to be had by using a fax machine in the domestic environment – faxing birthday messages to your friends, for instance – is then suggested in the zoomorphic, almost cartoonesque, shape of the machine itself, as is the case in the NEC Spax 5, first exhibited in 1991. Equally, the fact that the machine could be hung on a wall signals that its status is the same as that of a domestic telephone.

□R. Barthes, *Mythologies* (1957); T. Hawkes, *Structuralism and Semiotics* (1977); *Design Issues* Vol. 5, No. 2 (1989; the whole number is devoted to product semantics)

Productivism is a term that is often used interchangeably with CONSTRUCTIVISM. Both were generated in revolutionary Russia in 1920 and 1921 and broadly describe an artistic involvement in the mass-produced industrial object. However, while Constructivists approached the notion of 'production art' from their own artistic standpoint, grappling with form-making using a variety of materials, the Productivists worked from the industrial context. Christina Lodder argues that Productivism was largely a theoretical position held by critics of Constructivism such as the art theorist Nikolai Tarabukin and was thus never underpinned by the manufacture of actual artefacts.
□Lodder (1983)

products are not only manufactured goods, the term also applies to the services that are offered and marketed as products by companies who do not make durables or FAST MOVING CONSUMER GOODS for sale. Such companies generally take advantage of the mechanisms of BRANDING, MARKET RESEARCH, advertising and MARKETING, and include airlines, banks and insurance corporations.

Propst, Robert (b.1921) was a painter and inventor who met Hugh DePree, the president of HERMAN MILLER, at the ASPEN INTERNATIONAL DESIGN CONFERENCE in 1958. DePree subsequently formed a research division within the company with Propst as its director. Propst researched office dynamics, and his ideas were published in 1968 in *The Office: A Facility Based on Change*. In this book he anticipated the effects of the information technology revolution, which he and George NELSON incorporated into the design of office furniture with their Action Office (1964) and Action Office 2 (1968). In the second of these, they developed systems for cable management and did away with the hierarchical structures of traditional office layout and furniture. Instead, they created decentred pools of activity, encouraged by the move towards a system in which desktops, shelves and storage units hang off the panels that divide space in the office.

PTT (Posterijen, Telegrafie en Telefonie) is the Netherlands' postal and telephone service, and has also been the country's leading patron of modern design throughout the 20th c. This is due mostly to the efforts of Jean François van Royen, who joined the company in 1904. He

*Interior of a post office in Amersfoort, the Netherlands, by Total Design for **PTT** (1993).*

stamp design course there in 1951. In 1967 the course was closed down, and this gave way to a flurry of avant-garde creativity under the influence of international art movements such as Minimalism, POP and Conceptualism. Designers who subsequently worked for the PTT included Gert DUMBAR, Jan van TOORN and the celebrated cartoonist Joost Schwarte. A new CORPORATE IDENTITY was commissioned from Dumbar's Tel Design and Wim CROUWEL'S TOTAL DESIGN from 1968. This was redesigned in 1989 when the PTT was privatized: Studio Dumbar's Dawn Barrett provided a four-layered programme intended to cope with the diverse levels of commercial activity within the company. As a private company, it was subsequently unable to act as a coherent patron of design and therefore ceased to provide support for Dutch graphic design as a cultural activity.
□E. Bezemer and P. Hefting in *Holland in Vorm: Dutch Design 1945–1987* (ed. Stedelijk Museum, Amsterdam, 1987); G. Forde, *Design in the Public Service: The Dutch PTT 1920–1990* (1990)

had studied law at the University of Leiden, graduating in 1903, and was particularly interested in the arts (he was greatly influenced by the English reforming theorists William Morris, John Ruskin and Walter Crane). He started in 1904 as a clerical assistant in the PTT's legal office but during the ensuing decade began to put pressure on the company to undertake a more rigorous design policy with regard to its stamps, promotional literature and posters. Such a policy was achieved largely as a result of his growing involvement and reputation in private publishing and in the Netherlands Association for Crafts and Industrial Art. In 1927 the PTT established a publicity department within which van Royen had particular influence, and throughout the 1930s the Modernist graphic designer, Piet ZWART, provided designs for stamps and publicity material. Van Royen's resistance to the Nazi invasion of the Netherlands led to his death in a concentration camp in 1941.

Immediately after World War II the PTT established an art and design department with the aim of reviving its prewar achievements. The results were rather restrained, with greater emphasis on engraving and illustrational techniques than photography. The department's aesthetic adviser, W.F. Gouwe, established a

Push Pin Studio (f.1954) is a graphic design studio formed in New York by Milton Glaser

Seymour Chwast's cover for the December 1976 issue of Push Pin Graphic, *the* **Push Pin Studio**'s *magazine.*

and Seymour CHWAST. During the 1960s, Glaser in particular became well known for his innovative posters, often including a flattened, distorted perspective. His most famous image is possibly from his Bob Dylan poster of 1967. At the same time Chwast loosely explored historicist references (*see* HISTORICISM), employing 19th-c. vernacular typographic styles, for instance. The Push Pin Studio was influential in 'loosening up' standards in typography and illustration in New York by introducing 'vernacular' typography and freer handling of illustration. During the 70s the studio moved into CORPORATE IDENTITY. It is also noteworthy for its unrelenting self-promotion, producing several highly illustrated books about itself and its members.

Pye, David (1914–93) trained as an architect at the Architectural Association, London, and specialized in the design of wooden buildings until World War II, when he served in the navy. After the War he was invited to teach furniture design at the ROYAL COLLEGE OF ART, London, where he became professor in 1963. In 1968 he published *The Nature and Art of Workmanship* and in 1978, *The Nature and Aesthetics of Design*. Both in British craft and design theory and as a craftsman, writer and teacher his influence was seminal. In particular he was instrumental in shifting the conceptions of many away from the assumption that craft meant handwork and one-off production, and that design meant machine-based production for mass manufacture. He challenged the 'form follows function' axiom (*see* FUNCTIONALISM) by suggesting that objects do not necessarily function in ways we expect, and that their ability to work depends less and less on their form. He also demonstrated that the craftsman may act as a scientist in researching, for instance, the properties of materials for their own sake and not for any productive end. He thus challenged the traditional understanding of craft as a unification of manual and mental labour.

R

Race, Ernest (1913–64) was a British furniture designer known principally for his chairs designed in the CONTEMPORARY STYLE after World War II. He studied interior design at the Bartlett School of Architecture in London (1932–35) and soon went into production of his designs with the Race Fabrics firm (1937–39). After the War he founded Ernest Race Ltd to design and manufacture his furniture and this became Race Furniture Ltd in 1962. He also designed for ISOKON (1962–64), with whom he explored PLYWOOD, designing the attractive Penguin Mark 2 Donkey bookcase (1963). His Antelope and Springbok steel-rod chairs (1950) were markedly organic, representing a shift away from more traditional styles in English furniture, such as that produced by Gordon RUSSELL. They also made economical use of materials, which not only made them light and easy to handle, but also avoided extravagance in the face of postwar shortages. □H. Conway, *Ernest Race* (1982)

Radical Design was a tendency that emerged in the late 1960s and, like ANTI-DESIGN, aimed to break the tenets of 'GOOD DESIGN'. It differed from anti-design, however, in that its political will to attack the ideological structures of the mainstream was stronger. Thus its exponents (e.g., the studios ARCHIGRAM, ARCHIZOOM, SUPERSTUDIO and UFO) produced Utopian proposals and manifestos which incorporated architecture, planning and design

Wooden bowl carved by **Pye** *in 1980.*

Race's Antelope chair designed for the 1951 Festival of Britain.

destined to change people's attitudes to the shaping of the environment. Often the emphasis would be on user-intervention, altering the object to serve the consumer's particular needs. In addition, the subversion of dominant visual languages of design was seen as necessary, in order to undermine the visual codes used by mainstream Western capitalism. These proposals lost their vigour in the 1970s, due mostly to the West's economic depression, as it became evident that they would never be carried out. They did, however, form an important background to the NEW DESIGN of the 1980s.
☐G. Celant in Ambasz (1972); P. Navone and B. Orlandoni, *Architettura 'Radicale'* (1974)

Rams, Dieter (b.1932) was born in Wiesbaden, Germany, where he studied architecture and interior decoration at the School of Art (1947–48 and 1951), and was also apprenticed to a carpenter (1948–51). He then worked in an architectural office in Frankfurt until 1955, when he joined BRAUN as a designer. He became director of the design department (1960–80) and from 1980 was a member of Braun's management. Rams developed a sleek, austere product aesthetic which became syn-

onymous with Braun, with German design in general and, more widely, with the INTERNATIONAL STYLE. His personal design philosophy certainly expresses a belief in clearing 'the chaos we are living in', so that 'visual noise' in products is toned down – forms are reduced to their barest essentials, giving way to smooth white surfaces and an absence of colour or texture. He is notable for advances he made in ENGINEERING DESIGN, for instance in the introduction of a transparent plastic for the lid of a turntable and the double-shell casing for portable radios. He also designed furniture for the furniture company, Vitsoe, where, as in his work for Braun, he displayed an interest in creating complete systems that allow the user flexibility in arrangement.
☐F. Burkhardt and I. Franksen, *Design: Dieter Rams &* (1981)

Rand, Paul (b.1914) studied at the Pratt Institute (1929–32), Parsons School of Design (1932–33) and under George Grosz at the Art Students League (1933–34), all in New York. At the age of 23 he was art director of *Esquire* and *Apparel Arts*. Influenced by his studies he was strongly drawn to principles of design found in the European MODERN MOVEMENT in the early 1930s which he brought to these magazines and book jacket design. His designs thus broke from a symmetrical arrangement of isolated elements of image and type, bringing them together into a dynamic continuum, by mixing a simplistic yet expressive combination of colour field, symbol and type. He designed a series of covers for the bimonthly cultural

'Snow White's Coffin', a radio and record player made by Hans Gugelot and **Rams** for Braun in 1956.

magazine *Direction* (1938–45), work that was distinguished by his use of PHOTOMONTAGE, full-bleed and historical reference. In the 1950s he began to undertake CORPORATE IDENTITY work, creating the IBM trademark in 1956.

□P. Rand, *Thoughts on Design* (1946, 1970); *The Trademarks of Paul Rand* (1960); *Design and the Play Instinct* (1965); *Paul Rand: A Designer's Art* (1985)

Rationalism is an aspect of Modernism (*see* MODERN MOVEMENT) that makes the most economical use of materials, space and visual codification. It was also the term for Modernism most used in Italy and Spain.

Raymor (f.1940) was founded in New York by Irving Richard. It acted as a distributor of household objects with a policy of sponsoring modern design. It sold work by contemporary and Scandinavian designers (e.g., George NELSON, Hans WEGNER and Ettore SOTTSASS).

Read, Herbert (1893–1968) was one of the foremost theoreticians of the avant-garde in Britain in the 20th c. He was born in North Yorkshire and worked as a bank clerk before studying law and economics at Leeds University (1911–15), where he was a member of the Leeds Arts Club. This was a period of formative influence on Read: between 1910 and 1920 Leeds was second only to London as a centre of the English artistic avant-garde. Following service in World War I he moved to London in 1919 to work for the Treasury before taking up a post in the department of ceramics at the Victoria and Albert Museum (1922–31). He was professor of fine art at Edinburgh University (1931–33) and then returned to London to work as a freelance writer and editor of the *Burlington Magazine*. It was during the 30s that he wrote his best-known books: *Art Now* (1933), *Art and Industry* (1934) and *Art and Society* (1937). After this decade he turned more to social and political writing, though he acted as a director of the DESIGN RESEARCH UNIT from 1943 to 1945 while its main members were on World War II service. *Art and Industry* was a seminal book in the development of a design discourse of the MODERN MOVEMENT in Britain. It was heavily influenced by the Dessau BAUHAUS – indeed, in a 1932 report Read had proposed the creation of an experimental institute of art in Edinburgh based on that institution – and several Bauhaus masters,

Rand's *poster*, Alfred North Whitehead *(1965).*

with whom Read was in touch, assisted in its preparation: László MOHOLY-NAGY helped with the picture research and Herbert BAYER designed the first edition in 1934. Another formative influence on the book may have been Eric GILL's writing. *Art and Industry* itself involves a clear Modernist position calling for 'new aesthetic standards for new methods of production,' which in turn would come from 'abstract form'. It was received positively for raising the standards of discussion in design, but was also criticized for concentrating too much on abstract arguments and ignoring the real material conditions of society and the economy. In the later editions (1944, 1953, 1956 and 1965) its Modernist drive was progressively watered-down – the radical design by Bayer was abandoned in 1944, and references to Continental Modernism (Walter GROPIUS, Moholy-Nagy etc.) were reduced. As such, the book itself provides interesting historical evidence of the destiny of Modernism in Britain. □R. Skelton, *Herbert Read: A Memorial Symposium* (1968); G. Woodcock, *Herbert Read: The Stream and the Source* (1972); *A Tribute to Herbert Read: 1893–1968* (exh. cat., City of Bradford Metropolitan Council Art Galleries and

Museums, Bradford, 1975); D. Thistlewood, *Herbert Read: Formlessness and Form* (1984); R. Kinross, 'Herbert Read's *Art and Industry*: A History' in *Journal of Design History* Vol. 1, No. 1 (1988)

Realism is a term that covers architecture, design, literature and film in Italy of the late 1940s and early 1950s. It represented a rejection of the rhetoric of the preceding Mussolini years when government-sponsored cultural practices were characterized by their grand gestures – buildings, monuments and heroes designed to impress. Equally Realism meant a rejection of the Grand Plan suggested by the MODERN MOVEMENT before World War II and instead examined the everyday. In architecture and design this meant the use of local materials and vernacular styles, a supreme example of which was Gio PONTI's Superleggera chair (1956), which was based on traditional chairs from the fishing villages of Chiavari. These attitudes were echoed by avant-garde architects and designers such as Oriol BOHIGAS in Spain at the same time.

Renner, Paul (1878–1956) began his career as a painter, having attended art schools in Berlin, Karlsruhe and Munich. In 1926 he became director of the Munich School for Master Book Printers, but was dismissed by the Nazi regime in 1933. He is known for his SANS-SERIF Futura typeface, developed in the 1920s, which he employed in posters together with a diagonal orientation and abstract geometric forms, common among avant-garde posters of the time.

Republican Posters of the Spanish Civil War were mostly produced in Barcelona. They represented the political aspirations of the Republican side from the foundation of the Second Republic of Spain in 1931 up until the end of the Spanish Civil War in 1939. The strength of their design owes something to Barcelona's historical links with Paris prior to this period, and the Purist influences of A.M. CASSANDRE and Jean CARLU are clear. They might also owe some debt to Russian CONSTRUCTIVISM, although the posters' bold abstraction and use of PHOTOMONTAGE may often be coincidental or have arrived indirectly. Josep Renau, a master of photomontage, was the leading poster designer of this movement. He, along with other designers such as Carlos

Poster by Pepe for greater agricultural productivity published as part of the **Republican Posters of the Spanish Civil War** *campaign in Valencia (1937).*

Frontseré, Llorenç Goñi and Jaume Solá, was a member of the *Sindicato de Dibujantes Profesionales* (Union of Professional Graphic Artists) which acted as a focus for their efforts. Upon the Republican defeat in 1939, many of the movement's practitioners either went into exile or were unable to continue in the same vein under the dictatorship of General Franco. Enric Satué suggests, however, that had the Republicans won the Civil War, this movement would have established Catalonia as an important centre of postwar graphic design.

□C. Frontseré, *Carteles de la República y de la Guerra Civil* (1978); *No Pasaran! Photographs and Posters of the Spanish Civil War* (exh. cat., Arnolfini Gallery, Bristol, 1986); E. Satué, *El Disseny Gràfic a Catalunya* (1987)

Retro is a term used frequently to describe the popular re-edition from the early 1960s of Victoriana, ARTS AND CRAFTS, ART NOUVEAU and CONTEMPORARY STYLE designs.

Ricard, André (b.1929) was born in Barcelona of French parentage. He was sent to London to learn English in the early 1950s and there he

*The Octano sink designed by **Ricard** for Sangres (1987).*

became involved in design work associated with the Festival of Britain. On returning to Spain, he began to design 'humble objects' in his family's pharmaceutical supply firm, though still not fully aware of such a concept as industrial design. It was through contact with the growing theoretical literature on industrial design, in particular that of Raymond LOEWY whom Ricard first met in 1956, that he formed a clearer picture of the role of the industrial designer. Subsequently, besides being Spain's pioneering product designer, he also published three books, *Diseño ¿Por Qué?* (Why Design?, 1982), *Diseño y Calidad de Vida* (Design and Quality of Life, 1985) and *Hablando de Diseño* (Talking about Design, 1986), was vice-presi-

dent of the INTERNATIONAL COUNCIL OF SOCIETIES OF INDUSTRIAL DESIGN (ICSID) (1963–67 and 1976–79) and organized its 'Design for Rescue and Relief' project in the 1970s. He is highly important in the consolidation of Spanish design at an institutional and theoretical level, and his product design (e.g., for Moulinex, Metalarte and Gaggia) demonstrates a clear Modernist tendency (*see* MODERN MOVEMENT).

Rietveld, Gerrit Thomas (1888–1964) was born in Utrecht in the Netherlands and is most famed for his Red/Blue chair, constructed in 1918, and for his involvement with the DE STIJL group, of which he became a full-time member in 1919. In that same year Rietveld established an independent architectural practice, working within the guidelines of De Stijl ideas and philosophies. In 1924, with Truus Schröder, Rietveld designed and built the Schröder House, the most complete architectural expression of De Stijl ideas. Rietveld's position as a modern architect allowed him to participate in the founding of the CONGRÈS INTERNATIONAUX D'ARCHITECTURE MODERNE (CIAM) in 1928. From this point, up until his death in Utrecht in 1964, Rietveld continued to practise as an architect although not always in the distinctive idiom of the De Stijl group.

Rodchenko, Aleksandr (1891–1956) was a leading proponent of Russian CONSTRUCTIVISM. He studied at the Art School in Kazan (1910–14) and then moved to Moscow, where he studied briefly in the graphics department of the Stroganov School of Applied Art. In 1915 and 1916 he became acquainted with Kasimir MALEVICH and Vladimir TATLIN. He had already been influenced by FUTURISM and had begun to produce abstract and Cubist paintings and, from 1918, three-dimensional constructions. In 1917 he designed some lamps from overlapping and intersecting planes for the Café Pittoresk in Moscow. With his wife, WARWAWA STEPANOVA, and Alexei GAN, he formed the First Working Group of Constructivists in 1921. He also taught composition at the VKHUTEMAS (1920–30). The 20s represent his most prolific period as a graphic designer. From 1923 he designed posters for government trading organizations, the cinema, the journal *LEF* until 1925 and then *Novyi LEF* (1927–29). In *Novyi LEF* and in his cinema posters, he

*A plywood prototype for a chair by **Rietveld** (1927).*

began to use his own photographs in PHOTO-MONTAGE, producing, along with an investigation of the expressive potential of typography, vigorously striking results. He also designed the interior and furnishings of the Workers' Club as part of the Soviet contribution to the PARIS EXPOSITION DES ARTS DÉCORATIFS ET INDUSTRIELS, 1925.

Rörstrand (f.1726) was a ceramics factory founded in Stockholm, which moved to Gothenberg in 1926 and was bought by ARABIA in 1983. It is known for having produced some distinguished ART NOUVEAU designs by Alf Wallander at the turn of the century.

Royal College of Art (f.1837) was founded in London as the School of Design, the result of a government Select Committee on Arts and Manufactures which recommended the foundation of a school to train teachers and assist local schools. This was partly in response to impressive developments in design education in France, Prussia and Bavaria, who also constituted a threat to Britain in trade. It took its present name in 1896, soon after which Walter Crane became principal and W.R. LETHABY its professor of design. When Robert Darwen was appointed principal in 1948 its emphasis moved more from the fine arts to design. It remains Britain's only fully postgraduate art and design school and, since Darwen, has boasted among its staff figures such as Vico MAGISTRETTI, Daniel WEIL, Ken GARLAND and David PYE

Rodchenko *used photomontage for the cover of a series of detective stories (1924).*

and graduates such as Robin DAY and David Hockney.

□C. Frayling, *150 Years of the Royal College of Art* (1987)

Rubik, Ernö (b.1944) is renowned today as the inventor of the Rubik's Cube and other logic puzzles. He was a tutor at the Hungarian Academy of Craft and Design in Budapest, and, following his successes with the Cube, had built up the Rubik Studio, the largest design consultancy in Hungary, by the mid 1980s, with a number of colleagues from design education. Formed in November 1983, the Rubik Studio specializes in product and industrial design centred on PLASTICS technology.

Ruhlmann, Jacques-Emile (1879–1933) was a designer of luxury furniture most remembered for bringing ART DECO to its opulent extreme. He was born in Paris and inherited his father's successful building and decorating firm in 1907. He exhibited his furniture designs at the Salons d'Automne from 1913 and after World

*A table with a movable top of amboyna root and ivory inlay made by **Ruhlmann** in 1925.*

Furniture by **Russell** *from the mid-1920s showing the influence of traditional crafts in his work.*

War I built up Etablissements Ruhlmann et Laurent, a large furniture workshop. He also designed carpets, textiles, fittings and so on, becoming an *ensemblier* – that is, designing all the components of a room. His greatest triumph was at the PARIS EXPOSITION DES ARTS DÉCORATIFS ET INDUSTRIELS, 1925, where he furnished the Hôtel du Collectionneur. Up until then he had largely designed in a stripped-down mid-18th-c. style. However, in the late 1920s he began to introduce more MODERNE elements such as CHROMIUM, TUBULAR STEEL and black lacquers. His furniture was distinguished by its opulent materials, such as mahogany and inlaid ivory, and unsurprisingly, therefore, was never put into industrial production.

Russell, Gordon (1892–1980) was educated in Chipping Campden in the Cotswolds, the home of C.R. ASHBEE's Guild of Handicraft from 1901. Russell repaired old furniture for his father's antiques business from 1908 and as a soldier in World War I he described himself as a 'Designer of Furniture'. Upon demobilization he became a partner in his father's business, while also experimenting in furniture design. He was an early supporter of the DESIGN AND INDUSTRIES ASSOCIATION, but was also influenced by the ARTS AND CRAFTS movement, and thus advocated a craft ethic in design. In 1922 he wrote a pamphlet, *Honesty and the Crafts*. In 1927 the Russell Workshops Ltd was formed to manufacture his designs, and in 1929 he founded Gordon Russell Ltd with a showroom in London. The Wall Street Crash in 1929 resulted in a severe reduction in the antiques market in the USA, and subsequently the English market for luxury furniture almost disappeared. Russell's simple furniture thus found a ready market in such circumstances. He also designed radio cabinets for Murphy radios in the early 1930s. As a member of the Board of Trade's committee on furniture during World War II, he developed the UTILITY line of furniture which maintained its popularity through the 1950s. He was a member of the Council of Industrial Design from its foundation in 1944 and later became its director (1947–59) and a founder of the Design Centre in 1956. □K. Baynes and K. Baynes, *Gordon Russell* (1981); J. Myerson, *Gordon Russell* (1992)

S

Saab (f.1937) stands for Svenska Aeroplan Aktiebolaget (Swedish Aircraft Company) and was founded on the directive of the Swedish Government to manufacture military aircraft. It produced the J21 in 1944, the first aircraft ever to be equipped with an ejection seat. With no demand for military aircraft in the postwar period, Saab studied other options, including prefabricated houses, fitted kitchens, motorcycles and cars. Cars designed specifically for the difficult local driving conditions were seen as the most viable option. The Saab 92 (1950) was designed by a small, inexperienced team headed by Gunna Ljungström, with technical drawing by Sisten Sason. The company's background in aeronautical engineering showed in the streamlined bodywork. This basic shape remained the same until the more box-like 99 appeared in 1967.
□ B.-E. Lindh, *Saab: The First 40 Years of Saab Cars* (1987)

Saarinen, Eero (1910–61) was the son of Eliel SAARINEN. He is known as one of the most adventurous postwar architects, in particular for his TWA terminal building at Kennedy Airport, New York (1961). But he was also, like Charles EAMES, a pioneer of organic furniture (*see* ORGANIC DESIGN) using PLASTICS and PLYWOOD.

He emigrated with his parents to the USA in 1923 and studied sculpture in Paris (1929–30) and architecture at Yale University (1931–34), where he won a travelling scholarship to Europe for two years. On his return in 1936 he joined his father (as well as Charles Eames and Harry BERTOIA) as a teacher at the CRANBROOK ACADEMY OF ART; he also joined his father's architectural practice, which he continued after Eliel's death in 1950. From 1940, however, he made significant contributions to furniture design: the following year he and Eames won a prize at the Organic Furniture competition at the MUSEUM OF MODERN ART, New York. His interest in organic shapes was inherited from Alvar AALTO and Marcel BREUER but also, perhaps, from his Scandinavian design background, much of which also moved into a softened form of Modernism at the same time. The slender legs of his Womb chair (1946) emphasized its simplicity while its seat provided a more sensuous presence. In his Tulip chair (1956) the base and seat were visually, if not materially, incorporated by the inclusion of a central stem to provide a sculptural continuum.
□ A. Temko, *Eero Saarinen* (1962); E. Iglesia, *Eero Saarinen* (1966); A. Saarinen (ed.), *Eero Saarinen on His Work* (1968); R. Spade, *Eero Saarinen* (1971); R. Kuhner, *Eero Saarinen: His Life and Work* (1975)

Saarinen, Eliel (1873–1950) was a Finnish architect who, at the beginning of the 20th c., distinguished himself with several buildings

Tulip chairs by Eero **Saarinen** *(1956).*

and interiors which placed him in the vanguard of design along with such men as Peter BEHRENS. He was a frequent traveller and, in 1923, having won the $20,000 second prize in a competition for the design of the Chicago Tribune Tower (first prize went to Frank Lloyd WRIGHT), emigrated to the USA. He joined the staff of the University of Michigan before becoming involved in the foundation of the CRANBROOK ACADEMY OF ART from 1924. In 1932 he became its president and was responsible for bringing Charles EAMES, Harry BERTOIA and his son Eero SAARINEN together on its teaching staff – one of the most fruitful conjunctions of designers in the history of American design.

☐ A. Christ-Janer, *Eliel Saarinen: Finnish-American Architect and Educator* (1979)

Salón Internacional de Diseño del Equipamiento para el Hábitat (SIDI; International Salon of Design for Home Furnishings) (f.1984) was born out of Spain's first design magazine, *On* (f.1978). Under the direction of Carme Ferrer and Carme Llopis, SIDI grew as a response to the need to commercialize Spanish design. It thus established itself as an umbrella organization for companies manufacturing and EDITING furnishings and provided a platform for their stands at furniture fairs. Beginning with its first appearance at the Valencia Furniture Fair in 1984, SIDI gradually consolidated the image of Spanish design in the international market through presentations at nearly all the major European furniture fairs. SIDI is open to all comers and, while it is not responsible for the entire sector of furniture production in Spain, its members' exports grew between 1983 and 1988 by 449%, with the USA and France heading the list of buyers.

sans serif is the general term for a typeface without a serif. The serif is the terminal stroke at the top or bottom of the main strokes to be found in roman typefaces.

Sapper, Richard (b.1932) was born in Munich but is mostly associated with Italian design. After studying a wide range of subjects at the University of Munich (1952–55) he worked as a designer with Mercedes-Benz. In 1957 he moved to Milan to work in the studios of Alberto Rosselli and Gio PONTI and in 1959 he and Marco ZANUSO began a design partnership that was to last until 1975.

Sapper's kettle 9091 designed for Alessi in 1984.

Bringing in his German background in engineering, he, along with Zanuso, helped develop Italian product design in the early 1960s. They produced the Doney 14 television (1962) and the Algol 11 television (1964), both for BRIONVEGA, as well as the TS 502 radio (1964). These were all markedly innovative in their internal workings and also displayed the modish Italian style of gentle curves in their casings, thus bringing Italian products into strong competition with their German counterparts. Other notable projects include the 1972 Tizio plastic and aluminium table-lamp for Artemide and the Bollitore whistling kettle of 1982 for ALESSI. From 1980 Sapper was a consultant to IBM.

Savignac, Raymond (b.1907) is a French graphic designer noted for his humorous and colourful approach to advertising posters. He started out as a tracer-sketcher at the Compagnie des Transports Parisiens in 1922. In 1924 he joined the advertising agency Lortac and was assistant to A.M. CASSANDRE in the 1930s. He worked consistently through to the 1990s, his clients including SNCF, Air France, *Life* magazine and CITROËN.

Scarpa, Tobia (b.1935), the son of Carlo Scarpa, studied architecture in his native Venice (1953–57) and then worked as a designer at the VENINI glassworks until 1961. In partnership with his wife Afra, he has since worked as a freelance designer, with clients including B&B ITALIA, CASSINA, KNOLL and Flos. The Scarpas are best known for their soft furnishings, such as the Sirana chair for Cassina (1968).

Schawinsky, Xanti (1904–79) was born in Basle and became a student at the BAUHAUS in 1924, where he worked in the theatre department alongside Oskar Schlemmer. Following the school's relocation from Weimar to Dessau in 1925, he taught stage design and painting. In 1929 he moved to Magdeburg to head the city council's graphic arts studios. He worked as a freelance graphic designer in Berlin (1931–33) and then in Italy until 1936, during which time he produced posters for OLIVETTI that incorporated a bold use of PHOTOMONTAGE and little text. In 1936 Josef ALBERS invited him to teach at BLACK MOUNTAIN COLLEGE in the USA, where he subsequently remained for the rest of his life. He designed the North Carolina pavilion for the NEW YORK WORLD'S FAIR, 1939.

Schenk, Roland (b.1933) studied graphic design at the Basle School of Arts and Crafts (1948–51) where he was influenced by the Modernist poster designer, Armin HOFMANN. He then moved to Paris, returning to Switzerland in 1959 to become art director of *Du* in the same year. In 1966 he worked on the German weekly, *Quick*, a scandal sheet on which he learnt the journalistic skill of using pictures and words to grab the reader's attention. The following year he moved to London to work on *Town*, part of the Haymarket publishing group. He was later able to move within the organization to *Management Today*. Since working on *Du*, his stylistic traits have included

*A poster by **Savignac** advertising Air France (1956).*

shunting the letters of SANS-SERIF headlines close together, placing them off-beam and asymmetrically and positioning text up close to the photograph. Together with Willy FLECK-HAUS, art director of *Twen*, and Herb LUBA-LIN, Schenk has been an important influence on the design of trade magazines.

Schleger, Hans (1898–1976) was born in Kempen, Germany. He studied painting but then worked as a publicity manager and film-

*Veronica chairs, designed by Tobia and Afra **Scarpa** for Casas Mobilplast (1986).*

Schwitters' *collage,* Mz 158, Das Kotsbild (*The Kots Picture,* 1920).

set designer in Berlin, until he moved to the USA in 1924. After a short spell in advertising and magazine design, signing his work Zéró, he emigrated and settled in England in 1932. He became one of the leading commercial artists of the 1930s and 40s, working for Shell, London Transport, Government bodies and the General Post Office among others. In the 1950s he set up the design studio Hans Schleger & Associates and became a pioneer in CORPORATE IDEN-TITY work in the UK. His approach was particularly influential, due to his insistence on comprehensive company research and close involvement with the client. His projects included MacFisheries, Finmar Furniture, Fisons, ICI and the John Lewis Partnership.

Schuitema, Paul (1897–1973) was born in Groningen, the Netherlands, and studied as a painter during World War I. He soon turned to graphic design and from the early 1920s was adviser to Berkel, a manufacturer of kitchen equipment. From 1926 he made use of photography and overprinting with typography in bold compositions. This had some parallels with the work of fellow Dutch designers, Piet

ZWART and Hendrik N. Werkman. He was an influential teacher at the Royal Academy in The Hague (1930–62).

Schwitters, Kurt (1887–1948) studied at the Academy of Dresden, the Berlin Academy and the Technical College in Hanover, the city of his birth. From 1918 he was an exponent of DADA, his work being published in Tristan Tzara's Dada magazine, *Der Zeltweg.* He also lectured throughout Europe spreading the Dada message. He is chiefly known for his Merz collages for the journal *Merz,* which were creations of paper, glue, paint and found objects that reflect a Dadaist outlook. He also maintained a commercial art studio in Hanover, where he designed pamphlets, posters and other advertising for a number of clients, including the city of Hanover itself. In 1929 he worked under Walter GROPIUS as a typographer for the Dammerstock modern housing exhibition in Karlsruhe. His poster for this event, with its SANS-SERIF type and clean composition, reflected current Modernist (*see* MODERN MOVEMENT) interests in graphic design. In 1937 Schwitters left Nazi Germany and moved to Oslo and then in 1940 he escaped the German invasion of Norway and fled to Scotland, spending his last years in England.

Scott, Douglas (1913–90) studied silversmithing at London's Central School of Arts and Crafts and worked in the London office of Raymond LOEWY (1936–39). While at the Loewy studio he worked on fridges and vacuum cleaners for Electrolux. After World War II he set up his own design office and instigated Central School's first industrial design course. In 1949 he founded Scott-Ashford Associates with Fred Ashford. He is best known as the designer of the Routemaster double-decker bus for London Transport (1953). After this experience in engineering, with his new company, Douglas Scott Associates (1955–76), he continued to produce enduring designs in transport and products ranging from baths to public telephone kiosks. From 1976 to 1979 he was professor of industrial design at the Universidad Nacional Autonoma de Mexico (Autonomous National University of Mexico).

☐ J. Glancey, *Douglas Scott* (1988)

Secession is the name given to the Austrian version of ART NOUVEAU. It takes its name

Alfred Roller's poster for the **Secession's** *sixteenth exhibition in 1903.*

from a group who seceded from the conservative Academy in Vienna to form the *Wiener Sezession* (Vienna Secession) in 1897. While primarily consisting of artists and architects, several of its members, including Josef HOFF-MANN, Koloman MOSER and Joseph Maria OLBRICH, designed furniture, metalwork and ceramics. The group also exhibited the work of foreign designers including Charles Rennie MACKINTOSH. The Secession still exists but has been of little importance since the 1920s.
☐R. Weissenberger, *Die Wiener Sezession* (1972)

SIDI *see* SALON INTERNACIONAL DE DIS-EÑO DEL EQUIPAMENTO PARA EL HABITAT

Sipek, Borek (b.1949) was born in Prague and studied furniture design there before moving to Hamburg to study architecture. From there he went to the Institute of Industrial Design at the University of Hanover and then taught design theory at the University of Essen. After considerable international attention following the design of his sister's home, 'The Glasshouse', he moved to Amsterdam, wishing to avoid the more Rationalistic (*see* RATIONALISM) leanings in design he had encountered in Germany. Developing his designs from observations of behaviour, he also built stories around each one, and though he does not admit any direct influences, East European Expressionism is one of those that are indirect. His design work extends from architecture, to furniture and to cutlery for DRIADE.

soft-tech is a term that emerged in the mid-1980s. It normally describes the modification of electronic hardware (e.g., hi-fi systems), giving it curvilinear forms and warm colours. This was, in particular, to be found in Japanese designs by such companies as Yamaha and Sharp. Their designs, drawing on BIOMOR-PHISM and HISTORICISM, were intended to supply more human and humorous connotations, thus confounding a common view that Japanese design is overly functional in appearance. This was to some degree due to the influence of MEMPHIS and POSTMODERNISM in Japan in the early 80s. It was also part of a general shift in Japanese design – not least aided by the enormous spending power of some consumers – towards more witty STYLING in products. The widespread use of American RETRO Modern can also be seen as part of this.

*The **Sony** Walkman (1978).*

Sony started life as Tokyo Tsushin Kogyo (TTK, Tokyo Telecommunications Engineering), which was founded shortly after World War II by Masaru Ibuka and Akio Morita to produce small-scale electrical components. 1950 saw the introduction of the 'G' Type, the first commercially available Japanese tape recorder, the success of which contributed to the continued expansion of TTK. In 1955 the company manufactured the world's first transistor radio which was marketed world-wide under the brand name 'Sony' (taken from the Latin *sonus*, meaning sound). Since the mid-1950s Sony has consolidated its position as one of the most innovative of the Japanese electronics manufacturers, introducing the revolutionary Trinitron television in 1971, the Walkman during the 1980s and then contributing to the technology behind the compact disc (CD) and digital audio tape (DAT). Sony has also expanded into the entertainment business, acquiring the US giant CBS Corporation for $2 billion in 1987.
□N. Lyons, *The Sony Vision* (1976)

Sottsass, Ettore (b.1917) is one of the most important designers of the 20th c. He was born of Italian parents in Innsbruck. After a childhood in Trento, he moved to Turin with his parents in 1928 and enrolled to study architecture at the Polytechnic there in 1934, graduating in 1939. As a soldier during World War II he was based from 1943 in Montenegro, where his childhood interest in rustic, folk traditions was encouraged by the Alpine setting – he produced some designs for cloth that were printed by local craftsmen. After the War he joined the Giuseppe Pagano group of architects in Turin, though his interest in two-dimensional design continued in the form of book covers and scarves. In 1946 he moved to Milan, where he and Bruno MUNARI organized the first international show of abstract art. His own sculpture of the time combined NEO-PLASTICISM with more spontaneous shapes found in the work of Surrealist artists. Similarly, in a chair design presented at the 1947 TRIENNALE he combined the rectilinearity of RATIONALISM with more organic shapes – a unification that shows Sottsass to be at the centre of Italian design consciousness of this period.

By applying his artistic knowledge to design, Sottsass was able to combine his aesthetic, technical and social interests. At the time this was achieved mostly in industrial ceramic, furniture and lighting projects. Thus in the 1950s, with the aid of PLYWOOD, PLASTICS and metal sheet and rod, he broke from FUNCTIONALISM and began to revive the ORGANIC DESIGN styles found in craft activities such as ART NOUVEAU. This approach received much international attention via *DOMUS* and the NEO-LIBERTY movement.

These early years of energetic experimentation laid the ground for his move into product design after 1955. In 1956 he spent several months in the studio of George NELSON in New York. His American experience caused him to take account of mass-consumption and the 'instant values' or speed of the advanced commercial world; with the added influences of POP art and Abstract Expressionism this reinforced his interest in the immediate and sensuous qualities that may be invested in designs. And in a number of interiors executed in the late 1950s he experimented with colour as a spatial element, investigating the ways in which it defined and affected interiors.

In 1957 he began his collaboration with OLIVETTI: their arrangement, which has been maintained ever since, was that Sottsass should be taken on as a consultant with a team of other consultants, separate but employed directly by the company. His designs for Olivetti introduced technical advances while often adjusting the status of the object. In his first major project with Olivetti, the Elea 9003 computer (1959), he reduced the height of the cabinets so that operators could see each other; he introduced overhead ducts for cables, allowing the expan-

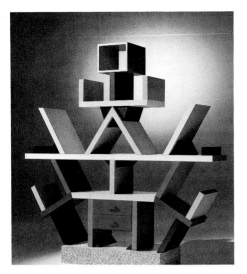

Sottsass's 1981 Carlton room divider for Memphis used colourful print laminate.

sion of the system; colour-symbolism was included to relate parts to each other; in short, its technical and sculptural potential was explored to the full. The object's symbolic function was further developed in typewriters: the Praxis 48 (1962–63) incorporated the carriage into the base, allowing a neater, more compact and decorative appearance. His last consumer product for Olivetti, the Valentine typewriter (1969), which was extremely light and made of red plastic, was tailored almost as a fashion accessory.

Sottsass's designs, which questioned the status of objects, resulted from extensive research and travel. In 1961 he travelled to India and subsequently produced a set of ceramics entitled 'The Ceramics of Darkness' (1963) in which he set out to elevate the object beyond its everyday function. His 'Ceramics to Shiva' (1964), with their decoration of dots, circles and other shapes, were to function as 'spiritual diagrams', by reflecting back to the viewer suggestions of mental and psychic life. In 1965 he produced a series of furniture for Poltronova which incorporated signs from the mass environment – the Lotus table is reminiscent of Mickey Mouse's foot, for instance. Other pieces suggested traffic lights, signage and mechanical equipment. In this way he reversed the status of furniture from high to low cultural positions.

Thus, in playing with visual language and creating new readings of familiar objects, Sottsass was a pioneer of POSTMODERNISM without ever reverting to HISTORICISM. His subversion of accepted standards of 'GOOD DESIGN' and his easy movement between art, craft and design were also important in making him a forerunner of ANTI-DESIGN and subsequently the NEW DESIGN. The groundwork for these new attitudes was thus laid in the 1950s and 60s.

During the early 1970s Sottsass produced little design for mass production. He spent alternate periods in Milan and Barcelona, where he was of considerable importance among more radical designers. He was also concerned with alternative living environments, an interest seen in his work for the important 1972 exhibition, Italy: The New Domestic Landscape at the MUSEUM OF MODERN ART, New York. In 1975 he was a founder-member of the Global Tools group and began work with STUDIO ALCHYMIA in 1979. However, his disagreement with Alessandro MENDINI, who did not share his commitment to creativity as a social force, led him to leave the Alchymia group in 1981 and form MEMPHIS. In 1980 he also formed Sottsass Associati, a studio that provided an umbrella for many young designers starting out during

Design for a building by **Sottsass** *(1983).*

that decade. He continued to design and travel with gusto, finally completing his first architectural project in 1990, while he also continued his research into textures and surfaces. The consistent brilliance of his designs is testimony to his eminently conceptual approach to design.

☐ F. di Castro (ed.), *Sottsass Scrapbook* (1976); P. Sparke, *Ettore Sottsass Jnr.* (1982); J. Burney, *Ettore Sottsass* (1991)

Spiekermann, Erik *see* METADESIGN

Stam, Mart (1899–1986) was a Dutch architect and designer, originally named Martinus Adrianus Stam, who was associated with members of the BAUHAUS and of Russian CONSTRUCTIVISM. He is best known as the inventor of the TUBULAR-STEEL cantilever chair, designed in 1924, which was made with lengths of straight tubing with elbow pieces, as he did not have access to pipe-bending techniques that would have enabled the tubing to be bent in one piece. The augmented springiness resulting from this construction was corrected in 1926. In the same year, both Ludwig MIES VAN DER ROHE and Marcel BREUER took up the idea and Breuer's cantilever chair, which exploited Stam's innovations, was manufactured by THONET from 1928. Stam worked as an architect in the Soviet Union (1930–34) before taking up directorships of art academies in Amsterdam, Dresden and East Berlin from 1939 until his retirement in 1966.

☐ B. Blijstra, *Mart Stam: Documentation of his Work 1920–1965* (1970); G. Dorthuys, *Mart Stam* (1970)

Stankowski, Anton (b.1906) studied painting under Max BURCHARTZ in Essen (1927–29). He then moved to Zurich, where he stayed until 1937, establishing himself as a leader in experimental photography and constructive art. In 1948 he moved to Stuttgart, where he worked as a graphic designer. His research in photography and painting was transferred to typographic and graphic design, in which he became adept at creating pictograms, often influenced by CONSTRUCTIVISM.

Starck, Philippe (b.1949) ranks along with Raymond LOEWY – who was also French – and Javier MARISCAL as a designer of international 'pop star' status. The son of a successful aeronautical engineer, he abandoned his architectural studies to work for the fashion designer

A screen, Le Paravent de l'autre, *designed by* **Starck** *in 1991 and produced in 1992.*

Pierre Cardin. In the early 80s he achieved wide public acclaim by designing furniture for President Mitterrand's private suite in the Elysée Palace. He also designed pieces for the Italian furniture company DRIADE and a set of shelves for the Spanish company Disform. His designs exhibit a strong BIOMORPHISM which influenced much furniture design of the late 80s. His flamboyant lifestyle (he keeps a motorcycle in every major European city, all started with the same key) and skill at self-publicity combine with an irrepressibly prodigious output of designs (he claims to design chairs in less than 15 minutes). He is therefore obviously supported by a strong backup team which ensures that these designs ultimately appear as a diverse range of products: from pasta, toothbrushes and a lemon-squeezer – which took on an iconic value in the homes of the early 90s chic – to large interior commissions such as the Starck Club in Dallas, Texas. In 1990 he completed his first architectural commission which was the headquarters of the Asahi Beer Company. Typically, he chose to top the building with a vast root-like form, giving it a convincing sculptural presence.

Starowieyski, Franciszek, (b.1930) was a leading designer in the second wave of the POLISH SCHOOL of poster design in the 1960s. He studied at the two academies of fine art in Poland in Warsaw and Cracow in the 1950s. A prolific designer of film and theatre posters, he has also worked as a set designer, mural artist and illustrator. His graphic style has been described as a 'Gothic Surrealism' for the way he utilizes a vocabulary of skulls, mutating bodies of women, bulging eyes and hook-beaked birds. His poster for his own retrospective exhibition in 1985 at the MUSEUM OF MODERN ART, New York, displayed classic elements of his style: crudely hand-rendered letter forms and a disturbing image of an eye, out of scale and spilling across a face in profile. In the 1970s Starowieyski was awarded prizes at a number of international poster competitions (including São Paulo and Chicago).
□Danuta Wróblewska, *Polska Grafika Współczesna* (1983)

ingly active as a graphic designer through this decade and the next, working with the poet, Vladimir Mayakovskii.

stile floreale *see* STILE LIBERTY

Stile Industria (1954–63) was an Italian design magazine edited by Alberto Rosselli and published in Italian and English. Throughout the late 1950s it was a vital force in the international establishment of Italian design both aesthetically and theoretically.

stile liberty (or stile floreale) was the Italian version of ART NOUVEAU. It derives its name ·from the British decorative arts retailer LIBERTY & CO., which established commercial links with Italy at the turn of the century. It was mostly applied to architecture and some decorative arts rather than to product or graphic design and reached its zenith at the Turin International Exhibition of 1902. It was revived in design as NEO-LIBERTY in the 1960s.
□G.P. Weisberg, *Stile Floreale: The Cult of Nature in Italian Design* (1988); *Journal of*

Sports clothes by **Stepanova**.

Stepanova, Warwawa (1894–1958) is most often noted for her avant-garde textile designs. She was, however, a leading proponent of Russian CONSTRUCTIVISM and, with Alexei GAN and her husband, Aleksandr RODCHENKO, was a founder of the First Working Group of Constructivists in 1921. Born in Lithuania, she attended the Art School in Kazan (1910–11). In 1912 she moved to Moscow and attended the Stroganov School (1913–14). She taught at the Fine Art Studio of the Academy of Social Education from 1921 and in the textile faculty of the VKHUTEMAS (1924–25). She was also involved in the journals *LEF* (1923–25) and *Novyi LEF* (1927–28). During the 20s she was involved in Futurist literature (*see* FUTURISM), producing her own books. She became increas-

Decorative and Propaganda Arts Vol. 13 (1989; *Stile Floreale* Theme Issue)

Streamform was a decorative style widely used by such American designers active in the 1930s and 40s as Raymond LOEWY and Norman BEL GEDDES. Its main ingredient was a teardrop form – often the outcome of STREAMLINING – which was applied to any object regardless of its function and which gave the impression of aerodynamism and speed. Walter Dorwin TEAGUE and Bel Geddes even spoke of the teardrop as a kind of platonic ideal to be achieved, a final solution to transportation design. The notion that a conception of modernity could be infused into three-dimensional forms had in some ways been previously

expressed by Italian proponents of FUTURISM.
□D.J. Bush, *The Streamlined Decade* (1975)

streamlining is a term which is similar to STYLING, in that it is concerned with the addition of surface effects after the interior workings of an object have been determined. The difference is that it is derived from aerodynamic form and is thus to be seen in car styling developed in particular at GENERAL MOTORS by Harley EARL and by the CHRYSLER CORPORATION during the 1930s and 40s and taken to extremes in the 1950s. However, with its dynamic connotations it also found its way into product design. Thus Raymond LOEWY's Coldspot refrigerator (1932) also appeared, strangely, to be aerodynamic. Streamlining overlaps somewhat with the organic shapes of products facilitated by the development of PLASTICS after World War II.
□F. Weingartner (ed.), *Streamlining America* (1986); O. Boissière, *Streamline: Le Design Americain Des Années 30–40* (1987)

Studio Alchymia (f.1979) was originally founded in Milan as a gallery by the architect Alessandro Guerriero, although it later became a design studio. Guerriero offered designers space to exhibit their prototypes, thus freeing them from the constraints of industry. This allowed for a second wave of ANTI-DESIGN in Milan in the second half of the 1970s, though by now that movement had become more international. Thus the designers he approached in 1978 included Ettore SOTTSASS, Alessandro MENDINI, Andrea BRANZI, the UFO group, Trix and Robert Haussmann, Daniele Puppa, Michele DE LUCCHI and Paola Navone. The name 'Alchymia' was deliberately chosen to confront the rational approach of the MODERN MOVEMENT, instead suggesting the mystical; it looked to popular rather than high culture. Its first two collections, shown in 1979 and 1980, were ironically called 'Bauhaus 1' and 'Bauhaus 2'. Its forms included KITSCH references and motifs recalling imagery from the 1950s – an obvious source in the collections' aims to amalgamate design and everyday life and culture. Mendini became the Studio's key spokesman in the 1980s and he remained preoccupied with the ultimate inability of design to change society. He wrote, 'The avant-garde is fated to play an isolated, aristocratic, restricted and brief role: a kind of enervating programme of self-immolation consumes it

and destroys it before it becomes widely acceptable.' Thus Studio Alchymia described itself as 'post-avant-garde'. In many respects, Alchymia was a forerunner of the more commercial MEMPHIS.
□B. Radice, *Elegia del Banale* (1980); Branzi (1984)

Studio Boggeri (f.1933) is a Milanese graphic design studio founded by Antonio Boggeri. Among the many important designers to work with it were Max HUBER, Bruno MONGUZZI, Bruno MUNARI, Bob NOORDA and Xanti SCHAWINSKY. Thus, much of its output combined an experimental exploration of photography with inventive typographic layout stemming from the indirect influence of the SWISS SCHOOL. It received considerable international attention in the late 50s and early 60s when Italy was perhaps better known for its furniture and product design.
□P. Fossati (ed.), *Lo Studio Boggeri 1933–73* (1974); B. Monguzzi, *Lo Studio Boggeri 1933–1981* (1981)

styling involves the application of surface effects to a product after the internal mechanism has been designed. The intention can be either to disguise or to enhance the relationship between form and function. Invariably it is used as a device for stimulating consumer demand. While styling may be seen as an 'optional extra' in terms of engineering, it is nevertheless important in terms of taste and style.

It is most closely associated with American design between the 1920s and the 1950s and with STREAMLINING in particular. Designers such as Walter Dorwin TEAGUE, Raymond LOEWY, Henry DREYFUSS and Norman BEL GEDDES created forms for goods which emphasized their modernity and speed. Especially in automobile design, the outward appearance of the product changed faster than its inner workings. Built-in OBSOLESCENCE made customers believe that their car was out of style. Given its broad definition, styling takes on all kinds of issues, including KITSCH, MARKETING and FUNCTIONALISM and has often been the cause of virulent debate. Such debate probably originated with the Victorian reformer Henry Cole's campaign for design that was appropriate to the function of an object and continued through to the Functionalist activities of Dieter RAMS at the ULM HOCHSCHULE FÜR GESTALTUNG

By the 1980s designers and manufacturers had to take into account such factors as safety, ERGONOMICS and cost-effectiveness. Styling is now integrated into the whole design process from the outset and not merely applied as an afterthought. Furthermore, automobile designs are no longer altered annually; instead, designers seek image control so that car styles do not date so rapidly.

☐ V. Packard, *The Waste Makers* (1963)

Suetin, Nikolai (1897–1954) studied at the Institute of Art and Practical Work in Vitebsk, Russia (1918–22), and became a member of Kasimir MALEVICH's UNOVIS group in 1919. He moved to Petrograd in 1922 to teach alongside Malevich and worked on Suprematist architecture projects with him (*see* SUPREMATISM). From 1923 he worked at the Lomonossov state porcelain factory in Petrograd, where he applied Suprematist designs. He was artistic director there from 1932, by which time his designs had reverted to a folk realism. In 1935 he painted Malevich's coffin with a black square in homage to Suprematism.

Supergraphics entails the application of large-scale graphics to architecture. Words and images are incorporated as part of the building, rather than as an added afterthought, as is the case with advertising hoardings. It emerged as a

Barbara Stauffacher Solomon used **Supergraphics** *for the interior of the Sea Ranch Swim Club, Somona, California (1966).*

term in the mid-1960s and, in drawing attention to a building's symbolic function through the use of images and text, may be seen as a developmental aspect of POSTMODERNISM. Robert VENTURI was an early exponent of Supergraphics.

Superstudio (f.1966) was a design and architecture group that worked in ANTI-DESIGN or RADICAL DESIGN and was formed in Florence along with ARCHIZOOM. Its members were Cristiano Toraldo di Francia, Alessandro and Roberto Magris, Piero Frassinelli and Adolfo Natalini. They worked on real and Utopian architectural designs and film projects. The group's increasing disillusionment with mainstream design was reflected in its catalogues and exhibitions up until 1973. It envisaged an environment in which everyone had a basic, neutral space to inhabit without the need for objects, and therefore production and consumption. Its Quaderni tables of 1971, manufactured by ZANOTTA, imposed a plastic-laminate grid pattern on the carcass, reflecting Superstudio's visionary architecture projects, so that rows of such tables appeared to stretch into infinity.

☐ Ambasz (1972)

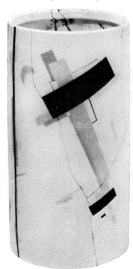

Suetin *applied Suprematist patterns to ceramics such as this vase (1929).*

Suprematism was a concept developed by Kasimir MALEVICH and first demonstrated in an exhibition of his paintings in Petrograd at the

Il'ya Chashnik used the abstract forms of **Suprematism** *to decorate a dinner service in 1923.*

0.10 Gallery in 1915. In 1916 he gathered a group of artists together and published a Suprematist journal entitled *Supremus*. The concept was expressed by the reduction of the picture to a Euclidian geometric arrangement of forms in pure colours, designed to represent the 'supremacy of pure emotion'. Such reductionism involved formal exercises which later fed into Malevich's Utopian projects for housing complexes from 1919 onwards. Malevich, Il'ya Chashnik and Nikolai SUETIN also applied these exercises to ceramics in 1921 and 1922 as did Lyubov' Popova to textiles (*c.*1924). Some proponents of CONSTRUCTIVISM saw this as little more than applied art, ignoring any functional requirements. Suprematism's reductionism of form and colour was, however, subsequently picked up by the DE STIJL movement.

Surrealism is an artistic approach sometimes used in design. It emerged as an art movement headed by André Breton following the demise of DADA in 1922. The poet Guillaume Apollinaire had used the term in 1917 and it was also influenced by Sigmund Freud's exploration of the subconscious through psychoanalysis. However, the Surrealists maintained that the subconscious was to be expressed by poetry or imagery, 'free', according to Breton 'from the exercise of reason and every aesthetic or moral preoccupation'. The result was either the careful depiction of a dreamworld, as seen in the work of Salvador Dali or Giorgio de Chirico, or a more deliberate construction of strange conjunctions of found objects or disjunctures between titles and accompanying images. This second practice was more directly prefigured by Dada and in particular by Marcel Duchamp.

His interfacing of art and the real world and his plays on the meanings of objects were rediscovered in conceptual art in the 1960s and were also to be seen in the work of ANTI-DESIGN. Both approaches had frequently been seen in graphic design from the 1920s. Examples of Surrealist design are the advertisements designed in the 1930s by British artists for the Shell Oil Company (e.g., Paul Nash's surreal landscapes) and the posters designed by Surrealist artist Man Ray for the London Underground (1932). Many other graphic designers have used Surrealist techniques, in particular Milton Glaser (*see* PUSH PIN STUDIO).

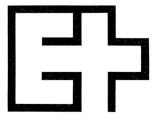

A **Swiss School** *logo for the Swiss National Exhibition, Expo '64, by Armin Hofmann.*

Swiss School, also known as the International Typographic Style, was a typographic style that developed in the centres of Zurich and Basle. Benefitting from Swiss neutrality prior to and during World War II, graphic designers were able to extend the experiments in typography and PHOTOMONTAGE made at the BAUHAUS. A tradition of excellence in graphic design was established by Ernst KELLER at the Zurich School of Arts and Crafts from 1918. Théo BALLMER, studying under Keller, introduced the idea of using a rigid grid system to organize the page, while Max BILL, who had studied at the Bauhaus (1927–29), contributed the typography of Herbert BAYER and the sometimes asymmetric layout, harmonizing contrasting and complementary relationships into an ordered whole. Other notable contributors to the Swiss style were Jan TSCHICHOLD, who emigrated from Germany to Basle in 1933 to teach at the School of Arts and Crafts there, and Anton STANKOWSKI, who was in Zurich from 1929 to 1937. Apart from its grid structure and careful layout of type across the page, the other characteristics to emerge during the 1930s and 1940s were the use of 'objective photography' – photographic images that do not make exaggerated claims on the subject matter – and its use in photomontage, the ranging left of text with a ragged right, and the use of SANS-SERIF type. Above all, it represented a precision and coldness that may on first consideration deny any sense of individual expression. To accept this as universally true of the Swiss School, however, would be to ignore the exuberant expressiveness of individuals such as Max HUBER or Armin HOFMANN.

The Swiss School became nationally accepted, thanks in part to governmental patronage of publicity, stemming principally from tourism campaigns which began at the beginning of the century. During the 1920s and 30s, the results encompassed the modern language of photomontage and the New Typography. At the Swiss National Exhibition of 1939, a large number of graphic works were exhibited, and since then an annual exhibition has been mounted to celebrate the best publicity posters. This verve for new graphic design fed into the expanding economy of the postwar period – Basle, for instance, was also the centre of Switzerland's important chemical industry which in turn patronized new design. It was through these industries that the Swiss School was launched internationally in the 1950s.

The typefaces Univers, designed by Adrian FRUTIGER in 1954, and Helvetica, revived by Max Miedinger in 1957, became international symbols of the Swiss School. Through the 1960s, Helvetica in particular was one of the most widely used typefaces in Europe. The International Typographic Style underwent greater dissemination following the appearance in 1959 of the journal, *NEW GRAPHIC DESIGN*. Its editors were four designers who played a major role in the evolution of the Swiss School: Richard P. Lohse, Josef MÜLLER-BROCK-MANN, Hans Neuberg and Carlo L. Vivarelli. This journal crystallized the philosophy and practice of the Swiss School. By the 1960s some Swiss designers, such as Siegfried Odermatt and Rosemarie Tissi (*see* ODERMATT & TISSI) and Wolfgang WEINGART, began to break down the general austerity of the style, introducing greater dynamism into the composition. Elsewhere the style underwent further investigation and development into the 1980s, for instance in the work of Wim CROUWEL in Amsterdam and April GREIMAN in Los Angeles.

system furniture is a term that refers to the design and production of a limited number of

The flexibility of **system furniture** *is demonstrated by Ettore Sottsass's Sistema 45 (1969), an office design for Olivetti.*

furniture elements which can be mounted in different combinations, thus providing a variety of configurations using the same basic pieces. This makes it the direct opposite of single-piece furniture, which does not belong to a 'family' of objects. It has been exploited in office furniture gradually since the 1940s, where the office layout shifted from the arrangement of desks in rows, with manager-overseer facing them, to the breaking up of the open space into small offices, divided by low walls. These walls usually doubled as storage spaces, a development that was prefigured by George NELSON for HERMAN MILLER with his 1945 Storage Wall. Nelson's 1964 Action Office, conceived in conjunction with Robert PROPST, was the first fully flexible, integrated and module-orientated walled office system, the concept of which was subsequently developed further.

Tatlin's *design for a Monument to the Third International* (1919).

T

Takahama, Kazuhide (b.1930) was born in Nobeoka, Japan, and graduated in 1953 in architecture from the Industrial University of Tokyo. In 1957 he went to Milan to set up the Japanese stand at the TRIENNALE, where he met Dino GAVINA for whom he designed a divan bed in 1958. In 1963 he settled permanently in Italy, designing furniture for CASSINA and B&B ITALIA, often combining Japanese and Italian influences.

Tallon, Roger (b.1929) is a pioneering industrial designer in France. He studied electrical engineering in Paris (1947–50) before becoming a designer with Studio Avas (1951–53). He then worked freelance until he became director of design research at Technès in 1963. In 1973 he founded Design Programmes, a multi-disciplinary team which gained international prominence through its design of the Corail train for the French railway network. In 1984 he joined Pierre PAULIN's ADSA + Partners and throughout the 1980s worked on the design for France's high-speed train, the TGV.

Tatlin, Vladimir (1885–1953) was a leading theorist of Russian CONSTRUCTIVISM. He studied painting at the Moscow School of Painting, Sculpture and Architecture (1902–4) and at the Penza Art School (1904–10). During his time at the latter he also frequently travelled abroad, principally to the Middle East. From 1910 to 1920 he was linked to exponents of Russian FUTURISM – illustrating books of their poetry – and became a leading member of the Moscow avant-garde. Immediately after the Revolution he became responsible for the implementation of Lenin's Plan for Monumental Propaganda. Moving to Petrograd in 1919 he began designing his famous Monument to the Third International, a model of which was exhibited in Petrograd and Moscow in 1920. The sources for this structure were various, ranging from the Eiffel Tower in Paris to the masts of ships. Tatlin's pre-revolutionary experiments with constructions of iron and glass expressing movement and tension and examining the materials' interrelationship may also be cited as sources. Tatlin was thus important in exploring the potential of a

A barometer by **Teague** *(1949).*

machine aesthetic, drawing on new constructional techniques. From 1921 he was involved in the Petrograd Museum of Artistic culture, setting up the department of material culture, which was concerned, in its widest role, with design in mass production. His subsequent teachings and writings were particularly involved in the cultural impact of materials. He taught industrial design (or rather 'production art', as it was termed by the Constructivists) at the VKHUTEMAS from 1927. In the 30s he returned to figurative painting.

☐ J. Milner, *Vladimir Tatlin and the Russian Avant-Garde* (1983); L.A. Zhadova, *Tatlin* (1984)

Teague, Walter Dorwin, Sr (1883–1960) was, alongside Raymond LOEWY and Norman BEL GEDDES, one of the USA's pioneer industrial design consultants. Born in Indiana, USA, he moved to New York in 1903 to become an artist. He studied at the Art Students League and briefly worked in an advertising agency. In 1911 he set up his own typographic office. By the mid-1920s he was also involved in PACKAGING and in 1927 began to work in industrial design. His first and long-lasting major client was Kodak. Teague developed a complete consultancy package for the company, providing accurate, up-to-date product appraisal and development. The subsequent Vanity Kodak was the first camera to function as a fashion element: its body and bellows were produced in a range of colours with a matching silk-lined case. Teague was also acclaimed for his design for the Baby Brownie camera (1933), which included an early application of PLASTICS. The

Bantam Special (1936) continued the miniaturization of the camera. Here, horizontal metal strips were not only decorative but also gave protection against possible cracking of the lacquer. The 1939 620 Special combined the view finder and the exposure meter. Thus Teague offered both technological and aesthetic innovations to his client. Other designs included the FORD and US Steel pavilions for the NEW YORK WORLD'S FAIR, 1939, Pullman coaches for the New Haven Railroad (mid-1930s) and the interior of the Boeing 707 (early 1950s). In 1944 he was the first president of the American Society of Industrial Designers. He is also distinguished as the author of a best selling book, *Design This Day: The Technique of Order in the Machine Age* (1940), in which he expounds a quasi-Modernist viewpoint, derived in part from a visit to Europe in 1926. His son, Walter Dorwin Teague, Jr, continued to run the consultancy after his death.

Telakowska, Wanda (1905–86) began her print-making and design career as a member of the Polish design group Ład (Order). After World War II, she ran the production department of the Ministry of Culture and, from 1950, was director of the Institute of Industrial Design, a research body in Warsaw. Through the worst excesses of the Stalinist period in Poland (until 1956), although an advocate of modern design derived from vernacular roots (she had continued the CRACOW SCHOOL tradition into the Communist period in Poland), Telakowska was a protector and sponsor of many Modernist designers (*see* MODERN MOVEMENT). She organized collaborative schemes to bring professional designers, folk artists and children together, resulting in a number of surface patterns for ceramics and textiles that were produced from the mid-1950s.

☐ W. Telakowska, *Wzornictwo moja miłość* (1990)

Testa, Armando (b.1917) worked in various jobs in his native Turin before studying at the Vigliardi Paravia School of Graphic Arts (1932–34). He worked freelance as a graphic designer until establishing a studio in 1946 which became an advertising agency ten years later. His advertising posters, such as those for Pirelli in the 1950s, used the visual language of SURREALISM with increasing subtlety and ambiguity through to the 1980s.

Thonet

*Production began on **Thonet**'s bentwood Chair No. 14 in 1859. 50 million had been sold by 1930.*

Thonet (f.1853) was founded in Vienna by Michael Thonet, a cabinet-maker from Boppard-am-Rhein in Germany who had experimented in bentwood, taking out a patent in 1841 and exhibiting at London's 1851 International Exhibition. Thonet underwent relentless expansion in mass-produced furniture: by 1900 it had factories all over Central Europe and produced 4,000 pieces a day, and by 1930 50 million of its Chair No.14 had been produced. It also manufactured a number of designs by Josef HOFFMANN, Adolf LOOS and Otto WAGNER. While keeping its old best sellers going, it maintained an active programme of modernization of its range. Using bentwood, Thonet had manufactured nesting furniture that was comfortable without extensive upholstery, sometimes using runners rather than legs. The company then moved towards TUBULAR STEEL in the 1920s, producing designs by Marcel BREUER, such as his Wassily chair (1930), thus coinciding with and popularizing the experiments of members of the BAUHAUS.
□T. Benton and B. Campbell-Cole (eds), *Tubular Steel Furniture* (1979)

Tomaszewski, Henryk (b.1914) is hailed as a father figure of the POLISH SCHOOL of poster design. He studied graphics under Mieczyslaw Kotarbinski at the Academy of Fine Arts in Warsaw (1934–39), where he himself became head of poster design in 1951 and later professor of graphic design in 1955. His designs are simple and direct, often using a simple collage approach, which is then silk screened.
□J. Bialostocki, *The Graphic Arts in Poland 1945–1955* (1956); B. Kwiatkowska, *Henryk Tomaszewski* (1959)

Toorn, Jan van (b.1932) worked as a freelance graphic designer in Amsterdam from 1957. He was a tutor in graphic design at the Gerrit Rietveld Academy from 1968 and became director of the Jan van Eyck Academy in Maastricht in 1990. His radical teaching and practice were highly influential on the younger generation of Dutch designers. His posters are marked by the use of provocative and sometimes shocking imagery – commonly with a strong political charge; type often 'floats' across the image to create a strong visual and semantic juxtaposition of the two. The strong emotional charge in his designs stems from his interest in investigating visual meaning as opposed to

__Tomaszewski__'s poster, Circus (1965).

*Van **Toorn**'s poster* la lutte continue *(1989).*

purely practical requirements. His work includes posters, postage stamps and literature for the Dutch PTT (post office) from the 1970s onwards.

Total Design (f.1963) was founded as a multidisciplinary consultancy in Amsterdam by Wim CROUWEL, Friso Kramer and Bennon Wissing. It soon became the Netherlands' most important studio, undertaking the celebrated CORPORATE IDENTITY scheme of the Dutch PTT (post office) (1978–79), which was the zenith of the SWISS SCHOOL influence on Dutch graphics.
□H.C. Boekraad in *Holland in Vorm: Dutch Design 1945–1987* (ed. Stedelijk Museum, Amsterdam, 1987)

Toyota (f.1933) was founded in Tokyo as a car manufacturer by Kichiro Toyoda, using capital from his father's automatic-loom-making company. Its first production car, the AA (1937), was very similar to the Chrysler Airflow (*see* CHRYSLER CORPORATION). Due to World War II needs and the postwar occupation, car production was interrupted (1944–49), but during the 1950s massive investments went into renovating the plant. A 'suggestion

system', whereby workers were encouraged to make constructive comments as to how production might be improved, was adopted, following a model seen at FORD in 1950. The difference, however, was that suggestions were increasingly implemented, and by 1960 production capacity exceeded 30,000. Its first car exported to the USA, the Toyopet (1958), was a dismal failure. However, through assiduous MARKET RESEARCH Toyota recognized that the market already served by imports of the VOLKSWAGEN Beetle was growing. So in 1960 an updated version of the 1957 Corona was launched to compete in product quality and performance, comfort and after-sales service. Thus Toyota's design approach was an integral part of an aggressive MARKETING strategy. It established factories in the Far East, South Africa and Portugal during the 1960s. In their STYLING Toyota's cars were perhaps unremarkable, but in the development and implementation of advanced electronics in cheaper cars, they broke new ground. Toyota is also noteworthy for the development of JUST IN TIME methods of manufacture in the 1970s, inspired apparently by a visit to an American supermarket by Kichiro Toyoda.

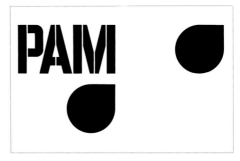

Total Design's *logotype for PAM Oil products* (c.1964).

Triennale is a triennial exhibition held in Milan. It began as the Biennale, first held in Monza, Italy, in 1923. It was conceived by Guido Marangoni to exhibit local, artisanal production, but soon passed on to show sophisticated design projects. In 1930 the 'International Biennial of Decorative Art' became the 'International Triennial of Decorative and Modern Industrial Art' and in 1933 it moved to Milan. Subsequently it became an important

Tschichold's *title-page for his manifesto on typography, published in October 1925.*

showcase and means of promotion of trends in Italian design.

□A. Panser, *Storia e Cronaca della Triennale* (1978)

Tschichold, Jan (1902–74) ranks among the most revered practitioners, theoreticians and historians of 20th-c. typography. The son of a type designer, he studied calligraphy at the Academy for the Graphic Arts and the Book Production Trade in Leipzig, where he was born. In 1923 he visited the BAUHAUS exhibition in Weimar and was profoundly impressed, in particular by the work of László MOHOLY-NAGY. A combination of this experience and a disenchantment with the prevailing typography of the time led him to embrace the Bauhaus's Modernist principles (*see* MODERN MOVEMENT). In October 1925 he published a manifesto in the Leipzig journal *Typographische Mitteilungen* (Typographic Notes), entitled 'Elementare Typographie' (Elementary Typography). Couched in an understandable language for the ordinary person, this manifesto was widely read and discussed. In 1925 Paul RENNER appointed Tschichold as a teacher of typography and calligraphy at the Munich

School of Master Book Printers. While in Munich he began to write *Die Neue Typographie* (The New Typography), which was published in 1928. This book was the very first publication in any language to attempt to lay down principles of typographic design for a wide range of applications. In this way, he introduced to a wide audience – including practical printers as well as avant-garde artists – the principles of 'the new typography'. He advocated a Functionalist's aesthetic (*see* FUNCTIONALISM): economy of expression, SANS-SERIF type and asymmetrical composition. The book itself, published in Berlin, was an elegant production showing that Tschichold had already assimilated traditional approaches to graphic production and was combining them with modern aesthetics. The book is dogmatic (coincidentally like Eric GILL's writings) and reveals a streak of Socialist idealism similar to that found in the work of William Morris. Tschichold was quick to recognize the importance of photography as a design tool in advertising. These elements may be seen in a series of Phoebus-Palast cinema posters.

In 1933 he emigrated to Switzerland to escape Nazi oppression. There he continued to write and practise as a typographer. He published *Typographische Gestaltung* (Typographic Layout) in Basle in 1935. It was translated and published in Denmark and Sweden in 1937 and in the Netherlands in 1938. It was not published in English – under the title of *Asymmetric Typography* – until 1967. Tschichold visited London in 1935, where he met Edward McKnight KAUFFER, Ashley HAVINDEN and Stanley MORISON and also designed the 1938 volume of *The PENROSE ANNUAL* (he later designed the 1949 edition). In 1935 he published an article in the Swiss printing journal *Typographische Monatsblätter* (Typographical Monthly), which stated that a symmetrical layout was acceptable. This apparent volte-face, although supported by much rational explanation, caused something of an uproar among dedicated Modernists, in particular Max BILL and Kurt SCHWITTERS. Tschichold, however, began to read the uncompromising nature of the new typography as having parallels with National Socialism, and returned to a more traditional typographic style, seeing the new typography as an alternative, not an obligation. In 1947, at the invitation of Allen Lane, he moved to England to revise the typographic design of Penguin books. Tschichold laid down

DEUTSCHE STAHLMÖBEL G.M.B.H.
BERLIN SW 61
TELTOWERSTR. 47-48

DIE NEUEN FEDERNDEN
STAHLMÖBEL
haben durch ihre Formschönheit, Zweckdienlichkeit
u. unerreichte Bequemlichkeit größte Erfolge erzielt.

FORDERN SIE KATALOG NR. 291

Advertisement for **tubular-steel** *furniture produced by Deutsche Stahlmöbel GmbH, Berlin, in 1930.*

strict standards for layout but not for typeface, which was to be chosen according to the book. At the end of 1949, his work for Penguin completed, he returned to Basle. His best designs for Penguin were published in a single book (*Designing Books*) in 1951, which was also published in Denmark, Switzerland and the USA, indicating the broad distribution of his work. During his remaining 23 years he continued to research and write on all aspects of the history of calligraphy, printing and book design. He also completed his last important typographical commission, the Sabon typeface (1965–68). □R. McLean, *Jan Tschichold: Typographer* (1975); P. Luidl (ed.), *Jan Tschichold* (1976); W. Klemke, *Leben und Werk des Typographen Jan Tschichold* (1977); J. Tschichold, *Die Neue Typographie: Ein Handbuch für Zeitgemäss Schaffende* (facsimile edition, 1977)

tubular steel was developed in Germany. The first generally successful process for its production was patented in 1885 by Max and Reinhard Mannesmann. It was differentiated from early piping systems by the absence of any seam between the two edges, which would limit the strength and spoil the appearance of the tube. Tubular steel's earliest application was for bicycles, using tubes of 95–380 mm ($\frac{3}{8}$–$1\frac{1}{2}$in.) outside diameter. Its use was extended to other areas of transport construction in the early 20th c.; a high strength to weight ratio made it an attractive substitute for wood, or for use in welded tubular structures, where it replaced riveted angle sections. The Dutch aircraft designer, Anthony Fokker, working in Germany, used welded steel tubing for his aircraft, the 'Spin' (Spider) Mark I of 1910, World War I acted as a catalyst for the material's develop-

ment and application. Fokker's innovations were handed over to the victorious powers after armistice in 1918. The development of portable welding equipment during the War also allowed for more flexible applications of tubular steel. The material itself was improved; in 1921 a patent was granted to the Maschinenfabrik Sack GmbH and Josef Gassen for a method of producing tubing with thinner walls that retained its strength.

The use of tubular steel increased dramatically in the 1920s. While the actual details of its use in automobile seats are still unclear, it is believed that it was this use that influenced Mart STAM in his application of the material to furniture in 1926. Stam's own use was first exhibited in the DEUTSCHE WERKBUND's WEISSENHOF SIEDLUNG and was a cantilevered tubular-steel chair, made up by Stam using gas conduit tubes and 'L' joints. Certainly the use of tubular steel formed part and parcel of the Modernist (*see* MODERN MOVEMENT) leanings of fellow Dutch architects and designers such as J.J.P. Oud, W.H. GISPEN and Piet ZWART, who were exponents of the DE STIJL movement and the 'Amsterdamse School' in the 1920s. As a relatively new technology, it coincided with an awareness of the development and expansion of the new architecture, with its aesthetic of pure materials.

Marcel BREUER also designed tubular-steel furniture, which was exhibited at the Weissenhof Siedlung in 1925. Among these first designs was his Wassily chair, first manufactured by THONET. Breuer and Ludwig MIES VAN DER ROHE both exploited Stam's innovation of the cantilever tubular-steel chair from 1926, incorporating the use of a CHROMIUM finish. Thonet continued to manufacture tubular-steel furniture in the 1930s. It was introduced into

Tusquets's Gaulino chair (1986) was produced by Carlos Jané.

Britain first by Cox & Co. in 1929 and then by PEL from 1931. Indeed, by the 1930s, chromed tubular-steel furniture was almost synonymous with the MODERNE style. It also began to be produced as CONTRACT FURNITURE for large corporations for office use, and even for village halls.

Despite the introduction of new materials such as PLASTICS into furniture, and the development of ALUMINIUM as a metal for seating, tubular steel has maintained its importance. This has been due largely to its continued competitiveness as a material: it can be produced and worked in small industrial units with relatively little investment in plant. Europe's leading area in the manufacture and working of tubular steel is in the West Midlands of Britain.

An important innovation in the use of the material took place in the mid-1970s with the development of epoxy finishing; this allowed a variety of surface effects to be applied, including a polyester finish, mostly for outdoor furniture, or a matt-black textured finish which became increasingly popular in the 1980s, as seen in the design work of Philippe STARCK and Marie-Christine Dorner. From 1987, the British designer Martin Ryan developed the spinning of tubular steel with the company Portfolio; it was thereby given a tapering effect, thus pushing the material once more beyond the standard association with the Modern Movement aesthetics of LE CORBUSIER et al. □ T. Benton and B. Campbell-Cole (eds.), *Tubular Steel Furniture* (1979)

Tusquets, Oscar (b.1941) graduated from the Barcelona School of Architecture in 1965 and then formed Studio Per with his classmates Lluís Clotet, Cristian Cirici and Pep Bonet. Having previously worked in the architectural studio of Correa-Milà, Tusquets was well connected with the avant-garde architects in Barcelona who would later make up the Barcelona School (a loose alliance of architects). He has often been seen as Spain's representative of POSTMODERNISM, mostly following his private house, the Belvedere de Regàs (1972). However, the label of Postmodernism is one that Tusquets himself would reject as being too orthodox and one that can only be applied by critics in its widest sense. His activities are varied, ranging from painting, through interior and product design to architecture. Likewise, the styles he adopts are eclectic, including POP, Modernista (*see* MODERNISME), Conceptual and neo-Classical influences. In 1973 Studio Per and others, in particular Xavier Carulla, formed B.D. Ediciones de Diseño, to produce designs that no one else would risk manufacturing at the time.

Typos (1981–82) was published just four times by the London College of Printing. None the less it is a useful source for graphic design historians, as it contains both analytical articles on past graphic designers and movements (e.g., the POLISH SCHOOL and Jan TSCHICHOLD) and up-to-date discussion of design theory. As its name suggests, its bias was towards typography.

U

UFO (f.1967) began in Florence as a small group of architects and other associated intellectuals motivated by RADICAL DESIGN. The group used such materials as papier mâché, POLYURETHANE and inflatables as well as literary quotes and linguistic theorems. The theoretical work of the group was very important, particularly in research into language. Among their collaborators was the writer Umberto Eco.

Ulm Hochschule für Gestaltung (Ulm College of Design) (f.1950) was founded as a private institution by Inge Aicher-Scholl and Otl AICHER following meetings with Max BILL in Zurich from 1947. Following the break in continuity caused by the rise of National Socialism and World War II, during which Aicher-Scholl's brother and sister had been executed by the Nazis, the Ulm project was primarily conceived as a rejuvenation of the BAUHAUS spirit. The teaching of design began

Utility *furniture (1942), by the Design Panel of the Board of Trade, chaired by Gordon Russell.*

in 1953 with Josef ALBERS, Johannes ITTEN and Ludwig MIES VAN DER ROHE as visiting tutors. In 1955, with Max Bill as its director, the school opened officially in new buildings. Bill was succeeded by Tomás MALDONADO in 1956 with Hans GUGELOT in the directorate. The central concern was to revive Walter GROPIUS's idea of co-operative endeavour, as well as the humanization and systematization of design methodology. In its attempts to realize this, Ulm, like the Bauhaus, was thwarted by internal struggles. Its courses included semiotics, contextual studies and psychology. The school's design aesthetic has been chiefly associated with the coolly industrial, stylized forms produced by Dieter RAMS and Gugelot for BRAUN. Maldonado left in 1967. When, in 1968, the local authorities starved the school of financial support, it being too radical for their tastes, its teachers refused to continue, and it closed down.

□T. Maldonado in *Rassegna*, No. 19, special issue on Ulm (1984); M. Krampen and H. Kächele (eds), *Umwelt, Gestaltung und Persönlichkeit: Reflexionen 30 Jahre nach Gründung der Ulmer Hochschule für Gestaltung* (1986); IDZ, *IDZ Protokolle: Hochschule für Gestaltung Ulm* (1987); B. Rübenach, *Der Rechte Winkel von Ulm* (1987); H. Lindinger, *Hochschule für Gestaltung Ulm: Die Moral der Gegenstände* (1987); Centre de Création Industrielle, Paris, *L'Ecole d'Ulm: Textes et Manifestes* (1988); H. Roericht (ed.), *HfG-Synopse: Eine Synchron-Optische Darstellung der Hochschule für Gestaltung Ulm* (1988); H. Jacob, 'HfG Ulm: A Personal View of an Experiment in Democracy and Design Education' in *Journal of Design History* Vol. 1, Nos 3 and 4 (1988); R. Kinross, 'Hochschule für Gestaltung Ulm: Recent Literature' in *Journal of Design History* Vol. 1, Nos 3 and 4 (1988)

Unimark International (1965–77) was founded in Milan by Massimo Vignelli (*see* VIGNELLI ASSOCIATES), Ralph Eckerstrom and Bob NOORDA. After opening an office in New York within a year, it soon became one of the first truly global graphic design companies, with eleven offices in the USA, Europe and the Far East. At its peak it employed 500 staff but it foundered in the late 1970s due to the world economic recession.

Utility furniture and textiles were produced from 1941 to 1951 in Britain in response to the demands of a war economy. This was undertaken under the auspices of the Board of Trade which had Gordon RUSSELL as chairman of its Design Panel from 1942. This body issued or approved designs for production. Its origins in part go back to 1938, when Russell had started an association to produce dignified furniture at low cost on his own private initiative. Russell took the agenda from this venture into Utility, although the latter's activities were driven primarily by the need to ration materials in the short term and exert influence on the domestic manufacturing sector of the political economy (particularly in textiles) in the long term.

In furniture, much of Utility's output was the fruit of loosely applying principles derived from the ARTS AND CRAFTS movement, which were then transferred to mass production. Thus radical proposals were not necessarily made. Nevertheless, Russell offered goods of high quality at low prices and introduced high standards of integrity in design to a population that had been denied them by peacetime traditions in retailing which favoured poor-quality furniture. In 1948 controls on furniture production were lifted. This was not before, it has been argued, Utility had been promoted as a form of 'consumer protection' to counteract criticisms of the performance of newly nationalized industries under the postwar Labour government.

☐J. Daniels, *Utility Furniture and Fashion 1941–1951* (1974); H. Dover, *Home Front Furniture: British Utility Design, 1941–1951* (1991); P. Maguire, book review of H. Dover in *Journal of Design History* Vol. 5, No. 2 (1992)

*An Art Nouveau motif is seen in Henry van de **Velde**'s cup and saucer (c.1904) made for the Dresden porcelain factory, Meissen.*

V

Vantongerloo, Georges (1886–1965) was a sculptor, born in Antwerp, Belgium. He met Theo van DOESBURG in 1915 and participated in the founding of the DE STIJL group two years later. Although he withdrew from De Stijl in 1921, he continued to create abstract pieces and, in 1931, became part of the Abstraction-Création group in Paris, the city in which he died.

Velde, Henry van de (1863–1957) was born in Antwerp, Belgium, and studied painting there (1881–84) and then in Paris (1884–85). In Paris he came into contact with other Post-impressionist painters, though in 1892 he gave up painting for architecture and design. He was much influenced by the writings of John Ruskin and William Morris (indeed, reflecting the late 19th-c. Anglophilia, he changed the spelling of his first name to the English form). By the end of the 19th c. he had founded his own decorating firm and factory near Brussels and his curvilinear ART NOUVEAU furniture designs were well known. Moving to Berlin in 1900, he designed in almost every field, including advertising graphics. In 1902 he was appointed to set up a school of applied arts in Weimar, and designed its building. This was the precursor of the Weimar BAUHAUS. His ideal was the *Gesamtkunstwerk* (total art work), in which he would design not only the building but all its fittings also. In 1907 he was a founder-member of the DEUTSCHE WERKBUND, where he championed an artistic approach. This led in 1914 to disagreement with Hermann MUTHESIUS, who believed in the standardization of design. In the same year, as an enemy alien at the outbreak of war, he had to resign his post at the Weimar school; among those he recommended as his successor was Walter GROPIUS. In 1917 he moved to Switzerland and then in 1920 to the Netherlands, returning to Switzerland in 1947.

☐L. Ploegaerts and P. Puttemans, *L'Oeuvre Architecturale de Henry van de Velde* (1984); K.-J. Sembach, *Henry van de Velde* (1989)

Venini (f.1925) is a Venetian glass-making company noted for its progressive design policy. Its founder was Paolo Venini, a Vene-

*Robert **Venturi**'s tea and coffee service (1983) designed for Alessi.*

tian lawyer who bought the Murano glasshouse of Giacomo Cappelini. Originally a maker of ornamental glass, it began to show more avant-garde pieces at the Monza Biennale in 1923 and subsequently at the Milan TRIENNALE. Venini glass is distinguished by its high quality, use of colour and strong abstract forms. From the 1950s it commissioned designs from Franco ALBINI, Gio PONTI, Massimo VIGNELLI and Tapio WIRKKALA. From 1959 it was run by Venini's son-in-law, Ludovico de Santillana.

Venna, Lucio (pseudonym of Giuseppe Landsmann) (1897–1974) was one of the most prolific graphic designers of Italian FUTURISM. Born in Venice, he moved to Florence in 1912 where he worked with the illustrator Emilio Notte and met the leaders of Futurism, Filippo Tommaso Marinetti and Umberto Boccioni. In 1917 he and Notte published the manifesto 'Fondamento Lineare Geometrico' (Basic Linear Geometrics) in *L'Italia Futurista*. In 1922 he abandoned painting to concentrate exclusively on applied graphics and founded the Studio Venna-Innocenti, collaborating with the Innocenti publishing house until 1928. His design work included covers of *Gran Sport* (1930–32), advertising for Debenham & Freebody, London, and work done as artistic director of *Scena Illustrata* (1937–59). □ M. Fidolini, *Lucio Venna dal Secondo Futurismo al Cartellone Pubblicitario* (1987); G. Fanelli and E. Godoli, *Il Futurismo e la Grafica* (1988)

Venturi, Robert (b.1925) is an American architect who is known as a father of POSTMODERNISM. This is in part due to his book, *Complexity and Contradiction in Modern Architecture* (1966), originally delivered as a series of lectures at the MUSEUM OF MODERN ART,

New York. He countered the formalism of the MODERN MOVEMENT and the subsequent INTERNATIONAL STYLE with the belief that architecture and design should embrace the eclectic visual landscape already at hand. He extended this thesis with the architects Denise Scott Brown and Steven Izenour in *Learning from Las Vegas* (1972), in which he calls for architects to be more receptive to the tastes and values of 'common' people rather than erecting 'heroic' self-aggrandizing monuments. Thus he draws attention to the symbolic forms used in demotic structures such as hamburger kiosks, doughnut shops and gasoline stations, and sees the cityscape as a pattern book of signs that can be taken up and reused. This approach specifically owes something to the writings of Roland Barthes on semiotics, but it also has some relevance to POP design, ANTI-DESIGN and the researches of such Italian designers as Ettore SOTTSASS. It is by no means insignificant that the starting point for this theory is an appreciation of the everyday object and its design rather than architectural and urban planning. Venturi designed a tea and coffee service for ALESSI (1983) and furniture for KNOLL in 1984, both of which are eminently, even flippantly, decorative in effect. His theories may be criticized for their cynical plundering of popular culture and for a loss of the vision and Utopian drive intended by proponents of both RADICAL DESIGN and the Modern Movement itself.

video graphics is a branch of graphic design which, as it is for televisual presentation, includes the dimension of time in its practice. Graphics in television may be used in many ways: for title sequences, to explain data using graphs or maps, or in intermediary spaces between programmes to reinforce the television or video company's CORPORATE IDENTITY. The medium means that graphic images must be planned to be read within particular spaces of time, to be set against moving images and/or to be animated. Its pedigree is in film, a major pioneer in this being Saul BASS. His title sequences for films such as *The Man with the Golden Arm* (1959) were influential on early television graphics in the creative use of drawn, animated imagery and type. In 1963 Bernard Lodge produced the first video graphics using video techniques rather than artwork for the BBC's *Dr Who* series; this was done by exploiting the picture distortion effects that occur when a video camera is

*Stacking melamine mugs (1972), designed by Massimo and Lella **Vignelli** for Heller.*

directed at a monitor. Lodge went on with Colin Cheesman to develop video graphics using COMPUTER-AIDED DESIGN (CAD). The development of video graphics was subject to the development of television itself – in Britain, for example, it did not have an immediate effect, despite the appearance of highly sophisticated CAD programmes, such as Paintbox and Harry, in the mid-1980s. Competition from satellite and cable television as well as pressure on television monopolies in the later 1980s ensured greater channel BRANDING and thus a greater call for graphics to put over the station's corporate identity. The animation of logos meant that their basic design had to be subject to variations. At times, they may merge to create a flow of images rather than a set of discrete units. This visual phenomenon had already been predicted by Raymond Williams in his book *Television: Technology and Cultural Form* (1974). This phenomenon was made more acute as video graphics were increasingly aimed at technical effect to interweave with programmes rather than more cultivated or mature results in the late 1980s.
□D. Merritt, *Television Graphics: From Pencil to Pixel* (1987); J. McClellan, 'TV in the Age of Eye Candy' in *Eye* Vol. 1 (1990)

Vignelli Associates (f.1971) was founded in New York by the Italian architects Massimo and Lella Vignelli who moved to the USA permanently in 1965 to work for UNIMARK

International. Vignelli Associates' work includes furniture, tableware and interiors, but the studio is best known for its graphic design. The hallmark of its three-dimensional design is a combination of simplicity, clear colours and vitality, while its graphic design makes an expressive use of typography while maintaining a grid structure derived from the SWISS SCHOOL. Its CORPORATE IDENTITY programmes include KNOLL (1966) and the New York department store Bloomingdale's (1972). □E. Ambasz, *Design: Vignelli* (1980)

Visible Language see JOURNAL OF TYPOGRAPHIC RESEARCH

VKhUTEMAS was the name of the avant-garde art and design school founded in Moscow in 1920. It is an abbreviation of *Vysshie gosudarstvennye kyhudozhestvenno-tekhnicheskie masterskie* (Higher State Artistic and Technical Workshops). Its forerunner was the State Free Art Studios which was founded in 1918 following the abolition of the Stroganov School of Applied Art and the Moscow School of Painting, whose establishment had encouraged the abandonment of Academic Realism in painting

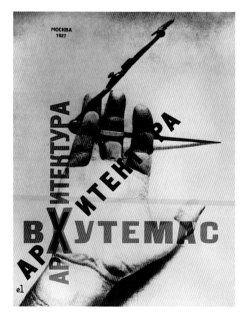

El Lissitzky's cover for Architecture *and the* **VKhUTEMAS** *(1927).*

Assembly line for the prewar
Volkswagen *Beetle.*

for Western European movements such as Impressionism, Cubism and FUTURISM. In reality there was a complex debate among its students between the traditionalists and the avant-garde. This resulted in the foundation of the VKhUTEMAS in which the pure fine art bias gave way to a mission to respond to the actual psychological and material needs of post-Revolutionary Russia. Thus the school was structured to allow for the training of artists for industry, but also for the cultural transformation of the country. As such it was the natural ground for the promotion and development of Russian CONSTRUCTIVISM. Among its staff were Aleksandr RODCHENKO, Warwawa STEPANOVA, Gustav KLUTSIS and El LISSITZKY. The textiles and ceramics faculties maintained close links with industry. The amalgamation of the metal and woodwork faculties in 1926 created the Dermetfak; much innovative furniture and product design came out of this body which was guided by the Constructivist ideal that the form of an object should be determined by the material from which it would be made. Many prototypes were produced, though, despite the plan to link with industry, none went into production.

The VKhUTEMAS played a similar role in the development of modern design in the Soviet Union as did the BAUHAUS in Germany, and there were several personal links between the two organizations via, for instance, Wassily Kandinsky and El Lissitzky. Like the Bauhaus the VKhUTEMAS also underwent considerable internal disagreements. Partly as a

result it became the VKhUTEIN in 1928 which in turn dissolved in 1930.
□ Lodder (1983)

Volkswagen (f.1938) was established in the new town of Wolfsburg, Germany, to manufacture the car that became known the world over as the 'Bug' or the 'Beetle'. It originated in 1933 when two motorcycle companies, NSU and Zundapp, signed a contract with Ferdinand PORSCHE for the development of a small car. This was followed in 1934 by a contract made between Porsche and the Reichsverband der Automobilindustrie (Reichs Union of the Automobile Industry) to construct a 'People's Car'. Adolf Hitler was personally interested because the idea not only provided a counterpart for the *Volkswohnung* scheme (People's housing), but it also provided a cover for his military plan to build a network of *Autobahns* (motorways) throughout Germany.

Hitler laid the foundation-stone for a manufacturing plant in Wolfsburg on 26 May 1938. Production of the People's Car – called the KdF-Wagen – was postponed by the outbreak of World War II, during which Volkswagen produced 100,000 military vehicles. From 1945 the Wolfsburg works were under British administration and the Beetle went into volume production. Its revolutionary features included a rear-mounted air-cooled engine, its distinctive body, designed by Erwin KOMENDA, and its remarkable cheapness – Hitler had promised it at under 1000 DM. In 1949 Volkswagen returned to German control and, under the plant manager Heinz Nordoff, proceeded to make the Beetle the dominant car in its class in Europe and then in the USA, due in part to a brilliant advertising campaign. This was stepped up by the agency work of Doyle Dane Bernbach from 1959, with its laconic style countering the lavishness put over by Detroit STYLING which peaked in 1958.

In 1950 Volkswagen put its popular van into production. By the early 1970s it was realized that the company was too reliant on the production of small cars, and it began to diversify and broaden to include medium- and larger-sized saloons and estate cars. They also replaced the Beetle with the Golf (1974) in Western markets – production of the Beetle stopped in Germany in 1979 but continues in Mexico and Brazil. The Golf was designed by Giorgietto GIUGIARO: this water-cooled car was the first of many similar fuel-efficient hatchbacks that appeared in the 1970s. By the 1990s Volkswagen was noted not just for the efficiency of its models, but also for its drive towards environmentally friendly production, promoting the recycling of parts as well as materials in the production process.

□K.B. Hofinger, *Beyond Expectation – The Volkswagen Story* (1954); T. Shuler, *The Origin and Evolution of the VW Beetle* (1985)

Coronation tea set designed by Star **Wedgwood** *for King George VI's coronation in 1937.*

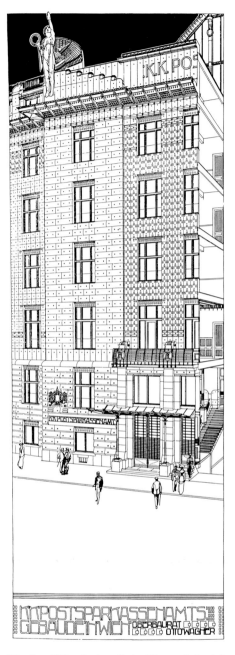

The Post Office Savings Bank, Vienna, designed by **Wagner** *in 1904.*

Wagner, Otto (1841–1918) was a leading architect of the Vienna SECESSION. At the turn of the century he became City Architect and employed such architects as Joseph OLBRICH and Josef HOFFMANN. He is also accredited as an early pioneer of the 20th-c. MODERN MOVEMENT. Furniture designed for his Postal Savings Bank in Vienna (1904–6) was produced by THONET and, in its starker FUNCTIONALISM, is invariably cited as a forerunner of Modernist developments a decade later.

Wedgwood, Josiah & Sons Ltd (f.1759) is a Staffordshire pottery, renowned for its early industrialization of the production process. It maintained a leading world position in industrial ceramics, with directorship passing through five generations of the Wedgwood family. Following the depressed market of the late 1920s, the company was reorganized and began to experiment in new directions. Some of its ware, designed by Eric Olsen from 1931, was markedly ART DECO in style, though it also produced more Modernist pieces, such as those designed by Keith MURRAY. From the 1950s the firm underwent considerable expansion; by the 1980s it employed about 2,500 people and headed a group which incorporated a wide range of ceramic manufacturers, including Susie COOPER Ltd.
□M. Batkin, *Wedgwood Ceramics 1846–1959* (1982)

Wegner, Hans (b.1914) trained as a cabinet-maker in Copenhagen (1927–31) and remained there to study furniture design at the School of Arts and Crafts (1936–38). He later worked in the office of Arne JACOBSEN (1940–43). From the late 1940s he designed a series of chairs for the furniture manufacturer Johannes Hansen which helped establish Denmark's postwar international reputation in design. His designs are characterized by their attention to detail, their structural complexity, physical and visual lightness, their elegance and the fact that they are mostly made using natural materials.

Weil, Daniel (b.1953) studied architecture in Buenos Aires and then industrial design at London's ROYAL COLLEGE OF ART (1978–81).

Wegner's E-legged chair (c.1949).

Weil's Cambalache AM/FM Radio (1982).

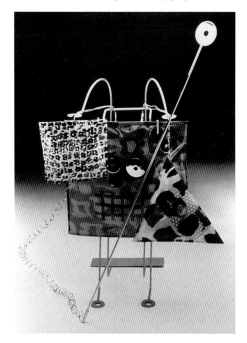

He came to international recognition through a series of clocks, radios and lights which he designed for and immediately after his degree show in London. These were encased in plastic bags, revealing their workings; his point was that it was only 'tradition' that boxed radios up and restricted their visual language. Through the 80s, he and Gerard Taylor worked with ALESSI, KNOLL and Ettore SOTTSASS on various interior, product and furniture projects, invariably characterized by a questioning conceptual approach. In 1991 he was made professor of industrial design at the Royal College of Art and became a partner of PENTAGRAM Design in 1992.

Weingart, Wolfgang (b.1941) is sometimes referred to as the father of CALIFORNIA NEW WAVE graphics. This is due to his systematic departure from the strictures of the SWISS SCHOOL, his subsequent teaching in Basle from 1968 and frequent international lecturing, especially in the USA. After a three-year apprenticeship as a typesetter from 1958 in Stuttgart, he travelled to Basle where he enrolled at the School of Arts and Crafts, studying briefly under Emil Ruder and Armin HOFMANN. Neither was of significant stylistic influence on Weingart, but Hofmann did introduce the notion of a systematic approach to learning. Weingart worked freelance in Basle for several years and then after Ruder's death in 1968 he was asked to join the faculty. His teaching and practice in the 70s broke away from the Swiss School's formats of grid system, asymmetry and use of text ranged-left with a ragged right. Instead he explored wide spacing between type, the combination of different type sizes and the use of 'demotic' letterforms, such as a typewriter script. The results may be seen in issues of *Visible Language* (*see JOURNAL OF TYPOGRAPHIC RESEARCH*) which he designed in 1974. During the 70s he also began to experiment with film montage, stacking and layering film positives to create juxtapositions of images, text and textural effects. This often featured enlarged halftone dots. Fascinated by the process as opposed to the finished result, he showed how visual subtlety and complexity may be produced without the aid of an APPLE Macintosh computer, allowing, perhaps, a slower, more considered approach – his work prefigures the more computer-based activities of exponents of the California New Wave. He said in an interview published in the graphic design magazine, *Eye*, 'I see type as a kind of picture that speaks. I'm a maker not a thinker. What's reflected here is my activity, not my inner being.'
□ W. Weingart, *How One Can Make Swiss Typography* (1972)

Weissenhof Siedlung (Weissenhof Estate) was an entire housing estate created by the DEUTSCHE WERKBUND for its Stuttgart exhibition of 1927. Participants in the project included Peter BEHRENS, Marcel BREUER, LE CORBUSIER and his brother Pierre Jeanneret, Josef Frank, Walter GROPIUS, Adolf LOOS, Ludwig MIES VAN DER ROHE, J.J.P. Oud and Mart STAM. The theme of the exhibition was 'The Home', and thus the interior furnishings, which included early examples of TUBULAR-STEEL furniture, were an important aspect. The project was dogged by administrative problems, but the estate was inhabited until 1939. After years of decay, the surviving buildings became historical monuments in 1956 and were restored in 1968.
□ Deutsche Werkbund, *Bau und Wohnung* (1927); K. Kirsch, *The Weissenhof Siedlung: Experimental Housing Built for the Deutsche Werkbund, Stuttgart, 1927* (1987)

white space is a term primarily used by exponents of the SWISS SCHOOL and quite literally means the blank spaces on a page, free of type or imagery. It may be used to make type more legible or to introduce greater vigour in the impact of an image.

Widmer, Jean (b.1929) studied under Johannes ITTEN at the School of Arts and Crafts in Zurich (1945–50). He took courses at the Paris Ecole Nationale des Beaux-Arts from 1952 and was then art director for the SNIP advertising agency, Galeries Lafayette and the magazine *Jardins des Modes* (1955–70). He founded his own agency Visual Design in 1972 and was in charge of the CORPORATE IDENTITY of the CENTRE DE CRÉATION INDUSTRIELLE, Paris (1974), and, in collaboration with Bruno MONGUZZI, the Musée d'Orsay (1983–87). He is important as being among those who introduced the typographic style of the SWISS SCHOOL to France and as a teacher of Pierre Bernard of the GRAPUS studio.

Wiener Werkstätte (Vienna Workshops) (1903–32) was an Austrian-based association of

The logotype by Josef Hoffmann for the **Wiener Werkstätte.**

arts and crafts workshops. In 1897, a group of artists and designers left Vienna's Künstlerhaus (the Artists' Association) to form an independent artists' association, known as the SECESSION. Its aim was mostly to procure private patronage in the absence of an effective system of commercial galleries or a supportive programme of government commissions. The Secession's magazine, *Ver Sacrum*, promoted its ideas, which included a call for unity of the arts. The art critic and Secession member Hermann Bahr dreamed of a 'tremendous studio, a colony of workshops where the artists will work with the craftsmen . . . with OLBRICH at the head, with Engelhart, Professor Böhm, Zelezny and the multifariously artistic Koloman MOSER, who would all work together, day after day, in large workshops, on the close implementation of their projects.'

Koloman Moser and Josef HOFFMANN made Bahr's vision a reality with a number of activities that culminated in the devotion of the Eighth Exhibition of the Secession in 1900 to handicraft. Hoffmann stated that the exhibition 'strives to achieve an identical goal within any nation: to impart appropriate form to modern perception.' As an international exhibition, therefore, it included designs by Charles Rennie MACKINTOSH and C.R. ASHBEE. It is such contact, in particular with Ashbee and his Guild of Handicraft, which Hoffmann later visited, that led to the foundation of the Wiener Werkstätte in 1903 with the financial support of a rich banker, Fritz Wärndorfer.

The Wiener Werkstätte, Produktiv-Gemeinschaft von Kunsthandwerkern in Wien (Vienna Workshops, Production Co-operative of Artist Craftsmen in Vienna) eventually incorporated bookbinding, metalwork, leather-work, jewelry and furniture, as well as Hoffmann's own architectural practice. It soon became the Viennese centre of progressive design and rapidly secured an international reputation. Its first exhibition, held at the Hohenzollern Kunstgewerbehaus (Hohenzollern House of Arts and Crafts) in Berlin, coincided with the October 1904 issue of *Deutsche Kunst und Dekoration* (German Art and Decoration) devoted to the Wiener Werkstätte. By 1905 it employed over 100 craftsmen. This factory-size group of workers may give it an ambiguous status in the face of current debates on craft and mass production. However, seen in the context of turn-of-the-century Austria, which had not undergone such advanced industrialization as other European countries, it may be argued, as Jane Kallir does, that the Wiener Werkstätte 'was geared to deal with the industrial situation as it existed in early 20th-c. Austria but not to change with it.' Thus, it worked on an international scale, both in Europe and in the USA, with various subsidiary groups offering interior design and its implementation.

The first major commission, won in 1904, was the Palais Stoclet in Brussels. Until 1915 the Werkstätte's style was characterized by this building's severe rectilinear design and an inability to cater for popular tastes or budgets. From that date, with the growing dominance of Dagobert Peche, a shift towards a more eclectic and curvilinear style can be detected. In 1928, 25 years after its foundation, it enjoyed a brief upturn in its fortunes but, despite the philanthropic support by industrialists such as Otto Primavesi, the rich patronage it required was scarce and it went into liquidation in 1932.

☐ T. Benton, S. Muthesius and B. Wilkins, *Europe 1900–1914: The Reaction to Historicism and Art Nouveau* (1975); P. Vergo, *Art in Vienna 1898–1910* (1981); W.J. Schweiger, *Wiener Werkstätte: Design in Vienna 1903–1932* (1984); J. Kallir, *Viennese Design and the Werkstätte* (1986)

Wirkkala, Tapio (1915–85) studied sculpture in Helsinki (1933–36) and worked as a designer for the glass and ceramics manufacturer Iittala (1946–85). In 1946 he designed the famous Kantarell vase which formed part of his show at the Milan TRIENNALE of 1951 which won three Grands Prix. This show helped establish 'Scandinavian Modern' as an internationally recognized style. His glassware explored the full potential of the material as well as its optical effects. He also worked with Raymond LOEWY

Wirkkala's *Puukko knives, produced from 1963 to 1987.*

(1955–56) and VENINI (1959–85). Among his other famous designs figure Finnish currency (1952), four stamps for the 1952 Olympics, the all-purpose Puukko steel and black nylon knife made by Hackman since 1963 and porcelain vases produced by Rosenthal since 1975.
□P. Berengo Gardin, *Tapio Wirkkala* (exh. cat., Triennale, Milan, 1984)

Wolff Olins (f.1965) began life as a London-based multi-disciplinary design consultancy with about twelve professionals and with a common aim of wanting to take on large projects. Among its early projects was a design programme for the London Borough of Camden, possibly the first CORPORATE IDENTITY for a local authority. It then worked on relaunching a paint company, Hadfields, which was struggling in the face of such dominant companies as ICI's Dulux, Hoechst's Berger and Reed's Crown – the 60s was the age in which giants emerged in all industries. With a new company logo of a fox symbolizing cunning, shrewdness and independence (it must be remembered that corporate identities are conceived as much if not more to inculcate and maintain a sense of loyalty among the company's staff as to present a particular exterior image), Hadfields was to maintain its position among the competition. Subsequently, Wolff Olins was instrumental in establishing corporate identity on the business map of indispensable requirements by the end of the 60s. The company expanded through the 90s to become one of the world's most significant corporate identity specialists, with offices in London, Barcelona, San Francisco and Copenhagen and over 130 personnel. Their projects have included the Bovis hummingbird identity (1973), the Q8 petroleum retail stations network (1986) and the controversial redesign of the British Telecom corporate identity (1991).

An armchair designed by **Wright** *(c.1904).*

Wright's *drawing for Willitt's House, Highland Park, Illinois (1902).*

Wright, Frank Lloyd (1867–1956) was primarily known and revered as an architect, though he is also of importance as a design theorist. Born in Wisconsin, USA, he studied engineering at the University there (1885–87). In 1888 he joined the architectural office of Louis Sullivan, the architect closely connected with the development of the theoretical concept, FUNCTIONALISM. He left in 1893 to set up in partnership with Cecil Corwen and then on his own in 1896. Wright's interest in Japanese architecture combined with Sullivan's influence to produce a style that departed from European theoretical ideals and embraced ORGANIC DESIGN. His subsequent architectural projects were often characterized by an emphasis on the horizontal, a tendency to sit low in the landscape, asymmetry, simplicity, a lack of representational forms and the use of natural materials. His Kaufmann House, best known as Fallingwater (1935–39), is often regarded as the zenith of his architectonic vision: the private house straddles a stream, its stone vertical elements support interpenetrating horizontal planes that are constructed in reinforced concrete. Thus the building sits in harmony with its woodland surroundings while at the same time demonstrating the expressive power of its own materials. This latter aspect is also regarded as a departure from the principles of the European MODERN MOVEMENT, which some believe sought greater neutrality in architectonic form.

The tension between modern and traditional found in Fallingwater also pervades Wright's furniture designs. The combination of a strong rectilinearity and traditional materials often gave his pieces an uncomfortable and heavy appearance. Thus, despite much promotion on his part, they never received wide acclaim. It was mainly through his architecture and his prolific writing and lecturing, therefore, that Wright extended the principles of organic design and maintained a decorative tradition in design.

□F. Gutheim (ed.), *In the Cause of Architecture: Essays by Frank Lloyd Wright for the Architectural Review 1908–1952* (1975); R. Sweeney, *Frank Lloyd Wright: An Annotated Bibliography* (1978); B. Pfeiffer, *Frank Lloyd Wright* (1991)

Y

Yokoo, Tadanori (b.1936) is a Japanese graphic designer. He has worked for several printing and advertising firms (1954–65), including the Nippon Design Center in Tokyo (1960–64). Since then he has worked freelance. His poster design gained him an international reputation in the mid-1960s; it was distinguished by its visual density, mixing Japanese and English images and text.

Z

Zanotta (f.1954), formed by Aurelio Zanotta, was based in Lissone, Milan, and set out initially to produce mainstream domestic furniture at its small plant in Nova Milanese. In 1958 it began to experiment in modern pieces and in 1965, in collaboration with Mario Scheichenbauer, it started to manufacture pieces by avant-garde designers such as Gae AULENTI, Vittorio Gregotti and the CASTIGLIONI brothers. From then on it maintained a policy of being designled and of using relatively new materials such as expanded POLYURETHANE foam. Its inflatable chair, Blow (1967), by DE PAS, D'URBINO E LOMAZZI is an example of such innovation. Since the late 1960s Zanotta has also produced many re-editions, including the Castiglioni brothers' Mezzadro chair (1957) in 1970 and Hans CORAY's influential Spartana chair (1938) in 1971.

□S. Casciani, *Mobili come Architetture: Il Disegno della Produzione Zanotta* (1984)

Zanuso, Marco (b.1916) was born in Milan and studied architecture at the Milan Polytechnic (1935–39). After service in World War II he established an architectural office in Milan, working on many architectural projects, such as OLIVETTI's headquarters in São Paulo and Buenos Aires. He was also editor of the magazine *Casabella* and served on the Milan city council (1956–60). In 1948 Zanuso was asked by Pirelli to produce some designs using the foam rubber that the company had developed as a potential furnishing material. As a

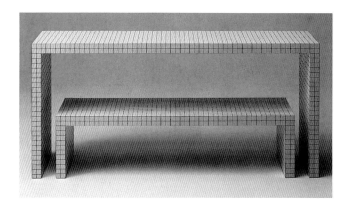

The Quaderna tables designed by **Zanuso** *for Zanotta (1970–71).*

result of his work, the Arflex company was formed as an offshoot of Pirelli, and Zanuso was given the key position of taking designs from conception through production to the finished result. Thus he moved increasingly towards design projects. His Lady armchair (1951) for Arflex was among the first to exploit the aesthetic implications of foam rubber, a material that made it possible to translate the streamlined aesthetic of metal objects such as cars into furniture. Like much Italian design of this period, in particular that of Joe COLOMBO, his designs (e.g., a 1957 sewing machine for Borletti or a 1962 television for BRIONVEGA) achieved a minimalist as well as a sculptural presence. He worked with Richard SAPPER from the late 1950s to the early 1970s, producing the innovatory TS 502 radio in 1964 and the first chair made entirely out of polythene for ZANOTTA in the same year.

☐G. Dorfles, *Marco Zanuso: Designer* (1971)

Zapf, Hermann (b.1918), a native of Nuremberg, began to study calligraphy privately at the age of 17. His two major sources were Rudolf KOCH's *Das Schreiben als Kunstfertigkeit* (Writing as a Talent) and the German edition of Edward JOHNSTON's *Writing & Illuminating & Lettering*. In 1939 he went to work in Paul Koch's foundry in Frankfurt, and it was there that he was put in contact with the Stempel foundry, for whom he began to create typefaces. He also wrote a book of calligraphic alphabets, *Feder und Stichel* (Quill and Gouge, 1941). After service in World War II he became the design director of Stempel. His Palatino typeface (1949) was based on Renaissance forms; this elegant typeface quickly became popular in the West Germany of the immediate postwar period where there was little choice in faces. He also published *Das Blumen ABC* (The Flower ABC, 1948) and the first volume of his *Manuale Typographicum* (Typographic Manual, 1954). This manual, the second volume of which appeared in 1968, covers 18 languages and over 100 typefaces. Each page consists of a typographic expression of a quotation on typography.

In 1956 Zapf left Stempel to concentrate on his own work. He has since designed Optima (1958), which he called a 'serifless roman' (*see* SANS SERIF). Foundries such as LINOTYPE, BERTHOLD and the INTERNATIONAL TYPE-FACE CORPORATION have all benefitted from his designs, the last of these with fonts in digital format. He also published *About Alphabets* (1960) and *Typographische Variationen* (Typographical Variations, 1963). Thus his prodigious designing and publishing output make him an important figure in the development of 20th-c. typography.

☐H. Zapf, *Hermann Zapf and his Design Philosophy* (1987)

Zenit (1921–26) was a leading avant-garde periodical published in Yugoslavia and dedicated to radical aesthetics such as free verse ('words in space') and abstraction in art. It was produced in Zagreb and later in Belgrade. Founded and edited by Ljubomir Micić, this journal reveals many of its editor's contradictory views. Micić was clearly influenced by various Constructivist notions (*see* CONSTRUCTIVISM), such as that of the 'artist-engineer', and by the MODERN MOVEMENT, as seen in his advocacy of artistic and typographic

Modernism (in 1922 covers were designed by El LISSITZKY and Lajos KASSÁK). Yet he also advocated a particularly virulent and mystic strand of Pan-Slavism and Serbian nationalism opposed to the 'perverse culture' of Europe, that owed much to Russian Symbolist thought at the turn of the century. Micić's ambitions for a Greater Serbia seem to have impaired his ability to notice the extremely advanced designs, akin to the work of László MOHOLY-NAGY, produced by artists such as August Cernigoj in Slovenia. *Zenit* was eventually closed by the authorities on the mistaken grounds that it was a Marxist publication.
□ *The Journal of Decorative and Propaganda Arts*, Yugoslavian theme issue (Autumn 1990)

Zolnay (f.1851) grew in the 1870s to become the largest ceramics manufacturer in the Austro-Hungarian Dual Monarchy before World War I and was based in Pécs, Hungary. Its success lay, for the most part, in the international demand for its high-lustre glazed domestic wares and, above all, its Eosin wares, which had a shiny metallic finish. Zolnay commissioned designs from a number of well-known artists and designers, such as József Rippl-Rónai, who was associated with the Hungarian ARTS AND CRAFTS movement. It also produced high quality industrial ceramics, such as porcelain electrical fittings, and the architectural tiles that gave Hungarian Secession buildings, designed by architects such as Ödön Lechner, their particular character. After World War I the Zolnay company fell into decline through mismanagement and the difficulties in which Hungary found herself after the treaty of Trianon in June 1920.
□ E. Hárs, *Zolnay Kerámia* (1988)

Zwart, Piet (1885–1977) is influential in graphic design for his combination of the architectonic control of the DE STIJL movement and the poetic expression of DADA. He studied at the School of Arts and Crafts in Amsterdam (1902–7) where little formal division was made between design disciplines. He went on to teach drawing and history of art at a girl's school in Leeuwarden and in 1911 began to work in furniture and interior design. After service in World War I he came into contact with members of the De Stijl group, although he never joined them, regarding the movement as too dogmatic. He worked with the architect Jan Wils (1919–21), for whom he designed a

A vase made at the **Zolnay** *factory, Pécs (c.1900).*

letterheading which clearly echoed Theo van DOESBURG's typography and layout for the *De Stijl* magazine. In 1921 he moved to the architectural office of H.P. BERLAGE, where he began to produce advertising designs for a firm of flooring manufacturers in The Hague. From 1925 he devoted most of his energies towards graphic design. He is noted for his sensitive, yet playful 'collaging' of type to create rhythmic compositions with dynamic contrasts of size and weight and of black form on the white page. He was also architectural correspondent of the daily newspaper *Het Vaderland* (1925–28). He developed an interest in photography and began to introduce photographs (from 1928 using his own) and PHOTOMONTAGE into his graphic design. During the late 1920s he designed for the Dutch post office, the PTT, producing, for example, a series of stamps in 1929. He was also a guest teacher at the BAUHAUS in 1931. During World War II he was arrested by the Nazis and held as a hostage. In the late 1940s he returned to industrial design and developed the famous Bruynzeel kitchen, a forerunner of the modern fitted kitchen.

Chronological chart

Where no further information is given, a date refers to the date of foundation, or publication in the case of a book.

	USA	Great Britain and Ireland	Belgium, the Netherlands and France	Scandinavia
Before 1910	1905 Frank Lloyd Wright makes first trip to Japan	1898 Heal's first furniture catalogue 1902 C.R. Ashbee's Guild of Handicraft moves to Chipping Campden 1907 Dryad founded by Harry Peach	1904 Jean Francois van Royen joins Dutch PTT 1905–11 Josef Hoffmann's Palais Stoclet, Brussels, designed and built	1904 Georg Jensen workshop, Copenhagen
1910–19	1913 First Model T Ford manufactured on production line system 1919 Lloyd Loom	1913 Omega workshops 1913 Ambrose Heal becomes chairman of Heal's 1915 Design and Industries Association	1913 Citroën 1917 De Stijl launched	
1920–29	1925 Cranbrook Academy of Art 1926 Container Corporation founded; develops first cardboard packaging 1928–29 Buckminster Fuller develops Dymaxion concept 1929 Museum of Modern Art, New York	1922 Stanley Morison joins Monotype Corporation 1929 Susie Cooper Pottery	1922 Eileen Gray founds Jean Desert in Paris 1923 Le Corbusier's Vers une Architecture 1925 Paris Exposition des Arts Décoratifs et Industriels 1927 W.H. Gispen begins manufacture of Giso lamp 1928 First CIAM, Paris	1929 Alvar Aalto designs Stacking Stool

·rmany, ʌitzerland and stria	Eastern Europe	Italy and Spain	Japan	Technology
·7 Vienna ·ession ·3 Wiener ·rkstätte ·4–5 Hermann ·thesius's *Das ·glische Haus* ·5–6 Peter ·rens designs ·G corporate ·ntity ·7 Deutsche ·rkbund	1902 Cracow School initiated 1902 Gödölő Workshops	1899 Fiat 1902 Stile Liberty reaches zenith at Turin International Exhibition 1908 Olivetti 1909 Futurist manifesto launched 1909 Alfa Romeo	1898 Toyoda (later Toyota) Company	1910 Tubular steel used in Fokker Spider Mark 1 aeroplane
·6 Dadaist movement, Zurich ·9 Bauhaus ·nded in Weimar	1911 Czech Cubism initiated 1915 Kasimir Malevich launches Suprematism in Petrograd 1917 Constructivism emerges in Russia	1919 Fiat Lingotto factory begins production	1918 Matsushita	1912 Monotype produces Imprint, first original typeface for mechanical composition
·5 Isotype formu-·ed by Otto ·urath ·5 Bauhaus ·ves to Dessau ·7 Weissenhof ·dlung, Stuttgart ·7 Herbert Bayer ·signs Universal ·eface	1920 Devetsil Group 1920 VKhUTEMAS 1920–21 Productivism established in Russia 1921–26 *Zenit*, Yugoslavia 1926 Praesens group	1923 First Triennale in Monza 1927 Cassina 1928 *Domus* magazine		1924 Mart Stam designs tubular-steel cantilever chair 1925 Chromium made commercially available

Chronological chart

	USA	Great Britain and Ireland	Belgium, the Netherlands and France	Scandinavia
1930–39	**1932** MOMA exhibition, The International Style **1934** Chrysler Airflow launched **1934** Raymond Loewy develops Coldspot refrigerator **1937** Harley Earl designs Buick 'Y' Job **1939** New York World's Fair	**1931** Eric Gill's *An Essay on Typography* **1931** PEL **1932** MARS **1933** Henry Beck designs London Underground map **1935** Industrial Design Partnership (*see* Misha Black) **1936** Nikolaus Pevsner's *Pioneers of the Modern Movement*	**1932** *De 8 en opbouw* **1937** Paris Exposition Universelle **1939** Citroën 2CV launched	**1931** Den Permanente, Copenha **1939** Arabia becomes Europe's gest manufactur of porcelain
1940–49	**1942** MOMA exhibition, Organic Design in Home Furnishings **1948** Sigfried Giedion's *Mechanization Takes Command* **1949** Buckminster Fuller develops geodesic dome	**1941** Utility **1943** Design Research Unit **1946** Britain Can Make It exhibition		**1943** Ikea, Swed **1946** Tapio Wirkkala design Kanttarell vase **1949** Finn Juhl designs Chieftai chair
1950–59	**1951** Aspen International Design Conferences begin **1956** Saul Bass designs credits for *The Man with the Golden Arm*	**1950** Ernest Race designs Antelope and Springbok chairs **1951** Festival of Britain **1952** Independent Group **1959** Alec Issigonis's Mini	**1957** Citroën DS launched	**1950** Hans Weg designs 'The Ch

rmany, itzerland and stria	Eastern Europe	Italy and Spain	Japan	Technology
0 50 million net No. 14 irs have now n produced 2 Bauhaus es to Berlin 3 Bauhaus es 4 Walter pius moves britain 7 Gropius and zló Moholy-jy move to the 3 Volkswagen tle launched 8 Herbert Bayer Ludwig Mies der Rohe move he USA		1930 Pininfarina 1933 Studio Boggeri		1937 Polyurethane developed
	1949 Soviet Socialist Realism imposed throughout Eastern Europe	1946 Piaggio launches Vespa motor scooter	1948 Honda	1940–45 PVC, polystyrene, Perspex and polythene developed
0 Ulm Hochule für taltung 4 Adrian tiger designs vers typeface 7 Max Mieder designs Helca (see Swiss ool) 8 New Graphic ign, Zurich		1953 Stile Industria 1956 Gio Ponti designs Superleggera chair for Cassina 1956–57 Fiat 600 and Nuova 500 launched 1957 Ettore Sottsass begins collaboration with Olivetti	1957 GK Industrial Design Associates	1950s CAD originated at Massachusetts Institute of Technology 1957 Icsid 1958 Berthold introduces first commercially available photosetting system, Diatype

Chronological chart

	USA	Great Britain and Ireland	Belgium, the Netherlands and France	Scandinavia
1960–69	**1966** Robert Venturi's *Complexity and Contradiction in Modern Architecture*	**1960** Reyner Banham's *Theory and Design in the First Machine Age* **1963** Archigram **1964** First Habitat store opened **1964** Minale-Tattersfield **1965** Kilkenny Design Workshops	**1963** Total Design, Amsterdam **1969** Centre de Création Industrielle, Paris	
1970–79	**1971** Victor Papanek's *Design for the Real World* **1972** Robert Venturi and Denis Scott Brown's *Learning from Las Vegas*	**1972** Pentagram		**1972** Jacob Jensen designs Beogram 4000 **1979** Ergonomi Design Gruppen, Sweden
1980– present	**Mid-1980s** California New Wave graphics emerge	**1981** Michael Peters Group **1981** Ron Arad's One Off studio	**1985** Plan Créatif, Paris **1990** Philippe Starck designs 'Juicy Salut' lemon squeezer for Alessi	

ermany, vitzerland and ustria	Eastern Europe	Italy and Spain	Japan	Technology
60 Dieter Rams ade director of aun design partment 68 Ulm Hochnule für Gestalng closes	1960 Council of Design and Industrial Output Aesthetics 1964 First Warsaw International Poster Biennial (*see* Polish School)	1964 Marco Zanuso and Richard Sapper design BrionVega 'Algol II' television 1965 Unimark, Milan 1966 Superstudio, Florence 1966 Archizoom, Florence 1968 Oriol Bohigas's *Contra una Arquitectura Adjetivada*		1963 Icograda Mid-1960s Medium Density Fibreboard first appears in the USA
		1972 Italy: The New Domestic Landscape exhibition, New York 1974 Giorgietto Giugiaro designs Volkswagen Golf 1979 Studio Alchymia	1970 Shiro Kurumata designs Drawers in Irregular Forms chest 1972 Honda Civic launched	
82 Frogdesign	1983 Rubik Studio, Budapest	1981 Memphis 1982 Domus Academy, Milan 1983 Alessi Programma 6 launched 1988 Javier Mariscal designs Cobi mascot for the Barcelona Olympics		1983 Colorcore launched by Formica 1984 Apple Macintosh PC launched

Bibliography

General

Banham, P. Reyner, *Theory and Design in the First Machine Age* (London, 1960). Reappraisal of aims and achievements of Pevsner's *Pioneers of the Modern Movement*.

Campi, Isabel, *Història del Disseny Industrial* (Barcelona, 1987). Catalan language survey of industrial design history. Useful discussion of non-'Western' experiences.

Forty, Adrian, *Objects of Desire* (London, 1985). History of design told from the point of view of changing marketing and consumer patterns.

Giedion, Sigfried, *Mechanization Takes Command: A Contribution to Anonymous History* (New York, 1948). Landmark publication tracing rise of industrial design through technological development.

Greenhalgh, Paul (ed.), *Modernism in Design* (London, 1990). Excellent collection of essays reviewing the destiny of Modernism in various countries.

Heskett, John, *Industrial Design* (London and New York, 1980). History of industrial design as interaction of individuals and industry.

Livingston, Alan and Isabella, *The Thames and Hudson Encyclopaedia of Graphic Design and Designers* (London and New York, 1992). Comprehensive guide to the international development of graphic design from *c.*1840. Places all aspects of the discipline in the wider context of the history of fine art and illustration.

Meggs, Philip, *A History of Graphic Design* (London, 1983). Exhaustive history of graphic design highlighting achievements of individual graphic designers.

Pevsner, Nikolaus, *Pioneers of the Modern Movement* (London, 1936), republished as *Pioneers of Modern Design* (Harmondsworth, 1960). Account of development of design as progression from William Morris to Pevsner's view of the ultimate destiny of Modernism – the Bauhaus.

Satué, Enric, *El Diseño Gráfico desde sus Origines hasta Nuestros Dias* (Madrid, 1988). Thorough historical account of graphic design with 'suggestive' interpretations and useful coverage of designers beyond Meggs's book.

Sparke, Penny, *Consultant Design: The History of the Designer in Industry* (London, 1983). Analytical survey which covers the diverse roots of consultant design.

———, *An Introduction to Design and Culture in the Twentieth Century* (London, 1986). Useful 'contextualized' account of design.

Historiography

Conway, Hazel (ed.), *Design History: A Student Handbook* (London, 1987). Useful introduction to eclectic discipline of design history and guide to methodologies and sources for its study.

Walker, John, *Design History and the History of Design* (London, 1989). Discussion of different approaches to design history.

Theory

Attfield, Judy and Pat Kirkham (eds), *A View from the Interior: Feminism, Women and Design History* (London, 1989). Alternative to standard readings of design history and indeed previous 'women's' design history, foregrounding the wider social position of women and their activities in and relationship to design.

Dormer, Peter, *The Meanings of Modern Design* (London and New York, 1990). Provocative reflection on the state of design at the end of the 80s covering notions of craft, technology and high design in their economic contexts.

Foster, Hal (ed.), *Postmodern Culture* (London, 1983). Collection of seminal essays on Postmodernism in art, philosophy, literature and design.

Pye, David, *The Nature and Art of Workmanship*

(Cambridge, 1968). Fascinating discussion and redefinition of meanings of craft and design.

———, *The Nature and Aesthetics of Design* (London, 1978). Continues the discussion.

Thackara, John (ed.), *Design after Modernism: Beyond the Object* (London and New York, 1988). Essays which collectively highlight the philosophical complexity of design 'after Modernism'.

Britain

Carrington, Noel, *Industrial Design in Britain* (London, 1976). Personal and almost parochial account of small group of designers who established consultant design in Britain.

Farr, Michael, *Design in British Industry: A Mid-Century Survey* (Cambridge, 1955). Wide-ranging survey, itself a reflection of a moralistic viewpoint of its time.

Huygen, Frederique, *British Design: Image and Identity* (London, 1989). Imaginative survey of cultural essence of British design.

McCarthy, Fiona, *A History of British Design* (London, 1979). Survey of British design told very much from an 'institutional' perspective (establishment of profession, rise of Design and Industries Association etc.).

MacDermott, Katherine, *Street Style: British Design in the 80s* (London, 1987). Attempt to bring together 'subcultural' (e.g., post-punk) and high design (e.g., Vivienne Westwood) aspects of British design.

Thackara, John, *New British Design* (London and New York, 1986). Survey mostly of prodigies of the Royal College of Art.

Whiteley, Nigel, *Pop Design: Modernism to Mod* (London, 1987). Discursive treatment of background to and rise of pop design in 60s Britain.

Eastern Europe

Adlerová, Alena, *České Užité Umeni 1918–1938* (Prague, 1983). Useful Czech language survey of interwar product and graphic design.

Bojko, Szymon, *Polska Sztuka Plakatu* (Warsaw, 1971). Survey of interwar Polish posters.

———, *Russian Revolutionary Graphic Design* (London, 1972). Pioneering study of hitherto unpublished movement.

Constructivism in Poland (exh. cat., Museum

Folkwang, Essen, 1973). Translates into English many of the key texts concerned with this movement.

Crowley, David, *Nation State and National Style: Design in Poland from the Vernacular Revival to the International Style* (Manchester, 1992). Through an analytical survey of Poland this book reveals the maintenance of the Arts and Crafts tradition in Central Europe.

Devetsil: Czech Avant-Garde Art, Architecture and Design of the 1920s and 30s (exh. cat., Museum of Modern Art, Oxford, 1990). Fascinating 'recuperation' of long-forgotten movement.

Huml, Irena, *Polska Sztuka Stosowana XX wieku* (Warsaw, 1973). Major survey of Polish applied arts in the 20th c.

Lodder, Christina, *Russian Constructivism* (London, 1983). Detailed and academic account of heyday of Russian art, design, practice and theory.

France

Capuis, Bernard and Ermine Herscher, *Qualités: Objets d'En France* (Paris, 1987). Amusing view of everyday French design classics from the Petit-Beurre biscuit and the Citroën 2CV to a Louis Vuitton suitcase.

Design Français 1960–1990: Trois Décennies (exh. cat., Pompidou Centre, Paris, 1988). Published to accompany review exhibition, its text is informative though a little confusing in places.

Levitte, Agnès and Margo Rouard, *Made in France: 100 Objets Quotidiens* (Paris, 1987). Celebratory survey of everyday objects manufactured in France.

Germany

Bertsch, Georg, *SED* (Cologne, 1990). Picture book of East German products and graphics with excellent essay outlining the theoretical background to design there until reunification. Published in French, German and English.

Campbell, Joan, *The German Werkbund: The Politics of Reform in the Applied Arts* (Princeton, 1978). Discussion of German design amidst its changing political climate.

Heskett, John, *Design in Germany: 1870–1918* (London, 1986). Persuasive re-evaluation of these crucial development years, placing

Bibliography

German design in its immediate cultural context.

Hirdina, Heinz, *Gestalten für die Serie: Design in der DDR 1949–1985* (Dresden, 1988). Painstaking portrayal of East German design and industry – and its collapse.

Naylor, Gillian, *The Bauhaus Reassessed: Sources and Design Theory* (London, 1985). Pioneering design historian revisits the Bauhaus (on which she first published a monographic study in 1968), bringing important insights to the subject.

Selle, Gert, *Design-Geschichte in Deutschland: Produktkultur als Entwurf und Erfahrung* (Cologne, 1987). Important account of German design and industrialization through the 20th c., featuring much material otherwise rarely published.

Whitford, Frank, *The Bauhaus* (London and New York, 1984). Academically sound and informative discussion of the school.

Italy

Ambasz, Emilio (ed.), *Italy: The New Domestic Landscape* (New York, 1972). Accompaniment to 1972 MOMA exhibition outlining major currents in radical design movement of the time.

Branzi, Andrea, *The Hot House: Italian New Wave Design* (London, 1984). Personal account of design and theory in a postindustrial age.

Fossati, Paolo, *Il Design in Italia 1945–1972* (Turin, 1972). Review of postwar achievements in design with profiles of ten leading Italian designers of the time.

Gregotti, Vittorio, *Il Disegno del Prodotto Industriale: Italia 1860–1980* (Milan, 1980). Detailed discussion of major advances in product design through 20th c.

Sparke, Penny, *Italian Design: 1870 to the Present* (London, 1988). Analysis of development of design in relation to social and economic change.

Japan

Evans, Sian, *Contemporary Japanese Design* (London, 1991). Theme-by-theme examination of the various fundamental characteristics of Japanese design.

Matsumura, Moritaka (ed.), *The Best of Japan: Innovations: Present and Future* (Tokyo, 1987).

Review of 1986 Nikkei Awards providing useful 'state-of-the-art' survey of mid-80s Japanese design.

Sparke, Penny, *Japanese Design* (London, 1987). Historical survey of major achievements in different design disciplines.

Thornton, Richard S., *Japanese Graphic Design* (London, 1991). Analysis of history and contemporary activity.

The Netherlands

Industry and Design in The Netherlands 1850–1950 (exh. cat., Stedelijk Museum, Amsterdam, 1986). Collection of essays by leading Dutch design historians to accompany exhibition. Surveys major individuals and companies across all design disciplines.

Overy, Paul, *De Stijl* (London, 1991). Important re-evaluation of the movement and its legacy by leading scholar on the subject.

Staal, Gert and Hester Wolters (eds), *Holland in Vorm: Dutch Design 1945–1987* (The Hague, 1987). Wide-ranging if idiosyncratic collection of essays.

Scandinavia

Beer, Eileene Harrison, *Scandinavian Design: Objects of a Life Style* (New York, 1975). Enthusiastic, illustrated account.

Lindkvist, Lennart (ed.), *Design in Sweden* (Stockholm, 1972). Dated but interesting account of Swedish design covering glass and ceramics through to furniture and product design, including discussion of social and political contexts.

Spain

Capella, Juli and Quim Larrea, *Nuevo Diseño Español* (Barcelona, 1991). Survey of emergent design by Barcelona impresarios.

Dent Coad, Emma, *Spanish Design and Architecture* (London, 1990). Wide-ranging survey.

Diseño en España (exh. cat., Barcelona Centro de Diseño, Barcelona, 1986). Publication to accompany travelling exhibition which includes essays on a wide range of historical and theoretical aspects of Spanish design.

Julier, Guy, *New Spanish Design* (London, 1991). Analysis of post-Franco Spanish design in political, social and economic contexts.

USA

Aldersey-Williams, Hugh, *New American Design* (New York, 1988). Profiles of major names in design of the 80s.

High Styles: Twentieth-Century American Design (exh. cat., Whitney Museum, New York, 1985). Illustrated collection of clearly argued essays to accompany exhibition.

Pulos, Arthur J., *American Design Ethic: A History of Industrial Design to 1940* (Cambridge, Mass., 1983). This is a well illustrated charting of design alongside the rise of the American consumer society.

————, *The American Design Adventure 1940–1975* (Cambridge, Mass., 1988). Continues the detailed examination.

Sexton, Richard, *American Style: Classic Product Design from Airstream to Zippo* (San Francisco, 1987). Explanation of large number of American cult objects.

Wilson, Richard Guy et al., *The Machine Age in America, 1918–1941* (New York, 1986). Excellent collection of essays discussing design, modernity and Modernism in the 'New World'.

Sources of illustrations

The following abbreviations have been used: *a* above, *b* below, *c* centre, *l* left, *r* right.

© A.C.L., Brussels 103*a*

By courtesy of Otl Aicher 16

Photo: Musée Air France, Paris 175*a*

Albright-Knox Art Gallery, Buffalo, New York, Gift of Darwin R. Martin 202*cr*

Alessi F.A.O., S.p.A. 17*b*, 161*a*, 161*b*, 174, 195

Apple Computer UK Ltd 20

Photo courtesy of Artek, Finland 14*a*

B&B Italia S.p.A. 28

BFI Stills, Posters and Designs 29, 156

Bang & Olufsen A/S 108*a*

Bauhaus-Archiv/Museum für Gestaltung, Berlin 17*a*, 31, 41*al*

Studio Bellini, Milan 34*b*

Black and Decker Ltd 39

Museum of Fine Arts, Boston 26*b*

Branson Coates Architecture 139

Braun UK Ltd 41*ar*, 167*b*

Kunsthalle, Bremen 108*b*

Galerie Brockstedt, Hamburg 194

The Brooklyn Museum, New York. Gift of the Italian Government 135

Cassina S.p.A. 27, 47, 153*b*, 159

Cheltenham Art Gallery and Museums 74

Ivan Chermayeff, Chermayeff & Geismar Inc. 49

Christie's 52*a*

Chrysler Corporation 50*l*

Seymour Chwast 51, 165*b*

Citroën UK Ltd 50*r*

Studio Joe Colombo 54*a*

Museo Civico, Como 87

Container Corporation of America 58*a*

Kind permission of Susie Cooper for Wedgwood & Sons Ltd 58*b*

Collection of Cranbrook Academy of Art Museum 60

Danese Milano/Photo Aldo Ballo 62*b*

Design Museum, London 54*b*, 110*a*, 144*b*

Design Research Unit 69

Photo courtesy Disabled Living Foundation 68

Driade 180

Dux Moebel, Sweden 125*r*

Centro Storico Fiat 80

Fiell 37*a*

Ford Archives, Henry Ford Museum, Dearborn, Michigan 83

Courtesy Barnaba Fornasetti 84

Photo courtesy of Buckminster Fuller Archives 75*a*, 86

Amigos de Gaudí 89

Courtesy General Motors, Detroit, Michigan 90

Giugiaro Design 92*b*

Milton Glaser 160

By kind permission of Guinness Brewing Worldwide Ltd Archives 35*a*

Calouste Gulbenkian Foundation, Lisbon 115*a*

Hackman Houseware Oy Ab., Helsinki 202*a*

Photo Fritz Hansen 199*a*

Sources of illustrations

Michael Havinden 98
Courtesy of Herman Miller Inc. 75*b*, 100 (Photo Hedrich Blessing/Nick Merrick)
Hille International Limited 63*a*, 157*b*
Howard Miller Clock Company 140
IBM (UK) Ltd 104
International Design Press Agency 125*l*, 170*a*, 192
Kaiser Wilhelm Museum, Krefeld 15
© The Knoll Group 42, 173
Leeds Metropolitan University 67, 96
Leicestershire Museums, Art Galleries and Records Offices 25
Prentenkabinett, Rijksuniversiteit, Leiden 155
Liberty Archive, Westminster City Archives, London 166
Liberty Retail Ltd 118
Courtesy Marlborough Gallery, London 32
Photo MAS 133
David Mellor Design 127
Memphis 41*b*, 63*b*, 114, 179*a*, 179*b*
Jan Mlodozeniec 158
Collection, The Museum of Modern Art, New York 131; Collection, The Museum of Modern Art, New York. Gift of Philip Johnson 64*b*; Collection, The Museum of Modern Art, New York. Given anonymously 134
Otto Neurath, *Bildstatistik nach Wiener Methode in der Schule* (Vienna, 1933) 106
Siegfried Odermatt 146
Olivetti UK Ltd 147*b*, 148, 185
One Off Ltd 21
Photo courtesy Frank den Oudsten 141
Photo John Outram 162
Bibliothèque Nationale, Paris 46*r*

Musée des Arts Décoratifs, Paris 116
Pentagram 152
Peret 153*a*
Pininfarina Archives 157*a*
Private Collection 95, 145, 168, 205
Photo Race Ltd 167*a*
Photo courtesy Gordon Russell 172, 193
Courtesy SCP Limited, London 52*b*
Some Bizarre/Virgin Records 44*a*
Sony UK Ltd 178
Sprengel Museum, Hanover 176
Barbara Stauffacher Solomon 183*a*
Stedelijk Museum, Amsterdam 170*b*
National Museum, Stockholm. Photo courtesy Georg Jensen, Copenhagen 91
© 1993, Walter Dorwin Teague Assoc. Inc., New York 187
Gebr. Thonet A.G. 188*a*
Jan van Toorn 189*a*
Total Design Amsterdam 189*b*; © Total Design Amsterdam 1993. © photo Roos Aldershoff 165*a*
Galerie Vallois, Paris 171*b*
By courtesy of the Board of Trustees of the Victoria and Albert Museum, London 14*b*, 26*a*, 107, 113*a*, 113*b*, 129, 151*b*
Vignelli Associates/Photo Mario Carrieri 196*a*
Trustees of the Wedgwood Museum Barlaston, Staffordshire, England 198*l*
Daniel Weil, Pentagram. Photo Richard Waite 199*b*
Wolff Olins Limited 59
Frank Lloyd Wright Foundation, Taliesin 202*b*
Yale University Art Gallery. Gift of the Société Anonyme 119
Zanotta S.p.A. 48, 64*a*, 204